Praise for
this is *not* how i thought it would be

"Kristin Maschka is a beacon of light in a sea of darkness about the possibilities for women looking to do 'mothering and more' with their lives. She is smart, well-educated about the details, and passionate in her quest to bring more knowledge to more women about more options. All women and men looking to juggle the multiple roles of parent, worker, spouse, and more should read this book, soon and often—it will change, and improve, their lives!"

—ED MCCAFFERY,Professor of Law, Economics and Political Science
at USC Law School and author of *Taxing Women*

"Women today are often blindsided by the clash between their expectations for their lives after becoming mothers and the reality of society's beliefs about motherhood. This book brings mothers' lives and realities into sharp focus and provides readers with a vision— and tips and tools—for building a brighter future for themselves and all mothers."

—JOANNE BRUNDAGE, founder and CEO of Mothers & More

"Kristin Maschka really gets it—motherhood is not all fuzzy blankets, first smiles, and pastel-colored nurseries. She's honest enough to admit that the joyful arrival of children can be accompanied by tremendous self-doubt, anxiety, and inner conflict. Mothers inherit a legacy of outdated assumptions, unfair expectations, and a fair amount of guilt no matter what they do. In relating her own experience with equal parts insight and hilarity, Kristin paints a nuanced portrait of what it really means to be a twenty-first-century woman with children. This book will delight, comfort, and educate you—don't miss it!"

—VALERIE A. YOUNG, National Association of Mothers' Centers (NAMC)

"Vast numbers of women are shocked to run into the Maternal Wall way before they get to the glass ceiling. [Maschka] offers plans for some elegant doors one can build in the Maternal Wall. Every working woman who is pregnant for the first time should read this book."

—KRISTIN ROWE-FINKBEINER and JOAN BLADES, cofounders of MomsRising.org
and coauthors of *The Motherhood Manifesto*

"All change begins with fresh ways of thinking. This brave and honest book jumps the needle out of the outmoded mental grooves we are stuck in when we think of mothering."

—ANN CRITTENDEN, author of *The Price of Motherhood* and
If You've Raised Kids, You Can Manage Anything

"*This Is Not How I Thought It Would Be* is a deeply candid, thoughtful, and in the end wonderfully practical book about how to navigate the shock that parenthood brings to even the most enlightened two-career couples. If you're a new mother wondering (in the few hours during the day when you're awake and conscious) why you're not 'having it all,' this book could save your life."

—SANDRA TSING LOH, author of *Mother on Fire*

KRISTIN MASCHKA

this is *not* how i thought it would be

REMODELING MOTHERHOOD TO GET THE LIVES WE WANT TODAY

BERKLEY BOOKS
NEW YORK

THE BERKLEY PUBLISHING GROUP
Published by the Penguin Group
Penguin Group (USA) Inc.
375 Hudson Street, New York, New York 10014, USA
Penguin Group (Canada), 90 Eglinton Avenue East, Suite 700, Toronto, Ontario M4P 2Y3, Canada
(a division of Pearson Penguin Canada Inc.)
Penguin Books Ltd., 80 Strand, London WC2R 0RL, England
Penguin Group Ireland, 25 St. Stephen's Green, Dublin 2, Ireland (a division of Penguin Books Ltd.)
Penguin Group (Australia), 250 Camberwell Road, Camberwell, Victoria 3124, Australia
(a division of Pearson Australia Group Pty. Ltd.)
Penguin Books India Pvt. Ltd., 11 Community Centre, Panchsheel Park, New Delhi—110 017, India
Penguin Group (NZ), 67 Apollo Drive, Rosedale, North Shore, 0632, New Zealand
(a division of Pearson New Zealand Ltd.)
Penguin Books (South Africa) (Pty.) Ltd., 24 Sturdee Avenue, Rosebank, Johannesburg 2196, South
Africa

Penguin Books Ltd., Registered Offices: 80 Strand, London WC2R 0RL, England

While the author has made every effort to provide accurate telephone numbers and Internet
addresses at the time of publication, neither the publisher nor the author assumes any responsibility
for changes that occur after publication. Furthermore, the publisher does not have any control over
and does not assume any responsibility for author or third-party websites or their content.

Unless otherwise noted, real names have been used, with the permission of those quoted.

Copyright © 2009 Kristin Maschka
Cover design by Rita Frangie
Book design by Pauline Neuwirth

PRINTING HISTORY
Berkley trade paperback edition / October 2009

Library of Congress Cataloging-in-Publication Data

Maschka, Kristin.
 This is not how I thought it would be : remodeling motherhood to get the
lives we want today / Kristin Maschka.
    p. cm.
 Includes bibliographical references.
 ISBN 978-0-425-22781-7
 1. Motherhood. 2. Mothers—Family relationships. 3. Work and family. 4. Parenthood. I. Title.
HQ759.M3714 2009
306.874'30973090511—dc22
                    2009021027

PRINTED IN THE UNITED STATES OF AMERICA

10 9 8 7 6 5 4 3 2 1

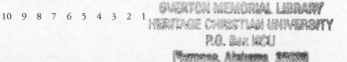

To David and Kate,
with love and gratitude.

Old-fashioned ways which no longer apply to changed
conditions are a snare in which the feet of women
have always become readily entangled.

—JANE ADDAMS

CONTENTS

this is *not* how i thought it would be

INTRODUCTION

the day the vomit hit the fan

WHEN OUR DAUGHTER, Kate, was born late one October evening, my husband, David, and I spent five days in a sleep-deprived fog together with our baby girl. David and I slept whenever Kate did. We woke up whenever she did. We ate when we remembered to eat. Sometimes we felt as if we'd slipped into a comfortable cocoon, cut off from the world and able to focus completely on each other and our baby. Whatever we felt, we felt it together and leaned on each other, sharing our new and overwhelming responsibility together.

And then David had to go back to work.

That morning, I sat in the rocking chair watching Kate in her crib. Early morning sunshine came in through the window, and our first day alone together stretched peacefully in front of us. Suddenly, Kate projectile vomited across the room, splattering it all over the wall. Stunned and panicked, I called David. He couldn't help me; he was in a meeting. I was on my own. So I called my mother, my friends, and my pediatrician who all assured me that projectile vomiting was not unusual for newborns. But, that vomit on the wall marked a turning point; it was the point at which our modern egalitarian marriage morphed into one you might see in a 1950s television show.

Each time baby Kate cried out at night, I dragged myself out of bed so that David could be fresh for work the next day. I then stumbled bleary-eyed and resentful through my own day. My formerly neatnik husband developed a blind spot when it came to dirty dishes and piles of dirty clothes. When I wasn't feeding Kate or changing her diapers, I spent every spare minute in the kitchen or laundry room. Instead of sharing everything, David and I mostly fought about everything, and my marriage was not the only aspect of my life that had gone completely haywire. Nothing about my life as a mother—not my marriage, not my identity, not my career—was how I expected it to be. I was mad, sad, and lonely. Plus, I felt guilty for even having those feelings. After all, what did I have to be upset about? We had a beautiful baby girl whom I loved to the moon and back. I had a roof over my head, food on the table, and a loving husband. Why did I feel so lost? How could I find my way again? I simply had to answer those questions. As far as I was concerned, the stakes had never been higher. I was losing my marriage, my career, and my money. I was losing myself.

I went after the answers to my questions with the doggedness of a sleep-deprived mother hunting for that magic special blankie. I read books. As the president of the national organization Mothers & More, I talked to mothers across the country. I talked to David late into the night. Now I can share what I learned. This book is a tale of my quest, written in hindsight, the way I might tell it to a friend over coffee.

David and I were able to figure things out after several years. We found our way to a marriage that, while not the same as before Kate, is a lot closer to what I envisioned. I found my way to a life for myself that, while not the same as before Kate, is much closer to what I expected and hoped it would be. I now know that the key to my quest was to take a different point of view. Specifically, I needed to step back and take "the balcony view."[1] I've always used the balcony view professionally. As a consultant on organizational change, my job is to get immersed in an organization but still step back far enough mentally to see what's really going on, to see connections that no one else has seen, and then to give objective advice about what could be done differently. Well, when I became a mother, I was so much a part of the drama unfolding on stage that I found it difficult to get up to the balcony. Difficult, but not impossible, and the more I took the balcony view, the more I was able to see both why my life had taken an unexpected turn and how I could get it back on track.

So, got your coffee? Good. Because here's the hardest thing I learned. I'm not as enlightened as I thought. And neither is David. And neither is the world around us. Come up on the balcony with me, and I'll share some of the snippets of my own drama that taught me those hard lessons.

FROM BASKETBALL TO A BABY

I grew up in a small town in Minnesota, the oldest of three girls. My father was an athlete in college, so I played ball from the time I could walk, which was unusual in the 1970s. By the time I was in seventh grade in 1980, my school had added a girls' basketball team. However, I noticed that the boys' team had twice as many practices, twice as many games, and practiced in the big gym with the shiny wood floor. The girls practiced in the cramped old gym with the concrete floor. I told my parents, "I want to play on the boys' team because they play more and get the good gym." With my parents' support, I went to the principal's office the next day, heart pounding. I quickly explained what I wanted to do and why. "Okay," he said, "we'll figure it out." I thought to myself, "Great! That was easy."

And then the boys' coach quit in protest.

On the playground a boy shouted at me some version of, "Girls can't play. You'll get squashed and it will serve you right!" I was confused, and I was angry. I could see so clearly that it wasn't fair that the girls' team was treated differently from the boys' team. Why couldn't everyone else see that?

I spent much of my childhood and young adulthood pointing out to people that it wasn't fair to treat boys and girls differently when it came to sports. Somehow, though, I convinced myself that this problem was limited to activities that involved a ball. I remember heading to college and pooh-poohing the idea of the need for women's studies. I never joined any women's activist groups in college. To me, both were relics of the past. Clearly, I could be anything I wanted to be. I figured playing sports was just the last frontier to conquer and now we could all move on.

I played basketball in college, too, and one winter, on the road for a game, I caught up with my aunt. She's younger than my mother, her sister, and her kids were much younger than I was at the time. I remember standing on a chilly New York City street when Aunt Ann put her arm around me and said, "You know, no matter how enlightened your future husband is, it will still be you that has responsibility for the kids." I smiled but quietly dismissed the warning. *I* was different. My future husband would be different. Times were different.

Over the next few years, I got married, got a job, and still didn't see any reason to shed my belief that women had made it. Sure, I heard a few inappropriate comments about women at work, but I figured the poor guys who made them were relics of the past, too. Overall, life was good. Best of all, David and I had a marriage of equals that was everything I had hoped it would be.

And then we had a baby, and I became a mother.

That's when the vomit hit the fan, so to speak. Five days later David went back to seventy-hour workweeks at the law firm so he wouldn't risk losing his annual bonus. While pregnant, my proposal to go part-time from a fifty-hours-a-week job had been turned down. I found a part-time job somewhere else but was laid off the day I came back from maternity leave. David and I did the math—taxes, childcare, work expenses—it was hardly worth it for me to work. So I didn't.

Motherhood threw me so many curve balls that all I could do was duck. My success in the workplace came to a screeching halt, while David's took off. My days of accomplishing long lists of "important" things were gone, replaced by days where getting a shower and four hours of uninterrupted sleep were reason enough to celebrate. I didn't even know how to introduce myself anymore. Was I a stay-at-home mom? A homemaker? Or later, a working mother? None of the labels felt right. My paycheck disappeared for several years, and a brand-new and unwelcome anxiety crept into my head. I was now completely financially dependent on David. But, what if . . . ? No, I couldn't think it. But, I couldn't *not* think it. What if . . . we got divorced?

David and I never talked about who would do what, but I ended up handling everything for our family. I gave Kate baths, clipped her toenails, and scheduled haircuts and doctor's appointments. I kept the family calendar, got gifts for friends' birthdays, and read parenting books and magazines. I planned meals, bought groceries, made the roasted chicken, and then usually ate alone. Because David worked. And worked. And worked. He got the cars fixed. He took out the trash. And worked. Even when I started working for pay again, some-how I was still the one researching preschools and keeping track of when Kate needed new shoes. I nagged. David defended himself. Mostly we either fought or retreated into stony, resentful silence.

I was confused and angry, but with whom? We loved Kate. David was working hard. I was working hard. But the division of labor wasn't working. Our work lives weren't working. Our *marriage* wasn't working. My aunt had been right. I had the enlightened husband, yet I was still the one who had responsibility for Kate. Why didn't I see that coming?

MENTAL MAPS

The world is a complicated place. Our brains try to help us navigate more easily by making some generalizations about things and then stuffing those generalizations into our subconscious. These subconscious assumptions, or *mental maps,* are the "images, assumptions, stories that we carry in our minds of ourselves, other people, institutions and every aspect of the world."[2] For example, "Stay-at-home moms watch soap operas and eat bon-bons." Mental maps filter what our eyes see. We tend to see what fits our assumptions, and we have big blind spots for things that fall outside our assumptions. That's why two people can see the same situation in two different ways. That's why I, armed with an assumption that women have made it, could go through life not really seeing any of the signs to the contrary and end up so shocked to find that my aunt was right.

Mental maps, even though they are subconscious, shape how we talk and how we act. If people have the mental map that "Girls can't play sports," then they are likely to use insults like, "You throw like a girl." They might then decide that "The girls can play in the old gym." Mental maps aren't right or wrong. They are broad generalizations, so by definition, they are not accurate all of the time.[3] Any particular mental map is good or bad based on how well it helps us navigate our lives. If we have mental maps that match our reality and what we want life to be like, then they can be quite useful. On the other hand, mental maps that are out of sync with our lives can make us pretty miserable and confused. From the balcony, I could see I had my own mental maps about mothers, fathers, work, money, and marriage that were painfully bad at helping me navigate my life. For example, my own mental map that "Stay-at-home moms watch soap operas and eat bon-bons" led me to believe I would have tons of time on my hands if I wasn't employed. Our mental maps led David and me to behave in ways we never expected. These assumptions made me feel as if something were wrong with me when I felt like I couldn't win no matter what I did. These ill-fitting mental maps left me confused about how to chart a course that worked for me and for my family.

REMODELING THE WHOLE HOUSE

Mental maps tend to be self-reinforcing because they are shaped by our environment and experiences. For example, everyone had always assumed girls weren't into sports: "Girls don't want to play." "Girls aren't strong enough to play." So parents didn't play catch with girls. Girls didn't get coaches or equipment or programs or teams or opportunities to play, at least not the same as boys got. Then people would say, "See? Girls aren't playing and aren't very good." Duh. Of course, if girls don't get to practice, they won't be very good. Of course if they aren't very good and people make fun of them when they try, girls won't want to play. It was a self-fulfilling prophecy, a vicious cycle.

What does this have to do with mothers, fathers, and families? Well, here's how I look at it. My husband and I live in a small craftsman bungalow that was built in 1919. It's beautiful, but it was built for the way people lived then, not the way we live now. Ninety years ago, people built houses based on certain assumptions they had about families, how family life would be lived, and what technology would be available. The bathroom and kitchen and closets are too small by today's standards. The dining room is way too big and formal. There are no ceiling fixtures and there are places for gas lamps on the walls. So my husband and I took out a wall to enlarge the kitchen. We built a huge deck off the back for a casual dining space. We installed closet organizing stuff so we could use every square inch of our tiny closets and ceiling fixtures so we could see. We turned the tiny garage into an office. We remodeled everything to make the house better fit our lives, so we could live the way we wanted.

About seventy years ago—during and after the Great Depression and World War II—our country went through a lot of changes. In response, people built the house we all still live in together today— our society. People built our house based on certain assumptions society had about mothers, fathers, money, marriage, and work. The primary walls of that house—what we say to each other, how our workplaces operate, the unwritten rules of behavior, and the public policies that make up the written rules—were built back then. We've all changed a lot over those seventy years. Most mothers are now employed at some point. Most families need two incomes to get by and get ahead. We have higher expectations about the care children need to thrive. Our lives have changed but we haven't remodeled the house. Mothers still do most of the housework and childcare, workplaces still assume real jobs are forty to fifty hours a week, and Social Security still assumes a woman will be financially dependent on a man her whole life. Oh, we've updated a bit, changed the decor, and refurnished a bit. Fathers are doing more housework and some mothers can get unpaid maternity leave for example. But we haven't moved any walls that need moving. We've been living in this communal house for so long, we've grown accustomed to the way it is. We don't notice the peeling paint so much. In fact, we have a tough time even seeing the walls and the assumptions embedded in them. We don't see how our lives today are completely out of sync with our old house. We don't realize that the house itself is keeping those outdated beliefs alive, reinforcing them every day. So we often bump into a wall here or a wall there, and we're puzzled. How did that wall get there? For example, I always thought I'd be able to keep working after I had Kate but bumped into a wall when my proposal to go part-time was turned down. When Kate arrived, the vomit hit the fan because David and I were living in a house that was totally out of sync with our reality and the way we wanted our family life to be.

Once I understood that the way the world around me thinks about mothers, fathers, money, marriage, and work influences my life every day, I had a better chance of making decisions that kept me from smacking into a wall. Once I understood that every aspect of our family life—our marriage, my job, his job, my identity, our money— is connected to all the others by vicious cycles, I understood why there was no quick fix and why tackling just one piece of the puzzle wouldn't do the trick. I had to remodel the whole house.

Remodeling Tools

Our mental maps often hang around long past their usefulness. Until something happens to break the vicious cycles that keep them in place. In 1972, Title IX was passed, laying out a new belief—a new blueprint. That blueprint said that girls and boys are both capable of playing sports and entitled to the benefits of playing. Therefore, Title IX required schools and colleges to offer girls equal opportunities to play sports. During the 1970s and 1980s, girls like me in towns across the country challenged the assumption that girls couldn't and didn't want to play ball, and today girls make up nearly half of the youth on sports teams, and we have female athletes the likes of Mia Hamm and Venus Williams and Candace Parker.[4]

When it came to motherhood, however, I found it a lot harder to figure out how I might make those shifts, because motherhood touches every part of my life. Plus, the sports thing involved me challenging *other people's* flawed assumptions. When it came to motherhood, I had to confront *my own* flawed subconscious assumptions too, not an easy emotional task. No one likes to admit her own blind spots.

Fortunately, shortly after I had Kate, I became the president of Mothers & More, an organization of thousands of mothers with chapters across the country. Since 1987, Mothers & More has supported women as they deal with the ways in which being a mother affects every aspect of their lives. Mothers & More made me part of a national conversation with mothers, and with twenty years of experience, the organization had figured out plenty of ways to help mothers deal with precisely the same questions that plagued me. Why do I feel so lost? How can I find my way again?

Through a mix of my own trial and error, my personal and professional knowledge, and my work with Mothers & More, I developed four powerful tools I used to remodel motherhood to get the life I wanted, tools that any mother can use to get from wherever she might be to wherever she wants to be.

- **Build a balcony.** Do what it takes to step back, get a balcony view, and see the invisible mental maps.
- **Draft a blueprint.** Clarify the beliefs and assumptions you want to build on and ask what life would look like if they were in place.
- **Remodel your life.** Experiment with doing what's on the blueprint. Does life fit better?
- **Remodel our house.** Experiment with doing something that helps remodel our house—society as a whole—and it will help you remodel your own life too.

Build a Balcony

Building a balcony takes conscious effort. Mental maps are invisible by design; it takes some work to bring them to the surface. People are really lousy at seeing their own subconscious assumptions and blind spots, so connecting with others is a key step. Talking with other mothers, hearing their stories, and reading books helped me build that balcony and get just far away enough from my own drama to get a different perspective. A well-built balcony is designed to help you see more of the world. In this case, the balcony also helps you see how your own life is part of larger patterns and influenced by vicious cycles so you can begin to ask about the mental maps lurking underneath them all.

Draft a Blueprint

Drafting a blueprint is the step we all tend to skip. We figure out what's wrong and why, and then we go straight to the tactical solutions. We collect recipes for twenty-minute dinners or give our husbands a honey-do list. If we decided to remodel the home we live in, would we start knocking down walls without a blueprint? No. I found that once I surfaced my own mental maps and the ones in the world around me, I could link imagination to action and ask myself, "What if I had a different belief? What if I subconsciously believed what I say I believe? Then how would I talk? How would I behave? How would the world operate?"[5] The new beliefs and the answers to my What if? questions became my draft blueprint—my very own guide to remodeling.

Remodel Your Life

To remodel my life, I had to act my way to a new way of thinking. I experimented by acting on the answers to those What if? questions to see if I'd found a better fit. Sometimes the experiments worked; sometimes they didn't. But experimenting with doing something differently was the only way to make a difference in my subconscious thinking. Over time, my life started to fit me better.

Remodel Our House

Along the way, I extended those experiments outside my own life and into the world around me to help remodel our collective house—society—as well. The very same mental maps that were tripping me up every day are the ones built into the world around us. Sometimes I couldn't remodel my own life fast enough, and doing things for other people was the only avenue I had for doing *something*—for acting my way to a new way of thinking. And inevitably it did; remodeling our house in turn helped me remodel my life.

As I share my story with you, you'll see these four tools running through everything. At the end of each chapter you'll find a list of remodeling tools to try out for yourself. Just to be clear, do not add everything on these lists to *your* to-do list. I imagine that list is plenty long already. Pick and choose, experiment, come back later and try something else. Remember, remodeling always takes longer than we think, right? There are always delays, hiccups, setbacks, and things happening out of order. That's okay, we just keep experimenting.

STORIES CAN MOVE THE EARTH AND THE SUN

Now, some of us may be more desperate for these tools than others. Not every woman feels as if the vomit hit the fan the moment she had children. However, judging from years of talking with mothers, many do. Some of us face different challenges at different stages of motherhood. Some mothers get hit by just a few things and some by everything at once. However, shocked or not, happy or not, employed or not, so many mothers experience these dilemmas in some form at some point in their lives. The mothers I've talked with are mothers who are employed full-time, not employed at all, and everything in between. They are mothers with six-figure salaries and mothers clipping coupons to afford the groceries. People might have notions that a mother in Wichita, Kansas, has little in common with a mother like me in Pasadena, California, or with a mother in Boston, Massachusetts, but they are wrong. I hear versions of the same stories in my small hometown in southern Minnesota as I do in conversations with mothers in Wisconsin and Georgia and Texas.

That said, what I will share with you is primarily my story, and my story is shaped by who I am—a married white woman with a college education and a professional job. Every woman's experience as a mother is shaped by race, class, religion, cultural background, marital status, and even geographic location. My story is not every woman's experience, and I don't intend it to be read that way. I'm offering my story as the best way I know to illustrate what I've learned. I know what I've learned will help many different mothers who have had similar, if not identical, experiences. As different as we all are, the countless mothers I talk with are all trying to make their way in a world that operates on a set of assumptions that are hopelessly out of date and out of sync with the lives we want to lead.

We're in esteemed company trying to remodel our lives and the rest of the world with new and improved beliefs about mothers, fathers, marriage, money, and work. In college, I studied the history of science and learned about paradigm shifts, the historic points in time when scientists shift their assumptions about how the world works. For example, a classic paradigm shift was when physics transitioned from Newton and the apple to Einstein and $e = mc^2$. Or long before that, when Galileo was threatened with torture and imprisoned for the last eight years of his life for demonstrating that the earth was not, in fact, at the center of the universe. I don't think we have to worry about imprisonment. In fact, shifting paradigms can be fun. Back in seventh grade on that boys' basketball team, a few minutes into our very first game, I went in, and a boy was assigned to guard me. I ran down the court to the right side of the basket and got a pass from my teammate. The boy guarding me stood several feet away just watching me. So I took a shot. *Swish.* His jaw dropped. Back and forth down the court we went. I ran to the right side again. Another pass. He still stood several feet away. Jump shot. *Swish.* He stared and shook his head. Back and forth one more time, I went down to the right side baseline. Pass. Jump shot. *Swish. Tweet!* His coach called a time out. As his coach yelled at him, I went to our huddle grinning. That boy had a mental map that girls couldn't play. He acted on that assumption by not bothering to guard me. When we returned to the basketball court though, he began sticking to me like glue. I had just shattered his assumption about girls and sports with three jump shots in thirty seconds. He would never think the same way about girls and basketball again.

That's the thing about mental maps. Buried in our subconscious they limit us. Out in the open, where we can challenge them and change them, mental maps can help us open up our minds and expand our options. We can change the world. The sun can move to the center of the universe.[6] And once it does, there's no going back. Our view of the world is changed forever.

1

the twilight zone

or why am i the one getting up
in the middle of the night?

WHEN DAVID AND I decided that it made financial sense for me to stay home after Kate was born, I didn't realize how completely it would change our lives. Our egalitarian marriage was gone, and we somehow crossed over into a black-and-white *Twilight Zone* episode in which, without warning, some bizarre force had taken over our brains. Our few days of new-baby bliss were forgotten and quickly replaced by a new order in which Twilight Zone Kristin was programmed to get up in the middle of the night, and Twilight Zone David was not. In the Twilight Zone, our modern notions of our marriage went out the window. Instead we found ourselves in an alternate universe, where the rules we obediently followed dictated that Twilight Zone Kristin cook, clean, and care for Kate and that Twilight Zone David work, work, and work some more.

And that was just the beginning.

One evening I returned from a Mothers & More chapter meeting. Baby Kate was asleep in her crib. I found David stretched out in front of the TV, sharing the couch with a huge pile of clean but unfolded laundry. I closed my eyes, tired and disappointed. When I opened my eyes and looked around the house, all I saw were things that needed doing. Here he had lounged for several hours leaning on a monster pile of laundry and hadn't folded a thing. I gritted my teeth and tried my best to be polite, "Couldn't you have folded some of that?" Twilight Zone David looked at me, genuinely puzzled. "But I had a long day at work," he explained. I'm not sure what made me crazier at that moment, the wrinkled clothes or the fact that he truly did not understand why I turned away to bang my head slowly against the wall.

So we were stuck in the Twilight Zone. During a weekend episode, I asked David to watch Kate while I finished paying bills in the office. Shortly after I buried myself in piles of envelopes, I heard the baby start wailing. My body reflexively tensed. Should I go to her? I didn't. David could handle it, and he needed the time with his daughter. *I* needed to completely finish one task that day uninterrupted or I would go insane *and* our credit card payment would be late. More crying. I resisted the urge to jump up. I tried to focus. I shut the door. I wrote a check. More wailing. Finally, I couldn't stand it anymore. Was he deaf? Was he dead? I marched to the front room to find David watching golf on TV and Kate fussing in her bouncy seat at his feet. Hands on my hips, I glared at him. "What?" he said. I pointed at Kate. Instead of getting the response I expected—that he would pick her up and I should go back to my office—Twilight Zone David said, "But it's my day off." "Day off?!" I blurted. "You have got to be kidding me. When's my day off?"

Time went by but the Twilight Zone's force still had firm control of our brains. When Kate was potty-training, that single task was pretty much the center of my universe for months. I knew where every restroom was within a ten-mile radius. I had stashes of clean underwear and pants for toddler Kate in every bag I owned, in the glove compartment, and anywhere else I could think of. During that time, David and I spent a night away for our anniversary. David packed a bag for

Kate and dropped her off at Grandma and Grandpa's house. Then he and I escaped and spent thirty-six desperately needed hours alone together. When we returned, David's mother said Kate had done just fine. "But," she said, "you only gave me the *one* pair of underwear she had on." Grandma had spent the weekend washing that one pair of underwear. Grandma wasn't bothered, but I was mortified—and flabbergasted. How could my intelligent husband not realize a potty-training child needed more than one pair of underwear, preferably a dozen? Twilight Zone David was defensive. "What's the big deal? She's fine." I felt like the Twilight Zone had robbed him of part of his brain, the part that could think several steps ahead and anticipate what Kate would need. He felt like Twilight Zone Kristin was obsessive-compulsive and had a superior attitude that drove him nuts.

We went through repeated episodes like this over several years. One time, when Kate was about three, David went into her room to get her to clean it up. From the kitchen, I heard his commanding voice deliver the directive. It shouldn't be so loud and sudden, I thought to myself. She needs time to transition. Kate stalled, "In a minute, Daddy." He got louder and more insistent. Don't do it, I predicted to myself, she'll just dig in her heels now. As if on cue, I heard Kate yelling back at David. In the other room, I silently shook my head. Within minutes, I couldn't stand listening to either of them, and I knew the more upset she got, the harder it would be for me to calm her down. So Twilight Zone Kristin swooped in to patch up a bigger mess than the one we'd started with. I yelled at David, "How do you not see what will happen when you do it that way? It's easier to just do it myself." Twilight Zone David stormed off, furious that I was coming to her rescue and undermining him.

The shadowy forces of the Twilight Zone made me say things I'd never said before. I started using the "good husband caveat." "*I love David, but* can you believe he forgot to pack extra underwear for a three-year-old?" I complained bitterly to friends, "*David is a great guy, but* it drives me crazy that I have to keep track of everything that needs doing!" I couldn't figure out how to express both my complete exasperation with the man and my deep love and respect for him.

To be fair, Twilight Zone David was just as perplexed and just as exasperated with me. He got annoyed at the things *I* didn't see. The kitchen trash could be overflowing, and I'd keep trying to stuff more in rather than take it out myself. When he came home from the office at night, the house, baby Kate, and I would all be wrecks, and he'd ask, "What exactly did you do all day?" He was appalled that I could spend all day with only Kate and the house to worry about and then sincerely and vehemently protest that I had not had a spare minute that day for myself or for cleaning the house or for making something for dinner. From his perspective, I was the one that got to stay in that cocoon at home with Kate while he slaved away at the office.

He constantly reminded me how much he was working. He told me I didn't understand the demands his clients placed on him. He was finally hitting his stride in his career, and I didn't care and I didn't offer any of the support or encouragement we'd always given each other. He resented that all Twilight Zone Kristin did the minute he got in the door was complain about how hard it was to be me. David spent the day with clients and his bosses yelling at him. Then he came home at night to me and Kate yelling and crying at him, or at least near him. He confessed later that he often didn't want to come home at all. In his words, "You were insane!" Not surprising, a regular feature of our warped black-and-white world at the time was a daily flareup over who was doing what and who was working harder.

I quickly discovered that we were not alone. In fact, I'm convinced that if you pull ten random mothers off the street, give them some margaritas and a chance to chat, in less than five minutes the conversation will quickly become a release valve for frustrations about who does what at home. I know that's what happens when I have margaritas with my friends. "He just does not *see* stuff that needs to be done," says a mother in Maryland. "The kids are in bed, he's watching basketball, and I am mopping the floor, clearing up homework papers, returning fourteen hundred small plastic objects to their proper toy bins, putting videos back in their boxes so they can be located . . . and he's watching basketball."[1] Often, another mother will say something like, "Well, you just have to tell him what you need him to do." Only to be met with volcanic responses such as, "But that's the point, I don't *want* to have to tell him what to do! He's an intelligent human being. I don't want the sole responsibility for figuring out what needs to be done and delegating it." I didn't want a minion I could order around either. Sharing the tasks wouldn't get us anywhere, if I still had the responsibility to delegate all those tasks.

These conversations among mothers unfold along one of two tracks. On the one track, we stay at the level of jokes and laughter about our husbands. Having had a chance to vent safely and blow off some steam, the conversation just moves on to other things—though it often circles back to venting about who does what. Sometimes this same track runs off the rails because someone in the group reveals too much information or emotion. Her jokes take on a bitter edge or her voice gets louder or she says something particularly damning about her husband. Not knowing how to deal with it, feeling more and more uncomfortable, the rest of us get quieter, sympathize, and then try to change the subject.

On the other conversation track, we move to trading explanations and advice. Someone often says mothers are simply wired to handle family stuff better. "It's so universal," we say to each other, "biology must be behind it." We cobble together bits of science to bolster the argument. Different hormones, different wiring in our brains, breast-feeding, and loose evolutionary theory along the lines of men as hunters and women as gatherers and caretakers. We match it to our experience. "Fathers can't seem to multitask the way we do; mothers seem to be more nurturing," we observe. The advice we offer each other is usually the path of acceptance, something along the lines of: "It's universal. It's biology. Just accept it and adapt, and everyone will be happier."

These conversations depressed me, even when I was an active participant in them or even the instigator of them. The most we got out of them was a release. I found it comforting to know I wasn't alone and to have a place to let the frustration out so my husband didn't get the full brunt of it, but that wasn't enough. None of the conversations seemed to help me figure out what to do about it. As my friend Carol lamented, "I feel as though I have to take responsibility for dressing three children plus me, while he shaves and showers and checks his e-mail. I want to fix it—complaining doesn't fix it and no one is helping me figure out how to fix it."

I had grown up being taught that men and women were equally capable of everything else, so I didn't want to believe that remembering to pack underwear and folding laundry were somehow exceptions to that rule. Given what had happened to David and me though, I now had my own doubts. The sinister forces of the Twilight Zone seemed immutable enough to be genetic. Plus, if I chalked it up to biology, I could avoid something I found very scary—the conflict that might rear its head and the risk to our relationship if I pushed too hard to do things differently. I wanted Kate to believe men and women were equally capable of everything, yet here I was wondering silently to myself, "Could it be that women are naturally better at caring for family after all? Or is there some other explanation? An explanation that might leave an opening for doing it differently?"

CRUNCHY WAFFLES:
Practice Makes a Perfectly Vicious Cycle

Then one morning later on, as David and I rushed through the morning routine to get Kate to preschool, I asked him to make her a waffle. When the wailing started, I returned to the kitchen, picked up the toaster waffle, and promptly scolded David. "Of course she won't eat that. It's crunchy from the toaster!" For at least a year,* I'd been microwaving the toaster waffles every morning so they would be soft. In that moment, it dawned on me that we did have a problem—and I was part of it. I was the only one who knew crunchy waffles were unacceptable because I was the only one who'd been preparing them for Kate. Yet I was blaming David for *toasting* a *toaster* waffle!

---

*I promised to disclose that the time period of "one year" was challenged by David when he read this. "No way were you doing that for a year!" To which I replied, "How would you know?"

I knew that biology could not have endowed me with a genetic ability to know when toaster waffles should be toasted or nuked. I saw the vicious cycle we'd fallen into. I just did everything and with so much practice, I was better at everything. Kate depended on me. David knew I would do everything and wasn't even sure he knew what "everything" was. And I silently, and sometimes not so silently, resented being responsible for everything. Pondering it some more, I realized the vicious cycle had started before Kate arrived.

When David and I found out I was pregnant, as if by some invisible directive, I got busy. I read a stack of books about child development. I signed up for parenting magazines and websites. I researched car seats, strollers, and baby food. Pretty soon, even though we took the childbirth class together, I knew a lot more than David did about babies. I was annoyed he didn't make an effort to learn more, but at the same time I enjoyed being the expert.

After Kate was born, we just got deeper into the vicious cycle. After our first five days together, David was back at work ten or twelve hours a day. As a matter of survival and sanity, I became acutely attuned to Kate over the next year; how long we could be out of the house before she melted down, how to make sure we had at least two pacifiers and her special blankie whenever we went out, when she would nap, how to get her to go to sleep, what she would eat, how to calm her down or make her laugh. I also did everything else family-related; groceries, planning and making meals, bills, laundry, and cleaning.

Even when I returned to employment, the cycle we were already in continued, and now I resented even more that I was doing everything. I rarely asked David for help. Yet I still got annoyed when he didn't do things. I was still the one keeping track of when she needed vaccinations and whether we'd given her some mineral oil for that unpleasant constipation issue. Before she started kindergarten, I went to four stores to find uniforms that would be comfortable. I special-ordered a backpack recommended by a magazine, aligned our family's sleeping schedule with the school schedule, read books to Kate about what school was like, and packed lunches stocked with her favorite foods. On the second day of school, when we got back home after dropping her off, I blew up at David for not doing any of it. Poor guy. He didn't know that I was freaking out or what he should be doing.

I had this odd combination of feelings—resentment about doing it all, but at the same time a pleasant feeling of superiority from being better at it. Which feeling came out, depended on my day, sort of like Dr. Jekyll and Mr. Hyde. On a good day, if David was trying in vain to get baby Kate to sleep, I'd flash him a patronizing smile, scoop her up, put her in my sling, and work my magic. On a bad day, I'd lash out. When I spent an hour bathing baby Kate and getting her to sleep, only to find David reading the newspaper with the dirty dinner dishes piled in the sink behind him, I would fly into a rage. "Are you blind? How can a college-educated man like you not even see what needs to be done around here?"

I'll bet I was a joy to live with.

I was making myself miserable too. I felt solely responsible for Kate's behavior. David's family invited us all to a fancy restaurant for a birthday dinner with toddler Kate. We both knew toddler plus dark steakhouse full of adults equals a recipe for disaster. David and I took turns walking her around and trying to keep her entertained, and just as our food was set down on the table, the inevitable meltdown happened, and the three of us got up to go home. The meltdown was a given. What surprised me was my own embarrassment and my anger with Kate. Deep down I felt people saw her behavior as a reflection on my mothering skills, much more so than on David's fathering skills.

I even felt responsible when something wasn't my responsibility. Every Tuesday, elementary school Kate needs to be picked up after school and dropped off at her theater class. David's mother, Ida, helps us out with this task, bless her, or I'm not sure we could get Kate to class. The Tuesday before a holiday break, I was going to be out of town so we asked Grandma to take chauffeur duty. At 5:30 that night, I got a call on my cell phone from Kate's school. Kate was in the after-school office saying that her grandma should have picked her up. I quickly called David on his cell phone. "My dad just called," he said, "Grandma forgot. She feels terrible. I'm on my way to school to get Kate." I felt awful too. When I saw Kate, her eyes got big and she whimpered, "I missed the last rehearsal before the break." My heart clenched. I should have been there to take her myself. I shouldn't have gone out of town. In other words, Grandma forgot, and *I* felt guilty.

It dawned on me that no matter what David and I said about mothers and fathers sharing responsibility for family, we somehow knew that the world around us would judge us, and we would judge ourselves and each other, against what mothers and fathers were *supposed* to do. Packing only one pair of underwear for a three-year-old reflected on me as a mother, even if it was David's task at the time. Forgetting to pick up Kate for theater class made me feel guilty, even if it was Grandma's task at the time. Mothers always feel as if they have the responsibility, even when someone else is doing the task. Depending on our personality and our situation, this sense of sole responsibility can turn us into control freaks or keep us in a constant state of anxiety and guilt.

The morning David made a crunchy waffle, I came to the hard realization that this wasn't entirely David's fault. I was part of the problem. Remembering or forgetting underwear wasn't biology, at least not completely. After the first five days of Kate's life, David never had responsibility for any of the family tasks. I'd just done them, invisibly, and now I expected him to see them all and know how to do them. I had to face up to the conflict inside me. On the surface I believed, and wanted to believe, that mothers and fathers could and should share responsibility for children and family, but I was acting as if I believed caring for family was *my* responsibility. I was acting as if I believed I was supposed to be better at it and that if I wasn't, other people would see me as a total failure. David was also acting as if I were better at it and had responsibility for it. He and I were feeding the vicious cycle ourselves, but how had it gotten started? Was biology the reason I had started to just do everything and the reason David had let me? How did we end up acting on beliefs we thought we had soundly rejected?

VICIOUS JUICE CYCLES:
Who Tells Mothers to Buy Juice?

One day, I went to get a juice box from the refrigerator to put in pre-school Kate's lunch. After I shut the fridge door and turned around, I stopped. Something wasn't right. I opened the door again and read the juice box package more closely.

> "Juicy Juice is a proud partner with Scholastic, supporting *moms* in their effort to raise kids that are 100% healthy." (emphasis added)

Not families, not moms and dads, not parents, just *moms*.

I had been buying the same juice for years, yet I had not noticed that the package assumed *I* was the one solely responsible for raising my daughter. I'm sure a clever marketing person used the language intentionally. I bet mothers buy more juice for kids than fathers do. Of course, I don't think mothers are embracing the juice-buying responsibility just because the copy on the container is directed to them, but marketing language perpetuates the assumption that moms are buying the juice, creating a vicious juice cycle.

I didn't want to think I'd fallen prey to social conditioning, but I began to see messages about mothers and fathers and about who does what all around me as if someone had given me new glasses that suddenly brought everything into focus. I love reading magazines, but my clearer vision made it difficult to enjoy them. In a popular parents' magazine an ad for children's cold medicine described it as, "*Mommy's* new favorite mucus fighter!"[2] Another ad showed a kid buried in dirty tissues and under him it reads, "*Mom* worries when a cold makes it hard for *her* kid to breathe."[3] Wait a minute. Is Mother the only one charged with fighting mucus, the only one who should be worrying? Why doesn't it say parents worry, or moms and dads worry, or even simply we worry when our kids can't breathe? While we're at it, why do they call them "parents" magazines at all, when they are clearly targeted to mothers? On *Parenting* magazine's website the banner announces, "What Parenting *Moms* Are Clicking On Now!"

How about television? Family sitcoms follow a standard formula explained by my friend Kristie: "Completely hot mom takes care of house and kids—plus overweight or bald, sometimes both, dad who can't seem to figure out how to dress himself let alone help out around the house." A surefire formula for comedy is the ineptitude of fathers, played out in such movies as *Daddy Day Care*. Television advertising? As Renate observed, "When was the last time you saw a diaper commercial that shows a father changing a diaper? Or bathing a baby? Dad's the one holding the video camera." Now, I don't think there's a vast media conspiracy to keep mothers buying juice and making waffles and to keep fathers away from vacuum cleaners and diapers. I think magazines and television writers and advertisers quite rationally respond to what is already a deep cultural assumption: that Mother is the one taking care of the kids and the house and Father is clueless. They use this assumption to serve their own interests. People will buy movie tickets to laugh at the dad who can't diaper a baby. Mothers who have so much to do will buy magazines and other stuff to help us get it all done.

Even so, how could the media have converted us so easily into Twilight Zone Kristin and Twilight Zone David? It would likely take more than just the media to brainwash both me and David. What else was going on?

WHEN BABY-SITTING ISN'T BABY-SITTING: A Daily Double Standard

I realized that on multiple occasions other people said or did things to show they assumed I had primary responsibility for our daughter and my husband had responsibility for certain other things. When David and I went to the car dealership, for example, they addressed him. When we went to a teacher conference at preschool, they addressed me. When people wanted to arrange a play date with Kate, they called or e-mailed me. I got an e-mail from a mother who was asking friends what to do about her son being bullied, and she asked if she should call the boy's *mom*. Why not his dad? Or his parents? My friend Barbara told me, "My mother-in-law always assumes every-thing is me. She directs all feedback/opinions/suggestions to me, way out of proportion to how we actually share parenting." Daily, moth-ers get the message that they are responsible for family.

After Kate was born, I went to *"Mommy* and Me" classes. Where are the "Daddy and Me" classes? Or the "Parents and Me" classes? Mothers are expected to be or become the experts. Dads are expected to be clueless about kids, so it's okay for them to *be* clueless. As Cindy protests, "My husband gets SO much social support for his jokes about not knowing what baby things are, how to diaper, etc. It makes me want to throw up all over these supposedly progressive males in my circle of friends and family." Or as Margot shared, "When I take a business trip and . . . (my husband) watches the kids for two days he is given such praise although I have done all laundry and prepared all meals, etc. . . . before I leave. When he goes on a business trip it is just a given that I can handle all when he is gone." Most everyone has an invisible mental map, a set of subconscious assumptions, that says mothers are responsible for and should be good at family; fathers stumble alongside. This mental map creates a double standard for mothers and fathers, setting the bar unattainably high for mothers and insultingly low for fathers.

In an e-mail conversation, Kiki explained how the double standard popped up one day at her workplace. A co-worker asked her if she would bake a casserole for "Bob" and Kiki asked why. The woman replied, "Well, you know his wife left him and he has to raise his kids all by himself, so we are going to help him out. We are going to get together and make some meals so he just has to come home and heat it up so he won't have to cook or go grocery shopping, and we'll work out a car pool to take his kids to their sporting events so he won't have to leave work to do it and whatever else we can do to help him. . . . Because he is raising his kids all by himself—we HAVE to help him." Kiki then asked her co-worker, "Where is my casserole? I am raising my kids all by myself and I make at least $10,000 a year less than Bob. Where is Betty's casserole? Her husband left her years ago and she's raising her kids all by herself. What makes Bob's situation so different from Betty's or mine?" Her co-worker responded as if it were obvious, "Well, 'cause he's a man, . . . and we HAVE to help him." The assumptions underneath her co-worker's words and actions were that "Bob" couldn't care for family because he's a man, but a woman in the same situation would be able to do it all, no problem.

As my friend Tod told me, the double standard can be just as annoying for fathers. One weekend, Tod took care of his two young girls while his wife was out of town. He said many people sought him out to ask how things were going. "It was nice to get some extra attention and know that there was help available to me, but it also made me wonder how many people made the same effort to seek out my wife when I was out of town. Further, many people asked how the 'baby-sitting' was going. It left me feeling sidelined in my own children's lives. Was I really no more involved than the girl down the street that earns $10 an hour to keep an eye on the kids?" Poor Tod, can you imagine someone telling a mother how great she is to baby-sit her own children while her husband is out of town?

Even our children pick up these assumptions no matter how careful we may be to avoid them. After a special family meal, Kara encouraged her son to help by saying that after she had spent time on the cooking, she was sure he'd be happy to help clean up the kitchen. Her eight-year-old son said, "You mean do the dishes? But I'm *not a girl!*" Kara and her husband were stunned. She and her husband share the chores. They were consciously trying to model balanced family roles. Yet when she asked her son why he thought dishes were a girl thing, he sheepishly said, "I don't know, Mom, I really don't. I wasn't trying to be mean or rude. It's just what I thought. I'm sorry." He was telling the truth. He didn't know why he thought what he thought, and it wasn't because his Y chromosome knew that doing dishes was for girls. For eight years, his perfectly tuned social radar had been picking up signals about what it means to be a boy or a girl, a father or a mother. The messages his mother and father were trying to send were just one blip among many books, TV shows, innocent comments, and observations he'd made of other families. Even if we manage to break the vicious cycle within our own family, we're up against forces that keep the cycle going across generations.

A comment here or an advertisement there seems to be such a little thing. In fact, we might not even notice any given comment or juice box label because there are so many. But taken together, they are evidence of a much larger problem lurking beneath the surface, assumptions about mothers and fathers so deep and so pervasive that they have become effectively invisible even though they have a powerful influence on our lives. Assumptions so powerful and invisible that in my own home, David and I, as enlightened as we intended to be, spent years as Twilight Zone David and Twilight Zone Kristin, acting in ways that constantly conflicted with our expectations of each other and our marriage.

HOPE FOR BREAKING THE CYCLE

Frankly, I was relieved to find that biology might not explain why I could calm Kate so much better than David or why I saw dirty laundry and remembered to make pediatrician appointments and he didn't. If mothers were supposed to be naturally gifted at caring for children, that would have made me a freak of nature. Hardly anything mothers are supposed to be able to do came naturally to me. Even breastfeeding, the most natural thing of all, was a disaster for me despite the very "unnatural" help of several breastfeeding consultants and pumps and plastic contraptions.

Fortunately, while I know women, like my sister, who took to motherhood like a fish to water, I also know other women, like me, who did quite a bit of flopping around before we could swim. I know men, like my uncle, who was a single father of two young children and one of the most caring, gifted parents I've known. I also know men who are uncomfortable around their own babies and most comfortable in the office. I'm thankful that I realized I was not a freak of nature. Nature seems to have quite a wide range of how "naturally" different men and women take to caring for family.

Now, I'm not denying that men and women have biological differences. However, science increasingly finds that it's not that simple. Some evidence says women are actually more different from each other than they are different from men.[4] Plus, biology is not destiny. Even if many mothers excel at certain family tasks that doesn't mean caring for family *should* be every mother's sole responsibility. The biology piece of "who does what at home" is a lot smaller than we tend to think. Sure, biology plays the biggest role in kicking off the vicious cycle. Mothers have the monopoly on childbirth and breastfeeding, for example. So if a mother gives birth, by necessity she'll need some time to recover. Add in breastfeeding, and mother ends up spending a lot of time with a new baby. That in turn can feed assumptions both mothers and fathers may have that she's the expert and he's just a bystander. However, after the first months of an infant's life, just about everything it takes to care for family can be done well by mothers *and* fathers. But by then, in many cases, the vicious cycle has already kicked in and can be hard to break.

Hard, but not impossible. So now I had hope. Even if the world around us was one big vicious juice box cycle, if David and I had crossed into the Twilight Zone in part because of our own mental maps about mothers and fathers and our own vicious cycle, then maybe we could do something about it. Maybe there was a possibility that David and I could remodel so that we shared responsibility for family and didn't drive each other nuts. So where in the cycle could we aim to break it?

Let's review. Growing up, David and I each developed an invisible mental map that *mothers are responsible for and are naturally better at children and family*. Our baby arrives, and five days later, David goes back to work. Driven by our assumptions and sheer necessity—and yes, especially initially by biological things like breastfeeding and hormones—I take over everything and get better and better at taking care of Kate and keeping track of appointments and planning meals and everything family related. We spiral helplessly into the Twilight Zone.

So going back to the beginning, what if we didn't have that invisible mental map? What if we had a different one? The trick to breaking down mental maps is to surface them so we become consciously aware of them. Once we can see the assumptions, then we can link our imagination to action.[5] We can imagine: What if we had a different belief? What if instead we held a belief that

Mothers and fathers share the responsibility and are equally capable of caring for children and home.

If we believed this, what would we say to each other and to others in our daily lives? How would we behave and what decisions would we make? How would the world operate if this belief were universal? Armed with our answers, we can then experiment by acting on the answers to see if our new belief is a better match for our lives, a more useful blueprint for building the lives we want.

So I asked myself, what if David and I believed that

Mothers and fathers share the responsibility and are equally capable of caring for children and home.

What would we say? Well, sometime after the crunchy waffle and juice box incidents, I noticed that I often use the word *I* when I should use the word *we*. Someone might ask what school-age Kate will be doing over the summer, and I say, "*I* decided on swim camp for her then a few weeks of theater class." Well, technically, I filled out the forms, but David and I had decided together what would be best for the summer.

I also realized I often asked David to "help me out" with something at home. The words sound polite but also mean I am assuming that the dishes or the clutter or the figuring out how to deal with Kate's nightmares are my responsibility and he is helping once in a while. Instead I tried saying things like "We need to tackle the dishes" and "Let's see what we can find out about how other people deal with monsters under the bed." If we had a new mental map, we might even help other people talk differently. When Amy's husband said she was the better parent, she quickly corrected, "No, I'm the more *practiced* parent." When Tod was complimented for baby-sitting his daughters, he politely corrected that he was parenting. When we use language that reflects what we want to believe, we shift our own mental maps and those of the people around us.

So how might we *behave* differently? If David and I really believed mothers and fathers shared the responsibility and were equally capable, then I would encourage David to get more practice, and David would look for more opportunities to practice and remind me to let him do it his way. I'd bite my tongue when he did things differently from the way I would. Quite from luck, we stumbled into providing David with some crash courses. When I started traveling for business about once a month when Kate was in preschool, I worried about how David and Kate would manage. They managed just fine—which both pleased me and made me a bit put out that they didn't depend on me quite as much as I had assumed. I think those trips proved to all three of us that David could take care of Kate and everything else just as well as I could, and our mental maps shifted even more.

I know mothers and fathers who were much more proactive than David and I were about making sure both of them got practice. Jeanne described a situation that at first sounded just like what happened to David and me. "As I took maternity leave and my husband continued to work for pay, I became the de facto expert on our baby. I was attuned to his rhythms and what his cries meant, and became practiced in those little things that add up." But Jeanne and her husband were smarter than we were. "What we did," she explained, "and what we recommend to anyone who can do it, is when I went back to work my husband took time out of his job to be the primary caregiver for a while. With our first son he took off two months. With our second it was one week. As a result, while I was on maternity leave I made an effort to communicate the things my husband would need to know when he took over. . . . My husband also got to become an expert on our baby in his own right. That experience set the stage for our parenthood being divided as evenly as we could."

The earlier couples have an opportunity for each to practice and become experts at caring for children and family, the harder it is for that vicious cycle to set in and the easier it is for them to intentionally arrange things the way they want them at any given moment in their lives. As Scott Coltrane, a sociology professor, sums up, "If couples deliberately divide tasks early in the relationship, a pattern of sharing becomes self-perpetuating. If couples assume that sharing will happen on its own, women end up doing virtually everything."[6] If we believe mothers and fathers share the responsibility for family, then we should be deliberate about figuring out how to share.

David and I hadn't been deliberate about figuring out how to share responsibility for family before Kate arrived. However one time when Kate was still a baby and we were arguing about who was doing their fair share at home, David challenged me to make a list of what we each did. Here's a short sample:

STUFF I DO	STUFF DAVID DOES
• Keep family calendar.	• Take out the trash.
• Pay bills.	• Plan investments.
• Plan meals, make list, buy groceries.	• Get car oil changed.
• Make breakfast, lunch, and dinner.	• Make household repairs.
• Notice when we need clean clothes and do laundry.	• Mow the lawn.
• Give Kate a bath every night.	• Clean litter box.
• Notice when Kate outgrows her clothes and get new ones.	

The two lists were different and not just in length. As Judith Stadtman Tucker, Mothers & More member and founder of the Mothers Movement Online observes, men "tend to do tasks that are less time sensitive than the household or caregiving tasks that women do. Women are more likely to be responsible for the things that must be done on a daily basis at a certain time, like preparing meals for children or helping with homework."[7] Mothers are also more likely to be responsible for the tasks directly related to children's needs. That's one reason a father can feel he's doing his fair share, while mother feels she's doing much more. He may be doing everything that is typically expected of fathers, he may have a long list, but it's very different stuff. Mowing the lawn and changing the oil don't happen every day, and even the cat litter can wait a day or two. Feeding a toddler or making sure a child has everything he or she needs for school the next day can't wait. Making my own list helped me see that I did have responsibility for a whole lot of stuff and that my stuff was fundamentally different from David's stuff. Understanding that gave me the confidence and the language I needed to talk with David about how we could divide the tasks differently.

WHY CAN'T WE SHARE THE FAMILY WORK EVEN THOUGH WE WANT TO?

As I came to understand more about how David and I had slipped into the Twilight Zone, we were able to take some baby steps toward sharing the family work. However, we still felt like we had one foot stuck in the Twilight Zone, and I was stumped as to why we couldn't escape completely. Why couldn't we manage to really share the responsibility for family even though we wanted to and even though we could see this vicious cycle? We couldn't escape completely because "who does what at home" was just one of many self-perpetuating cycles we were stuck in, and they were all connected to each other. We were also dealing with vicious cycles around things like work, and money, and time. We had trouble escaping the Twilight Zone because the larger problem was a web of invisible assumptions about mothers, fathers, marriage, money, work, time, and our very identities. David and I were tangled up on opposite sides of that web. Before we could really understand completely what was happening to *us*, I needed to get myself untangled and deal with what was happening to *me*.

REMODELING TOOLS

Each of the items in these lists lets you try out one or more of our Remodeling Tools: Build a Balcony, Draft a Blueprint, Remodel Your Life, Remodel Our House. Try one or two yourself, or better yet share with some friends over coffee…or margaritas.

▶ Flip through a women's magazine or parents' magazine and look at the ads. How many have images or language that reflect an assumption that Mother is the natural caregiver and has responsibility for the family? Can you think of other examples of a magazine, commercial, TV show, or other media reinforcing the idea that mothers are naturally better at taking care of children and family? Point them out to your spouse or your friends. Write letters to the companies or publishers pointing out the problem with the messages they are sending.

▶ Listen to your own words and the people around you. Do you ever use *I* when it probably should be *we*? Do you notice mothers using the "good husband caveat" or fathers joking about being clueless? Do other people talk as if they assumed the mother has responsibility for kids and family? Politely point it out when you can. Even simply noticing it yourself helps you surface and shift your own assumptions.

▶ Make your own "Stuff I Do" list, and if you're married or have a partner, make a "Stuff My Spouse Does" list. How long are the lists? How are the tasks different? Simply making the lists can help you see the reality behind how you feel about who does what.

▶ What could your family do to build confidence that both mothers and fathers can and should take part in caring for family? Can Father take the kids on his own for a day or a weekend or more? Can Mother take responsibility for a home repair job? No matter how you share responsibility now, what would take one or both of you out of your current comfort zone?

▶ If you and your family truly believed *mothers and fathers share the responsibility and are equally capable of caring for children and home,* what would you say? What would you do differently? How would the world operate?

2

the mother of all to-do lists

or why didn't anyone tell me

how hard this is?

WHEN I WAS pregnant, the covers of my pregnancy magazines featured cheerful, fit moms doing yoga with their babies.
At the time, the images felt inspiring. I imagined how rosy my life
would be with a baby. After Kate was born, the magazine pictures of
smiling, put-together moms who made their own baby food and ran
multimillion-dollar businesses from their homes didn't inspire me. I
just felt unworthy. All I could seem to get done in a day was a shower
and maybe a trip to the park—and that was a good day.

Magazines, newspapers, radio, and books told me everything I
should be doing and all about the dire consequences if I slipped up.
Breastfeed for at least a year or risk infections and IQ points. A child's
academic achievement is linked to the mother's education level so
spend lots of time talking and reading to your child or sacrifice more
IQ points. Don't forget safety! Buy the right car seats, teach your
child how to avoid strangers, check the playground equipment, keep

track of toy recalls, baby-proof your entire house and the grandparents' homes as well. Constant vigilance is a must. Constant attention
to nutrition is too. Make your own baby food. The jarred stuff is full
of junk. Don't give them sweets, not even juice, and limit TV or risk
obesity and diabetes.

Education is the only way to get ahead in the information age in a
global economy. So do your research and then use whatever bribery or
flattery it takes to get your kids into a good school or they are doomed
to work at McDonald's until they die. Teach your kids to be independent, but be sure to show plenty of love and affection and spend lots
of quality time together. Teach them how to fall asleep on their own,
but go to them when they cry at night or they'll develop abandonment issues. Get them involved in sports and music classes, but don't
overschedule and don't put on too much pressure. Oh, and emotional
intelligence is even more important for success than IQ so be sure to
teach manners, how to get along with people, and self-awareness.

What?! I was caring for baby Kate around the clock, I was sleep
deprived, I was effectively parenting solo, I'd lost everything in my
former life—my colleagues and friends, my income, my work, my
sanity—and I was being told that no matter what I do I will end up
causing my daughter permanent physical, psychological, intellectual,
or economic damage? I finally decided I should just set aside money
for Kate for the time she would have to pay for "Therapy for All the
Things Your Mother Messed Up." No wonder all those mothers were
doing yoga on the magazine covers, though I suspected a bottle of
wine might also do the trick.

Wine and yoga only last so long though. I needed a place and
some people to talk to about what was going on. You'd think with all
the "Mommy and Me" classes and mothers' groups, this would have
been easy. It wasn't. I sat on the carpet at "Mommy and Me" class in
a circle of fellow bleary-eyed, vomit-stained mothers with infants in
carriers. When I tentatively said that being a mother was much more
difficult and nerve-wracking than I had expected, some would com-
miserate briefly but close off the conversation with an upbeat, "But
it's all worth it!" When I ventured to ask if anyone else felt they were

losing themselves, their sanity, and their marriage, some would agree that getting sleep or time for themselves was a challenge. Then they would quickly offer parenting tips or parenting books they used. I didn't know what to make of these responses. How to take care of Kate wasn't my problem. Taking care of *me* was. Surely there was something very wrong with me. No one else seemed to be struggling! Everyone else seemed to have it under control or they were just more patient and virtuous. I loved Kate too much to reveal to anyone else that I couldn't live up to what everyone seemed to think mothers should be.

Why hadn't anyone told me how hard this would be? Why was my expectation of motherhood so different from my reality? Why wouldn't anyone talk to me? Was it possible I was the only one who'd ever felt this way?

WHAT'S HAPPENING TO *ME*?

Several months after Kate was born, I made one of my regular calls to my own mother. Frantic and tired, I scolded her. "Why didn't you tell me it was this hard?" Trying to empathize, she told me her story. I was two when my middle sister arrived. My dad was away working by day, in law school at night, and in the reserves on the weekend. My mother was alone in a new city with no car. And my sister, Sarah, had colic for nine months! My mom would sit downstairs and try to read books to me as Sarah cried upstairs. I sputtered, but I just scolded her again. "So, why didn't you tell me it was this hard?" She couldn't really say. Why hadn't I ever asked? I couldn't really say either. Something had kept me from asking my own mother about her story, and something had kept her from telling it.

I find it easy to talk to other mothers about certain things. Even at the playground or the PTA meeting, mothers who barely know each other exchange stories about toddler tantrums and teenage mood swings. We'll trade tips on how to get kids to wipe their own backsides or how to do their homework. With mothers we know, we don't hesitate to joke or even complain about our spouses. But that wasn't what I needed. I needed to go deeper, and I needed to talk about *me*.

I needed to be able to tell someone that I missed my old job, my old life, my friends, and my colleagues and not worry that he or she would take that to mean I didn't love Kate. I needed to talk about how underneath my jokes about my husband, I was really angry at him. I was scared of what that anger might do to my marriage. Could we survive the number of fights we were having? Given the tension, could we even talk to each other to figure out how to recover our relationship? I also needed to talk about how taking care of a baby all day was . . . well, draining. And, truth be told, boring a lot of the time. I needed to talk about how none of this seemed to be turning out the way I thought it would. I needed to talk long enough and deep enough to understand what was happening to *me*. Except, no one would talk to me, and I was afraid that it wasn't happening to anyone else. I was stuck.

One of the books I read while I was pregnant mentioned a group called Mothers & More. [1] I had joined online back then. Little did I know how much I'd need that connection. In desperation, with my three-month-old in tow, I trekked across Los Angeles to a Mothers & More chapter meeting. I blurted it all out. I told them my chest felt tight all the time, and I didn't know why. I said I was in love with my baby and my husband, but I was mad, sad, stressed, and lonely and felt guilty for having all those feelings. "We know," they said. "We feel it too."

A weight lifted from my chest. I wasn't alone. We were all different: some young and some not so young, some employed and some not employed, some were dealing with postpartum depression and others were simply trying to deal with the unexpected parts of their experience. Certainly not everyone was reeling as hard as I was, but we also had so much in common. We loved our husbands and our children, but we felt like we couldn't win no matter what we did. We felt like the expectations of a "good mother" were hopelessly out of reach and left no room for *us*. Until we'd found each other, we'd felt alone, reluctant to reveal our confused and conflicted truth. I left the meeting with a feeling of hope, of camaraderie, and, most important, of knowing I was definitely not alone. Maybe this conversation could go deep enough to help me understand what was going on and figure out a different way.

I found that mothers across the country often feel alone, sometimes even when they are together. One mother confessed, "I've always felt very much alone in my role as mother—once I finally made friends with other mothers, we were 'alone' together in that every aspect of our children's lives was our responsibility, including how they reacted to situations and behaved."[2] Like me, mothers find it easy to talk about some things, and others are strictly off limits. My friend Carol told me, "Revealing the common is no big deal—revealing the big stuff, the stuff that really alters the way you see yourself as a mother is much harder. I don't reveal those things because I don't want others to judge me or judge my children." We are reluctant to open up because we're afraid of being judged against an invisible, sky-high set of standards. We don't go deep in conversation about all the ups and downs, the happiness and rage, the anxiety and contentment that comes with motherhood, because we're afraid we're the only ones who feel this way. We're afraid it's some failing of ours and—worst of all, what we can't bear—we're afraid someone will think we don't love our kids or that we are "bad" mothers. My friend Rosemary, an actress, described motherhood as "a constant audition, for the most demanding critics." Yes! That's how I feel. But who are the critics? Who set these standards anyway? And how do we get that person fired?

ADDING TO OUR TO-DO LIST

With the help of my friends, I was able to step back far enough to unpack that assumption from the last chapter that *mothers are responsible for and are naturally better at children and family*. From the balcony I could see that everything I expected of myself or felt other people expected of me had built up over time like fossilized layers of rock. Judith Stadtman Tucker, the founder of the Mothers Movement Online, told me, "It's not just in the last fifteen or even fifty years that our ideas of motherhood have changed. Our ideas about mothers' responsibilities and abilities and the right way to bring up children have changed profoundly throughout American history." Mothers have been adding to our to-do list for a couple of hundred years now, creating the Mother of All To-Do Lists. We haven't been able to check anything off or give anything to someone else, and every item on that list has a dire consequence for *not* doing it. From my balcony seat, I started examining more closely everything I felt I was responsible for in our family.

HOME AND WORK BECOME DIFFERENT DIMENSIONS

When Kate was born, one of the big changes in our lives was how David and I separated from each other each morning. David went out in the world to make money, to fight for our survival, to compete, to be a mover and shaker. I stayed at home and cared for Kate, but "home" wasn't just our actual house, though I spent lots of time there. "Home" was a different dimension, a cocoon where time moved more slowly, where fighting and competing weren't allowed, where, if I did my job, we would be protected from the world out there. Things I read and people I talked to told me that as a mother I was, "holding civilization together where civilization begins—in the home."[3] The year Kate was born, a popular parenting expert said that my task was nothing less than to "lay the foundation of morality, a person's sense of right and wrong."[4] Boy, that's a lot of pressure for one person.

It wasn't always this way. During colonial times, fathers were in charge of everything, and everything happened at home. Mothers and children were laborers, overseen by Father. Everyone worked from dawn to dusk to feed, clothe, and shelter the family. Fathers made decisions about disciplining children and usually dealt the punishment themselves with a switch from a nearby tree. Fathers made decisions about whether children would go to school or work in the fields. Mothers were expected to have lots of children and knew that many would die in childhood. Mothers were told these deaths might well be punishment for their own sins, one of which was a tendency to love their children too much.[5] Though mothers were doing the tasks of daily care, mothers with their "unruly passion" weren't to be trusted with the responsibility of raising children[6] or the children might not grow up at all.[7] How did we get from mothers can't even be trusted with children to my sense that I was the *only* person who could be trusted to raise my child right?

Two revolutions happened, that's what. The American Revolution pulled fathers into the work of building and fighting for the new country. Mothers were given the task of raising the citizens of the fledgling democracy, the sons and daughters of the revolution. Mothers were to raise sons who had the moral character and basic education to participate in the creation of this new nation. Daughters should be taught to support those men and to raise the next generation of citizens. For the good of the republic, mothers had patriotic work to do at home while fathers were on the front lines.[8]

Then came the Industrial Revolution. What was once family work supervised by father was physically divided into father's work and mother's work; his was out there and hers was at home. Father left home every day for the factory. Most mothers didn't. At least the prevailing opinion was that a proper lady shouldn't, though poor women and women of color often worked in those same factories. As industry became the engine that fed families, made clothes, drove the economy, and made the world go around, mothers got an additional set of duties. The growth of industry, everyone assumed, unleashed greed and competition only men could handle. Given the cold and calculating world out there, men needed a refuge from it at home. Boys needed to develop a moral compass to guide them when they entered that world. The nation needed a force for good and a model of virtue that would keep us all from spiraling to the dark side of our greedy natures. Mothers were thus called on to protect us all from ourselves by looking after Home Sweet Home while fathers went out in the world to fight for economic survival. Plus, now that families depended on wages to survive, mothers were responsible for making sure boy children grew up to be obedient workers and could earn enough money to support their aging parents.[9]

The shift in mothers' roles was so dramatic that by the late 1800s, while fathers were still masters of the house, "child rearing was synonymous with mothering" and the "overall image of both was one of pervasive sentimentality mixed with purity, piety and patriotism."[10] Over time, everyone came to consider mothers naturally superior at raising children and caring for the home. Mothers, it was assumed, had the natural instincts for love and compassion. Mothers smiled and withstood the most difficult times and greatest sacrifices, in part because women were expected to be submissive and in part because their inherent virtue meant that the love of their children made it all worthwhile.[11]

As the protectors of the nation's virtue and future, mothers gained a moral and practical authority in the home that they hadn't had before and didn't have outside the home. On the flip side, this responsibility came with serious consequences for messing up.[12] If a good citizen and worker was a credit to his mother's love and attention, then a child gone astray was her failure to serve her country.[13] Janna Malamud Smith, psychologist and author of *A Potent Spell,* details the history of how fear has been used to get mothers to follow advice they are given. She observes that mothers became "deities when they are 'good,' and scorned, harmful failures when they are 'bad.'"[14]

When I looked back at this long history, I could see the origins of my invisible belief that Kate was my responsibility, that it was my responsibility to make our home a cocoon of love separate from the world out there, that civilization itself depended on me, and that if I couldn't do all that without complaining then, well, I was a failure. I could see how several items had ended up on my own Mother of All To-Do Lists.

❑ Raise the citizens of the democracy while the father goes out and builds it.
❑ Raise the workers of our economy while the father goes out and competes in it.

❑ Build children's moral character.

❑ Raise children who can financially support their elderly mother and father.

❑ Make your home a haven from the cutthroat culture of industry.

❑ Stand as a model of virtue for society.

❑ Do all of the above with the patience and serenity of a saint.

EXPERT ADVICE

When I had Kate, I felt compelled to read scores of parenting advice books, all told in the same calm, usually fatherly, voice. Ninety-seven of every hundred American mothers read at least one parenting book, but most read more than one.[15] Judging from the numbers, we read the same ones. Dr. Benjamin Spock's *Baby and Child Care*, first published in 1946, has outsold every other book except the Bible.[16] When I was pregnant, I read Spock and Sears and Brazelton and *What to Expect When You're Expecting,* and then I would summarize them over the phone for my sister, also pregnant at the time. She had stopped reading them because they stressed her out too much. But wait, if I am so naturally superior at doing all this, why the heck do I have to read so many books and take classes on how to do it?

Mothers have been bombarded with expert advice for centuries. However, in the last century, science ramped up the advice, setting up a contradictory expectation of mothers as naturally superior at family but dependent on science to do it right. Science had become the key to progress on so many societal fronts. Mothers, then, must have scientific training and advice as well.[17] Over a century, and on my own bookshelf, doctors and experts assured mothers that, with careful study, we could gain the knowledge and skills to expertly guide not only the physical but also the increasingly important emotional and intellectual development of our children. Despite the fact that these experts switched to mostly gender-neutral language by the 1970s, a century of experts, mostly men, spoke to mothers, not parents. If mothers didn't study or ignored the experts and went with their instincts, then their kids would grow up into maladjusted adults who couldn't function or support their own parents.[18] At the same time, we were told by icons like Dr. Spock himself, "Trust yourself. You know more than you think you do."[19] As Sharon Hays, author of *The Cultural Contradictions of Motherhood,* points out, Spock opens with his "trust your instincts" message but then follows it with nearly *nine hundred pages* of expert advice.[20] Ann Hulbert, who chronicled the past century of advice in her book *Raising America: Experts, Parents and a Century of Advice about Children,* sums up "the conflicting child-rearing counsel of an entire century" in this way: "Trust your instincts and train your insight, follow your baby's nature and spare no effort on her nurture—relax and enjoy those first years and don't forget for a minute that your child's future is at stake."[21]

Paradoxically, the rise of the scientific expert adviser for mothers and our dependence on him *raised* the status of mothers. On the one hand, the experts were telling us we couldn't handle it on our own. However, they also elevated taking care of family "to the status of a scientific profession."[22] Mothers, who for a long time couldn't vote or own property or pursue careers, had complete control over the care of children and the home, which now required the equivalent of an advanced degree to do properly. That's why I felt compelled to read an entire library of books even when I also felt taking care of family was somehow supposed to come naturally. That's how two polar opposite tasks got added to my Mother of All To-Do Lists:

- ❏ Follow all of the latest scientific advice about caring for children's physical, emotional, psychological, and intellectual well-being.
- ❏ Relax and listen to your natural, maternal instinct.

DUELING EXPERTS

Reading and listening to all that expert advice made my head spin. Different experts seemed to contradict one another. Some told me I needed to do whatever it took to bond with my child, become attuned to her shifting needs, and respond unfailingly. Others told me I was supposed to be able to set limits, teach her independence, and be the parent. So no matter what I did, I felt as if I were failing someone's test.

For example, before Kate was born, I took a breastfeeding class that advised breastfeeding on demand and painted a lovely picture of the mother-child bond. Except once she arrived, Kate fought every attempt to breastfeed. The hospital sent us home with an industrial-strength breast pump. Every three hours I would wrestle my stubborn seven-pound baby for a half hour at my breasts. Then I would spend another thirty minutes giving her a bottle since David wasn't around to do it. I'd put her down in her crib to spend another forty-five minutes hunched over the breast pump only to start it all again an hour later. My back screamed with pain.

One night five weeks later, a breastfeeding consultant visited us and taped plastic tubes to my chest so that Kate could try to breast-feed and get formula at the same time. When she left, I looked up at David with tears in my eyes and tubes down my chest. "There's no way I can tape myself into this contraption when I'm home alone," I said. "I can't do it anymore. I need to stop and just go with the bottle." David was relieved. My back was relieved. But I felt guilty for months. I hadn't been able to bond and respond at all costs.

Sleep was another problem area. On the one hand, by the time Kate was born, "co-sleepers," those small bassinets that attach to an adult bed, were a hot baby registry item. Some books I read advised a family bed as the most natural way to promote bonding and responding to a child's needs. On the other hand, some books I read said co-sleeping was unsafe, would keep the child from learning good sleep habits, and could even keep her from learning to be independent period. Those experts said the right thing to do was to teach Kate to sleep on her own by not going to her when she cried. I didn't know what to think, but David and I already knew our child was a wriggler. If we did the co-sleeping thing, we might not sleep through the night until she left for college. So we went with the "teach her to sleep on her own" approach. I would sit in the kitchen watching the timer, flinching at each cry, waiting until the schedule said I could go in to comfort her. Except I caved regularly and rocked her to sleep. I wasn't truly able to set limits and teach independence.

When we look again at the last century of expert advice to mothers, two camps have been rehashing the same debates the whole time: rigid feeding schedules with a bottle vs. breastfeed on demand, potty train by two years vs. wait until the child shows interest, let the baby cry it out vs. rock him or her to sleep, set limits with clear punishments or talk through problems together. The list extends from babies to teenagers.[23] Mothers have been stuck in the middle wondering whom to listen to and suffering from uncertainty and self-doubt no matter what they do. As I dealt with questions of feeding and sleeping, zealous experts and mothers made the case for each camp. The differences were fundamental. It was about what you believe, not the simply practical—what works. As Hulbert explains, "Two poles have defined America's child-rearing advice from the very start. . . . How much power and control do, and should, parents wield over a child's journey from dependence to independence? How much freedom and intimacy do children need, or want, along the way? And, the implicit question lurking not far behind both of those over the past hundred years . . . What do the answers imply about mothers' rights and responsibilities?"[24] While in practice David and I tend to pick and choose from advice across the spectrum, a century of conflicting advice placed two more conflicting responsibilities onto my growing Mother of All To-Do Lists:

- ❏ Bond with your child; let your unique child's evolving needs guide your care; and spend the time, money, and emotional energy necessary to respond to those needs unfailingly.
- ❏ Be the parent, set limits and consequences, enforce discipline, encourage independence, and avoid being overly indulgent.

FLYING SOLO

I also felt I had to do everything myself when it came to Kate. Or at least I had to feel awful if I wasn't doing it all myself. For example, David's parents have always pitched in to take care of Kate. As I increased my employment and his mother retired, Grandma pitched in even more. Elementary school Kate goes to Grandma's when she is sick and neither David nor I can stay home from work to be with her. Grandma also picks her up at school at least once a week for an afternoon together. Kate stays overnight when David and I need a date night. Grandma and Grandpa love spending time with Kate, and David and I wouldn't survive a month without them. Still, I feel bad every time we call Grandma and Grandpa for help. Even when Kate is sick and my paid work has stacked up, I'll try to keep Kate at home in the morning watching TV so she isn't at Grandma's all day. Somehow, I feel like we—no actually, *I*—am supposed to be able to do all the family care on my own. I've even heard people ask judgmentally, "Why would a woman have children if she didn't want to raise them?" as if a woman didn't deserve to have kids if she doesn't do every minute of the raising herself. Yet, I've never heard that said about a father. How did doing it all solo get added to our list?

Doing it all on our own began back with our two revolutions and the separation of work and home. She took the responsibility for home, and he took responsibility for earning money. Once that split occurred, mothers didn't expect fathers to help much at home. However, that didn't mean we were caring for children and home all on our own. For a long time, mothers shared "women's work" with grandmas and aunts and older siblings. However, the rise of the scientific mothering experts meant we could no longer really trust any of those folks to take care of children right because mothers are the naturals and the only ones who've undertaken the study required. Today, babies are supposed to sleep on their backs, breastfeed as long as possible, and car seats require an engineering degree to install correctly. How was I supposed to get advice from or hand off my child to anyone, like my mother or David's, who put their own babies to sleep on their tummies, went straight to bottles, and never used a car seat? The avalanche of advice from experts about every stage of childhood and the dire consequences we are told awaits our children if we don't follow it fuels a distrust of family members who might pitch in to help, a distrust of childcare as an option, and even a distrust of our own husbands. I confess, often I didn't even feel I could trust *myself* to do everything right, let alone anyone else.

A lot of the people mothers used to share housework with aren't around anymore. As more families depended on father's earnings rather than the family farm, families started moving to where father could get a job. Most mothers today no longer live in the same house with grandmas and aunts, and they often live hundreds of miles away from their extended families. Older siblings are now required to be in school. Mothers were assigned responsibility for family a long time ago, and over time the people we were allowed to share that responsibility with were peeled away from us. That's how I ended up with this additional item for the Mother of All To-Do Lists:[25]

❏   Do everything on your own; your spouse and extended family aren't around and would probably mess it up anyway.

SUPERMOM

So far, my to-do list is pretty much the same as the one my own mother had when I was born in 1968. However, several items have been added since then. The mothers in the magazines I read weren't just making their own baby food. They were running successful home businesses or marching up the career ladder, too. They looked good, like they exercised more than once a year and had the time and money to buy clothes in actual outfits. Often, they were pictured in the arms of a smiling husband.

I never saw the iconic Enjoli perfume ad when it came out; I was two. I know it by heart anyway. "I can bring home the bacon, fry it up in a pan, and never ever let you forget you're a man." The 1970s and 1980s added several items to my growing list. As more employment and education opportunities opened up for women, the definition of a successful woman and mother expanded to require a successful career too. Plus, Supermom looks thin and fabulous all the time and has an equally fabulous marriage.[26] So there are three more tasks for the Mother of All To-Do Lists:

❑ Compete in the economy yourself and build a successful career.
❑ Look fashionable and sexy.
❑ Make your marriage fabulous.

GET AHEAD AND STAY AHEAD

There is one item we get to scratch off the list, but we'll just quickly replace it with another. With the creation of Social Security in the 1930s, and then pensions, and then retirement savings plans, mothers no longer had to raise children who can earn enough to put a roof over their elderly parents' graying heads. David and I don't expect Kate to support us. Either we save for ourselves or our own contributions to Social Security allow us to claim benefits when we get old. Interesting to note that the only item we've scratched off the list is also the only item that actually returned a concrete benefit—financial support in old age—back to the mother and family. Instead, I have a heightened responsibility to make sure *Kate* can get ahead and stay ahead financially.

For example, my own mother never agonized about where to send me to preschool. Preschool was simply a place for me to play with other kids a couple mornings a week. My mother never agonized about where to send me to elementary school. I went to the elementary school in our neighborhood. David and I, however, started agonizing about education while I was still pregnant. Did we need to get on a waiting list for preschools now? Was our neighborhood school going to be good enough or did we have to save up for private school or move to a different neighborhood? What schools did she need to attend to get into a good college?

My parents signed me up for piano lessons and T-ball. Today, every three months, I figure out what programs are being offered, what activities we think Kate would enjoy, what experiences she ought to have, and what we can afford. Ballet? Soccer? Theater? Guitar? Building rockets? I bought a book on financial smarts for kids and set up an allowance system for Kate to teach her the basics about managing money. Every year, I lament that we haven't been able to figure out a way for her to learn a foreign language before she turns twelve and the language development part of her brain switches off.

I am not the only mother fixated on making sure my daughter has the best education and every experience she needs to get ahead. Mothers talk about this topic easily and constantly because dealing with it always seems to rest with us. We do the research and visit the schools. We share tips on the best teachers in the next grade and the worst summer camps. We talk about whether our kids are overscheduled or underscheduled. When did researching, coordinating, and chauffeuring to a continuous curriculum of learning opportunities get added to my Mother of All To-Do Lists?

WELCOME TO THE INFORMATION AGE
AND THE GLOBAL ECONOMY

Companies no longer keep employees for decades in return for loyalty. Instead, employees face cycles of layoffs and downsizings. The price of a college education grows faster than everything else.[27] At the same time, decent-paying jobs for people *without* a college education are disappearing just as fast. Manufacturing and many professional jobs are moving to countries with cheaper labor, forcing everyone to compete for jobs with thousands of people all over the world. Employers are cutting health benefits and retirement benefits. The gap between people who make a little and people who make a lot is getting wider. We know our children will need every advantage we can give them to get or hang on to a middle-class lifestyle.

We also know that nearly every other middle-class mother is paranoid about giving her kids an advantage. So if I'm *not* paranoid, my kid could be the one who doesn't get into Harvard because I missed the deadline to sign up for the "Art of the Masters" class for six-year-olds. The economic insecurity is real, but the resulting competitive paranoia leads us to do crazy things and makes us ripe targets for people who want to sell us stuff. One day in the doctor's office, out of nostalgia I picked up a pregnancy magazine and saw an ad for a "prenatal education system." You strap a contraption onto your pregnant belly to play the alphabet and maybe Einstein's theories I guess. So while we're no longer focused on raising children who can support us in our old age, we are even more focused on doing whatever it takes—or whatever we think it might take—to make sure our children can support themselves financially.

Then there's also the way my responsibilities for nutrition, health, and safety have been ramped up. Growing up, my family had a drawer in our kitchen full of Twinkies and Ho-Hos, yum. My daughter doesn't even know what a Twinkie is.* I've never given her one. The more science shows that we are what we eat and the more headlines we read about the epidemic of childhood obesity, the more responsibility mothers have for making sure children eat right and exercise even when there's a fast-food chain on every corner and not much physical education happening in school. Safety requires a heightened awareness now too. Some of it is practical, like bike helmets and car seats and recalls of toys from China. Some of it is born of a media-induced fear that is often out of whack with real risk, like not letting my daughter play in the front yard like I did as a kid for fear someone

---

* In fact, when Kate read this chapter, she asked, "What's a Twinkie?"

will abduct her. In the span of a generation, the expectations about what mothers need to do to raise our children well have grown exponentially. So while I can scratch one task, at the same time I add two more items to my Mother of All To-Do Lists that my own mother never had on hers.

❏ Spend whatever time, energy, and money necessary to be sure children get the education, life experience, and financial literacy they will need to compete in the global economy, cling to the middle class, and avoid poverty.

❏ Maintain constant vigilance around nutrition, health, and safety.

THE MOTHER OF ALL TO-DO LISTS

So now we can review my full list, keeping in mind that several of these items have expanded over time. Martha Stewart has ratcheted up the standard for "making your home a haven." Celebrity mothers on the covers of all the tabloids have ramped up the "look fabulous and sexy" standard. The list is a growing beast.

❏ Raise the citizens of the democracy while the father goes out and builds it.

❏ Raise the workers of our economy while the father goes out and competes in it.

❏ Build children's moral character.

❏ Make your home a haven from the cutthroat culture of industry.

❏ Stand as a model of virtue for society.

❏ Follow all of the latest scientific advice about caring for children's physical, emotional, psychological, and intellectual well-being.

❏ Relax and listen to your natural, maternal instinct.

❑ Bond with your child; let your unique child's evolving needs guide your care; and spend the time, money, and emotional energy necessary to respond to those needs unfailingly.

❑ Be the parent, set limits and consequences, enforce discipline, encourage independence, and avoid being overly indulgent.

❑ Do everything on your own; your spouse and extended family aren't around and would probably mess it up anyway.

❑ Compete in the economy yourself and build a successful career.

❑ Look fashionable and sexy.

❑ Make your marriage fabulous.

❑ Spend whatever time, energy, and money necessary to be sure children get the education, life experience, and financial literacy they will need to compete in the global economy, cling to the middle class, and avoid poverty.

❑ Maintain constant vigilance around nutrition, health, and safety.

❑ Do all of the above with the patience and serenity of a saint.

OUR MASKS

Whew! No wonder I couldn't get any other mothers to talk to me or tell me up front how hard being a mother can be. Who would want to let slip that they might be letting down our democracy, our economy, or the moral fabric of society or dooming their own children to stunted growth, maladjustment, and poverty? Not me! So instead we put on "the mask of motherhood," which is the term used by Susan Maushart, sociologist and author of *The Mask of Motherhood: How Becoming a Mother Changes Our Lives and Why We*

Never Talk about It. The mask of motherhood is her term for "the brave face that women put on to convince the world that the job of mothering is unproblematic, straightforward and 'instinctive.'" [28]

Our masks take on all manner of shapes. In those first six weeks after Kate was born, many mothers said things to me like, "Oh, isn't it wonderful? Aren't you so happy?" I wanted to roar at them, "No, it's hard work! I'm barely holding it together. Why are you pretending you don't know that?" But instead, I faked a smile and agreed. Another mother, Meg, shared her mask. "People would ask me if I loved staying at home, and I'd say, 'Yes,' when really what I wanted to say was, 'Well, not really.' " After Susan's first child was born, she returned to her job but said, "I couldn't talk to anyone there about the struggles of being a new mom. My husband's sisters . . . had older kids so they just kept telling me 'it's a phase,' and my family was out of town. I felt completely alone, confused and totally stressed. It was like I had to have a split personality—totally keeping home at home and work at work. . . . I had to always be aware of who I was talking to and what 'face' to wear."

My friend Rosemary was right. Motherhood is a constant audition for the most demanding critics, so we've all become superb actresses. Motherhood is one big *American Idol* episode: Can she sing? Can she dance? Can she juggle? The clincher is: Can she do it all and *smile* the whole time? Getting dinged as a mother stings far worse and far deeper than any humiliation host Simon Cowell can heap on a hapless *Idol* candidate in front of millions of viewers. Our love for our children is supposed to make it easy for us to handle this ridiculously long to-do list with a smile on our face and nary a complaint. If the smile wavers for an instant, it's the *love* that gets questioned. We can't bear that, because the one thing we're all sure of, in the midst of all this conflicting advice and our own confusion, is the absolute depth of the love we have for our kids. So we keep the smile on and avoid conversations that might expose that love to any questions or doubts—our own or anyone else's. We each go on thinking we are alone, an isolated case, and that there's nothing we can do about it but grin and bear it.

WHAT IF WE COULD REALLY TALK WITH EACH OTHER?

True change occurs only in the context of relationships.
—MARY PIPHER, WRITING TO CHANGE THE WORLD

We can do something about it. We can talk to each other. We need other people to listen to us and point out what we can't see about our own ways of thinking about the world. As Tracy says, "Discussing these issues has bolstered my self-confidence and lessened my guilt for not conforming to some outdated, false ideal." We need to be mirrors for each other, helping each other see all the invisible, outdated mental maps about mothers, fathers, marriage, money, and work that trip us up every day.

Now, in some ways we're surrounded by people—including mothers—talking about motherhood on blogs and talk shows, in magazines and books. However, surfacing our mental maps takes a special kind of conversation, one that happens in a safe community of long-term relationships. Conversations like that do not happen in anonymous posts on websites or blogs where those relationships are missing. Yet they happen all the time in places like Mothers & More meetings or other virtual or in-person groups where relationships are in place. In a community of relationships, we are less judgmental and more forgiving of each other so as not to burn bridges. In a community of relationships, I come to know that you want the best for me, so when you help me question my own thinking, I can more easily hear it and not get defensive.

What if we wanted to create spaces and relationships for these kinds of conversations? First we'd all agree that:

- We all love our children to the ends of the earth.
- We love our husbands too.

And we'd add in a Mothers & More belief.

- All mothers are unique.[29]

The first two beliefs remove our fear that something we say will be taken to mean we don't love our children or spouses enough. The last belief—that each of us is unique—reminds us to suspend judgment of each other as individuals so that we can feel safe sharing the stories that will help us examine our assumptions and the larger patterns in those stories. Together these agreements are the first step toward getting up on the balcony together.

Next, we'd start sharing stories about our experiences as mothers. "I love my husband, but can you believe he didn't know the waffle had to be soft?" That triggers someone else. "How is it husbands don't know these things? Mine didn't know how to microwave frozen chicken nuggets." Before we get too carried away in the stories, we'd pause to ask if anyone sees any mental maps underneath a story or a pattern of stories. Who's assuming what? Do our actions or anyone else's reflect outdated mental maps? Where do the assumptions come from? Someone asks, "How would he know not to make the waffle crunchy if you'd always made the waffles?" Someone else suggests, "Maybe our husbands have a mental map that we have responsibility for the kids, which may come from the fact that we do everything." Together we can surface outdated subconscious assumptions like *Mothers are responsible for and are naturally better at children and family* and the Mother of All To-Do Lists that goes with it.

On paper it sounds easy, but getting to that point is tough, often emotional work. Even Maushart says, "To recognise the extent to which my own personal life was structured by assumptions I thought I explicitly rejected . . . shocked me. It made me realise that the problems I could see 'out there' were part of the very structure of my consciousness. It's a notion I still find scary (on a bad day) and intensely challenging (on a better day)." Confronting our own blind spots can make us angry, resistant, confused, or embarrassed that our subconscious has been misleading us.

There's a prize for all that hard work though. If we can get those mental maps surfaced, then we can examine them, question them, and decide whether they are useful or not and whether we want to try out some new ones. Here's where we link imagination to action and have our *What if?* conversations. If we believed *Mothers and fathers share the responsibility and are equally capable of caring for children and home,* how would we behave, what would we say, and how would the world operate? We talk about possible experiments and we share experiments we've tried that have succeeded or failed. Someone shares, "I take one week making breakfast and school lunches and he takes the next. That way we both know how to do it." Then we go out and try some experiments of our own and come back together for conversation.

One of my own experiments has been to be open and honest about my experience of motherhood and to try to be a safe space for others to be honest without any judgment. When Kate was six months old, an alumni representative from my college visited me. She asked what motherhood was like because she was considering starting a family soon. I warned her that I was going to be honest and then told her about all of the different feelings and experiences I'd had. She listened quietly, and when she left I was sure she thought I was crazy. Instead, she e-mailed a few days later to thank me for being honest and that it was really refreshing to talk about motherhood in a meaningful way. Laura does the same thing I do. "I am a firm believer in truth in motherhood, so I keep telling people my true feelings. . . . I know in my heart that my frustrations and anger during moments of motherhood don't reflect my feelings for my daughter or my aptitude as a mother. I'm at peace with the dichotomies, but this took many years of talking, writing and discussing motherhood myths and taboos." Talk. Experiment. Practice. And talk again. Challenge yourself every day, and eventually it will mean changes in those deep, hidden and outdated mental maps.[30] Conversations that help me remodel motherhood to get the life I want? Yes, for that I'd trade in both the yoga and the wine, thank you very much.

REMODELING TOOLS

- ▶ Find a way to connect with other mothers in a space that feels safe to be open and honest about motherhood. Find or start a local chapter of Mothers & More (www.mothersand more.org). Check out the National Association of Mothers' Centers (www.motherscenter.org). A local book club or a spin-off from a book club could use this book and other books I have suggested to have conversations. Shoot, pick a chapter in this book and just have a margarita night!

- ▶ If there's nothing local in person, go virtual, but with care. Join a well-moderated e-mail discussion group. Don't expect casual conversations or anonymous blogs or websites to serve as well as something that allows you to build longer-term relationships with other mothers. We need deep enough conversations to see and then question our own mental maps.

- ▶ The absolute *best* online discussion forum for these issues is the Mothers & More POWER Loop. Launched in 2000 by Mothers & More members Debra Levy and Judith Stadtman Tucker, the POWER Loop is available to members and brings together mothers across the country for a wide-ranging discussion that connects our personal stories to the news, research, and bigger picture around motherhood and society. Past special guests have included Susan Maushart, author of *The Mask of Motherhood*, and many of the authors listed in this book (www.mothersandmore.org/Advocacy/powerloop.shtml).

- ▶ If a good friend or colleague asked you tomorrow to share your honest experience of motherhood, what would you say? What do you think it would be most important for her to know about your story before she goes into motherhood? What would you have the most trouble sharing? Why?

▶ Watch the news and magazines for articles that implicitly—or explicitly—add more to the Mother of All To-Do Lists. For example, I read an article that made mothers responsible for disaster planning in their communities and another that implied mothers should be taking the lead on going green. Write letters to the editor questioning the assignment of all these responsibilities to mothers alone.

▶ Pick up a book. Books count as talking with someone else. Better yet, suggest that your book club or friends read a book together and then talk about it.

  ◆ *The Mask of Motherhood: How Becoming a Mother Changes Our Lives and Why We Never Talk about It* by Susan Maushart

  ◆ *A Potent Spell: Mother Love and the Power of Fear* by Janna Malamud Smith

  ◆ *Brain, Child: The Magazine for Thinking Mothers* (www.brainchildmag.com). *Brain, Child* was created as "a source of smart writing that delved into the meatier issues of that life-altering experience: motherhood."[31]

3

oxygen masks

or why am i at the bottom

of my own list?

MY DAUGHTER AND I fly to Minnesota a lot to see my family. In fact, she's had a frequent flyer card since she was three months old. Whenever we fly, as we settle into our seats the airline attendant gives safety instructions and inevitably says, "Should the cabin lose pressure, an oxygen mask will drop from the panel above you. Please put on and fasten your own mask before assisting small children or others traveling with you." Sure, easy for you to say. When I let myself imagine the scenario, I worry. Could I really put on my own mask first with my child struggling in the seat next to me? I hope so, because by not taking care of myself first, I would risk both of us. Even when the need to take care of myself first is so crystal clear, it's hard to imagine. Mothers have trouble giving ourselves permission to take care of ourselves. Putting my oxygen mask on first to save my child is okay for a mother. Hard to do, but justifiable. Putting on an oxygen mask simply because I need and want oxygen is not.

When mothers do talk ourselves into going out with friends or going to the gym or going after our dreams or just going to sleep, we often use the airplane oxygen mask justification. I tell myself, "If I get enough sleep, then I'll be a better mother to Kate tomorrow. I'll have more patience to deal with repeated tantrums." Or "I need to get out to a Mothers & More meeting because 'if momma ain't happy, ain't nobody happy.' " Or I decide to go for a run because I need to be a good role model for Kate by eating healthy and exercising regularly. All of these are true, of course, yet, I have a tough time imagining David saying to himself or to me, "You know, I really need to go play poker with the guys tonight so I can be more emotionally available for Kate tomorrow." He goes because he wants to, he enjoys it, and he needs a break. He needs some oxygen.

I, on the other hand, feel like my days are a series of decisions about whether to steal time away from Kate and my family that seems rightfully theirs and not mine. If I walk the neighborhood for a half hour before I pick up Kate then I've stolen the half hour we could have spent together before dinner. If I finish that last report while Kate reads a book then I'm stealing the time I could have played with her. Shouldn't I finish the report after her bedtime and give up an hour of sleep instead? If I slip out to a yoga class Sunday morning while Kate watches TV and David is still asleep, then I've stolen the time I could have used to hang out with them both over breakfast. Shouldn't I give up the yoga and walk around like a hunchback the rest of the week instead?

Our subconscious assumptions, and everyone else's, are that *mothers are completely fulfilled by caring for family* and *mothers who are employed or pursue personal fulfillment are selfish.* Mothers are at the bottom of our own to-do lists. Since the Mother of All To-Do Lists is all-encompassing and never-ending, we often don't even get to ourselves. As Bonnie told me, "I have definitely neglected myself for my children. Why? I don't know. Because I'm supposed to put their livelihood before my own? I honestly don't know when it happened. I never think of myself, because I don't have time."[1] By the time we've knocked ourselves out to do enough for our families, we've given up time with friends, time for exercise, time for personal interests like reading, time for the things we're good at and enjoy doing. In short, we've given up time for our own life. With no time or energy left for the things that make us who we are, we're left wondering to ourselves, "Who am I now?"

IDENTITY PIE

Before Kate arrived, I had a pretty full life. If I think of my identity as a pie, the pan was completely full. I had healthy slices of Wife, Employee, and Me—my personal interests, my relationships, and my health. When Kate was born, I had to find room for another huge piece of pie, one labeled Mother. The Mother piece started to crowd out all those other pieces, all the pieces that together make up my More.[2] All aspects of my life changed. How and where I spent my days changed—from doing workshops in an Internet company to doing dishes at home. Who I interacted with every day changed— from well-dressed adults to babies and the occasional mother or nanny in the park. How much I got to be with my husband changed from hours a day to minutes or none at all. How frequently I could exercise or read or go out with friends changed from nearly every day to once in a blue moon. The things I lost as a result of those changes—my career, my paycheck, my colleagues, my time with my husband, my own interests—were all things that were deeply important to me and felt like major losses. Mothers I talked to shared the same sense of loss. Patti-Jean said, "I've somehow lost my 'more.' It got relegated to the back burner some time ago, and got replaced by the things my kids and husband are passionate about." As another mother described so well: "I felt my identity shrivel up and wither."[3] If we lose our More, we lose ourselves. The appearance of the Mother piece of pie presents us with a psychological pie dilemma we have to solve to find ourselves. How do I integrate this huge new piece of who I am into my identity pie without making a big old mess and leaving myself at the bottom of the list?

The answer is to get up on the balcony and reflect on how becoming a mother and the series of changes we experience as mothers are similar to other life changes people experience. William Bridges, who wrote the book *Transitions: Making Sense of Life's Changes,* explains change as the external event or situation that is different, whereas transition is the internal psychological response we have to the change. It doesn't matter if the change is a welcome one like a new baby or an unwelcome one like losing a job. People are people. They go through three stages of transition in response to any change: the Ending Zone, the Neutral Zone, and the New Beginning Zone.[4] I had used these concepts with companies and employees in my work as an organizational change professional. Of course, it took me several years to recognize that these concepts also applied to everything I was going through as a mother and to my identity pie dilemma in particular.

THE THREE STAGES OF LOSING THE NAP

So let me quickly illustrate the three stages of transition with a mother story. As both a baby and a toddler, Kate was always a solid sleeper. One of the things that protected my sanity in those early years was the two- or three-hour nap she took every afternoon. That nap gave me time to sleep if I needed it, clean the house if *it* needed it, or even get on the computer to respond to e-mail. Eventually, though, David and I both noticed that Kate was starting to stay up later and later at night. I was having a tougher time getting her to go down for her afternoon nap. She was grumpy most of the evening. My friends told me it sounded like she was ready to get rid of the afternoon nap.

No way, I said. *I* was not ready!

Faced with the threat of a change—no more naps—I entered the Ending Zone. Every change means the loss of something that came before it, an ending. I kicked off my Ending Zone with a healthy dose of denial. No, she wasn't ready to give up the nap, I'd insist. She must be sick and that's why she's out of sorts. As she got grumpier, I switched to frustration and anger. What will I do if she stops taking the nap? She *has* to sleep. I was angry with Kate when she wouldn't go down for a nap. I couldn't let go. Most people I talked to must have thought I was completely overreacting to the change, which was of course an expected developmental step. Really, I was reacting to what I felt I was losing. Giving up the nap meant I would lose something very precious to me, time to myself. I was going through a transition. I was a big old mess.

As it became clearer that the nap was going away whether I liked it or not, I entered the Neutral Zone, that place in between the old and the new where everything is up in the air. My old routine was gone. I could no longer count on a two- to three-hour nap every day, but I hadn't figured out a new routine yet. I was worried our afternoons would become a battle of wills. What was I supposed to do all afternoon with her—especially when I could count on her being grumpy by 5 P.M.? I knew if I let her fall asleep between 5 and 7 P.M., then she'd be up all night. I had to experiment. Would it work to give her quiet time in her room in the afternoon like some books advised? Nope, Kate didn't do quiet time, at least not alone. She was too wriggly, too busy, and wanted to be with me if she was awake. Did it work to hang out at home in the afternoon playing? No, because it drove me stir crazy. Did it work to get out of the house in the afternoon—to the park, to a friend's house, to the grocery store? Well, yes, except for the grocery store idea, judging from a meltdown in the produce aisle.

After several weeks of experimenting, I entered the New Beginning Zone, that place where the change starts to feel comfortable and even presents new opportunities. I'd finally accepted that the nap was gone forever. I realized there were some benefits to the change. Before, we had only had a three-hour window in the morning to get out of the house because I had to have us back in time to get down for that precious nap. Now we could take a day trip to the aquarium or go to an event at the library scheduled in the afternoon. I hired a teenager to come over one afternoon a week to play with Kate while I got other stuff done at the house. She and Kate became long-lasting friends. The change began to work for us, a new beginning.

BACK TO IDENTITY PIE

So what does all this have to do with pie? Becoming a mother forced me to deal with the question of how to integrate this huge new Mother piece of who I was into my identity pie. From my balcony view, I saw that becoming a big old mess in response to a big change is pretty normal; it's part of the Ending Zone. The Ending Zone we inevitably enter when we become mothers can be a head-on collision for some of us and a speed bump for others. Joanna, a friend of mine from college and a trained singer, stopped singing when her children were born. She told me, "Walking away from singing, the expression that is so defining of me—physically, mentally, artistically— the thing that in so many ways makes me more myself than anything else, was without question the hardest thing I had to do when I became a parent. I felt the loss of it profoundly." The depth of that sense of loss depends on how many changes there are, what we feel we're losing, and how important those things were to us.

For me, leaving my job after Kate was born was one of my big losses. A friend, on the other hand, arranged a half-time schedule with her employer when she had her first child. She hung on to part of her paycheck, her job, and her time with her colleagues. Her sense of loss was not as great as mine was so her transitions were easier. She moved quickly through the Ending Zone and the Neutral Zone and settled into a New Beginning, where motherhood fit into her life quite nicely. When she had her second child, that's when she crashed. The cost of childcare doubled, her employer started asking for more time, and eventually she quit. With that change, she felt more loss and reentered the Ending Zone. Of course, leaving a job doesn't always feel like a loss. I know many mothers who left the workforce like I did but didn't feel the shock I did because they had always wanted to care for their children themselves and some even hated their jobs. Giving up a job you hate or at least don't care much about for something you've always wanted to do won't feel like as much of a loss. On the flip side, having to stay in a job you hate when you have a desire to care for your own children can feel like the loss of a dream.

The point is that from the outside, all anyone can see is the change; women who became mothers. From the outside, no one can see our internal transitions. They cannot know how big or small the losses feel that come with our particular Ending Zone or how that impacts our sense of who we are. It's no use comparing ourselves to other mothers and thinking, "She's not struggling so why am I a mess?" Or "*I'm* not struggling so why is she floundering?" It's foolish for anyone to judge how a woman responds to motherhood. The core change, having a child, may be the same, but the array of related changes, the transitions, and the feelings of loss are all different because we're all different.

Mothers do have something in common as they deal with these transitions, the mental maps about mothers: *Mothers are completely fulfilled by caring for family* and *Mothers who are employed or pursue personal fulfillment are selfish.* Lurking in our subconscious, these assumptions make it harder for us to move through the stages of transition and get to that New Beginning. We quickly scoop out big chunks of every other part of ourselves, big chunks of our More, to make room for Mother. Giving up so much of our existing identity so fast can make our sense of loss and confusion more dramatic and harder to recover from. Because my own subconscious told me that a good mother loves taking care of family and never complains, I thought I was supposed to feel only joy about becoming a mother. I did feel joy. I also felt a sense of loss. Yet I resisted admitting that I had lost anything because then I wouldn't have been a "good mother." Our "mask of motherhood" from the previous chapter hides our reality from everyone else and also keeps us in denial. Stuck in denial, we get stuck in the Ending Zone, unable to deal with those feelings of loss, and unable to move to the Neutral Zone where we might be able to experiment with some other options for fitting Mother into the pie pan.

MOMMIES ARE WOMEN WITH CHILDREN

When I was in fourth grade, my bespectacled teacher, Mr. Petti-grew, led our class in a performance of *Free to Be...You and Me* in our elementary school gym. Along with such gender-bending classics as "William's Doll," there's a song called "Parents Are People" and the opening says, "Mommies are people, people with children."

My ten-year-old brain thought, "Well, duh!" Talk about stating the obvious. What else would they be? That ten-year-old girl grew into a twenty-something woman who got to be a person in ways women before me hadn't. I played college basketball. I got two degrees. I got offered jobs teaching middle school and jobs on Wall Street. I lived in a co-ed dorm. I lived on my own. I lived in Japan. I lived with my fiancé. I kept my own name when I got married. I was a woman. I was a person. I was free to be me. I was free to expect that the world wouldn't have a problem with that.

Years later, having forgotten most of the songs, but harboring a warm, fuzzy feeling about the fourth-grade performance and Mr. Pettigrew, I bought a CD of *Free to Be...You and Me* for school-age Kate. She and I turned it on and sang along as we picked up beads and dirty socks off her floor. Eventually, "Parents Are People" began to play and the words and tune came back to me. "And now mommies are women, women with children."

Marlo Thomas's pep-squad voice stopped my now thirtysomething brain in its tracks. My life as a mother flashed before my eyes. I did not feel like a "woman with children." I felt like a "mommy," and being a mommy required giving up much of what made me a woman, a person. What I had given up flashed before me. I gave up small things like a shower everyday, and big things like my job and what came with it: achievement, a paycheck, and colleagues. I lost time to exercise and to read and to travel. I lost time with my husband. I lost my name and became "Kate's mom." I lost my firm grip on who I was, because mommies are *not* supposed to be people. Mommies are supposed to be mommies, round the clock, giving up their own lives to meet the needs of their children and families. I get it now, Marlo! I want to be both. I want to be a mommy who loves her child, and I want to be a woman too. I sang along, loudly and badly, as Kate sort of stared at me like I'd lost my mind.

Women with children are mothers and also so much *more,* all at the same time. That's how the organization Mothers & *More* got its name. Talking with other mothers gave me a place where it was okay to talk about what I'd lost along with what I'd gained, making it easier to move into the Neutral Zone. Once I got to the Neutral Zone, I spent a long time there trying to understand what was happening both inside and outside of me. I didn't want to be "selfish," but I needed and wanted to be *me.* How could I move from feeling like a mommy to feeling like a woman with children? Do I really have to choose between caring for my family and my More?

CAN AMBITION AND MOTHERHOOD COEXIST?

One major part of our More is ambition. Although many women start life with lofty childhood ambitions, over time many also come to have a conflicted relationship with ambition. They avoid using the word to describe themselves. They associate it with being self-ish, greedy, and stepping on other people on the way up the career ladder. They don't think of themselves as ambitious if they aren't gunning for the CEO's office. Understandably, they associate ambition with men because so many women are discouraged from going after their ambitions.[5] Becoming a mother often brings our conflicts about ambition front and center. Some women, having watched their own mothers as trailblazers in the workforce and seeing the sacrifices of time and energy and family, decided that ambition would have to take a backseat. They would make their families a priority. On the other hand, many women like me, embraced our ambitions for much of our lives.

My own mother had a college degree but was never employed after she had children. I remember thinking to myself as a child, "That's not going to be me. I'm going to do more than 'just' watch the kids and keep the house clean." My own parents told all three of us girls we could be anything we wanted to be. For me that meant *not* getting trapped by motherhood.[6] I find it hard to admit that now because I love and respect my mother so much, but that's what I thought. No matter what baggage we carry, mothers today often feel we have to decide between our families and our ambitions. We sense that we can't have both because our subconscious tells us that *mothers are completely fulfilled by caring for family* and *mothers who are employed or pursue personal fulfillment are selfish.* That doesn't leave a lot of room for ambition. Should a "good" mother be able to let go of ambition? What is this thing called ambition anyway?

Anna Fels answered those questions for me. Reading her book *Necessary Dreams: Ambition in Women's Changing Lives* was like laying on a couch with Dr. Fels sitting, legs crossed, in a chair next to me holding her notepad and asking, "So tell me about your childhood." So I did, and along the way, she explained what ambition is and why mothers shouldn't have to let it go.

WHY WE NEED AMBITION

When I was a child, I wanted to be chief justice of the Supreme Court. My childhood ambition was not a wish—like for a pony. I would have to work hard and learn new skills to achieve my goal. Given that my father and grandfather were lawyers and the title I wanted was a pretty prominent one, clearly I also wanted to be recognized by other people for my unique achievement. In *Necessary Dreams*, Fels explains that *ambition* is a word that describes the combination of these two proven human psychological needs. I've adapted Fels' concepts into a simple equation.[7]

> Desire to get good at something
> + Desire for others to recognize that we got good at it
> ―――――――――――――――――――――――――――――
> AMBITION

Fels points out that we can see these human drives at work in our children when they do a new task over and over again and revel in their own mastery and then say, "Mommy, Mommy, look at me!"

This is different from simply wanting to be popular or being overly concerned with what others think of us. People are driven to master things. We enjoy the process of getting good at doing stuff. As Cindy told me, "I want to feel highly engaged and challenged intellectually with what I am doing. . . . I love that kind of thing." But people are also driven by recognition. We love the applause. Research into human behavior shows that people are powerfully motivated by recognition from others that is specific to us as individuals, accurate, and meaningful.[8] As Katie says, "I want people to notice! I'm a 'praise junkie' and always have been." In other words, people are ambition addicts. Mothers are no different. So when we experience the two components of ambition together—the pleasure of doing something well and the recognition for it—it can make for a very memorable moment. That explains why I so vividly remember a seemingly mundane event from when Kate was a toddler. At the time, my days taking care of toddler Kate ran together, leaving a string of unfinished tasks behind. I might empty just the top half of the dishwasher before she woke up from her nap. I couldn't seem to finish a conversation or a meal or even an e-mail. As soon as I cleaned the kitchen, it was dirty again. Don't get me wrong, I enjoyed a lot of what I was doing. However, days of doing but never getting done are draining.

One day, our family computer crashed. I was thrilled! In one of my lives before Kate I was the technology guru at a school; fixing computers, running wires, troubleshooting cryptic messages. I ordered a new hard drive. I watched for it in the mail every day as if I were expecting a lottery check. When I finally saw it sitting on the porch one day as we returned from the park, I got excited butterflies in my stomach. That night, I told David, "I need an hour, just one hour, uninterrupted, to install this hard drive."

So I locked myself in our home office. I sat on the wood floor among the dust bunnies and started unplugging wires and cords. I dragged out the gray computer box. I popped it open and laid out the directions on the floor. I unscrewed teeny tiny screws, took new parts out of their protective foil. I blew out the dust inside the computer, inserted end A into slot B and then put everything back together. I hopped into the office chair and powered up the computer. The welcome screen greeted me and I clicked open the new hard drive and smiled. Jumping up, I ran in to David. "I did it!" I announced, as if I had just found the cure for cancer. My body felt a rush of adrenaline. David looked at me a bit strangely, "Great, dear, thanks." My chest puffed up with pride as I strode back down the hall to the computer.

After spending my days caring for Kate, something I felt I had no hope of mastering—more on that later—and something for which no one was giving me any meaningful recognition, I needed an ambition fix. That computer hard drive was my fix. Installing the new hard drive gave me a chance to practice a skill in which I had developed proficiency. My announcement to David was my plea for recognition of my awe-inspiring skill. To this day, I remember that mundane task as well as I remember Kate's first birthday party.

Our jobs and our professional skills are often major suppliers of our ambition fixes. When I facilitate a meeting, I get in the zone. I've got my markers, and I'm diagramming stuff on the white board. I'm listening to the lengthy monologue of one person and trying to figure out what the heck she is really trying to say. I've got my eye on the team member who doesn't participate very often, trying to pull him in. I'm making connections between what different people are saying. My brain cells are firing, people respect my skills, and I love it. I love it so much that I found out it was folly to think I could give it up for very long, and I often volunteer to do it for free. A paycheck is certainly a form of recognition, but volunteer work has other rewards and can be just as powerful an avenue for ambition. As Anna told me, "I am more ambitious now than ever before. I am putting my time into unpaid volunteer work, and I am becoming more noticed doing this than I was ever noticed while in the paid work force." Employment and professional skills are not the only outlet for ambition. Our desire for mastery and the desire for recognition get played out in multiple other ways, depending on the person. I have a good friend in Minnesota who isn't employed, yet I think of her as quite ambitious. Cathy plays tennis competitively, winning trophies and going to tournaments. Her ambition comes out in sports. Brianne gets that sense of expertise from cooking. "Cooking is something that I can accomplish and that can be done from start to finish. I need that sense of accomplishment." The possibilities are endless; music, art, or the eclectic mix Katie shared with me, "I belly dance, make my own wine, and make toys for my daughter."

Fels helped me understand that even for mothers, who feel they are supposed to be taking care of everyone else first, ambition is a vital part of our identity that needs to be expressed. Mothers, like everyone else, have a deep drive to master skills and show them off. When we let the Mother piece of our identity cut off all the avenues for that need, the power drains out of our psychic batteries.

WANTING TO CARE FOR OUR FAMILIES

The challenge for mothers, Fels says, is that "In many ways, caring for children is the exact opposite of ambition."[9] Certainly there are skills required, but we never really know if we've "mastered" being a good mother, and no one is around to give us recognition. Our kids don't register all we're doing—at least they won't until they have kids of their own! Plus, getting recognition for doing what you are supposed to do anyway—be the mommy—can feel false and forced. Still, I felt I was supposed to master motherhood, so I read stacks of books and took classes. When the Mother piece of pie crowded out my other outlets for ambition, I channeled that desire to get good at something into caring for my family. Judging from my conversations, many mothers do that, whether they are employed or not.

However, wanting to care for our children and families is a fundamentally different desire from our ambition addiction. As Joanne Brundage, founder of Mothers & More, observed, "Most of us have a drive to care for our own kids even if we are a 'C' student at it." Wanting to care for our children has little to do with wanting to be good at something and more to do with purely wanting to be part of that relationship for its own sake. Mixing up the two desires

—ambition and the desire to care for our children—can leave us feeling inadequate and confused when motherhood can't be "mastered" and gives us so little recognition.

Honestly, this desire to take care of Kate myself was a surprise to me. My plan had always been to put ambition first. As a modern woman, shouldn't I be able to hand off caring for my children to someone else in order to go out in the world and be employed and pursue my ambitions? When we were kids, my middle sister, Sarah, was the one who was the nurturer and always knew she wanted children when she grew up. Small children made me very uncomfortable, and I was sure that I had too many other important things to do. When my daughter was born, I was shocked to find that I *did* in fact want to care for her myself. I was even somewhat ashamed that I couldn't bring myself to find a high-paying job and hire a full-time nanny. I knew that if I found a full-time job, we could afford quality care for Kate; I had a problem that I hadn't anticipated. I *wanted* to be with her more than a fifty-plus-hour-a-week job would allow. This wasn't supposed to happen. I thought I would be able to happily hand off much of the family work to someone else: nanny, childcare center, husband, *someone.*

So I picked up a book and lay back down on the therapist's couch. This time, Daphne de Marneffe, psychologist and author of the book *Maternal Desire,* helped me understand that the need to care for our families ourselves and the pleasure we get from it are completely normal and valid psychological needs. De Marneffe defined maternal desire as "the longing felt by a mother to nurture her children; to participate in their mutual relationship, and the choice . . . to put her desire into practice."[10] As Katie confirms, "I didn't think I'd feel this strongly, but I do want to be the one to take care of my daughter. . . . It isn't that I don't think others could do as well, but I want to be the one to enjoy it!" De Marneffe explained in an e-mail conversation that "so often this care has been misunderstood as purely self-sacrifice (which it can be in economic terms) or as some sort of shying away from opportunity or some sort of throwback to pre-feminist fifties values." Because of my own misunderstanding, I hadn't counted on having my own maternal desire. De Marneffe helped me understand that for both mothers and fathers, caring for our families can be "a vital part of what some of us experience as our authentic selves."[11]

De Marneffe also made the point that different mothers are at different points on the maternal desire spectrum: some with more, some with less. Thinking about my sisters, I could see her point. My sister Sarah and I always tackled the world in our own unique ways. I was always the leader, and Sarah was the follower. Sarah and her friends played with dolls. I could usually be found curled up with a book. So it doesn't surprise Sarah and me that we now tackle motherhood differently. We fully expect our sister, Jane, will tackle it her own way too if she has children. Sarah and I are simply different people, and we fall on different places on two spectrums: the ambition spectrum and the maternal desire spectrum. Sarah is on the high end of the maternal desire spectrum but was surprised to find that she didn't want to completely lose her ambitions. I happen to be on the high end of the ambition spectrum, so I hadn't counted on having my own maternal desire and worried that it somehow made me less ambitious.

Each mother has her unique place on the spectrum of maternal desire. Each mother also has her unique place on the ambition spectrum. Unfortunately, the world around us expects women to decide between being a mother *or* more. My pair of psychologists told me otherwise. Fels says that motherhood introduces new and different dimensions to our lives; "loving and being loved, seeing your children develop, sharing their experiences, taking on a new aspect of identity, entering into new communities, . . . it can be one of life's richest experiences."[12] The desire to experience the richness of caring for our children and the desire to pursue ambitions are both valid human needs. What's crazy is to expect mothers, for us to expect ourselves, to choose only one or the other of these essential pieces of a whole life.

WHAT IF MOMMIES WERE WOMEN WITH CHILDREN?

So what would happen if we imagined ourselves into a world where "Mommies are women with children?" What if we let go of the mental maps that *mothers are completely fulfilled by caring for family* and *mothers who are employed or pursue personal fulfillment are selfish*? What if we let go of the idea that mothers have to decide between being a mother or being more? What if we didn't have to be at the bottom of our own to-do list? What if instead we truly believed the following core Mothers & More beliefs?[13]

- All mothers are unique.
- A mother is more than any single role she plays at any given point in her lifetime. She is entitled to fully explore and develop her identity as she chooses: as a woman, a citizen, a parent, or an employee.
- The transitions women make into and through motherhood are challenging and can be difficult.

What would we say? How would we behave? Well, we would stop using the oxygen mask justification. For example, we would trade in "I need to go after my own dreams so I'm a good role model for my daughter" for simply "I want and need to go after my own dreams." For example, one day Debra was talking to another mother and discovered the woman was a musician with the symphony. Debra said to her, "One day your kids will see you playing up there." The mother replied, "I don't care what they see or what they think. I'm doing this for me."

With these updated beliefs, we would look at the changes mothers experience in the same way people deal with other major life changes. We would know that even celebrating a welcome change like having a baby will come with some losses and an Ending Zone. With our new beliefs, mothers would feel comfortable asking themselves and each other questions that can help get us through that zone.

- What has changed? How much and how dramatically?
- Is the change something I wanted or expected?
- What did I lose and how important were those things to me? How do I feel about those losses?
- Do I really have to lose those things completely? Can I compensate somehow?[14]

If we adopted all our new beliefs, then once through the Ending Zone, we would feel okay about wallowing in the Neutral Zone, that place where everything is up in the air, and we're trying to figure out what comes next. We would be able to reflect on what the change means and listen to ways other mothers are experimenting with fitting the Mother piece in without losing too much of the More.

For example, Angie realized she'd pushed to the back burner two pursuits that made her happy: reading and scrapbooking. A change in her frame of mind brought them back. "After my daughter goes to bed, I let myself do one or the other instead of doing more work around the house or at my desk. My husband is 'off duty' once we put her down, her day is done, so I decided mine should be too!"[15] Barbara had a similar epiphany. "A few years ago, we signed our daughter up for horse-back riding lessons. That's an activity I always loved as a child, but I never got lessons because that was an expensive hobby. After driving her to weekly lessons for a few months and envying her, I finally had a click where I said, 'How come we can afford it for her and not for me?' I couldn't think of any way in which that made sense. So I finally signed up for the riding lessons I'd always wanted."[16] My own experiments included taking an online writing class when Kate was a baby, something I could fit in around caring for a baby. I also recruited Grandma and Grandpa a few nights a month so I could start a Mothers & More chapter and volunteer on a community task force. The more I experimented, the more confident I felt that making room for my More was not just okay but necessary.

The point isn't that our More will or should be the same as it used to be or even that we'll find it and then we're set for life. As one mother explained, "I am working on finding my 'more' again, although it has to be a kind of toned-down modified 'more' for now. Time, a traveling spouse, and kids who need help with homework and reading have replaced it. For now, I do a two times a year get-away with my college friends to remember that my 'more' was being incredibly artistic, funny and loved." *For now* is a good phrase to use. It reminds us that we're experimenting and that whatever change we're dealing with as a mother, it won't be the last. My friend Joanna, a singer, casually mentioned to her church choir director that she'd be willing to sing when the choir was off. To her surprise, pretty soon, he was composing music for her to sing. She told me, "While I am singing far less frequently than before I had children, I am able to do it in such a way that is also vastly more satisfying. The other happy surprise is that I think I have grown artistically because the experience of being a parent has been so personally enriching." The Neutral Zone gives us a chance to experiment with new ways to integrate both the More and the Mother pieces into our identity pie, a pie that will end up looking different but, we hope, will still come out whole.

I knew I'd started to enter the New Beginning Zone myself one night at a Mothers & More chapter meeting when Kate was finishing preschool. My friend Christine asked a few of us, "Does it ever get better? Will I know who I am again?" Without thinking, I found myself answering, "Yes. In fact, in some ways I feel more myself than I ever have." That's the prize waiting in the New Beginning Zone. Recovering any More at all is necessary to our most basic sense of self, but the real prize is having the opportunity to reflect on what we want that More to be and at the same time folding in the richness of the Mother piece.

These days, both my paid work and my community work are connected to public education. That's partly because of Kate, of course, but, at the same time, it's about me. Public education is a passion I've always had but never created an outlet for pursuing until now. Becoming a mother also made me ask myself, "What's missing that I want to include in my More?" Now I am writing again, something I'd given up for a long time. I have more close friends, especially women, than

I've had since I was in college because being a mother has connected me to communities of women through Mothers & More and communities of families through schools. Having Kate confronted me with the question, Who am I now? and forced me to come up with a better, richer, truer answer to that question than I'd ever had before. I'm a mother and more. I am more myself than I have ever been.

REMODELING TOOLS

▶ Create your own Identity Pie Chart. Carolyn Pape Cowan and Philip Cowan used this exercise when they worked with couples groups, but you can use it on your own or with some friends.[17] Consider the different aspects of your life, and then draw a pie chart showing how big each part feels, regardless of how much time you spend on it. What feels too big? Too small? What's been lost? Now draw a chart showing how you would like your life to feel. How big is the difference between the two charts? What is one small thing you could do to close the gap? Go to a website like www.hallmark.com. Pick a card, write yourself a reminder of what you want to do, and schedule it to be sent to you six weeks from now to remind you of your commitment to yourself.

▶ What were your childhood ambitions? What are your ambitions now—things you want to be good at and want to be recognized for? List the things you've mastered and enjoy doing. List the things you'd like to master. What do other people recognize you for? Are there things you do or want to do that you need some recognition for to keep you going? Who could you ask to feed you that recognition?

▶ Where would you place yourself on the spectrum of maternal desire? On the spectrum of the need to feed your ambitions? Does thinking of yourself as a mommy feel any different than thinking of yourself as a woman with children?

▶ A really powerful tool for getting comfortable with your own strengths and ambitions is the "Reflected Best Self" process described in the short article "How to Play to Your Strengths," published by Harvard Business Review and available from Harvard Business Publishing. (http://harvardbusiness.org.)[18] The idea is to ask a select group of people for feedback on your strengths and only your strengths, and use that to analyze who you are at your best. I still return to my analysis when I need a reminder about who I am and what I'm good at doing.

▶ Ask other mothers, "What's your More?" Catch yourself and other mothers when you use the oxygen mask justification and remind each other that it's okay to get oxygen simply because you need oxygen.

▶ If you believed these new beliefs, what would you say? What would you do differently?

- ◆ All mothers are unique.
- ◆ A mother is more than any single role she plays at any given point in her lifetime. She is entitled to fully explore and develop her identity as she chooses: as a woman, a citizen, a parent, or an employee.
- ◆ The transitions women make into and through motherhood are challenging and can be difficult.

▶ Are you in transition right now? You might be in the Ending Zone in response to some changes in your life and in the Neutral or New Beginning Zone about other changes. Whether it's a change in nap times or a new job or second child, consider the change and ask yourself:

- ◆ What has changed? How many changes and how dramatic?
- ◆ Is the change something I want or expect?
- ◆ What did I lose and how important are those things to me?

▶ You can try a few things to help yourself get through an Ending Zone. Identify what you are losing. Money, relationships, time, control, activities you love? Then:

- ◆ Give yourself permission to ask whether you really have to lose those things. Are there ways to make up for the losses?

- ◆ Give yourself permission to mourn the loss. Mourning a loss doesn't mean you can't also celebrate a welcome change.
- ▶ Pick up a book.
  - ◆ *Transitions: Making Sense of Life's Changes* by William Bridges.
  - ◆ *Necessary Dreams: Ambition in Women's Changing Lives* by Anna Fels.
  - ◆ *Maternal Desire: On Children, Love and the Inner Life* by Daphne de Marneffe.
  - ◆ *Mojo Mom: Nurturing Your Self While Raising a Family* by Amy Tiemann.

4

identity whiplash

or who am i now?

FOR ONCE I was looking forward to wearing hose and heels. I dressed like a professional for the first time in the six months since Kate's birth. David and I left Kate asleep in Grandma's arms as we drove into downtown Los Angeles. We were headed to a ritzy hotel for a college alumni event. We'd both gone to the same college and expected to see a lot of people we knew. We joined the dressed-to-impress crowd in the banquet room, wineglasses and hors d'oeuvres in hand. The game of one-upmanship had already begun. The question came quickly from the first person we talked to, "So what are you doing now?" My husband answered that he was in his second year at a prestigious law firm. I answered, "I'm at home taking care of our six-month-old." The response was, "Oh. Isn't that wonderful." Pause. "So tell me, David, what kind of law are you practicing?"

Hey, what about me? All night I felt invisible. No one was interested in what I had to say. No one took me seriously. Everyone knew

I was a fellow alumnus, but once someone knew I was a mother who wasn't employed, he or she seemed to think I was watching soap operas all day. I was crushed. Somehow the arrival of the little girl we loved so entirely made me feel like I was *in* a bad soap opera, one where the heroine gets amnesia and her whole life seems foreign to her.

Welcome to Identity Whiplash. Rolling merrily along, I naively assumed that after having Kate I was the same person I'd always been. Then *wham!*, I started colliding with unexpected reactions from other people that I didn't see coming. I thought beliefs like *homemakers don't have brains* and *employed mothers neglect their kids* were long gone. Yet, I kept crashing into them in my own head and in people around me. Someone give me a neck brace.

I remember just weeks after Kate was born going to our insurance agent's office to make some key financial decisions for me and David. I grilled the agent about the various policies. Satisfied that I had competently narrowed in on the policy I wanted, we got down to logistics. Address? Phone number? Husband's employer?

"And what do you do?" the agent asked innocently.

I hesitated. Trying to be helpful, the agent offered, "The category we have in the computer is homemaker."

A minute ago, I had thought of myself as the capable, get-it-done kind of person that I am. But when he said *homemaker,* in a jarring flash, I saw what he saw. My baby was asleep at my feet, curled up in the yellow and navy plaid car seat. My bulging diaper bag teetered precariously on the chair next to me. I was wearing a badge of baby vomit on the sleeve of my right arm—the one I'd been using to sign documents. I might as well have had *MOM* tattooed on my forehead. As nice as he was, I figured he saw what I saw, because to me the word *homemaker* conjured up images of a smiling woman in a red apron in the kitchen while the important, demanding work of the real world gets done somewhere else. My brain couldn't fit the two pictures together—me as capable person and me as homemaker. Fumbling, I faked a smile and said sure that's fine. We finished signing documents quietly, and I left as soon as I could.

That night I cried to my husband. I knew I didn't want to be thought of, nor did I think of myself as, a homemaker. At the same time, I felt guilty for being so upset about the term. *I* knew taking care of my family was important. *I* didn't think caring for my family had somehow robbed me of my intelligence. I had learned very quickly that taking care of my family and not being employed was some of the hardest work I'd ever done. So why couldn't I wear the label homemaker with pride?

I couldn't because I knew what other people thought of homemakers. So I too looked down my nose at homemakers. Subconsciously, I looked down my nose at myself. Every time the world reminded me of that subconscious conflict between who I thought I was and how people now looked at me, I crashed.

Ouch.

One day years later, not long after I'd returned to employment, I sat in the park watching preschool Kate climb the monkey bars. A few other mothers sat nearby and they watched a nanny they knew approach with a stroller. One mother shook her head and disapprovingly said something like, "You know, I don't understand why a mother would have children just to pay someone else to raise them." My face burned. Kate was now in childcare several days a week. The unspoken assumption underneath her words was that *employed mothers neglect their kids so they must not really love them.* I wanted to stand up and shout, "How dare you claim I don't love my child simply because I'm employed!" But I didn't. Why? Because I have to confess that when I'm employed, I often feel guilty and worry that I'm not taking care of Kate as well as I should. I usually don't have any actual evidence that she needs more time with me. It doesn't matter. I can zoom along happily juggling employment and family until—*crash!* I smash into a comment like the one overheard at the park, and it reminds me of the subconscious assumption that *employed mothers are neglecting their kids,* and I'm sent reeling.

So who am I—a caring mother *or* a competent person? How did I end up with these competing versions of who I can be as a mother? Why do I care so much about what other people think of me?

WHO I AM DEPENDS ON YOU

I always believed that my identity was something I created. I believed that the question to be pursued was "Who am I?" not "Who do all of you think I am?" I prided myself on being someone who didn't care what anyone else thought. Psychologists, however, know that peer pressure isn't just a middle school thing. They've known for a long time that who we think we are depends on what other people recognize about us and how they treat us. People have very finely tuned radar we use to pick up on words, actions, and body language. That radar tells us what others think of us and what they recognize about us. Our subconscious and our identity care an awful lot about what other people think.[1] Our identity is not created in isolation. It exists only because of the web of relationships we have with other people and the world around us.[2]

Our mental health and our happiness depend on other people accurately recognizing who we are and on the identity that springs from our interaction with them. For example, going back to our definition of ambition, we have an internal desire to master skills, but we also have a desire for that mastery to be recognized by others. Sure, some of us need more external validation than others, but the basic need is there for all of us. Because it feels good, we gravitate toward doing the things that get us recognition. Then those things take on more and more importance for who we are. On the flip side, we may struggle to hang on to parts of our identity that don't get recognized. We probably all have examples of this in our childhood families. In my family, doing well in sports got lots of recognition, so that became a healthy chunk of my identity. Music? Not so much. So music isn't a large part of my identity.

The assumptions people have about us also affect our ability to reach our full potential. If a teacher is told his students are high achievers, those students will outperform a similar group of students taught by a teacher who is told her group is low achieving.[3] Assumptions influence expectations, which affect behavior. In turn, that behavior—what people say and how they treat us—shapes how we think of ourselves.

A lifetime of watching mothers portrayed in certain ways, or listening to what people say about mothers, or seeing how other people treat mothers shapes everyone's assumptions about mothers—including the mothers themselves. So let's add an additional two outdated mental maps to the ones from previous chapters.

- Mothers are responsible for and are naturally better at children and family.
- Mothers are completely fulfilled by caring for family.
- Mothers who are employed or pursue personal fulfillment are selfish.

AND

- Employment is a woman's path to fulfillment and equality.
- Mothers who are not employed are dull.

Like a vicious cycle, these assumptions about mothers lead people to talk about and act in certain ways with mothers. Their behavior and speech continually reinforce the outdated assumptions that *homemakers are dull* and *working mothers are selfish*. Mothers carry on as if the world had changed along with them, until *wham!*, like a car accident, they crash into one of these outdated mental maps. Diagnosis? Identity Whiplash.

"YOU LOOK LIKE *JUST* A MOM"

Mothers who have spent time being employed and spent time not being employed can often describe what Identity Whiplash feels like in one breath. Stephanie went to a new hair salon with her son and was chatting with the owner. She told him that she was a lawyer and taking time off to care for her son. She told him about her volunteer work in the community and that she was rehearsing for a play. She whizzed along telling him about her interesting life. Then *bang!* She hit the wall of his assumptions. He said, "Wow. How deceiving. You look like *just* a mom." Translation, he hadn't expected a mother to have such an interesting life, to be a mother and more. Stephanie later shared her reaction, "What the heck does that mean anyway? Would he have said that if I had come in wearing one of my suits for court? I do know that I get treated much differently by sales people when I go to the store in casual clothes with my son than when I used to stop after work when I was wearing my suits and heels." She gets treated differently because in the one instance she's got the MOM tattoo, her clothes and her kid. In the other instance, she has her suit and heels and her after-work arrival time to identify her. She has a VIP tattoo (short for Very Important employed Person). Another mother got Identity Whiplash reactions from her friends. "The friends I once had 'left' me because all of a sudden I was a mother. I had a baby not a lobotomy. I still read, dance, go to the movies, etc. Why can't a woman be a mother plus all things she was before she had a child???"[4] Her friends harbored the same assumptions as Stephanie's salon owner; mothers are *just* mothers—not interesting people with full lives, not women with children.

Even our spouses fall into this vicious cycle, jarring our identity by treating us differently after we have children or depending on if we are employed or not. Alison vented, "I . . . work part-time with my husband and in the midst of stressful projects I have to admit to telling (ok screaming at) him that I am a college-educated woman, not a moron! I have even remarked to him in calmer discussions that while I know he respects me being home and thinks I'm competent at that, I did feel more intellectually respected by him when I was working." Our husbands don't do this intentionally. When we become mothers, our husbands' mental maps about mothers get flipped on. In Alison's case, his mental map that *mothers who aren't employed eat bon-bons all day and their brains turn to mush* got activated, and he started to treat his wife differently because of that assumption. This is the power of the subconscious. Men who have lived with us for years can end up treating us and even thinking of us in strikingly different ways once we become mothers.

IMPLICIT ASSOCIATIONS:
Doing What We Believe, Not What We Say

To understand why Identity Whiplash is so common, I found it help-ful to understand a thing called an "implicit association." Several years ago, researchers from Harvard developed a simple type of computer test revealing that below the level of our awareness, we have associations between certain people and certain traits—a specific type of mental map they call implicit association. We may have a subconscious asso-ciation between two things, say men and science and another associa-tion between women and liberal arts. The computer test asks us to pair words or images in those categories, and we're supposed to do it so fast that it's automatic. We hum along pairing male words or images with science words or images. However, if we're asked to pair the *opposites* quickly, say *women* with science and *men* with liberal arts, it takes us longer—by seconds or fractions of a second. We take just a bit longer to *consciously* overcome our subconscious associations to give the right answer. The longer it takes us, the stronger the underlying association is. The stronger the underlying association is, the more likely we are to behave in line with that association and not according to what we *say* we believe.[5] We'd like to think our beliefs and behavior are totally under our conscious control, but our subconscious beliefs can differ dramatically from what we say we believe when asked.[6]

If our implicit associations just stayed there, buried in the back of our brains, we wouldn't need to worry about them, but they don't. Our subconscious beliefs can make us say and do things that are the polar opposite of what we *say* we believe.[7] For example, while most people will tell you they believe white and black people should be treated equally, they often behave according to a very different sub-conscious belief. In just one of dozens of studies, researchers sent out five thousand identical résumés. Some were given a typical "white" name like Emily or Brendan, and others were given a typical "black" name like Lakisha or Jamal. White-sounding names got 50 percent more callbacks from employers.[8] People acted on their subconscious associations without even realizing it.

WHY MOTHERS CAN'T WIN

While the Implicit Association Test (IAT) doesn't specifically look for associations with mothers, it does check for subconscious associations of men with careers and women with home/family. I figured I could pass this one with flying colors. No way do I associate men with careers and women with family. To my complete surprise, I struggled to pair female names with career words and male names with family words. At the end, the computer screen said, "Your data suggest a strong association between Male and Career." I was horrified, embarrassed—but I wasn't alone. Most people have an implicit association of jobs and careers with men, and home and hearth with women.[9]

Other researchers have found other subconscious beliefs people have about mothers in particular. One study asked people to rate the competence level and warmth level of different roles. People rated businesswomen as high in competence, close to businessmen and millionaires. In other words,

> woman
> − children
> + job
> ―――――
> rich genius

They rated the competence of housewives as comparable to the elderly, blind, "retarded," and disabled, though they also gave them high ratings for being caring and nurturing.[10] So that means,

> woman
> + children
> − job
> ―――――――――――――――――――――――
> dependent dimwit who cares a lot about other people

Mothers find themselves shaken when they run into these associations in action. My friend Barbara was at a meeting of her fellow computer geeks. The speaker said to them all, "I'll try to explain it so my mother could understand it." Barbara told me that it dawned on her that she remembered others making similar remarks in her economics Ph.D. program, and then she said, "It was always clear to me that [the phrase] meant someone untrained, possibly stupid. This was the first time since I became a mom that I'd heard it. I felt kicked in the stomach." She felt kicked in the stomach, and I did too when she told me the story, because we were both now in this category—someone assumed to be stupid simply because she was a mother.

This association between mothers and dimwittedness causes a lot of pileups at intersections where we meet people we don't know, and they ask innocently, "So what do you do?" My friend Bev attended a backyard luau one evening and in the glow of the tiki torches she had an interesting chat with another woman about houses, music, and government. The woman shared that she had a career in art and had chosen not to have children. She asked what Beverly did. Beverly answered that she was a stay-at-home mom. The woman's face went blank. She half-smiled, and then, Beverly said later, "Looking *above* my head, she promptly excused herself and joined the conversation just behind me, as if I had conveniently vanished . . . this was the first time someone had literally looked over me as if I was, well, salami." Beverly thought of herself as an interesting person—the two of them were already having an interesting conversation. Yet as soon as Bev answered the What do you do? question, she slammed into this woman's assumption that no matter how interesting a *woman* Beverly might be, mothers who are not employed are not interesting.

But wait, there's more. People also subconsciously believe that employed mothers are less family-oriented, more selfish, and less sensitive to the needs of others than nonemployed mothers.[11] In other words,

> woman
> + children
> + job
> ———————————————
> rich genius who is selfish and neglects her family

For mothers who are employed, often the questions after "What do you do?" cause Identity Whiplash. Kristie, the sister of a good friend of mine, is employed full-time. When she responds to "What do you do?" with her job title, she says people immediately quiz her about what she's not doing. "When do you pick him up? (incidentally I don't, my husband does) What do you do when he's sick?" Before kids, Kristie's answer probably let her glide right through this intersection. As a mother, she gets through the first light and then plows into a deep belief that employed mothers could not possibly be caring for their kids well enough.

Sometimes the crash comes from a comment someone intends as a positive. My friend Jackie was employed full-time for a long time and then switched to a reduced schedule. Her brother-in-law said, "Thank God you went part-time. We were worried you wouldn't see your kids until they graduated." Buried in his words is the assumption that when she was employed full-time, she couldn't possibly have been giving her kids the time and attention that a mother should.

Okay, then working part-time must be the solution to this math problem, right? Nope. Mothers who work part-time actually get all the negative associations and none of the positive ones.[12] So that means,

$$
\begin{array}{r}
\text{woman} \\
+ \quad \text{children} \\
+ \quad \text{part-time job} \\
\hline
\end{array}
$$

dimwit, slacker employee who is selfish and neglects her family

Bouncing off her brother-in-law's comment, Jackie turned around and hit head-on the opposite reaction at work. When she went to a reduced schedule, she started getting less-challenging assignments and comments about how she "must not plan to be around long." A reduced schedule stamped her with the MOM tattoo and flipped on her colleague's assumptions that mothers aren't that serious about their jobs. Reduced schedule = bad employee. At this intersection, mothers get sideswiped coming and going.

No wonder we feel like we can't win. In the subconscious of the people around us, we can't! If people see you with a baby on your hip, or hear that you are a stay-at-home mom, they will treat you as if you were not so smart but care a lot about other people—and they won't even realize they are doing it. You may feel as if you had been demoted, no longer taken seriously, but you may also feel like people see you as a good mother. If people see you in a suit at a meeting or hear that you are a working mother, then unintentionally they will treat you as if you were smart and capable but somewhat selfish and uncaring. You may feel like a competent, contributing citizen, but you may also feel people see you as a bad mother.

CONFLICTING EXPECTATIONS

Where do these conflicting expectations of mothers come from? While we'd like to believe that history is water under the bridge, sometimes we don't even notice when we're still drowning in it. Think back to our Mother of All To-Do Lists. By 1950, mothers had June Cleaver's To-do list: raise moral citizen-workers, make your home a haven, study the experts to make sure you do both well enough to avoid catastrophe, and do it all on your own because father's gone to work. Our friendly experts have told us along the way that a good mother "feels all her cares amply repaid"[13] by her child's development, saddling us with an assumption that "devoted mothering satisfies women completely."[14]

That part of our Mother of All To-Do Lists is where we get these three mental maps.

Mothers are responsible for and naturally better at children and family.

Mothers are completely fulfilled by caring for family.

Mothers who are employed or pursue personal fulfillment are selfish.

Therefore, women should not be employed.

Then by 1980, mothers added the Supermom list, including the task to get our own career. The women's movement of the 1970s made it clear that keeping all women restricted to one role, housewife, was not fair, and cut women off from employment as a path to fulfillment, independence, and equality. As women poured into the workplace, our additional pair of assumptions took root:

Employment is women's path to fulfillment and equality.

Mothers who are not employed are dull.

Today, mothers are expected to label ourselves as one or the other; a stay-at-home mom, like June Cleaver, or a working mother, like Supermom. June gets to act on her maternal desire and is caring but dull. Supermom gets to act on her ambition and is competent but selfish. Take your pick, be dull or be selfish.

The rest of the world, however, is still hanging on to *all* of these conflicting assumptions, so mothers get mixed messages at every turn. On one hand, mothers get messages that they should be completely fulfilled by caring for family. For example, at a Mothers & More meeting one night, a mother approached me and told me that she wanted to go back to school to get an MBA. "That's great!" I encouraged, but her face was troubled. "I want to," she said, "but no one in my family and none of my friends understands. They think I have a perfect life at home with my kids and a husband who earns enough for the whole family. They keep asking why I would want to do that and why I would want to go back to work." A *Newsweek* article about a reality show in which a mother took a job quoted someone scolding: "Unless you're about to starve there is no reason for you to be at work. If you didn't want to raise your children, you should not have had them. It's child abandonment."[15] Messages like these that mothers should feel lucky when they don't have to work and that pursuing a career is really only okay for a mother if she absolutely needs the money stem from our

1950s assumptions that mothers are completely fulfilled by family, solely responsible for family, and therefore pursuing employment would be selfish.

On the other hand, mothers also get messages that they ought to be employed. My friend Kim went to a benefit luncheon one day and sat next to a legislative aide. The two of them had an intense discussion about the use of bond financing to solve a state budget crisis. The aide asked her what she did. Kim said she was at home caring for her child and used to teach economics. The aide responded, "It's such a shame for all that skill and knowledge to go to waste. I hope you come back to the workplace." Messages like these that a mother who isn't trying to be Supermom is not only wasting her own education but also letting down women everywhere stem from our 1980s assumptions that real fulfillment and equality come from employment and mothers who are not employed are dull.

Stuck in the Middle

Stuck in the middle, every week, whether I am working for pay or not, I ask myself: Shouldn't I be doing *more* paid work? Shouldn't I be doing *less* paid work? Sometimes I feel like I'm in one of those cartoons where Elmer Fudd has a little Elmer devil on one shoulder and a little Elmer angel on the other, each trying to tell him what to do.

On *my* left shoulder I have a mini-Kristin dressed as a 1950s June Cleaver housewife in a dress and pearls and a spatula in her hand. On my right shoulder I have a mini-Kristin as a 1980s Supermom in a pinstripe powersuit with a floppy bow tied at her neck and a briefcase in her hand.

JUNE CLEAVER MINI-KRISTIN: Dear, you know you love Kate. So what's not to love about changing diapers and sweeping and having a hot meal on the table when David comes home? What could possibly be more fulfilling than that? Besides, it's your responsibility. A mother's place is in the home caring for her family, not out there wheeling and dealing. You're lucky. You know, there are mothers who *had* to work even in the fifties.

How awful for them. [Then she lowers her voice] I know all that housework can be mind-numbing, but that's nothing a martini or a margarita can't cure. Right?

SUPERMOM MINI-KRISTIN: [She hits me with her briefcase and shouts] Hypocrite! Don't listen to her. She's so bored she's popping Valium as if it were candy. If her husband leaves her, she's toast. She has no money. No power. No voice in the world. And she's been brainwashed to think that being in charge of diapers and pot roasts is fulfilling! Getting a job with a paycheck, now that's the path to fulfillment, independence, and equality. You can hand off the childcare and housework to someone else. You can have it all—the career, the great kids, the fabulous marriage. You need to do it all, because that old version of motherhood is a quicksand of drudgery our sisters in the seventies fought to break us out of. Don't let her suck you back in! [Then her voice gets lower] Besides, our sisters said men would pick up their fair share of work at home and our workplaces and communities would rearrange themselves so both mothers and fathers can be employed. So what's to worry about? Right?

Most mothers have some version of these two voices in our heads. Our mini-1950s June Cleaver on one shoulder makes us think that if we are employed, something is wrong with us and we are selfish and neglecting our kids. We feel the need to justify our employment to ourselves and other people. For example, one evening at a crowded Mothers & More meeting in Minnesota, we sat on the carpet in small groups and introduced ourselves. The mother sitting next to me shared her name and then said, "I work full-time, *but only because I have to.*"

Our mini-1980s Supermom on the other shoulder makes us think that if we enjoy caring for family, something is wrong with us because employment is supposed to be fulfilling and family is supposed to be drudgery. As one mother confided, "It's like I'm a little '50s house-wife. *Love* figuring out what to make for dinner, making a shopping list, clipping coupons, going to the store, buying groceries, budgeting things on sale. *Love it!* What the hell is wrong with me??"

We're stuck in the middle, plagued with questions. Am I neglecting my kids and family because I need or want to work for pay this much? Am I neglecting my finances and my future because I'm not employed or not employed very much? Am I selling myself short or letting women down if I'm not trying to have it all and do it all? On the one hand, how dare anyone tell me "you can't have it all?" On the other, do I really want it?

WHO SAYS I CAN'T?

The familiar but troublesome phrase used to describe the conflict between these expectations of mothers is *You can't have it all.* Now, when Kate is struggling to do something new, David and I tell her never to say "I *can't.*" So why do people use that word with mothers? Why do we use it ourselves? We use it because, as Cindy told me, the phrase resonates as being "Shockingly, earthshakingly true." We use "You can't have it all," because it does reflect a reality, our frustration with the impossible goal of trying to be both June Cleaver and Supermom at the same time. While I tend to feel warm and fuzzy about "Free to Be…You and Me," other mothers I talk to feel they were duped by the same songs into believing they *could* have it all and now find they can't.

You can't have it all, is a classic example of how outdated mental maps sneak into our language and stay there, all but invisible. *You can't have it all* limits our options by chaining us to that set of conflicting mental maps. When we use that phrase, we are effectively saying that it's okay to expect mothers to have to choose between being June Cleaver or Supermom, between maternal desire or ambition, between being caring or competent, and between being dull or selfish. When we tell ourselves that we can't have it all, we may relieve the pressure we feel to do it all, but using the phrase also frees up the rest of the world to tell us we can't. As Freda shared, her older brother, who was single and had no children, commented that, "Motherhood isn't all it's cracked up to be. They told you you could have it all, but you can't."

Fathers aren't faced with the same dilemma. I noticed that David did in fact have it all—the job, the kid, the wife. His life hadn't changed much. If anything, at least from my perspective, he had everything he used to have plus the bonus of coming home to a cute baby. No one was telling David that he couldn't have it all. Why? Because *you can't have it all* is code for telling a *woman* she can't have what men have traditionally had—namely, a challenging, time-consuming job and a well-cared-for family. Well-cared-for, that is, by someone else: the wife. Another mother shared with me that her PhD adviser was disappointed when she and another female colleague decided to slow down their march to a tenured position to care for family. She said, "He seems to forget that his wife put her career on hold in order to cover for his parenting responsibilities at home, thus enabling him to be the superstar in the field that he is today while having kids who have grown up raised by a parent." The only way *he* could have it all, is because *she* didn't. Mothers are told we can't have it all and even come to *believe* we can't have it all because having it all has been defined as what fathers have had.

There's a similar phrase mothers themselves often use that is just as problematic, "You *can* have it all, but just not at the same time."[16] While the kids are little, mothers can leave the workforce for a few years to take care of family. Then, when everyone else in the family is ready, she can jump back into the workforce. Just make some tradeoffs and it can all work out. At first, I bought into this idea of "sequencing."[17] It matched my reality pretty well. I couldn't see a way for me to have it all when we had a baby and with David working seventy-hour weeks. Not when I knew most jobs I would apply for would also want fifty hours a week or more. I would spend a few years not employed, and then eventually when the time was right I'd go back to employment. Easy, right?

Except, the longer I went without a paycheck, the more freaked out I got. My retirement savings were at a standstill. As I talked with other mothers and started learning more, I realized that reentering the workforce years down the road and even finding part-time employment and part-time childcare would be much harder than I had naively assumed. I worried about what would happen to me financially if, after years out of the workforce, I ended up divorced or if something happened to David. The idea that you can have it all, but not at the same time by taking time off and jumping back in later started to feel like a risky gamble. Having taught middle school, I knew Kate would need plenty of parent time as a teenager too, so leaving the workforce for the baby years wasn't going to solve that issue. Plus, I knew this was a gamble only a few mothers could take. I happened to be able to afford to try having it all, but not at the same time. Plenty of mothers I knew couldn't. So having it all, but not at the same time hardly counted as a solution to the conflicting expectations mothers face. And, hey, as David's career took off and I felt my own identity wither, I realized the whole thing simply didn't feel fair. I felt like I was being compelled to put my life on hold, to live a "deferred life," deferring all the things I wanted to do, while he wasn't.[18] Telling mothers, or telling ourselves, that they can have it all, but not at the same time is yet another way our language reinforces the idea that only mothers have to make tradeoffs; fathers don't.

WHAT IF MOTHERS COULD HAVE A WHOLE LIFE?

In the last chapter, we imagined what we would do differently in our own lives if *mothers* believed:

- All mothers are unique.
- A mother is more than any single role she plays at any given point in her lifetime. She is entitled to fully explore and develop her identity as she chooses: as a woman, a citizen, a parent, or an employee.

Now it's time to imagine, if *everyone* held these beliefs, how would the world operate? Let's start with language. If everyone held our new beliefs, then people wouldn't tell mothers *you can't have it all* or *you can have it all, but not at the same time*. No matter how they are used, these phrases are thick with history and assumptions. The phrases keep us from taking risks to experiment with ways to create lives that include both caring for others and pursuing ambitions and employment. As Kimberley told me, "'You can't have it all' is a defeatist attitude, which is not indicative of how I think about and see the world." So let's try some alternatives. Joanne Brundage, founder of Mothers & More says, "The 'having it all' positioning sounds greedy and self-centered, but having a life with some balance of all the pieces of who you are and what you have to contribute to the world sounds pretty reasonable, sane, and healthy to me." We can talk about mothers wanting a whole life or an integrated life, something fathers and most everyone wants.[19]

While we're talking about language, how about if we end the use of the term *mommy wars?* Whenever anyone chastises working mothers or dismisses stay-at-home mothers, it activates the worst incarnations of the mental maps and keeps them alive. That hurts all mothers and families. We can respond with equal outrage in both instances. Whenever a mother is made out to be bad because she's poor, or single, or an executive who works long hours and even whenever a mother is made out to be good because she fits some idealized version of motherhood, we can call it out. Mothers & More gives out an Apple Pie in the Face Award to people or organizations that "divide mothers or trivialize our struggles to combine caring for our families with paid work over our lifetimes."[20] For example, *Dr. Phil* got Pie in the Face for a "Mom vs. Mom" episode, which sensationalized the divide between employed mothers and mothers who are not employed. Mothers can refuse to allow outdated mental maps and the way the media plays on them to divide us.[21] As Mothers & More Board President Debra Levy pointed out in an e-mail discussion, "Stay-at-home mothers become working full-time moms in the blink of an eye if necessary or imposed, or desired. Full-time employed moms decide it is time to get off the treadmill and take stock and seek more time. Our lives are a continuum of such adjustments. Let's envision a world where mothers can move along this continuum of work/life and not be ridiculed or made vulnerable in the process of living the kind of life that will make them whole."

How do we break down our own implicit associations and the ones other people have? We can't think our way out of them, we have to *act* our way out of them.[22] One way is to expose ourselves and others to examples that don't fit the stereotype. Joan offered this example. "Being a stay-at-home mom for part of your child's life is not by definition an impediment to becoming a Supreme Court Judge or a Secretary of State. Just ask Sandra Day O'Connor and Madeleine Albright." Even simply imagining in some detail a mother who is both employed and a caring parent or a mother who is not employed and very accomplished helps counteract our hidden assumptions.[23] An even better way is to develop close relationships with people who challenge these outdated mental maps.[24]

While everyone naturally gravitates to groups of people who are like him or her, this is one time when mothers should make an effort to get close to mothers who are different. If you are employed and hang out only with mothers who are employed, then chances are you'll unwittingly end up with a stronger subconscious belief that mothers who are *not* employed are dull. If you are not employed and hang out only with mothers who are not employed, chances are good you'll end up with a stronger subconscious belief that mothers who *are* employed are selfish and neglect their kids.[25] Your identity looks out for *you*. Your subconscious will pick up signals from other people that back up the mental maps that make you look good. "I'm employed so I'm smart and capable." Or "I'm not employed so I'm caring and nurturing."

In my local Mothers & More chapter, I am surrounded by mothers in all different kinds of employment and life situations. Getting to know them bolsters what I want to believe—that mothers can be competent and caring, regardless of their employment status. Hanging out with them helps me see what I want to be and what I want

to believe. I want to be both/and. I don't want to have to be either/
or. I want to be a mother and a capable worker when I am employed.
I want to be seen as a competent and interesting person and as a
caring person. My relationships with mothers who are different from
the way I am also challenge *their* assumptions. In fact, I've made it
my personal mission to be a mother-myth buster, and not just with
other mothers. I took my one-year-old along with me to visit offices
where I was doing volunteer work. I made it a point to mention
my four-year-old when I facilitated executive-level meetings. With
intentional action, we can thwart our own subconscious tendency to
think in stereotypes and help others do the same.

If we want to shift to our new beliefs and avoid giving other mothers Identity Whiplash, we'll have to catch the subconscious assumptions in our own thoughts and speech. Laura, who was not employed,
realized that when a woman described herself as "at home" she was
thinking to herself, "Hmmmm, how much will *she* know about strategic planning." Laura would then say to herself, "Laura, you know
better. Stop being prejudiced." Like Laura, I have to admit, that even
when I'm an employed mother, I've caught myself thinking about
other employed mothers, "I wonder if her kids really get enough time
with her?" The more I talk with other mothers about these outdated
assumptions, the more I am able to catch myself when they show up
in my own thinking—before I put my foot in my mouth and give
someone else whiplash.

None of us wants other people to assume things about us that just
aren't true—even if it's unintentional. We each want to be seen as
unique. That conflicts with our subconscious brain's strategy of putting people into easily labeled boxes in an attempt to make sense of
the world. By breaking down the assumptions about mothers to protect our own identity, we can also start a ripple effect on the people
around us. We can make other people aware of their hidden assumptions, pushing them to think differently.[26] Together, if we change
enough of those beliefs in enough people, the epidemic of Identity
Whiplash will disappear. Then we can all get rid of this collective
pain in the neck.

REMODELING TOOLS

- ▶ Visit Harvard's project on implicit bias at https://implicit. harvard.edu/implicit/. Click on the demonstration site and take the ten- to fifteen-minute Gender-Career Implicit Association Test (IAT), which reveals the association most of us have between family and females and between career and males.[27]
    - ◆ Send the IAT link to friends and have them take the test. Talk about the results at a play group, coffee date, or family dinner.
- ▶ When you find yourself thinking, "Shouldn't I be employed more?" or "Shouldn't I be employed less?" pause and take a deep breath. Ask yourself, how much of this is you responding to subconscious beliefs you may have or to invisible expectations others have. Ask yourself how much of this is real. Do you have evidence that there's something to worry about?
- ▶ Protect your identity and become an incredible mother-myth buster!
    - ◆ Have you ever caught yourself falling into the trap of these subconscious assumptions—either when thinking about other mothers or about yourself? Perhaps the negative ones like employed mothers are selfish and mothers who aren't employed are dull? Or maybe the positive ones like employed mothers are more capable and mothers who aren't employed are more caring?
    - ◆ List ways in which you don't fit the assumptions. List mothers you know and how they don't fit the assumptions.
    - ◆ How could you make it obvious to others that you don't fit the assumptions?

◆ Rent a copy of the movie *The Incredibles*. Be sure to get a copy that has all the scenes that were deleted from the theater version. There's an alternate opening in which Elastigirl, now a stay-at-home mom hiding in the suburbs, takes on a woman at a neighborhood barbecue who sneers when Elastigirl answers the What do you do? question with "I'm a homemaker." The commentary from writer/director Brad Bird tells us he drew on an experience of his own wife for the scene.

▶ If everyone shared these beliefs, what would people say? How would people behave differently? How would the world operate differently?

   ◆ All mothers are unique.

   ◆ A mother is more than any single role she plays at any given point in her lifetime. She is entitled to fully explore and develop her identity as she chooses: as a woman, a citizen, a parent, or an employee.

▶ When someone says, "You can't have it all," have your own response ready. Maybe, "I think everyone should be able to live a whole life." When you see a newspaper or magazine use the phrase *you can't have it all,* write and tell the publisher why the phrase is out of date and give some alternatives.

▶ The Third Wave Foundation and their project "I Spy Sexism" provide a simple mechanism that can also be used to expose the mental maps about mothers. I Spy Sexism suggests that "[t]he first step is to sit up and take notice of what's going on around you. . . . Carry a notebook and jot down incidents that strike you as unfair."[28] Jot down incidents that reveal the outdated mental maps about mothers. Then, "[o]nce you recognize unfair behavior for what it is, the next step is to let your feelings be known."[29] Send a card or e-mail to the person or organization you noticed, the media, your elected officials, organizations you belong to that work on related issues, your friends, and your family. Visit www.thirdwavefoundation.org/advocacy/i-spy.

▶ Pick up a book.
   ◆ *Blink: The Power of Thinking without Thinking* by Malcolm Gladwell. See especially chapters 2 and 3.
   ◆ *The Truth behind the Mommy Wars: Who Decides What Makes a Good Mother?* by Miriam Peskowitz.
   ◆ *The Mommy Myth: The Idealization of Motherhood and How It Has Undermined Women* by Susan Douglas and Meredith Michaels.

5

baby vacations

or what did i do all day?

Quick! Without thinking.
Write down the first answer that comes to you:
How many hours did you work this week?
Hold on to that answer, we'll come back to it later.

MY FRIEND BETH came to my door bearing good wishes and a stack of novels. I was in the last weeks of my pregnancy, and Beth didn't have children yet either. "I thought you might like to read these once the baby comes and you stop going to work," she offered. That seemed to make sense to me. I should have tons of time on my hands. How hard can taking care of a baby be? So I gave her a thank-you hug and set the stack on the table.

Of course, once Kate was born, my bubble quickly burst. A few weeks after Kate was born, I got an e-mail from a single friend asking me, "So what do you do all day?" I sighed with exhaustion but my mind immediately thought, "Well, nothing really." I avoided replying to her. What *did* I do all day? I had no time to myself. Every minute was spent taking care of Kate or doing stuff around the house. I rarely had a minute to read the headlines on the front page of the newspaper let alone a novel. Every once in a while, I looked at the stack of books from my friend, sitting on our table for months, unread, in the exact same place I put them down. A year later, I did manage to find the time to simply return them to her, unopened and unread. Where did all that time go that Beth and I thought I would have?

Then when Kate was about six months old, we tagged along on my parents' vacation in the desert town of Palm Springs. While David rose early to catch a morning tee time, I rose early to prepare the morning bottle and change the morning diaper. As David played the ninth hole, and my parents played with the baby, I played house. I prepared bottles, did laundry, changed diapers, coordinated nap times, rocked her to sleep—all the round-the-clock stuff I'd been doing at home. I broke down, saying that nothing about this trip felt like a vacation to me. David quickly offered to stop golfing and pitch in. Then my mother and sister said, "But poor David, he's been working so hard. He needs a break." I nearly bit their heads off. "Excuse me!" I insisted, "I need a break too!" Though I couldn't really explain from what. Why would anyone need a vacation if they weren't "working"? Fortunately, my father chimed in, "Wait a minute; Kristin's been working hard too."

Working. Yes, he was right. I *was* working. I'd been working non-stop. I'd never thought of it that way. Growing up, my mother was never employed and I often wondered to myself, "What does she *do* all day?" What my dad did was work. Whatever my mom did was simply what moms do. So I figured leaving the workforce for a few years would be a break. Some break. Instead, I got completely sideswiped by how much time and energy and skill it takes to care for a child and for a family. My new boss threw tantrums several times a day. I managed pee, poop, and puke. I worked a sixteen- to twenty-hour shift every day with no breaks and was on call all night. I didn't get paid for any of it. I was exhausted from taking care of family and didn't have a spare minute for anything else, yet I realized that I had always acted and talked as if I believed caring for a family wasn't work and didn't take any time. How did I end up with an assumption, a mental map, so different from the reality? Why was it so hard for me to change my own assumption now that my very brutal daily reality was so different?

I started listening to mothers' stories and noticed they were also running into this assumption that *caring for family isn't really work, it's just what mothers do.* When Stephanie went to a workplace meeting a few weeks before her maternity leave ended, a male colleague said to her, "So, when are you coming back from your *baby vacation?*" Stephanie was bemused by his assumption and responded that, "The vacation is getting to come to work!" How can everyone say mothers have the most important job in the world and at the same time say that taking care of a baby is a vacation?

Another mother shared that she had recently attended a career seminar in her field. She asked the people in attendance how to explain in an interview the fact that for three years she had been caring for family and not employed. A colleague told her, "Tell them you've been in a coma. That way, you'll have better luck explaining why you haven't been doing anything for the past three years." Haven't. Been. Doing. *Anything?* I wanted to put that guy in a coma for her. Or better yet, have him spend a couple of months on his own taking care of two toddlers. Then he'll be begging to be put in a coma so he can take a break. Let me get this straight. I need to update my résumé, and I have two options:

Coma Patient (1999–2002) Responsible for lying in a hospital bed as machines breathe for me, tubes feed me, and nurses bathe me.

or

Family Care Provider (1999–2002) Responsible for . . . *everything!*

You're telling me I'm better off with the title Coma Patient? How is it possible that people can calmly assert that being in a coma—a coma!—is more productive, more contributing, more work than caring for family?

DIMWIT SLACKERS, BLIND SPOTS, AND FAMILY MATH

The assumption that caring for family is not work but a "vacation" and just what mothers do contributes to the epidemic of Identity Whiplash we talked about in the previous chapter. For example, Joanne Brundage, founder of Mothers & More, quit her job as a letter carrier to take care of her two kids. Shortly after that, a friend called her. Busy with her baby, Joanne didn't pick up the phone until the fourth ring. "Oh . . . sorry," quipped her friend, "did I interrupt a crucial moment in your soap opera?" The hidden idea that family time is leisure time feeds the "soap opera and bonbons" image of mothers. That idea is why people say, "Let me explain it so my mother would understand it." Our implicit associations have paired up *dimwit slacker* with *mother.*

Mother = Caring for family
Caring for family = Doing nothing productive
Doing nothing productive = dimwit slacker

Therefore, Mothers are dimwit slackers

Whether we're employed or not, when the world around us believes subconsciously that mothers are dimwit slackers, we collide with that belief unexpectedly—on the job, in our communities, and even in our own heads.

The idea that family work takes no time and is just what mothers do is one of the reasons our husbands sometimes—okay, often—have blind spots when it comes to family work. Mental maps act as filters for what we see and notice. If your husband has a subconscious assumption that family work is just what a mother does, he won't see what needs doing. As a result, mothers and fathers can end up with different ideas about who is working harder. As one mother said, "When I first started staying home my husband was frustrated. Eventually he admitted that he didn't think I was doing enough." He didn't think what she was doing was work, so he concluded he was working much harder. If a father believes that, he's unlikely to pick up much extra family work at home. Our husbands just don't get it, in part because nobody gets it.

When mothers themselves subconsciously believe caring for family doesn't take any time, we can't understand why we never have enough time and why our employment suddenly doesn't fit. If mothers believe caring for family isn't work, then we're likely to feel we shouldn't need "help" from fathers to get it done. For example, after Kate was born, I wasn't employed for three and a half years but still felt like I was struggling to get everything done. When I returned to employment, I felt even more frazzled. David and I never talked about where the time for me to be employed would really come from. We took for granted that if Kate was in preschool for twenty-five hours a week, then I had twenty-five hours to be employed. Simple math, right?

```
    25 hours preschool for Kate
 -  25 hours employment for Kristin
    _____
    0 hours leftover
```

What we left out was all the other work that got done when I was with Kate myself. In those same twenty-five hours I was also running laundry, getting groceries, calling repair people, and paying bills. In those same twenty-five hours I would notice that Kate needed bigger pants and get them or remember that she should see the doctor and take her there. The preschool took care of *Kate* for twenty-five hours, it did not, however, take care of everything else I was doing. Of course I was frazzled. David and I both assumed I should still do everything else too because I was employed fewer hours than he was. We didn't realize what we'd done. I had traded twenty-five hours of taking care of Kate while I also did a bunch of other things for twenty-five hours of employment *plus* many more hours doing the bunch of other things that still needed doing.

```
    25 hours preschool for Kate
 -  25 hours employment for Kristin
 +  10 hours other family work
    _____
    10 hours of work leftover that don't fit anywhere =
    Frazzled Kristin
```

That unpaid work had been so invisible to us that David and I simply didn't factor it into our family math. Most everyone assumes that if you have good childcare (which is not cheap or easy to find) for the hours you are employed, it's an even trade. Even having learned that lesson once, I figured that when Kate started grade school full-time I could easily increase my employment or at least I would find it easier to be employed, but I didn't. I was doing different things but not fewer things. One day I picked Kate up at school, and she said she'd had a bad day. That was all she would say. After three hours of hanging out, getting groceries together, making dinner while she sat doing homework at the kitchen table, all the while gently returning to what had happened and giving her time to open up, I finally learned about a spat with a friend, and we talked through what she could do about it. School-age Kate isn't physically with me nearly as much and taking care of her now involves a lot of emotional support and a lot of just being together. I hadn't factored that time into my calculations. I hadn't noticed that caring for family is vital work that takes time, energy, and skill or that an assumption that *caring for family isn't work, it's just what mothers do* complicates our daily lives by giving our husbands blind spots, labeling mothers as dimwit slackers, and messing up our calculations about time and employment. Where did this mental map come from?

INVISIBLE WORK:
It's *Just* What Mothers Do

Everyone makes a wonderful fuss over mothers. We all spend a lot more money on Mother's Day than Father's Day. When we want to describe something as pure and wholesome, something that everyone agrees is good, we say it's like mom and apple pie. We remind adults to call their mother. Mothers and motherhood have a very special pedestal all their own. I figured joining the ranks up there on that pedestal meant I would effortlessly fill the role of mother and bask in some of that glow. When I became a mother, I did get the flowery Mother's Day cards and felt the warm glow. What caught me completely off guard was that I found myself doing a bunch of work day after day that had been completely invisible to me before, and was still invisible to everyone else, as if you needed special x-ray glasses to see it. We praise mothers and motherhood—the role on the pedestal, but the work of caring is invisible. Why?

To see how family work became invisible, let's look at the difference between two families we know and love: Laura's family, as in Laura Ingalls; and Beaver's family, as in *Leave it to Beaver.* In Laura's world, Pa built the *Little House in the Big Woods* and hunted deer. Ma made clothes and grew vegetables. Neither got paid but both did the work necessary to feed, clothe, and shelter the family. Separated in time by the Industrial Revolution, Beaver's family looked quite different. Ward left each morning for work out there doing something, I'm not really sure what, and he did it for money. June cheerfully took care of everything at home, and she did it for the satisfaction of providing husband and children with a haven from the harshness of the outside world. What June did looked very different from what Ma did and was harder to see. Advances in technology meant that June's work didn't look as much like work as Ma's did. Mothers didn't have to can their own tomatoes from the garden anymore, or make their own clothes, or churn their own butter. More and more, mothers were responsible for caring for children's emotional, psychological, and intellectual well-being, which is not nearly as tangible as a can of tomatoes on the shelf.

What June did also looked very different from what Ward did. He got paid, she didn't. He was out there in the world with other people. She was alone in her home. Work got defined by the marketplace and measured in dollars. Companies paid dollars to employees. Employees produced products and services that other people paid for with dollars, all so that ultimately the company would make more dollars. Family work had no dollars attached to it so it was not productive work and faded further from view. Between Ma's time and June's time, as Ann Crittenden, author of *The Price of Motherhood,* says, unpaid family work was assigned to women and the work "disappeared."[1]

The mother pedestal itself also obscures our view of the work it takes to care for family. We can see this pedestal problem in action when we find ourselves confusing *mother* (the role and the relationship) with *family work* (the activities necessary to care for children and family). For example, I remember times when my exhausted, bedraggled self tried to talk to other mothers about how hard I was working caring for my family. I was looking for empathy. Inevitably though, they responded by talking about the idealized mother role rather than the work. I would say something like, "Boy, I was up all night taking care of a feverish toddler." Response: "Yes, but isn't motherhood a blessing?" Well, yeeessss, but that wasn't my point. We were speaking different languages. I was talking about the work. They were talking about the role and the relationship. Over time, the two have become one and the same.

Mother = caring for family
Caring for family = Mother

Allison had the same experience. She was out with her sister and her sister's friends, all young single women with no kids. Allison told me, "When I jokingly chimed in with my temper tantrum stories and sleepless nights in response to their job gripes I got a lot of 'Oh but you get to be home with the little darlings' kind of comments." She was talking about the work she was doing that was analogous to their workplace stories. They were talking about the mother role up on the pedestal. The work of caring for family has been absorbed into being Mother. So if we talk about caring for family in the same way other people talk about work, it just doesn't compute.

That pedestal Mother perches on has been a long time in the making. Remember, a few hundred years of history added these three items to our Mother of All To-Do Lists:

❏ Make your home a haven from the cutthroat culture of industry.
❏ Stand as a model of virtue for society.
❏ Do everything with the patience and serenity of a saint.

As Judith Stadtman Tucker, founder of Mothers Movement Online observes, "There's a long and complicated history of representing motherhood as a sacred calling." A long, long time ago so many children died that mothers spent a lot of time nursing sick children, grieving for lost children, and continuing to take care of home and family in the midst of that grieving. In that context of life and death, viewing motherhood as a sacred practice is not surprising. Over the decades, more than one adviser to mothers has likened motherhood to the sacred and the holy.[2] One even compared mothers to God, and of course we have the lines from a famous poem: ". . . The hand that rocks the cradle / Is the hand that rules the world."[3]

Today, child loss is much, much rarer in the United States and developed countries. The focus of caring for children has shifted away from nursing illness and toward developing emotional, psychological, and intellectual well-being. Yet the language and assumptions of motherhood as a sacred calling are still common, making the work invisible. People note "the unspeakably high calling of motherhood" and "the sacrifices that so many women make, day in and day out, to the raising of children, the nurture of the home, and the shaping of civilization itself."[4] One modern author stated, "Serving as your child's 'psychologist' and your home's 'facility manager' isn't work—it's the essence of life."[5] Wait, why can't it be both? My relationship with my daughter as her mother is absolutely one of the essences of my life. David's relationship with her as her father is one of the essences of his life. My love for my daughter is *why* I care for her and, in many ways, my reward for caring for her, but that doesn't mean that what I'm doing, the activities to care for her, should be automatically disqualified as work. The way in which family work has disappeared and been absorbed into an idealized version of Mother confounds us in our everyday lives and limits the ways in which we can think about sharing responsibility for that work within our families. This anachronistic assumption that *caring for family isn't work, it's just what mothers do* has also become part of our collective, outdated house—society—and that has real consequences for mothers and for families.

MY OBSESSION WITH SOCIAL SECURITY

A few months after Kate was born, I was standing in my kitchen reading the *Los Angeles Times* when I happened on a review of a new book, *The Price of Motherhood: Why the Most Important Job in the World Is the Least Valued,* by Ann Crittenden. I recognized in the review a chance to understand why motherhood had made a mess of me. I immediately ordered my copy online.

Reading furiously at nap time and at night I managed to finish the book in two weeks. Crittenden was the first of many guides I would find in books and in person that helped me understand the consequences of so many subconscious beliefs being entrenched in our society. Crittenden wrote about Social Security that: "Years spent caring for others, unpaid, are calculated as zeroes," "Years spent raising the next generation don't count," and "Because unpaid childcare ... is not counted as labor, caregivers earn zero Social Security credits.[6] I'd never thought twice about Social Security. I wasn't even thirty-five. Yet the words hit me like fists in my gut: "Zeroes," "Not counted as labor," and you "don't count." Are they serious? How could it be?

Well, that's what happens when beliefs like *caring for family isn't work, it's just what mothers do* get embedded in the policies people create. It's yet another example of a vicious cycle in which people hold beliefs, then act on those beliefs, and then set up the world to operate on those old beliefs. Then—voilà!—the old beliefs live on, deep in our subconscious, silently dealing out unexpected consequences for those of us who thought the beliefs were long gone.

When I sat at my desk late one night and used the Social Security Administration's own calculators, I looked at two scenarios. In one, I assumed that I continued to work full-time in my same line of work until retirement without stopping. In the other, I assumed that I left the workforce for seven years to care for my daughter and then reentered full-time.

Those seven years of doing "nothing" but raising a child cost me a half million dollars.

Why? Because Social Security was designed in the late 1930s, just before World War II, so its design sprang from the beliefs of the policy makers, both men and women, who put it together. They believed men would and should be employed. They also assumed that women would be taking care of family and would be married to one of those employed men. None of these beliefs was a stretch because at the time only a handful of mothers were employed and even fewer were unmarried.[7] Given those beliefs, the designers decided to tie benefits to employment history and earnings, giving more benefits to men who worked more years and earned more money. Women would be taken care of as dependents of those employed men.

Social Security is the same today. When you work for pay, you earn Social Security credits. The higher your earnings and the more years you work for pay, the higher your benefits. Time out of the workforce counts against you, whether you are twiddling your thumbs or raising three children. That's why seven years out of the workforce would have cost me a half million dollars. That mother pedestal is costing us a lot of money.

Social Security is a major government program that still touches every adult at some point in their lives, but the assumptions about mothers, fathers, work, and marriage embedded in it no longer match our reality. Now, most mothers are employed at some point in some way. Many are divorced or single and can't count on a male earner's benefits. In a still small but growing number of families, mothers are the primary earners. We've changed, but the rules stayed the same. Those rules sneak into our subconscious. Family work still doesn't count as a contribution and mothers still pay the price. When assumptions like this are part of the fabric of society, we can't escape their reach. Even for mothers who personally feel the work of caring for family is valued by their spouses and respected by family and friends, we all still get tangled up in rules based on a deep assumption that caring for family doesn't count as work because it's just what mothers do.

Social Security is just one example on a long list. Take family law. A judge is likely to look at the years a married mother spent caring for family and conclude that the work would count for next to nothing in a divorce.[8] Take state disability insurance programs. The programs apply only to people earning money. A mother, or anyone out of the workforce caring for family, who has an accident and becomes disabled won't be eligible for disability insurance benefits. Her family will have to scramble to find the money or family members to replace all the unpaid work she was doing. Take welfare programs. If a single mother cannot find a job and needs support from welfare, she'll be required to do thirty hours of mandatory work activities to get her welfare check.[9] Those activities include searching for a job and working for any employer *without pay*. However, taking care of her own children doesn't count as work toward the work requirement. Take workplaces. They still behave as if taking care of family were done magically by someone behind the curtain. The vast majority of jobs leave no room for the employee to care for family because workplaces were designed when employers could assume that the paid jobs would be done by men, while caring for family would be done by their wives. This mental map about family care not really being work is embedded not just in our own brains but also in our culture, public policies, and workplace practices.

FAMILY WORK:
What's It Worth to Us?

So what is work if it's not just the activities that make us money or make other people money? In a Mothers & More e-mail discussion, Jennifer pointed out that women economists have been challenging that definition of work for some time now. As Jennifer explained, "[economist] Margaret Reid promoted a concept of a 'third person' criteria . . . [it's work if] it's an activity that you could pay someone else to do and still receive the benefit. If you can't still receive the benefit of the action, then it isn't work." Okay, so if I paid someone to take a vacation for me, I wouldn't get any of the intended benefit— relaxation. That's why it isn't work. If I paid someone to mow the lawn, I still get the benefit—cut grass—so it is work.[10]

In real life we might not be willing to pay someone to take care of our families, at least not all the time. Remember, we have our own maternal desire. We enjoy caring for our families and value the relationships we build with them when we care for them ourselves.[11] We might also believe—correctly or not— that no one else can do it as well or that no one else will in fact interact with our children the way we will. In the theoretical world of economists, however, we can have our cake and eat it too. We don't have to *actually* pay someone else to do it. If in theory we *could* pay someone to do it and still receive most of the benefit, then the doing of this stuff counts as work.

What if we looked at what a typical mother does using this criterion? Here's a time diary from noon to 3:00 P.M. that a mother contributed to a Mothers & More survey.

> Spent time trying to get my 4 year old to pick up things he had thrown on the floor because I am tired of doing it, all the while trying to come up with strategies for making this task easier/ him more accountable/me less frustrated. Prepped and cleaned up snack. Checked e-mail and responded to messages re: a community arts and crafts fair I am co-planning. Spent some time playing with my son. Spent time wondering where I put our overdue bills, and then trying to figure out how to get them in the mail (which involves a drive to town), give my son a bath, get all the laundry sorted and then started, make dinner. Felt overwhelmed because was up late cleaning last night, so likely not strategizing as best I could under better circumstances. Back of mind thoughts are trip planning for a cross-country trip this week.[12]

What could this mother pay someone else to do? Just about everything—teach child to pick up, prepare food, clean up, deliver bills, bathe child, do laundry, plan trip, and even play with her child. She would still receive a lot of the benefit—a child who picks up, a child and family who are fed, bills that are paid, laundry that is clean, a trip that is planned, and a happy child. She would lose the intangible personal rewards of the work, but that's true of any work defined like this. Even if you feel particularly fulfilled by a well-trimmed lawn and decide therefore to do it yourself, mowing the lawn is still work because you *could* pay someone else and still benefit from the cut grass. Emotional rewards don't cancel out the tangible benefits or the fact that the activity is real work.

Emotional rewards don't cancel out the financial value of work either. Though especially when it comes to mothers, we're often told our care for our families is sullied by thinking of it in economic terms. As one author said of mothers, "Your compensation isn't measured in dollars, but in building a life that you love."[13] Gee, isn't it possible it can be measured both ways? Tons of people do paid work that shows their commitment to serving others; nurses, doctors, teachers, firefighters, soldiers. Plenty of people get paid big bucks to do work that they love: Michael Jordan, Bill Gates, Oprah. Career advisers tell us that doing what we love will bring us the most financial success. However, when it comes to mothers, loving the work is what gets us up on the pedestal. Talking about the work as having a financial value or cost sends us tumbling to the ground. The subconscious assumptions that home is a haven of virtue while the marketplace is full of vice and greed makes some people balk at applying dollars to home and motherhood for fear of contaminating the virtue. That's dangerous, though, because discouraging mothers and families from considering the financial value of family work invites financial risk.

During the time David was doing seventy-hour workweeks and my sole work was taking care of everything else, we knew I added what I'd call a quality-of-life value to the family. I did the stuff that helped us be less stressed, eat better, have fun together, show love for each other, sleep better—sometimes anyway—and live in a home that met at least minimum standards of cleanliness on most days. We also knew my work had a financial value. How did we know? Because we knew I needed life insurance even when I wasn't employed. Life insurance companies and financial advisers recommend policies to insure parents that are not employed, usually mothers.[14] If I died when I was the primary family person, David would have to pay someone to replace me and all that care I had provided. Or he might have to cut back on his own employment to make room to care for Kate. Families need life insurance not just to replace a parent's income but also for the cost of replacing the amount of family work the parent had been doing. Assuming that mothers are somehow dishonored by considering the economics of family work can lead families to make financial decisions based on a formula that leaves out a big chunk of the total work that sustains the family.

Sometimes people try to demonstrate the financial worth of unpaid family work by calculating a salary for the person doing it, but these calculations always sound inflated. In 2008, Salary.com pegged the salary for mothers who are not employed at $116,805 and at $68,405 for mothers who are employed (less because they pay for some childcare).[15] These calculations use typical salaries for specialists, such as psychologist, cook, and chief executive officer, to value the hours a mother spends doing similar activities. For example, one hour as a psychologist is worth $38.84, one hour as a cook is worth $14.26, and one hour as a CEO is worth $72.32. These types of salary figures seem too high because you'd never hire a whole team of specialists to do the work a mother (or father) does. We know that, if we wanted or had to, replacing some or all of the family work done by a mother or father wouldn't cost that much. So those numbers may give us an ego boost, but they aren't very useful for thinking about the value of family work.

We'd be better off thinking about the replacement value of the work like a life insurance policy would do. If a parent no longer provided care for the children and family, what would the family need to pay to provide replacement care of similar quality?[16] Nancy Folbre, economist and author of *Valuing Children*, calculates that a conservative estimate of the cost of replacing the time the parents spend caring for children (not including housework) is between $13,000 and $23,000 per year for a two-parent, two-child family.[17] Now, what it might actually cost to replace the care that parents provide to children depends quite a bit on how we define *quality care*, and families with higher incomes tend to spend more when they pay for childcare and education. However, these estimates were developed using solid data on time parents spend on childcare and median wages of childcare specialists so the numbers demonstrate that caring for children and family has a value, and that value can, in fact, be reasonably quantified.

FAMILY WORK:
What's It Worth to Everyone Else?

I had a conversation about family work and its value with my friend Becky one day. She later e-mailed me that, after we talked, she'd spent some time sitting with her kids and watching all the comings and goings at a major city center anchored by a large bank. She imagined their stories; the mother who was counting on Grandpa to pick up her daughter after school so she could run the sales department; the father whose wife had made everyone breakfast, made him a lunch, and gotten the kids to school so he could be on time to his job as a bank teller; the accomplished older man whose parents had cared and provided for him and whose wife had reduced her employment schedule during key times to care for the family so he could pursue the jobs that ultimately led to his promotion to CEO. Watching the people, she realized just how much unpaid work it took behind the scenes, past and present, for all those people to be doing what they were doing in that moment.

Caring for our own families contributes to our community's bottom line. Caring for children develops adults that contribute to the economy. They have jobs, and they contribute taxes. Those children, whose care shows up as zeros on our Social Security statements, are the ones who will actually fund the Social Security checks for everyone in our generation. In this age of information and globalization, the long-term health of any country's economy depends on the development of people—the creation of human capital. Now, I don't typically sit with my daughter to help her with homework and announce, "Time to create human capital!" However, *my* investment of time in helping her understand fractions has benefits for her *and* economic benefits for both the local and larger community.

Of course, children aren't just investment portfolios and future earnings are by no means the best measure of a person's value. People are valuable as people. People contribute to society in ways that the market can't measure. As Folbre points out, simply calculating future earnings would mean neither "Van Gogh or Mother Teresa was worth much" and a "daughter is worth less than a son" because she's likely to earn less.[18] Our commitment to care for our children and families is a promise we keep even if there's no financial return on our invest-ment.[19] Yet our commitment has spillover benefits to the community. Our communities enjoy a higher quality of life when families care for each other. We get children who grow up to be doctors and take care of us, mechanics who keep our cars running, aides who care for us when we get old. When families care for each other, we all enjoy less crime, fewer unemployed people, and fewer homeless.[20] Caring for our children—past, present, and future—means more responsible adults, good citizens, and more kindness and caring every day for all of us.

While both the intangible social values of family care and the value of the human capital families develop can be translated into dollars, the complexity is more than I can deal with here. Some might argue that there's too much guesswork involved in putting a dollar figure on any aspect of caring for others. Yet, somehow people have managed to figure out ways to value futures on pigs and ways to value ideas for inventions that haven't even been manufactured yet. There's a sur-prising amount of guesswork involved in measuring our economy, so that shouldn't stop us from calculating a value for family work. For example, we can ask our basic cost of replacement question again, this time using the question that Folbre uses to frame her calculations. "If parents were unwilling or unable to provide care to their children, what would *society* need to pay to provide substitute care of acceptable quality?"[21] Well, at $13,000 per year per child for the time spent on childcare *alone* and nearly seventy-four million children in the United States in 2006, that's well over a trillion dollars.[22] In fact, the organi-zation Redefining Progress estimates that the value of parenting plus housework in the United States in 2004 was about $2.5 trillion— equal to about a third of the gross domestic product (GDP).[23]

WHAT WE DON'T MEASURE CAN HURT US

Why do all this theoretical math? As Folbre says, "Even crude approximations of the social value of family work, used judiciously, can help call attention to its contributions."[24] However, we can't even get crude approximations if we don't measure family work in the first place. As a country, we are careful to measure investments that are important to us. Our government spends $500 million a year measuring a variety of labor statistics: who is employed, what they do, how much they get paid.[25] We spend $50 million measuring the GDP,[26] which is "the market value of goods and services produced by labor and property in the United States."[27] The government spends those millions of dollars collecting and reporting economic data so that businesses can make decisions about where to build a factory or how many people to hire and what to pay them. The data are used by local, state, and national governments to determine how a piece of legislation will impact people and the economy and what types of services are needed by their communities.[28] People use the economic data every day to make good, informed decisions that affect a lot of people.

Because we measure dollars so well, if I pay my neighbor to take care of my kids, and she pays me to take care of hers, we will all be able to see that paid work show up in the numbers. The GDP increases. However, if each of us cares for our own children—*poof!*—the work and the value disappears. The GDP decreases. The work becomes invisible. It reminds me of that philosophical riddle: If a tree falls in the forest and no one is around to hear it, does it make a sound? In this case, we might ask: If a person falls down from exhaustion doing the feeding and clothing, mopping and comforting, organizing and chauffeuring but no one is around to see it or measure it, does it count as doing something?

Why should I care if there's a data table in some obscure government office measuring family work? Well, what if I told you that having that data explains a universal kitchen argument between mothers and fathers? She says, "I'm doing everything. You're not doing your fair share! You've got to help out around the house more!" He says, "But honey, I'm doing a ton. Way more than my dad ever did. You just don't appreciate it." No one wins, because they are both right. He is doing twice as much family care as his father did, but she increased her time, too, so she's still doing twice as much as he is.[29] We know this because of the American Time Use Survey (ATUS). The 2003 ATUS is the first U.S. government-conducted comprehensive measurement of how we all spend our time, including the time we spend caring for family. The data from the survey, along with a few much smaller, less detailed snapshots done every ten years or so since 1965, tell us that both mothers and fathers are right.

On a grander scale, having time data challenges the conventional wisdom about a lot of things. For example, many people claim that mothers and fathers are employed more hours than they used to be, so parents—and especially mothers—must be spending less time with kids. That's why kids today are having so much trouble, so they say. Not true. Together, mothers and fathers are spending *more* time with their kids today than they did in 1965.[30] Without the ATUS we wouldn't know that. Without good data, we can easily fall into the trap of accepting the conventional wisdom explanation of a problem and blindly trying solutions that won't work.

When communities and governments don't have good data, we can get misguided solutions on a grand scale. If we don't know how many people are providing unpaid care to children, grandchildren, or elderly relatives and how that impacts them, how can a commu-nity plan to provide enough paid childcare and eldercare? If we don't measure the family work, we won't know who is providing most of it—men or women, old or young, rich or poor—or how providing that unpaid work affects their well-being. As mothers and fathers spend more time with children and on employment, what are they giving up—sleep, community involvement, or exercise? If we watch the GDP over time, we conclude the United States has been on a path of steady growth of productivity and prosperity. But wait, is part of that growth a result of women moving into the workforce—doing less of the invisible unpaid family work and more of the employed hours that count in the GDP?

David and I messed up our family math by not factoring in the invisible hours of family work that still needed to get done when I returned to employment. Not having—or not using—the data on all the family work getting done in our communities messes up our larger calculations about what is valuable, what is needed, and what is in the best interests of mothers and families. As a nation, we set ourselves up to make bad decisions, which often have unintended negative effects on mothers and on families. Conveniently, the absence—or ignorance—of the data means we can't see any problems, which as our children know makes it easy to pretend there's no problem. Tell a child to clean her room and she's just as likely to stuff all the toys under the bed where we can't see them. See Mom, no problem! Mothers and families are left trying to make our way through a world that reinforces every day that caring for family isn't work, that this work doesn't contribute to the economy, doesn't contribute to our society, and doesn't need to be factored into our decisions.

"So what?" someone might ask. When mothers or anyone else complains that caring for children and family is not appreciated or valued or measured, they often get dismissed as simply wanting a pat on the back to make them feel better. And yes, I for one would feel better if I could go through life without hearing people say that taking care of family is as productive as being in a coma. However, valuing family work isn't just about our feelings. It definitely isn't about arguing that more mothers should leave employment to do the family work because it is so valuable. Measuring family work, valuing it, and using that information makes it clear that unpaid family work creates healthy communities and a healthy economy and that placing the responsibility for family work mostly on women has major consequences for the well-being of mothers, families, and communities.

WHAT IF WE BELIEVED CARING FOR OTHERS IS WORK?

If we want to break down the outdated mental map that says *caring for family isn't really work, it's just what mothers do*, we'll need a replacement belief. So let's experiment. What if everyone believed instead:

> Caring for others is a vital human and economic activity and a public service.

What would we say? How would we behave? How would the world operate?

Let's start with what we would say. We would separate Mother (the role and the relationship) from the work (the activities necessary to care for children and family). When we talk about motherhood as a job or a profession or talk about mothering, we confuse the relationship with the work. Unintentionally, we imply that mothers are the only ones who can or should do this work and the work disappears into the role and can't be seen. With our new belief, instead of talking about motherhood as a job or a profession or even an ideal on a pedestal, we would try talking about being a mother as a relationship, a relationship a woman has with a child. We would experiment with talking about taking care of family as important unpaid work lots of people, not only mothers, do.

So now armed with our experimental ways of talking about mothers and family work, we can test out answers to the questions, Who am I? and What do you do? Within Mothers & More, we often talk about what labels to use for different mothers. *Full-time mom* doesn't work because it implies that employed mothers aren't mothers all the time. Try telling that to the mother on the job calling to check in on her sick child. *Working mother* doesn't work either. That one suggests that mothers who aren't employed aren't working. Try telling that to someone who has spent the whole day with two toddlers. Even *stay-at-home mom* seems so woefully inaccurate these days. How much time does a stay-at-home mom actually spend in her home and not in the car or somewhere else? And because many employed mothers have *home*-based businesses or *home* offices, even referring to employed mothers as *mothers who work outside the home* is problematic.

Home is a word that just muddies the waters no matter how we use it. Plus, I've found that if you have two different mothers, and both are employed, say, ten hours a week, one may call herself a stay-at-home mom and the other might call herself a working mother. They select a term based on how they think of themselves, which is fine, of course, but that also muddies the waters. What do the terms really mean if two mothers with the same employment situation call themselves by different terms? Even popular titles like family manager and family CEO hint that only mothers who are *not* employed can have these titles, when many mothers and fathers do work covered by these titles. So trust me, we've hashed this stuff through for over twenty years within Mothers & More. At the end of the day, we stick with the basic idea that when we talk about ourselves and about mothers in general, we try to separate the role of mother from the work of caring for families

We can think about answering the Who am I? and What do you do? questions in two parts:

Mother (relationship to a child)
+ Work (relationship to employment and/or volunteer
  work and/or family work)

Answer to Who am I? and What do you do?

The key to answering these questions is to start the answer with "I'm a mother, and . . . " So we might say to someone we're meeting, "I'm a mother, and I'm employed as an office manager." Or "I'm a mother, and I spend most of my time caring for my family." Or "I'm a mother, and I run a home-based business and I volunteer time at my children's school." Or "I'm a mother, and my primary work is caring for my family and I have a background in information technology." Experimenting with the switch is easier when you know what the first three words will be. At first switching away from our old language feels awkward and forced. With practice, we find our own words and rhythm, and it gets easier, especially if we use humor. When someone asks me, "What do you do?" I sometimes smile and say, "I help a very small person learn to get along with others, and I help grown-ups learn to get along with each other. Guess which one pays more?"

I've also stopped asking other people, "What do you do?" because I know how much I hate that question myself. Martha Bullen, author of the book *Stay-at-Home*, observed in an e-mail conversation, "My husband is English. He's pointed out that immediately asking 'What do you do?' when you first meet someone is a very American habit and is much less common in Europe. He said that question would be perceived as rude in England." We can experiment instead with alternatives. I've started trying to ask, "Tell me about yourself." Deb, another friend of mine, asks people, "What's important to you?" Kim has yet another approach, "Now when I talk to moms, . . . I like to ask what works for her about her life now, what she wants to see change, what she's thinking about for the future."

So what do we do when we want to refer to groups of mothers? Judith Stadtman Tucker, founder of the Mothers Movement Online, explains, "As someone [who has] spent A LOT of time trying to articulate the types of work mothers do, I generally use 'employed mothers' or 'mothers who work for pay' instead of 'working mothers.'" Okay, that's simple and clear. Then all we need to do is use the flip side of those terms as a replacement for *stay-at-home moms*. So how about mothers who are not employed or mothers whose primary work is unpaid family care? To feel comfortable with this new language, we must feel confident in our own belief that *caring for others is a vital human and economic activity and a public service.* As Tracy says, her first step was "to read . . . books and talk with other moms to sort of get clear in my own mind how I felt about what was work to me." Remember, as I've mentioned before, we almost always need conversations with other people to help us surface our own mental maps and then shift them.

I found that talking differently about family work helped me change my own assumptions as well as those of others around me.

When I finally responded to that e-mail I got from my friend asking "What do you do all day?" I sent a long e-mail that listed what I'd been doing that day to take care of baby Kate. Feed Kate, clean up after breakfast, change a diaper, play with Kate, put her down for a nap, do a load of laundry, and so on. I make it a point to support other mothers and fathers talking about family work. If a mother tells me she's "just" a mother, I'll say, "There's no 'just' about it because caring for family is hard work." If a mother tells me that her job is so demanding she can't seem to get everything in her life done, I'll say, "Of course you feel squeezed. We often don't see just how much time and energy caring for our families takes on top of our jobs."

One year Mothers & More launched an annual Mother's Day Campaign with buttons that said "I Care. I Work. I Count." In a grocery store parking lot one day, another mother stopped me to say she loved the button. We talked for fifteen minutes as I explained the campaign and why counting family work as work was about so much more than appreciating mothers. The more time I spent trying to persuade other people that caring for family is real work, the more I came to believe it myself. The more I believed it myself, the more confident I was talking with David about sharing that work—and the more I was able to resist the ways in which my environment and my own subconscious were telling me that what I was doing wasn't really work.

IF WE BELIEVED CARING IS WORK, HOW WOULD THE WORLD OPERATE?

If we believed *caring for others is a vital human and economic activity and a public service,* how would the world operate? First, talking about caring for others as work and placing an economic value on it wouldn't be viewed as an insult or reason to think a woman is not a good mother. In fact, people would insist on measuring family work and understanding its financial impact on families and communities. The American Time Use Survey would be considered just as important as the GDP, or the census, or all those labor statistics. Our workplaces would be designed to make room for people to do the important work of caring for family. Family law would recognize time spent caring for family as a contribution to the family equal to a paycheck. People who were caring for family and not employed would be eligible for disability insurance and earn Social Security benefits. Single parents who need welfare support would be able to count caring for their own young children as work. In short, Mother would come down off the pedestal, and the work of caring for family would go up there instead.

HOW MANY HOURS DID YOU WORK THIS WEEK?

So now, do you remember that number you came up with at the beginning of this chapter for how many hours you worked this week? What was it?

If we believed *caring for others is a vital human and economic activity and a public service,* how would you answer the question now? How many hours did you work this week?

Did the number get bigger?

Good.

I'd be happy to trade in that mother pedestal for a world that believed and acted like caring for family is hard work with lots of value. Though I admit, I continue to find it hard to shift my own mental map. The beliefs are so deep and we're so surrounded by the vicious cycles telling us *caring for family is not really work, it's just what mothers do.* When I slip into old ways of thinking, my daughter often brings me back. One day I was fretting in my head while I was playing on the rug with preschool Kate. I said to her, because she was the only one around to hear me at the time, "Kate, I really want to do something important with my life." She looked up at me and said, "But ma, taking care of me is important work." I smiled and said, "You're right, Kate. You're absolutely right."

REMODELING TOOLS

▶ Conduct your own American Time Use Survey. Choose a six-hour block of your day, at least part of which you will spend with your children and family. Make notes about how you spend your time. Be sure to include mental work like making lists or planning meals. The first step in challenging the unconscious belief that caring for family isn't work is to make the work visible to yourself and your family.

▶ If we believed *Caring for others is a vital human and economic activity and a public service*, what would we say? How would we behave differently? How would the world operate?

▶ Looking for new language? Use these guidelines tested by hundreds of Mothers & More members over the years.

INSTEAD OF	TRY
• Working mother • Just a mom • Stay-at-home mom • Full-time mom	• Mother all by itself • Employed or working for pay • Not employed* or caring for family
• Motherhood is a job • Mothering	• Family work • Work of caring for family • Unpaid family work
• Does she work or stay home?	• Is she employed?
• Using *or*. • Is she working OR at home?	• Using *and* . . . a lot. (I'm a mother and . . .) • I'm a mother AND a bookkeeper AND a volunteer tutor. • I'm a mother AND I have a background in social work AND I spend most of my time caring for my family.

INSTEAD OF	TRY
• What do you do?	• Using new openers. (Tell me about yourself.)
	• Using humor, but don't be surprised if people don't get it! (From Stephanie: "I still tell people that I'm a lawyer. I just either say that I'm not practicing right now or that I quit my job with a firm to handle the affairs of one very demanding little client!")

* *Unemployed* has a specific technical definition as someone who is looking for employment.

▶ Using the guidelines, come up with your own experiments.
   ◆ What language do you usually use for talking about yourself and other mothers? What could you switch to?
   ◆ How will you answer the question, "What do you do?" Write an introduction for yourself trying out new language. Try writing how you would introduce a friend who is a mother too.
   ◆ What could you ask instead of "What do you do?"
   ◆ How do you feel using your experimental language in different contexts? For example, in a professional context it can be hard to feel comfortable leading with "I'm a mother," no matter what comes after that opening.
▶ Take these guidelines to your local newspaper or write a letter to the editor asking them to use new language.
▶ Review your life insurance and your spouse's. Have you factored in what it would take to replace the unpaid family work one or both of you are doing now?

► Visit the American Time Use Survey website (www.bls.gov/tus) to learn more about the study. Many other countries have conducted time-use surveys. In the United States, the first one happened in 2003 and is now threatened by budget cuts. Send a note to your elected officials and the secretary of labor expressing your support for collecting these data.

► Organizations that advocate for the elderly use information like the ATUS to calculate and publicize the dollar value of the work families do taking care of older relatives. How could you make people aware of how much care parents provide and that it is worth $2.5 trillion?

► Do you know if your local or state leaders know about and use the survey data? Print out the "General Overview" and the most recent economic news release from the ATUS website (www.bls.gov/tus), which summarizes the data from the most recent year. Take it to a city council meeting or your state representative's office and explain why it is important to you that they use these data. Note that the data can be broken down by state.

► Ask your local and state leaders how they are making sure we measure what we value, including unpaid care work. Many cities have adopted quality-of-life measures. Has yours? Does it include the work of caring for family as something to be measured? Another example is the Genuine Progress Indicator (GPI), an index created by the non-profit organization Redefining Progress that "enables policymakers at the national, state, regional, or local level to measure how well their citizens are doing both economically and socially" including measurements of unpaid care work. Visit www.rprogress.org to find out more.[31]

► Pick up a book.
   ◆ *The Invisible Heart: Economics and Family Values* by Nancy Folbre

SQUARE PEGS:
A FAIRY TALE IN THREE ACTS
ACT ONE

ↂ

Once upon a time there was a young and idealistic couple. They looked forward to the time when they would have a child. And they said, "When our child arrives we will both be home for family dinner together every night in our castle. We will both have time to read to and play with and care for our child. We will both have time to pursue our careers and interests and have time for each other. So we'll simply get jobs that add up to around seventy hours a week of work between us!" Pleased with their own foresight and planning, they continued in their fairy tale life, confident that they had planned for a happy ending.

And then the baby arrived.

And the happy ending went up in smoke.

6

i'm a square peg

or why doesn't my job

fit anymore?

BEFORE KATE WAS born, I was a manager at a high-tech company. I enjoyed what I did, but the workplace itself was toxic, and eventually I felt I'd hit the glass ceiling. After yet another promotion opportunity passed me by, I told David I was ready to make a change. "I'm ready to have a baby," I said. The next month, I was pregnant. David was just starting his first job at a law firm. Keeping up and getting ahead for him meant ten- and twelve-hour workdays, weekend work, and travel. My job was at least fifty hours a week and, given a recent merger, would now include coast-to-coast travel.

No problem. I'm a valued employee. I'll just propose a part-time schedule for myself. So I did my homework and put together a very thorough proposal to go part-time. I didn't even tell anyone I was pregnant. I based the proposal purely on business reasons. Doing my best to hide my queasy stomach and bouts of fatigue, I flew to the

East Coast and met with my new boss in his office. I pointed out the advantages of having me part-time on the West Coast and hiring someone else part-time on the East Coast in our new headquarters: lower travel costs, someone available in person in both locations, and the ability to hire two people with complementary skill sets and experience for the same money.

He listened but didn't even read my nifty memo before he said, "Sorry, can't do it." His budget gave him a head count of a fixed number of bodies. Full-time or part-time, I counted as a body. He couldn't hire a second person part-time on the other coast. My new boss was a really nice guy, but my options were clear to me. Full-time with coast-to-coast travel or no time.

So guess what? A few weeks later, I announced both my pregnancy and my resignation. I'd found a half-time director-level job at a different company five minutes from my home and accepted it as fast as I could. Pretty impressive, right?

Well, don't be too impressed with anything but my amazing luck. The founders of the new company were fellow alumni from my college. They were married, and she was due with her first child a month before I was. When I told them I couldn't accept the full-time job they offered because I was pregnant, they called me back to offer a different schedule. The catch was that the new company was a hundred times smaller and less stable. My offer was half-time at half-pay but no paid vacation or sick time, no health benefits, no retirement, no stock options—all of which I'd had for years. Still, I felt like I'd won the lottery. I'd be able to work a reduced schedule in an executive position close to home.

After five months in the new position while I was pregnant and then three months of maternity leave, my manager asked to meet with me. Funding was shaky, and they needed to cut costs. She laid me off that day along with several other people. For all my planning and plotting, I now had no job. Finding another company with a pregnant executive from my alma mater who would offer me a half-time executive position seemed about as likely as winning the lottery twice.

Something didn't feel fair about how I'd ended up with no job and no prospects, but what was it? No one had said they wouldn't hire me because I was a woman or because I was pregnant or because I was a mother. I left one company and gave up benefits at another because *I* had decided I needed to work a different schedule from everyone else. It seemed only fair that someone who worked more hours should earn more and get ahead faster than I would. Still, something just didn't feel right. Before I'd gotten pregnant, I'd been gunning for an executive job. Now, just a year and a half later, only six months into being a mother, I despaired about getting and keeping *any* job. I'd been told all my life that I could be anything I wanted. I had experienced success in the workplace. Now suddenly I felt like a square peg trying to fit into a round hole. What had happened? What could I do about it?

FIFTY HOURS, FIFTY WEEKS, FIFTY YEARS

My aunt Ann, whom you met in the Introduction on that New York City sidewalk, entered the workforce on the heels of the women's movement. In the 1970s she worked in publishing for ten years until in 1980 at age thirty-four, a senior editor at a national magazine, she had her first child. A colleague referred her to a nanny and told her she should come back to work quickly so she didn't bond so tightly with the baby that she couldn't leave. During her maternity leave, she and her husband tried to negotiate part-time schedules so they could each work three days a week. His employer said no; she realized that her editor would expect her to do full-time work on part-time pay, so she began making arrangements for full-time childcare. One week before she was to go back, she woke up with a panic attack in the middle of the night and realized she simply couldn't leave the baby. So she quit.

Twenty years later, Kate was born, and I faced the exact same problem and, as I quickly learned, so did many mothers. As one mother shared, "I have my MBA and 8 years of experience, but if I am not available 24/5 (sometimes 6 and 7), there is no room for me in corporate America."[1] Even in professions most of us think of as family-friendly, mothers find themselves struggling to fit in. Annie is a teacher, yet she described her reality as "Finding daycare at 6:30 in the morning as well as after school care until 5–6 P.M. so I can work the 50–60 hours per week required." Non-profit organizations are often thought of as more flexible employers, yet Lisa told me she interviewed at a non-profit who told her she would have to be in the office from 8:00 A.M. to 6:00 P.M., that it would be best if her childcare provider could do things like take the kids to the doctor, and that, "People here have children, but you'd never know it." Lisa got the message. As she describes, "It was all right to have children just as long as their care did not cut into the 50 hours you were expected to be at work." No matter the field or employer, everyone is expected to put in fifty hours and everyone is expected to keep family completely separate from the workplace. That's a tough fit for anyone with children.

Mothers also have a tough time fitting into jobs because most require fifty weeks a year. In other words, outside of a two-week vacation, if that's even available, there's not much wiggle room for days off to take care of a sick child, to take time off when kids are off from school, or to take time off after a baby is born. Employers are not required to provide paid sick leave in the United States, and even having paid sick days doesn't always mean you can use them to care for a sick child. Only three in ten workers are officially able to use paid sick days to care for a sick child.[2] There's also not much wiggle room for maternity leave. Even though just over half of all employees are eligible for twelve weeks of unpaid leave under the Family Medical Leave Act (FMLA), over and over I hear mothers describe how their employers require them to use up all their paid vacation and sick time during that same twelve weeks, leaving them with no cushion after the leave is over. Or employers require them to start using their unpaid leave before the baby is born if their doctor says they need to stop working a few weeks beforehand or won't extend it if the baby is born prematurely. Or they can't take leave at all because they can't afford to go twelve weeks without pay or aren't eligible for FMLA.[3] If you can't work fifty weeks a year, you just don't fit.

If you can't work fifty years in a row, you don't fit either. Employers don't necessarily expect people to work for one company their whole lives anymore, but they do expect to see continuous employment. Gaps in a résumé and switching jobs too often are standard red flags for hiring managers. As you may recall from the last chapter, one mother was told she'd be better off with Coma Patient on her résumé than admitting she left employment to care for family.

The round hole I was trying to fit into is defined by two mental maps:

- Jobs are one-size-fits-all, fifty hours a week, fifty weeks a year, for fifty years of our lives.
- Family and employment are separate.

What defined me as a square peg were two realities:

- My need to have enough time in my life to care for my family.
- The fact that both family and employment are core parts of my life hourly, weekly, and across the years.

WHAT'S NOT FAIR?

When Kate was four, she was fixated on understanding the concept of fair. She'd ask me, "Mommy, what's not fair?" and from the stories I told her, she would try to get her arms around the meaning of fair. I puzzled over that question myself. Okay, so we assume *jobs are one-size-fits-all, fifty hours a week, fifty weeks a year, for fifty years of our lives* and *family and employment are separate.* What's not fair about that? Isn't that simply a business requirement, completely unrelated to gender and thus completely objective, fair, and neutral?

When trying to figure out what's fair or not, a good person to turn to is a lawyer, or in this case a law professor. About a year after Kate was born, I found some expert help thinking about the What's not fair? question in a new way. Joan Williams is a law professor, the director of the WorkLife Law Center, and the author of *Unbending Gender*. Williams' book helped me understand that the assumptions about jobs and employment are actually tightly linked to gender. Like the other mental maps we've discussed so far, these two are a product of history and not immutable laws of physics or even laws of economics. Williams made a compelling case that together these beliefs have shaped a workplace that is not fair to mothers.

Let's review. Remember this item from our Mother of All To-Do Lists?

Raise the workers of our economy while the father goes out and competes in it.

Also, remember we talked about June and Ward Cleaver as an example of how work and home got separated into two different dimensions, with Ward being assigned to work and June to home? Remember the implicit association of men with careers and women with family? Our mental map that *mothers are responsible for and are naturally better at children and family* has a partner map that says *fathers are responsible for and are naturally better at employment and earning money*. Both beliefs were firmly in place as the Industrial Revolution took off. In a nifty bit of mental map math, added together, they give us our seemingly neutral assumptions about employment.

Mothers are responsible for and are naturally better at children and family
+ Fathers are responsible for and are naturally better at employment and earning money
Family and employment are separate
+ Jobs are one-size-fits-all, fifty hours a week, fifty weeks a year, for fifty years of our lives.

At the birth of our modern economy, family and employment *were* separate. Fathers were employed and earned money. Mothers were not employed and cared for family. Because of that reality, employers could reasonably assume that their employees, if they had children, also had a wife to care for them. So business structured jobs to fit that assumption. Jobs could be one-size-fits-all because for the most part, the men who filled them were one-size-fits-all. As a result, what Williams calls the "ideal worker" was born. An ideal worker can work fifty hours a week, fifty weeks a year, for fifty years of his life because when the ideal worker was created, he was a man with a wife at home.[4]

A BIT OF HISTORY

In the late 1930s and 1940s, these assumptions about jobs and employment were built into some very critical policies. At the beginning of the Industrial Revolution, fifty hours was a light week. Sweatshop hours of ninety and a hundred hours were common. Child labor was common. After years of campaigns for workers' rights, in 1938 the Fair Labor Standards Act (FLSA) fixed a reasonable workweek at forty hours and eliminated child labor. Given the dire economic times, the FLSA was also designed to get employers to hire more people. If an employee worked more than forty hours in a week, the company would now have to pay them more per hour—that is, overtime pay. The hope was that employers would then prefer hiring two people because that would cost less than paying one person to work tons of expensive overtime.[5] When this standard was set, a man could work forty hours a week because he had someone else caring for family. In fact, the expectation was that employers would strive to provide full-time jobs for men that paid a "family wage" that allowed him to support a wife and children.[6]

Then, a few years after the FLSA passed, during World War II, the United States implemented a wage freeze.[7] Companies started offering health insurance and other benefits as ways to get around the freeze and attract workers. In other words, it is an accident of history that today health insurance is provided by employers and tied to having a full-time job.[8] Linking benefits to full-time jobs messed up the FLSA overtime incentive to hire more people rather than work one person longer hours. Instead, employers today ask themselves, "Hmm, since I'm already paying a lot for this employee to have benefits, is it cheaper to pay him overtime to work longer hours or is it cheaper to hire an additional person who will also get expensive benefits?" As the cost of benefits goes up, as it has dramatically, increasingly the answer is that it is cheaper to work the one employee longer hours than to hire a second employee and provide benefits.[9] Along with other factors, this rational employer calculation has pushed that forty-hour standard workweek closer to a fifty-hour reality for many full-time jobs.[10]

IS ONE-SIZE-FITS-ALL FAIR?

Wow, I hadn't learned this history in high school. Once I understood that our assumptions about jobs were more accidents of history than business imperatives and more influenced by assumptions about mothers and fathers than I thought, I considered my own experience managing employees and asked myself, "What's not fair?"

In my first management job, years before Kate was born, most of my employees were young, unmarried, and childless, but one was a single mother of two school-age kids. Every afternoon, she'd get a call from them to report that they had arrived safely home from school. She'd worry about them at home alone. Some afternoons she would take or make several phone calls home. Sometimes she'd be absent because of a sick kid. In this company, absences and spending work time on "personal calls" were frowned upon. So I asked my boss, "What should I do about this?" "Lay down the law," came the answer. "We have to be consistent or everyone will take advantage of us." On one hand, that seemed fair—if we define *fair* as "everyone should be treated exactly the same way." On the other hand, from the balcony view Williams had given me, it was patently unfair. In hindsight, the job schedule and standards that fit my twenty-two-year-old single, childless male employee just fine weren't ever going to fit my thirty-five-year-old single mother employee. There wasn't much I could do about it though, so I laid down the law. Thinking about it now I get a guilty pit in my stomach.

In that same job, I remember a customer service representative in our call center who requested to start her 6:00 A.M. shift at 6:30 A.M. instead so she could drop her child off at childcare in the morning. She offered to work a half hour at the end of her shift. The supervisor, manager, and human resources representative went through much hand wringing and all agreed that modifying the shift was impossible and her request would be turned down. Once again, the argument was that fair meant treating everyone exactly the same. They didn't want to set a precedent of making schedule modifications that everyone might want. Everyone needed to work the shift they were assigned and work overtime on demand. It wasn't that they were trying to discriminate against women. It's just no one considered an alternative perspective about what was fair. Maybe the one-size-fits-all job with schedules dictated by the employer wasn't fair because it made it impossible for anyone with family responsibilities to do the job well, and the people most likely to have family responsibilities are women.

Imagine you woke up one morning in a bizarre dimension in which *clothes* were one-size-fits-all. One size for all adults over eighteen. People say to you, "Since it's the same for everyone, it's the best way to be fair. Plus, it's very efficient because the machines that make clothes can be built to make just the one size." You notice some people for whom the clothes fit very well. They seem perfectly happy with the one-size-fits-all approach and will explain how efficient and fair it all is. However, many people seem to be uncomfortable. They do their best to grin and bear it. You play along, putting on the clothes. Hmm, too tight in the chest and hips. You try to stretch them out. You avoid drying them in the dryer so they won't shrink. Still, you're uncomfortable every day. One-size-fits-all doesn't seem fair to you at all. The clothes just don't fit you. They don't serve their intended purpose. You think to yourself, what's more important here? A standard process for making clothes or achieving the purpose that each person have clothes that fit?

That's really not so different from what workplaces do. Workplaces define what's fair as a standard, one-size-fits-all work uniform that requires at least fifty hours a week, fifty weeks a year, for fifty years of our lives and expects us to keep family and employment separate. The uniform often requires overtime or travel on demand or relocation. No one really remembers the original reasons for the one-size-fits-all uniform and that it worked at the time because of reasonable assumptions about mothers and fathers. Now those jobs don't fit mothers or quite a few others. What's more important? Treating everyone the same so that we can serve the purpose of filling all those one-size-fits-all jobs? Or treating individuals as individuals so that we can serve the purpose of making it possible for more people to succeed and to contribute in their jobs?

The assumption that employers have a right to ideal workers has become more like the law of gravity—so well known and reinforced by our experience that we don't even question it anymore. Like our own heartbeat, we take it for granted. So it takes effort to ask ourselves, is it fair to women that since World War II, all our employment policies and practices have been designed around ideal workers, who by definition were men with wives to care for the family?[11] Is it fair that the FLSA stands largely unchanged after seventy years, but is now completely out of sync with families in which both parents are employed? Is it fair that benefits are attached to having a full-time job due to an accident of history and assumptions that a father's wages and benefits would cover his family's needs? Is it fair that mothers and fathers have changed so much, yet like dinosaurs lumbering in our midst, our policies, practices, and culture around work are well adapted to a world that no longer exists? My answer now to all of these questions is no, it isn't fair. So how do we remodel the practices and policies around employment? Williams answers, "Until mothers believe it's not fair, they'll never convince the courts, or employers or policy makers that it's not fair."[12]

CHALLENGING WHAT WE *THINK* WE KNOW
AND WHAT WE *THINK* IS FAIR

I spent many years challenging myself about what I thought I knew about mothers and employment, and then one October evening I spoke at a Mothers & More chapter in Minnesota. The title of my talk was "Work Options That Work for Mothers." After introducing myself, I said to the packed room, "First, I want you to talk to each other about these questions. What would your ideal employment situation be today? What would it be in five years? Think about how many hours a week you'd be employed, and in what field, and what kind of work." The room started buzzing with conversation. A few minutes later, after I finally got them to stop talking, I asked a few people to share.

Jane said her ideal would be to reduce her hours in her current job from fifty hours a week to about thiry, but she'd asked for that and was turned down. Kristy had left employment and said not being employed was ideal now, but in five years her ideal would be a job that would let her pick her kids up from school at 3:00 P.M. She figured she would have to move outside her technical field to find a job with an alternative schedule. Laura said she needed the income from her current full-time job, and it would be her ideal if she just had a bit of flexibility around start and end times to be able to drop off and pick up her kids. Cayla had found a job with the right hours—about twenty-five a week—but it was a low-paying service job that wasn't using her skills or advancing her career or providing any benefits. Everyone who spoke talked about their ideal as a job that left enough room for them to care for their families in a way they wanted and needed to over time.*

---

* Names used are not real names.

"So how many of you have your ideal right now?" I asked. A very few scattered hands went up. "Isn't it interesting," I continued, "that in a modern world where women have made it, where mothers can simply choose to be employed or not, and where workplaces are more family-friendly than ever, that there are surprisingly few of us that have anything close to our ideal employment situation? Isn't it interesting that for so many of us, our ideal is something different from what most jobs ask of us—fifty hours a week, fifty weeks a year, for fifty years of our lives?"

I went on to explain that they weren't alone. Eight in ten Mothers & More members said in a survey that their ideal job would be less than thirty hours a week. Other studies tell us that many mothers who are employed full-time would prefer part-time jobs. And, many mothers who are not employed at all would prefer to have part-time jobs, too.[13] Mothers know what their ideal is, but they don't have it.

That's not what I expected, I told my audience. Before I had my daughter, I wanted to believe that mothers aren't treated any differently at work. I wanted to believe the newspapers and magazines that said today's workplaces have tons of flexible options. I knew that most mothers are employed, and I thought that meant mothers are employed in the same ways everyone else is employed. Before I had my daughter, I believed I could simply choose to be employed or not or how much. I assumed that if a mother is employed, her job is what she wants or needs to do. If she's *not* employed, that's simply what she wants. But how can our employment simply be our choice if so few of us have the jobs we want?

We can't get work options that work for mothers, until we understand why work *doesn't* work for so many of us. We can't navigate the landscape unless we can see the boulders in our way. To see more clearly, we have to challenge what we think we know and what we think is fair. Tonight, I said to them, I'll share the insights I learned that convinced me that everything I thought I knew about mothers and employment was wrong.

INSIGHT:
Mothers Don't "Work" Like Everyone Else

I knew most mothers work. It's hard to read newspapers or magazines without being reminded that the number of mothers in the
workforce has doubled in just forty years to over 70 percent. So I
thought all mothers are employed and that they work like everyone
else. They don't. Even though mothers don't have their ideal, they
also don't work like everyone else does. If I had a backyard barbecue
for twenty couples and their kids, here's how the twenty mothers
and twenty fathers would likely be employed. Of the fathers, eighteen would be employed full-time, more than thirty-five hours a
week. Just one would be employed part-time, and one wouldn't be
employed. Of the mothers, only ten would be employed full-time,
four part-time, and six wouldn't be employed at all.[14] If I invited

How We Are
Employed

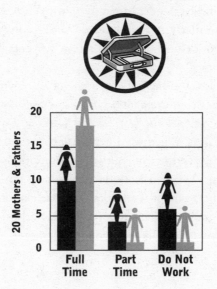

the same group back again five years later, the mothers would be much more likely to have shifted their employment up or down in response to additional children or the ages of their children.[15] The mothers would be much more likely to have left the workforce for family reasons.[16] As Williams says, "Our economy is divided into mothers and others."[17] Jobs that require overtime, jobs that expect someone else will handle the kids when they are sick, jobs that look askance at gaps in a résumé. In other words, the vast majority of jobs are just not mother friendly.

That is one of the reasons women are rare among executive ranks today.[18] Since half the workforce is women, and just over half the management and professional jobs are held by women, some people conclude that if women aren't at the highest levels, it must be because they choose not to seek these types of positions.[19] Lisa sure didn't feel like it was a choice. Lisa's boss announced that she was leaving and had always supported Lisa and praised her work. But, as Lisa explains, "She told me that she couldn't recommend me for her job because I had children, saying that her job would require more than 70 hours a week. My boss did not have children or other family responsibilities and ultimately selected a woman to replace her who was similarly unencumbered." Lisa didn't choose not to move up; she got defined out of the job by her boss before she even had a chance.

On the surface, the mental maps about employment seem like objective business requirements: *family and employment are separate* and *jobs are one-size-fits-all, fifty hours a week, fifty weeks a year, for fifty years of our lives.* When we dig a bit deeper though, we see that these mental maps spring from outdated assumptions about mothers and fathers. They have led workplaces to define jobs in such a way that often mothers cannot work like everyone else and still care for family. So yes, most mothers are employed, but don't let that fool you. Mothers don't work like everyone else.

■ ■ ■

INSIGHT:
Workplaces Aren't So Flexible After All

I thought workplaces were already flexible. It turns out that mothers are the flexible ones. As square pegs faced with round holes, mothers turn into Elastigirl, our hero from the movie *The Incredibles*. Mothers contort themselves to fit into employment or to move in and out of employment. Some mothers wake up in the middle of the night to finish paid work left undone when they put the kids to bed. Some quit and then struggle to get good jobs again later. Some start their own businesses or take freelance projects. Some move to different companies or positions once they have children to find a better fit. As flexible as mothers are, I discovered that workplaces haven't made nearly as much progress as I had hoped or as the media had led me to believe.

Often, mothers who request an alternative schedule get the same answer I did when my part-time proposal was turned down. No, because the structure of the budget and benefits assumes everyone is full-time. As one mother said, "I had ten years' experience with my state government agency and another mother and I requested a job-share. We were refused . . . they didn't want to have us both on the payroll because we would both have benefits and be considered full-time for payroll purposes."[20] When people with less than full-time schedules get full benefits and count as a full-time person in the budget, the manager concludes that it is expensive and complicated to allow people to work less than full-time. On the other hand, when people with alternative schedules get zero benefits, most employees won't ask for an alternative schedule because they can't afford to go without benefits or pay for their own benefits. No matter how you slice it, linking budget and benefits to full-time jobs limits the options employers can offer and employees can afford to take.

Even when workplaces create policies to provide flexible work options, whether people actually use those options depends on the individual manager and the organization's culture. Organizations are simply collections of people who will act on their mental maps. And most people still carry versions of these mental maps, consciously or subconsciously:

- Mothers are responsible for and are naturally better at children and family.
- Fathers are responsible for and are naturally better at earning money.
- Family and employment are separate.
- Jobs are one-size-fits-all, fifty hours a week, fifty weeks a year, for fifty years of our lives.

Mental maps are a lot harder to change than policies in the handbook. Mothers often discover that even companies that are lauded for being family-friendly don't always match their billing. One mother, her part-time request denied despite the company's policies, described having to go over her supervisor and the human resources department to two vice presidents who then "directed HR to implement the directives in place" and accept her request.[21] Yet another mother described getting the okay for a part-time schedule after her maternity leave, only to have it withdrawn when a new manager was hired.[22] A company might have fabulous programs and policies on paper, but individual managers may not go along with them or managers may change. The unspoken rules of the office often make it clear that using policies or programs for flexibility will keep you from getting ahead or that only certain types of employees are supposed to use them. As one mother explained, "I decided to leave when I looked at the department and saw that no one in the forty-person department had children under the age of fourteen. The company that I worked for has been in *Working Mother* magazine for ten years as one of the best places for mothers to work. The reality was if you were a professional person that made over $35,000, the work-life programs didn't apply to you!"[23] Employees know the unwritten rules, and over 40 percent of working parents who have access to flexible work options say they believe they will risk their jobs if they use them.[24] In the battle between well-intentioned policies and the unwritten rules of any workplace, unwritten rules win every time.

These mental maps are so deep that even proposed solutions are often based on the same outdated assumptions.[25] For example, some companies offer backup childcare services so that an employee doesn't have to miss work if their own childcare falls through or even if the child is sick. Other companies offer concierge services to pick up groceries or dry-cleaning or gifts for relatives. Such services sell themselves to companies by saying that the services mean employees will take fewer days off and do less personal business at work.[26] In other words, with these kinds of services, employees can function more like ideal workers and delegate their lives and family work to someone else. Many solutions try to help employees fit the one round hole better, rather than create holes of different shapes.

Other types of solutions, like company programs for parental leave and part-time work for parents of young children, are aimed at carving exceptions for mothers to the one-size-fits-all rule. Sometimes the programs are explicitly for mothers. Other times they are described as being designed for parents or even all employees. Either way, using them is almost always a black mark on the employee's record, so fathers are less likely to use them,[27] and employees without children view them as an unfair favor to parents. The result is a two-tier system with mothers on the mommy track and everyone else with the real jobs.[28]

Many mothers today have been employed for years before they have children, so they assume they'll have the good standing to ask for some flexibility, whatever the actual policies at their workplace. For example, when Carol's oldest entered kindergarten, she knew she would need a different schedule to match his bus schedule. "I had been working for the state for almost eight years (two years from being vested in the pension system), and thought my past excellent job performance and position as a supervisor would offer me more flexibility in terms of schedule—that I would be able to work some hours from home each day. It did not. I ended up leaving that job for a job that pays significantly less . . . but is much more flexible." Workplaces just aren't as flexible as mothers hope or expect, so mothers have to be so flexible it hurts.

INSIGHT:
Childcare Doesn't Make Everything Better

Within months of being laid off from my part-time job after maternity leave, I missed my profession so much that I volunteered for an obscure city task force so I could pull out my flip charts and markers once in a while and facilitate *something*. We found a great childcare center for baby Kate one day a week to give me some breathing room and a chance to figure out how to get a new job. Little did I know that even spotless childcare centers are Petri dishes. Kate was sick every other week from just one day with her playmates' germs. David didn't have the flexibility to stay home with a sick child. His parents were only five minutes away, but at that point they were both employed full-time. If Kate woke up with a fever, I was the one who would have to drop everything to stay home; even if I was scheduled to lead a meeting of fifty executives that day. That wouldn't work. We couldn't afford full-time help at home unless I was employed full-time. But I couldn't even look for work or take consulting projects without help at home in case Kate got sick. Before I had a child, I thought the basic solution to mothers being employed was childcare. Instead, I discovered that finding childcare options isn't simple or easy, and even when you have good childcare, that doesn't make everything all better.

Historically anyway, fathers delegated childcare to mothers. As mothers entered the workforce and if they were going to adhere to the one-size-fits-all jobs too, then—so the logic went—they would simply pass the baby on to someone else. Turns out there's nothing simple about that. What mothers and families face is the Bermuda Triangle of childcare challenges: quality, cost, and logistics. Is it good enough? Can we afford it? Is it available for my children on the days I need for the hours I need in a location that makes pick up and drop off possible? I was the one wrestling with all these questions with minimal involvement from David. The mental map that *mothers are responsible for and are naturally better at children and family* saddled us both with the assumption that if I wasn't caring for Kate myself, the childcare conundrum was still mine to solve.

Childcare is a conundrum because jobs are one-size-fits-all and so mothers find that either their childcare options limit the jobs they can have or the jobs they have limit the childcare options. For example, most childcare options are one-size-fits-all to match most jobs so even when mothers find an employment arrangement that works, often they can't find a childcare arrangement that matches. As one mother explained, "If day care provided a part-time option for infants, I would still be working part-time now."[29] My sister Sarah had to pay for full-time care to take a part-time job. On the other hand, if you work the long hours required by many jobs, your childcare options are also limited. Lisa found she couldn't use a childcare center and had to find full-time help at home because, "I couldn't do both pick up and drop off and be in the office as many hours as I needed to." In other words, the demands of her job dictated her childcare options.

Mothers and families are expected to make childcare fit the job, as opposed to being able to modify the job to fit the childcare. One mother said that she and her husband were both working second shifts when she got pregnant and there was no second shift childcare available. She asked to work first shift instead. "The two bosses that I had said no, and told me that if I wanted to stay there, I had to take a demotion [to get] a first shift job."[30] When the job and the best childcare options don't fit each other, mothers are the ones stretched in the middle. As Amy said, "I chose the daycare situation that I feel is best for the kids, and built my working life around it. But it makes for long days, compressed family time, vacation time spent to deal with illnesses instead of recreation, and professional challenges."

I assumed that at least once Kate was in our public elementary school, the built-in childcare would make my own employment much easier, but it didn't. Instead I was dealing with school start times that were out of whack with the workday, ending times in midafternoon before the end of a standard work day, random days when school was closed, researching after-school programs, and finding good childcare options for the summer. Schools are structured not only for a farming calendar in which summers off made sense but also for a time when it was reasonable to assume fathers all worked full-time and all kids had a mother who could pick them up midday and spend the summer caring for them.

Oh, and kids get sick, and when they are young, they get sick a lot. So even when we have childcare, the fifty-weeks-a-year requirement of that one-size-fits-all job becomes a problem. Half of mothers in the United States give up pay when they stay home with a sick child.[31] Even having access to paid sick days isn't a cure-all. As Carol explains, "In the twelve months after I returned from my first maternity leave, I never was able to work a full five day week because my child was ill so often—not with anything chronic—just stupid colds. But I got disciplined from my work."

Our kids' health isn't the only thing that can change. Our childcare arrangements themselves are always changing. As one mother explained, "You get a good situation and then your kid ages out of the program, or you get a different job, or the babysitter quits, or school is out for the summer, etc. It is always just temporary." Then there's the problem that even if we have good childcare options, we can't and don't want to delegate absolutely everything to someone else. From doctor's appointments to school plays to laundry, there's plenty of family work we still need or want to do ourselves. So even if we get through the Bermuda Triangle of quality, cost, and logistics and find childcare that matches our needs, childcare doesn't make everything better.

INSIGHT:
We Feel Lucky to Be Treated Unfairly

Remember I told you that when I was pregnant I found a half-time position at half pay and was told no retirement benefits, no health insurance, no stock options? It wasn't until after I was laid off that I finally asked myself, "Why had I felt like I'd won the lottery when in reality I'd given up more than my fair share of dollars?" I felt lucky because I shared the invisible assumption that real jobs are fifty hours, fifty weeks, and fifty years. I assumed that anything other than this ideal worker schedule was a favor—one that shouldn't be questioned too much lest it slip away. So I didn't even ask.

Because mothers have come to assume that it's perfectly reasonable for jobs to be one-size-fits-all, they think of themselves as exceptions. When we do find alternative employment arrangements, we usually talk about them as "accommodations" or "bending the rules" and consider ourselves lucky. As Susanna says, "My boss is extremely supportive of family and bends the rules in order to accommodate my family time. I worry about my future with this company if I'm not working for him. I know to appreciate him because I've worked at some companies and interviewed for some jobs that seemed openly hostile to mothers." Diane told me she lucked into a part-time job as a ceramic engineer. Her flexible hours make room for caring for her two daughters, her job is close to home, and she says, "Most importantly, I still get to be an engineer." Yet she has no health benefits or paid vacation because her company schedules her to work up to twenty-three and a quarter hours a week, just shy of the twenty-four hours that in this particular company would entitle her to health and vacation benefits. Diane and Susanna feel lucky because they know their arrangements are rare.

The mental map that *jobs are one-size-fits-all, fifty hours a week, fifty weeks a year for fifty years of our lives* has been embedded in employment policies and practices and makes most mothers' ideal of working less than fifty hours a week not so lucky in reality. Because she's working less than twenty-four full hours a week, Diane isn't eligible for unpaid leave under the Family Medical Leave Act since it effectively requires that someone work twenty-five hours a week for a year to be eligible.[32] Part-time workers rarely receive health, retirement, vacation, or sick leave benefits.[33] In fact, the federal law that governs employee benefits (ERISA) has thresholds that in effect prevent part-time workers from receiving pension benefits.[34] When I was laid off from my employer, I lived in one of only nine states where unemployment insurance covers part-time workers. In most states, only those who were working full-time and are still available for full-time work qualify for unemployment insurance.[35] Everything around us is designed for Williams' ideal workers.

When everything is designed for ideal workers, the not-so-ideal workers feel it in their paychecks. Gin looked for entry-level part-time work in retail, and she started with Target. She offered them school hours Monday to Friday and some weekends. Their computer wouldn't even create a schedule without a permanent weeknight every week. A weeknight would require childcare that the hourly wage they offered her wouldn't cover. So Gin felt particularly lucky to find a position at a department store where they jumped through hoops to work with her schedule. She said that "the pay is terrible" and she's not eligible for promotion unless she goes full-time. But she notes, "My family schedule was more important to me than pay." In Gin's case, the assumption that jobs are one-size-fits-all was built into the computer itself. Because she couldn't fit, she traded away pay for flexibility. Part-time workers earn a lot less per hour than full-time employees.[36] Part of this gap is because part-time jobs are concentrated in lower-paying occupations, but that hits women and mothers hard too. Half of women who work part-time are in the lowest paying industries, such as education, nursing, department stores, restaurants, and childcare.[37] As Gin experienced, when women want or need a schedule other than fifty hours a week, they are often limited to the lowest paying jobs even within low-paying industries.

So let's say we have a part-time employee and a full-time employee in the same job. Is it fair to pay less *per hour* and no benefits to someone who works a schedule other than the ideal? Let's ask a lawyer again, or in this case, a judge. When Linda Lovell filed a lawsuit against her employer she was working a 75 percent schedule, thirty hours a week, as an engineer. Her co-worker Charles worked 100 percent at the same job, but Linda's salary was less than 75 percent of the full-time salary of her co-worker. The Equal Pay Act says employers cannot pay an employee a lower rate than they pay employees of the opposite sex for equal work. Linda's employer argued that her different schedule meant that the Equal Pay Act did not apply, but the court disagreed. The court decided that the different pay rates weren't fair and said that an employer's justification for paying a lower rate has to be based on actual duties and training and cannot be justified solely by arguing that the woman works a reduced schedule.[38]

As Williams comments, "This case indicates that it's not fair to pay a woman with the same skills and job a depressed wage because she's working 30 hours a week. We have to realize that the traditional work schedule is designed around men's typical life patterns. It doesn't make sense to penalize a woman for not being able to work a schedule designed around men when they are doing the same work with the same training." What is fair is for men or women on different schedules to be paid proportionally. In Linda's case, assuming equal work and equal experience, what is fair is a 75 percent salary for a 75 percent schedule. The challenge is that while the Equal Pay Act applied in this case, it doesn't explicitly cover part-time workers and covers only wages not benefits or promotional opportunities.[39] By contrast, the United Kingdom guarantees proportional pay and benefits for part-time work. Paying a lower rate and no benefits to those on alternative schedules has been considered unfair and illegal there for decades.[40]

Yet mothers' need for flexible work and alternative schedules is so great, their availability is so rare, and our assumption that jobs are one-size-fits-all are so deep, mothers are often the first to say they are lucky to have found an alternative schedule even when it comes with low pay, no benefits, and little chance at promotion. Feeling lucky makes it hard to see what's not fair, and knowing these options are rare makes it risky to ask for what is fair.

INSIGHT:
Mothers *Are* Treated Differently at Work

I wanted to believe that in spite of everything I've talked about, once mothers are on the job, they are treated the same as any other employee. Instead, mothers told me things like, "When I was pregnant with my first child, everyone in my department was interviewed for additional responsibilities (and a promotion) except me."[41] Susanna said, "I even had a hiring manager ask me how I thought I could devote myself to my job and children." The reality is that a lot of people are still very conflicted about whether mothers should be employed at all.[42]

Most people have subconscious beliefs about mothers that influence how they treat mothers in the workplace. Remember the discussion in Chapter 4 about the unconscious stereotypes about mothers that prompted an identity crisis?

> woman
> – children
> + job
> _____
> rich genius

> woman
> + children
> – job
> _____
> dependent dimwit who cares a lot about other people

> woman
> + children
> + job
> _____
> rich genius who is selfish and neglects her family

> woman
> + children
> + part-time job
> _____
> dimwit, slacker employee who is selfish and neglects
> her family

In the workplace, these unconscious stereotypes lead not just to Identity Whiplash, but to discrimination. Even when the assumptions about mothers are silent and subconscious, they shape people's decisions and behavior in the workplace in ways that disadvantage mothers and often in ways that may be invisible to an individual mother. A study from Cornell showed that mothers were far less likely to be hired than others with equal résumés and were offered lower starting salaries. Fathers, on the other hand, were not penalized for being a parent and sometimes benefitted from having children.[43]

Employers view mothers as less capable than women without children and less competent than they were before they had children, and being a mother also decreases employers' interest in training and promoting a woman.[44]

Williams and the WorkLife Law Center she runs have led the effort to expose the way that subconscious assumptions about employment and mothers turn into discrimination—often unintended—in the workplace. Family responsibilities discrimination (FRD) "occurs when an employee suffers discrimination at work based on unexamined biases about how employees with family caregiving responsibilities will or should act."[45] Sometimes, this happens simply because people are oblivious to their own perceptions about mothers. They make employment decisions and act based on their subconscious assumptions about how mothers behave and what they want. Sometimes they even mean well. They believe they are helping a mother out by not considering her for a promotion to a job with travel.[46] Or as one pregnant customer service employee was told by her supervisor when she was fired, "Hopefully this will give you some time to spend with your children."[47]

Other times, employers have opinions about how mothers *should* behave and what they should want and have strong assumptions that mothers cannot be good employees. One employer said that, "Working mothers cannot be both good mothers and good workers. I don't see how you can do either job well."[48] Another mother was told that she "was no longer dependable since she had delivered a child; that [her] place was at home with her child."[49] A car salesperson, who was married with four children, had her supervisor tell her she should "do the right thing" and stay home with her children.[50] One senior vice president complained to a mother about "the incompetence and laziness of women who are also working mothers."[51]

These stories are all from legal cases, many of them successfully awarding thousands of dollars in damages to mothers for FRD. These types of lawsuits are relatively new but increasing rapidly.[52] Although there is no single federal law that prohibits FRD, many—but not all—cases are illegal as a form of sex discrimination under several federal and state laws.[53] For example, certain existing laws apply if fathers are promoted but not mothers. A single case in Pennsylvania under Title VII awarded a female civil engineer $3 million because she was passed over for promotions after the birth of her son. The president of the company had asked her, "Do you want to have babies or do you want a career here?"[54]

Mothers are treated differently at work, and increasingly courts are saying it's not fair. Even the former Chief Justice of the Supreme Court, William Rehnquist, said in a 2003 opinion that "the fault line between work and family [is] precisely where sex-based generalization has been and remains the strongest. . . . Stereotypes about women's domestic responsibilities are reinforced by parallel stereotypes, presuming a lack of domestic responsibilities for men. These mutually reinforcing stereotypes create a self-fulfilling cycle of discrimination."[55] So that's the nut of it, isn't it? It doesn't feel fair because it isn't. The Chief Justice said so himself.

MY CONCLUSION:
My Employment Choices Aren't Choices After All

Flush with all my insights, I concluded that my mistake had been thinking that my employment choices would be made in a vacuum, free of any external constraints or variables, with all possibilities open to me. When I could see the landscape as it was, rather than how I hoped it would be, I could see what I really had was a short list of lousy options to try to make me—a square peg—fit into that one round hole.

Like me, most mothers evaluate our short list of employment options based primarily on what's best—financially and otherwise—for our children, then our family, and then to a lesser extent, what's best for us personally.[56] If you ask mothers, those are the reasons they'll usually give for why and how they are employed or not. Mothers may not even mention inflexible workplaces as a factor in their choices. The mental maps that *jobs are one-size-fits-all* and *family and employ-*

ment are separate are so deeply embedded in our minds and invisibly in the walls around us that blaming workplaces for how they are structured feels like blaming the sun for rising.

However, those outdated mental maps shaped the workplace in such a way that I, as a mother who needed to be able to care for her family, had only a few options for making myself fit. I selected one of the few options I had by moving to a part-time job, but I didn't choose the lousy baggage that came with it—getting paid less per hour, losing my benefits, giving up the seniority that might get me a promotion, or leaving a stable company for a start-up.

Speaking of choosing, I think we need different language. I would say that each time I face a fork in the road about family and employment I've made the best *decision* I could given the constraints and my priorities. I prefer the word *decision* because it implies a much more complicated process of understanding the context and weighing pros and cons. *Choice,* on the other hand, makes me sound like I can choose my employment from an endless variety of options—like choosing cereal among the endless options in the cereal aisle.

Choosing cereal isn't nearly as painful or as complex as what mothers often face. As one mother described, "I thought I had it all figured out until I was forced to choose between full-time work (as opposed to previously part-time work) or be with my kids in the afternoons of middle and high school. This was a time when I was needed to a) make sure they didn't have an unsupervised house for sex or drugs; b) provide transportation to extracurricular events (sports and academic). I gave up work—painful *decision*" (emphasis added). Her *choice* would have been part-time work that let her take care of her kids. Without that option, she made a *decision* between the remaining two options based on what she believed was best for her children and family.

Switching our own words and thoughts to *decision* gives us more responsibility and more opportunities. Choices made in a vacuum don't require us to understand anything but our own wishes. Making difficult decisions about employment and family within a larger historical and social context means that if mothers learn that landscape well enough, we can make even better, more informed decisions.

ONE LAST INSIGHT:
His Job May Be the Biggest Problem

Now, let's go back to that October evening in Minnesota when I spoke with that roomful of mothers. After the women had shared their ideal employment now and five years down the road, I said to them, "Let me ask you another question." I paused for effect. "If you're married, when I asked you to think about how your own ideal employment would change over five years, how many of you assumed your spouse's employment would *stay exactly the same?*"

They looked around to see if anyone else was raising their hands. Then slowly, nearly every hand in the room went up. Several looked at me with open mouths, stunned by the realization that they'd made that assumption without batting an eye.

I smiled. "I did that too," I said. Most of us assume that *we* have to be the ones making room in our employment to care for family, that our employment will shift but his won't. Without realizing it, even our *ideal* is limited by our own subconscious beliefs about mothers, fathers, and employment. Our vision of what could be is clouded by our own assumptions about what mothers should be willing to do to take care of family, about what fathers wouldn't be willing to do, and about what workplaces shouldn't have to do. Mothers can navigate a lot of these barriers once we can see them and ask, "What if it were different?" I promise I'll tell you how I did. But here's the thing, I didn't do it on my own. Turns out, the biggest barrier to having the job *I* wanted was the job *David* had. We had to work together.

SQUARE PEGS:
A FAIRY TALE IN THREE ACTS
ACT TWO

∽

When the couple's happy ending went up in smoke, it was very hard to see through all that haze. The two got separated, and the young woman got very lost and very frustrated. She wandered the forest with the baby, struggling to find her way. She was very angry with her husband for not helping her. She became quite convinced that he was the one who had messed up the happy ending and was merrily traveling the forest without her.

But as she started to get her bearings alone in the forest, she caught glimpses of her husband far away in the smoky haze. As her sight became clearer, she realized to her surprise . . . he was lost too.

7

he's a square peg

or why doesn't his job

fit anymore?

WHEN DAVID AND I found out I was pregnant, he ran into his boss in the hallway a few days later and shared the news. The first words out of his boss's mouth were "Oh @#&!" Then, Kate surprised us by arriving three weeks early, which meant David would have to go back to work five days after her birth or lose his annual bonus. Within months of her arrival, David's boss wanted to send him to Korea for several weeks. I freaked out. So he told his boss, "Um, it would be hard for me to go with the new baby and everything." His boss was shocked. "Isn't your wife at home? I know if it were me, my wife would just grin and bear it." So David went to Korea. I did bear it, but I did not grin.

In those early weeks and months of her life, baby Kate and I spent many of our days quite peacefully and enjoyably. Until about 4:30 P.M. By then Kate and I were both tired and cranky. The house felt claustrophobic, and I was desperate for adult conversation. So every evening, Kate and I would sit on our front lawn in the grass together. I chose the front lawn for two reasons. One, I might catch a neighbor passing by for my only adult conversation of the day. Two, the moment David arrived home, Kate and I could pounce on him for some relief from each other. I kept the phone in the grass by my side. Starting around 5:00 I'd call David every half hour to find out when he'd be home. Inevitably, he'd be scrambling to wrap things up, and interrupting him every half hour didn't help his mood. Often, he'd say that he wasn't going to make it home before 8:00 or 9:00 or even later. "Fine!" I'd say, "Then I really don't care if you come home at all." Tears in my eyes, I'd hang up the phone. After all, by 9:00 Kate would be in bed and I would have collapsed in bed myself.

When Kate was eight months old, after endless weeks of David being at work all hours on all days, I hit the wall. I heard myself shouting the unthinkable at David. "If you can't figure out a way to fix this mess and spend more time with us and less time at work, I'm leaving with Kate for my parents' house in Minnesota, and I'm not coming back until you do!"

What had happened to the fairy tale happy ending we'd planned? The one where together we were employed seventy hours a week? Instead, he was employed seventy and I was employed zero, and we were falling apart. I thought to myself, if he would only manage his time better, he'd get home. If he drew some boundaries with his boss, he'd have a more reasonable workload. If he really understood how much I needed him, how defeated and drained I felt at the end of the day, he'd figure out a way to leave work and be home to share the load. This was *not* the plan for our family life that I had had in mind. I was *not* happy about it, and I blamed David.

Coincidentally, a month after I exploded at him, all three of us went to Minnesota on a planned family vacation. One day David took baby Kate across the street to the park all by himself. He pushed her in the swing. It was such a pure moment. Kate was laughing and happy. There was no one else around, just David and Kate in the whole green field in the sun. David choked up with emotion. He was so happy that he felt tears welling in his eyes. Since Kate had been born, nine months earlier, it was the first time he'd been with her by himself like this when it wasn't 2:00 in the morning.

At the time it happened, David didn't share his park experience with me. We weren't sharing much of anything with each other. He knew I blamed him for working all the time so he had stopped expecting me to support him. At the time, I couldn't even see how much our whole situation was making him miserable too. He had to make money and keep his job because that was the only paycheck now that I'd been refused one part-time job and laid off from another. He made plenty of money, but in return his boss and clients had priority claims on his time and energy. He wanted to do his job well, but his boss and colleagues assumed he could work and travel on demand because I would take care of everything else. I had made it clear to him that he could have either our marriage or his job, but not both. It was clear to him that if he devoted the time to his job that it required, then he would have little time left for his relationship with Kate. He couldn't win. Once I began to understand why I didn't fit any jobs anymore, I started to see that *David* didn't fit his job very well anymore either. For me, being a square peg in a round hole meant losing my career, my identity, and my earnings. For him, being a square peg in a round hole meant losing time with his child and quite possibly, losing his marriage.

I'm not sure I ever would have been able to see our situation from David's perspective without understanding my own situation first. From the balcony view, I'd learned how the mental maps about mothers, fathers, and employment complicated my own life. Now I had to consider the possibility that maybe David faced some invisible hurdles too. I had to consider the possibility that, even if it was convenient, maybe blaming David wasn't fair and wouldn't get us out of this mess. I had to ask and honestly answer the question, "Why did David seem to be a square peg trying to fit into a round hole too?"

INSIGHT:
Fathers Work Like Everyone Else,
But They Don't Always Want To

Except for five days off when Kate was born, David's work life didn't change much after her birth. He still worked the seventy hours a week his one-size-fits-all job required, but it was not what he wanted. While I'd learned that most mothers don't have their ideal employment situation, I discovered that fathers don't either. As Robert shared, "I am not as involved as I would like to be [at home]. This is completely a limitation of being the breadwinner and having a job that requires much more than forty hours/week." Robert has a lot of company. Yvonne told me her husband feels torn between being labeled a slacker for leaving at 5:00 P.M. to spend time with the family versus staying late and "abandoning the family to get more work done."

Many fathers would like to work fewer hours than they are and would like to be able to work some hours at home, yet only one in twenty works a schedule less than thirty-five hours a week.[1] Even more fathers simply want more flexibility and control over the hours they do work.[2] Both mothers and fathers feel a big gap between the jobs they have and the jobs they want.[3]

INSIGHT:
Fathers Get Steered into the Breadwinner
Role, Whether They Want It or Not

Before Kate came along, David and I thought of our careers as equally important and didn't expect to treat them otherwise when we had children. To our surprise, Kate's arrival forced us to decide his job was more important. And once we did that, we headed down a decision path that led us further and further away from the life we wanted. What forced us? One-size-fits-all jobs and subconscious assumptions about mothers and fathers.

Once Kate was part of our life, me working fifty hours a week and David working seventy wouldn't leave any room for the family life we wanted or the parent time we felt Kate needed. Not to mention the cost for the amount of childcare and help at home we'd need to make it feasible. So that was out. The option we wanted, each of us working thirty to forty hours, now seemed impossible, given my failed attempts to find and keep a job that was less than fifty hours a week and the fact that David's job was clearly fixed at seventy hours. So that was out, too. Having eliminated the two options that would have allowed us to continue placing equal value on both our jobs, we had to shift gears. If the only jobs immediately available to us were the one-size-fits-all variety, then at least one of us would have to have one of those jobs for the money and for the benefits. So which one of us?

Well, even though my job helped put David through law school, by the time we had Kate, his job was paying him twice as much as I could make. If we had to pick one primary job, then financially the logical decision in the short term was that his would be that job. If David had been able to keep his job at forty hours with a proportional salary, if I'd been able to keep one at thirty, the financial calculation would have been different, but we couldn't. As my friend Larry said about his own family's similar decision, "At that point it's a small business decision as much as an emotional one. What's more efficient? What makes the most sense economically? Our roles were driven by who was best suited to take on the role at that point in time." The problem is that despite the rising incomes of women, in the majority of families husbands still make more than their wives do.[4] So at this decision point, needing to hang on to one of the one-size-fits-all jobs, couples are still more likely to decide his job is more important.

Those economic calculations couples make are also influenced by employers, who are influenced by assumptions they have about mothers and fathers. Study after study shows that married fathers make more money when they have a wife who isn't employed.[5] Lisa said that when her sister quit her job after her baby arrived, "Her husband's company immediately gave him a raise, saying her being a stay-at-home mom made him 'more valuable' to the company because he would not be having to help do things like trade off staying home with a sick kid or pick up the baby at day care and he could travel whenever they wanted him to." Lisa was stunned. "I wonder what happens there to a woman who gets pregnant? . . . And I shudder to think what that firm might do if she were a single mom. Or what about a male whose wife does not quit her job and he wants to be involved in his kids' lives?" The fact that employers, often as a result of subconscious assumptions, pay married fathers more money and mothers less money steers the family calculations in the direction of deciding that his job is more important.

To be fair, this dynamic works in the reverse, too. If the mother earns more, and the couple feels forced to prioritize one job, hers may get priority. This scenario is rarer, but increasingly common, and may still end up leading the family away from the way they wanted to share employment. However, money isn't the only factor in these decisions. Amy was earning twice as much as her husband when they had their daughter, but she was still the one that cut back her employment. She explained that one reason was the social accept-ability of a mother cutting back. "There aren't many playgroups for stay at home dads," she said. "And the stigma attached to a man asking for part time, or taking time off and trying to come back to a career later, seemed so much greater." Once the one-size-fits-all job structure forces couples to prioritize one career, both money and cul-tural expectations steer them toward making the father the primary breadwinner.

What we often don't anticipate is the vicious cycle that begins with the initial decision for his job to be the primary one even if the intention is for the situation to be temporary. Kaarsten explained that once she shifted her employment down, her husband's career and salary took off. "Now he nearly brings in what we used to make combined. . . . If I were to go to work again we would sacrifice his ability to continue earning at that level or to continue to expand his career." Over time, the gap between what he can earn and what she can earn widens.[6] As Amy says, "The reality is that men earn more than women. Women believe their work is worth less in the short-run, thus there is greater pressure for us to 'opt out.' A self-fulfilling prophecy, because then we *really* make less than men!"

Only about two in twenty couples want to have the father as the sole earner, but five in twenty couples—like David and I—say they felt forced into that arrangement by the absence of other options.[7] Jennifer explains why it happened to her family. "Finding one permanent part-time job in my field is almost impossible, and finding two (so my engineer husband could also work part-time) is less likely than both of us being struck by lightning. So we are forced into the traditional husband works full-time and more and I'm a [stay-at-home mom], and people can say this is our 'choice.' " In this context, many families make entirely rational decisions to take on more traditional family roles than they would like to ideally and fathers tend to take on the main breadwinner role even when that's not what the father or the family wanted.

INSIGHT:
Workplaces Aren't So Flexible for Fathers Either

David took just five days off work when Kate was born. Then, his boss was shocked when David said he didn't want to go to Korea just weeks later; in the end David went anyway. Fathers often face even stronger cultural pressure than mothers not to use workplace policies like parental leave that make room for family. I've had fathers tell me that while other men knock off early to go golfing, they will get dinged on their evaluation if they leave early to pick up the kids too often. Employers subconsciously believe fathers are or should be more focused on their jobs, and that they have someone else, usually the mother, to take care of family. For example, if a mother leaves a work meeting early for family reasons, people are likely to think, "Typical. Mothers can't be counted on. They always put their families first." If the father leaves a meeting for family reasons too often, they are likely to think, "Slacker. Can't he get someone else to do that?"

Sensing that they will be perceived as less committed if they try for some flexibility, fathers are less likely to leave work early for childcare logistics and less likely to turn down assignments for personal reasons.[8] Fathers are told, directly or indirectly, that things like taking leave for a new baby are really just for mothers. Fathers are much less likely than mothers to take family or paternity leave,[9] which is too bad because fathers who do take paternity leave are more involved with their children down the road.[10] Unfortunately, if fathers do take leave, they often stick out like a sore thumb among the men at work. One mother said of her husband, "He rearranged his schedule to be home two days a week after taking a month off (unpaid) to help me take care of our premature twins. He was one of the very few at his plant to do so."

Just like mothers, fathers often find that wanting or needing flexible work limits their employment options. Kristie told me that rather than having "golden handcuffs," a job that pays so much you can't bring yourself to leave, her husband had "rubber handcuffs." He was stuck in his current position and couldn't get promoted because he wouldn't give up the flexibility to have time with his family. He, like so many mothers, was chained to a job that gave him flexibility but made him give up money and career advancement. Yet workplaces and the media talk about conflicts between family and employment as if mothers were the only ones who face them. For example, one of the most prestigious family-friendly workplace awards is a spot on the list of *Working Mother* magazine's The Working Mother 100 Best Companies. However, the conflicts fathers face stay largely under the radar and out of the headlines.

Family responsibilities discrimination happens to fathers, too. It just looks different. FRD often occurs when fathers try to use options for caring for family that are readily available to mothers. One state trooper requested the family leave he was legally entitled to and was told he could not take it "unless your wife is in a coma or dead."[11] A probation officer was told he couldn't use sick leave to care for his newborn even though mothers were allowed to do so.[12] A firefighter, who is a single parent with custody of his three children, was passed over for a promotion. His boss told him "he didn't want to hear this garbage" about having to pick up his kids after school and wrote a memo directing him to "make arrangements for other persons to take your children different places."[13] As with mothers, when fathers face FRD, it's not always illegal under current laws, but it isn't fair. Workplaces aren't nearly as flexible as many mothers would like, but fathers often have even greater difficulty using what little flexibility is available.

INSIGHT:
Today's Fathers Are Where Mothers Were Twenty-Five Years Ago

The more I used the balcony view to see what David and fathers in general were dealing with, the more I kicked myself for blaming David for all our troubles. Fathers are just as out of sync with workplaces as mothers are. Even though men had the workplace pretty much all to themselves for many decades and designed it to fit men and fathers, something major has changed: fathers' and mothers' expectations of fathers. Like David, many fathers today expect and even want to change diapers, or at least are married to women, like me, who not only expect them to change diapers but also to do dishes and help with homework too. While many of the dilemmas mothers face combining employment and family haven't changed much in the past twenty-five years, the experience of fathers and the way they think about their role has changed dramatically.

For the past twenty-five years, two-thirds of women have consistently reported that they reject the idea that it is much better for everyone involved if the man earns money and the woman takes care of the home and children. Over that same time, the number of men who reject traditional gender roles has doubled, going from one third up to match women at two thirds.[14] Young men today place a much higher priority on spending time with their families than generations before them, and 70 percent say they are willing to sacrifice pay to get it.[15] "Most Gen X men think fathers can parent as well as mothers and should be equally involved in kids' lives," says Sandra

Hofferth, a University of Maryland sociologist and demographer who studies family life.[16] Those Gen X fathers, born between 1965 and 1980, have changed how they act too. Fathers today spend much more daily time with their children than their Boomer fathers did and do more housework.[17] Fathers' involvement extends outside the home too. The National Parent Teacher Association, founded in 1897 as the National Congress of Mothers, elected its first male national president in 2007.[18] Our school's PTA has had a father as a president for three years in a row, and in our house, David's the one that holds a PTA position, not me. All indications are that men in Generation Y, born between 1980 and 1994 and now entering fatherhood, will spend even more time with their children.[19]

Workplaces operate assuming today's fathers will behave and fit into employment the way their Boomer fathers did, but fathers today are different. So they are more frustrated. Being torn between our jobs and our families is old hat for mothers, we've been feeling this way for over twenty-five years. The number of fathers who feel a conflict between employment and family has nearly doubled since 1977.[20] Brian Reid, who owns the blog RebelDad, has called this phenomenon the "daddy wars": "the increasing conflict between employers and fathers who want more flexible arrangements."[21]

In an interview, Michael Kimmel, author of *Manhood in America*, described firsthand the evolution among men and women that he's seen over the last couple of decades.

Twenty years ago when I started teaching about these issues, I would ask my students what are you going to do to balance work and family if you get married and if you have children. . . . Women would say, we're going to love each other. It's going to work out. The men would say, huh? Like the question didn't even register for them.

Now I ask my students, what are you going to do to balance work and family? The women say, well first, I'm going to have my first kid but I'm only going to take 4 months off because I want to get right back to work because I really want to keep my career going. But with my second kid, that's when I'm going to take 5 years off. Because I really want to be there for both kids when they are developing. Then I'm going to go back to my work because I will have made it possible for my career trajectory to come right back. The women have it all planned out. The men they say, we're going to love each other, it's going to work out. What I get from this is two things. The men are where the women were 20 years ago, but the question now makes sense to them."[22]

When it comes to combining family and employment, fathers now feel just as much like square pegs in round holes as mothers have for over twenty-five years.

INSIGHT:
Fathers Get Identity Whiplash Too

One evening, David took toddler Kate to a summer work event at a bowling alley. For the two of them, it was a rare outing alone together, and David was looking forward to father-daughter time. Yet, within minutes of arriving, a couple of his female colleagues swooped in. One popped Kate onto her hip, and they waved him off as if he were relieved of duty. "It was just weird," David said. They acted as if he wouldn't want to be troubled to take care of his own daughter. While I crash into assumptions that employed mothers are selfish and mothers who aren't employed are dull, David collides with assumptions that fathers are clueless and uninterested when it comes to family. Fathers get Identity Whiplash too.

Remember those mental maps?

- Mothers are responsible for and are naturally better at children and family.
- Fathers are responsible for and are naturally better at employment and earning money.

These maps create different cultural expectations for mothers and fathers. Mothers feel more pressure to be the ideal mother. Fathers feel more pressure to be the ideal worker. Fathers get Identity Whiplash when they step outside that stereotype to be involved with family.

Grandparents and extended family are a common source of Identity Whiplash for fathers. One mother and her husband visited her aunt and uncle after their first child was born. She said, "It was time for a diaper change so my husband did it. My uncle was in shock and declared that 'women's work.'" One day my friend Sonia was sitting with her mother-in-law as her husband vacuumed their house. Her mother-in-law turned to her and asked, "Why is my son vacuuming?" Sonia's answer, "Because the carpet is dirty." Her mother-in-law then turned to her son and insisted that she would do the vacuuming. Smart man that he is, Sonia's husband kept vacuuming. Yet he was stuck between his wife's expectation that he do his share around the house, and his mother's reaction that he was doing women's work.

On the other hand, fathers may also get a hero's praise when they are involved with family. One Saturday morning, my friend Chris took his two girls and his infant son to a coffee shop after the girls' ballet class. As he sat enjoying his coffee, juggling the baby, and corralling the two twirling tutus, he noticed people were watching him and whispering. Eventually, one woman came over and said something like, "Wow, that's amazing how you handle all three of them!" Chris later said to me, "It was as if I didn't have arms and was taking care of three kids. My wife has all three kids all the time and no one's ever said anything like that to her." My friend Tod says that when he's out alone with his two girls, other women seem to be eager to offer assistance. "If I am having trouble folding up a stroller, find myself short some Kleenex at the park, or one of the girls drops something in a store, it is not uncommon for a woman to step forward to give a friendly helping hand. This happens much more frequently than when my wife and I are out together with the girls." Tod is well aware of the double standard at work. "The overall gist of the interaction seems to be 'A dad out with his kids—great! Let's give him some help.' The two subtle messages are 1) that I need the help and

2) that what I am doing is extraordinary enough to justify offering the help. Not that I don't appreciate a little help, but I shouldn't be treated like a hero for doing what my wife does everyday. The bar is set so low for dads that if you don't melt off to the living room to drink a beer and watch the game, you get a lot more credit than you should."

Unfortunately, mothers often send these same mixed messages to fathers. I was chatting with a colleague over the phone one day, and she told me that in a couple of months, she was taking a full-time job and she and her husband would trade roles. He'd be the primary caregiver. She was a bit nervous about the transition. Laughing, she said that if she comes home at the end of the day and the kids are in one piece, and everyone's happy and fed, then she won't worry if the house is a disaster. Without noticing, she'd set the bar low for him before they'd even started. Another mother told me about a colleague of hers who goes through elaborate preparations anytime she has to go on a business trip. She writes out detailed directions for her husband, stocks the refrigerator, freezes meals, and arranges play dates. Mothers, myself included, are often guilty of sending our own husbands the message that we don't really believe they can learn to care for family as well as we do.

For fathers there's a fine line between being a hero and being a wimp. While a little family involvement is heroic, a lot is lame. Identity Whiplash of this type is easiest to see when mothers and fathers reverse traditional roles. While they are still a small percentage, a rapidly increasing number of fathers are leaving employment to care for family.[23] A mother who makes the decision to leave her job for family often gets praise from many people. Not a father. One father who was caring for his children said other men think he's lazy and women think he's gay or that he couldn't possibly care for children as well as a mother. With his wife working crazy hours, he finds himself in a complete role reversal—home with the kids all the time, feeling sad and alone. So while he's facing the same challenges a mother may have with a switch from employed person to person whose primary role is caring for family, he gets none of the praise a mother might get for being an ideal mother. Instead, his manhood is questioned for not being an ideal worker and for spending his time doing women's work.

Like many mothers, fathers who are not employed also crash into that mental map that *caring for family isn't work, it's just what mothers do*. Paul told me that when he tells other men he is not employed and cares for his family, the men a generation older tend to say, "You mean you don't *work* at all?" Fathers his own age dreamily talk about how great that would be and seem to be "as enamored with the idea of 'not having to work anymore' as they are of spending time with their children." Especially for fathers, employment is considered the only real work, caring for family is considered one long, lazy break.

More and more, fathers want to be involved with family. More and more, their wives are expecting them to be. Just as mothers have different amounts of maternal desire and ambition, each father has his own unique blend of paternal desire and ambition. When fathers act on their desire to care for their families, people around them react in conflicting and unexpected ways, and fathers get Identity Whiplash just like mothers.

MY CONCLUSION:
Mothers and Fathers Have More
in Common Than We Think

The mental maps and vicious cycles around mothers, fathers, and employment had messed up my career, but I had a bond with Kate I cherished. It was time for me to face the fact that those same mental maps and vicious cycles made David feel stuck and lost and frustrated too. David still had the job and the money, but he knew our marriage was hanging by a thread, and he wasn't able to have the relationship he wanted with his child. We had a lot more in common than I had ever let myself realize.

Maybe we'd better tackle this remodeling job together.

SQUARE PEGS:
A FAIRY TALE IN THREE ACTS
ACT THREE

⚮

The more the young woman got her bearings and the more she caught sight of her husband's struggles on the far side of the forest, the easier it was for her to see a path through the forest. The smoke seemed to lift more each day, until one day they found each other again.

Overcome with emotion to be reunited, they embraced as a family. They could see the castle in the distance. They agreed they still wanted the same happy ending. Jobs that allowed everyone to be home for family dinner every night in the castle. Jobs that meant both of them could read to and play with and care for their child. Jobs that let them both pursue their careers and interests and still have time for each other.

So they said to each other, "We can't get there the way we thought we could. There are a lot more obstacles than we thought, but whether or not we ever get to our happy ending . . . we'll find our way together."

8

square pegs together

or how do we make

our jobs fit together?

❧

WHEN I STOPPED blaming David and started empathizing with him instead, we started to have different conversations. Maybe the conversations were better because I wasn't pointing fingers and yelling, and he wasn't either. Instead of pointing fingers at him, I pointed out how unfair it felt for David's firm to expect the same crazy hours from everyone, regardless of their personal situation. Sounds just like what pushed me out of my jobs, I would say.

We talked about that fairy tale vision we'd had. The seventy- to seventy-five-hours-a-week goal, everyone home for dinner, time for Kate, and time for our careers and for each other. It was still what we wanted, but clearly seventy for David and zero for me wasn't going to get us there. We teased it out together over many conversations late into the night because that was pretty much the only time we had together. We concluded that the demands of his job were the first domino standing in the way of just about everything else we wanted.

I couldn't go up from zero hours unless he could come down from seventy hours. We literally couldn't figure out a way for me to be employed and still hold our lives together unless he worked less. Figuring out an employment option for me was inextricably connected to figuring out a different employment option for him. If he was going to have time with Kate, if I was going to have time to be employed, if we were going to have more time together for our marriage, if we were going to get any closer to our vision, he'd have to leave his job.

Even though we were still at least two years away from any actual changes, agreeing that our vision was still a vision we both believed in was a major turning point for us. We felt like we were on the same team again. Agreeing that his job was the first domino that needed to fall got us focused on working together to get where we wanted to go. But how? We had changed our conversation by stopping the blame game. We were helping each other see how the mental maps and vicious cycles around us were making us both crazy and frustrated. But with all these obstacles, where do we start?

WHAT IF WE HELD DIFFERENT BELIEFS ABOUT EMPLOYMENT AND MOTHERS AND FATHERS?

The beliefs that had been invisibly shaping our path so far were not going to help us get to the vision David and I had for our lives. We needed to get rid of the mental maps that weren't working:

- Family and employment are separate.
- Jobs are one-size-fits-all, fifty hours a week, fifty weeks a year, for fifty years of our lives.

And then we needed to replace them with ones that matched our vision.

- A variety of job structures to fit various stages of personal lives is best for people and organizations and communities.

- Family and employment can be integrated and complementary.[1]
- Mothers and fathers share the responsibility and are equally capable of employment and contributing to the family's financial security.

Now, many people find it hard to imagine a world built on these new beliefs. However, I'd been reading and talking to enough people to know that it was possible. The evidence that supporting families is good for business and good for employees has been piling up for years. Employees who feel their employer supports their family needs "are less stressed, feel more successful in meshing work and family life, are more loyal to the company, are more committed to their employers, are more satisfied with their jobs, and are more likely to want to remain with their employers."[2] When employers don't support family needs, they lose people both in spirit and body. As one mother reported in a survey, "I requested to return part-time after my maternity leave. This was initially agreed to but the offer was withdrawn when there was a change of CEO. . . . I decided not to return at all." In fact, in that same Mothers & More survey, eight of ten mothers who requested an alternative job structure and were turned down either left that job right away or stayed just long enough to find another job.[3] Losing employees, especially experienced employees, is very costly for employers,[4] yet the old mental maps are so deep that many managers and companies can't even see the evidence. As Margaret Heffernan, former CEO and author of *The Naked Truth: A Modern Woman's Manifesto on Business and What Really Matters*, confirmed in an online discussion, "This ancient division between work and life, in which there is no apparent flow of value from one to the other, is one of the most outmoded aspects of business today. Instead of updating their computer hardware, these companies would be better off updating their thinking."

There's also evidence that when employees have jobs that fit their family lives, the communities in which they live and work are better off. One mother explained, "Having worked part time for eight years . . . I have filled up my at-home time with a lot of volunteering: Girl Scouts, Sunday School, help in the classroom."[5] Part-time employees are more likely to volunteer and be active in the community than full-time employees. That might not be so surprising, but part-time employees are also more involved citizens than people who are not employed at all! As Robert Putnam speculates in his book *Bowling Alone*, people who are employed part-time have both a connection to the community through their employer and the time necessary to be involved outside their jobs.[6]

So if the benefits are clear in the research, then why haven't our workplaces remodeled themselves? Because the power of the assumptions built into the workplace culture, the policies, and our own subconscious are hard to break with facts and figures. If we assume workplaces and jobs built on these new beliefs are impossible and we've never seen anything like it in real life, facts and stats and reports won't convince us it is possible. Imagination and stories of people who've been there just might though. If mothers and fathers are to remodel their employment together, they need to be convinced that building on these new beliefs is feasible and have a picture of what it looks like.

WHAT WOULD INTEGRATING FAMILY AND EMPLOYMENT LOOK LIKE?

So let's drop the facts and figures for a moment and imagine some stories, shall we? First I'll think back to my first management job and my single mother employee and filter that scenario through our new and improved beliefs. What if I'd been able to offer her an 8:00 A.M. to 3:00 P.M. schedule with proportional pay and benefits? What if she'd been able to take it because it was a standard option used by men and women, with children or without, so there was no stigma attached to it? She wouldn't have spent her afternoons worrying about what her kids were doing home alone without her. The company would have gained her loyalty and her ability to focus when she was at work. As a manager, I would have had a way to match the job to the person, so that no one else in the department felt resentful that someone wasn't putting in the same hours but was getting the same pay.

Okay, now fast-forward to when I became pregnant myself. What if my boss hadn't had any artificial budget and payroll constraints and could have kept me half-time on one coast and hired someone else half-time on the other coast? I might have stayed with a company where I'd spent years building relationships and experience that made me more effective. My manager would have saved money on travel, gained the skill sets of two people for the price of one, and would have saved the cost of replacing me. I might have worked half-time locally for a while and then shifted back to full-time with travel when it made sense for me and my family. That might have given me the opportunity later on to pursue promotions to the types of management positions I wanted.

What if, when Kate was born, David had been able to shift to a thirty-five-hour-a-week schedule with no travel for a year or two or three? He might have stayed at a law firm that had invested enormous amounts of time and money training him out of law school. He might not have had to come home to a wife who, as he said, had gone insane from handling everything else herself.

Sound crazy? Pie in the sky? Well, would Deloitte, one of the largest professional services companies with more than 40,000 employees and billions in revenue, try to make this fairy tale a reality if it were really that crazy?

I was at a conference in California when I heard Cathleen Benko, Deloitte LLP's Chief Talent Officer, speak in a way I'd never heard corporate America speak before. I was shocked that instead of trying to celebrate and justify corporate efforts to make work flexible, she said flat out that flexible work arrangements are not the solution; they are band-aids and one-offs.[7] Why? For many of the same reasons I've covered in our stories—such as budget and benefits systems that are built for full-time employment only; perceptions that using flexible work programs is career suicide; and the reality that even if there is an official flexible work policy, using it is often managed and viewed as a one-time exception. Benko and her colleague Anne Weisberg wrote a book about how Deloitte and other companies are experimenting with a different approach. Both the book and the framework they've developed are called *Mass Career Customization*.

The simple idea behind Mass Career Customization (MCC) is that everyone, including the company, benefits when all employees can work with managers to customize their employment over time. As Benko and Weisberg explain, "Mass Career Customization moves organizations away from the one-size-fits-all view of career progression toward supporting multiple career paths, each designed and executed through continual collaboration between employee and employer."[8] The MCC framework makes the idea practical by providing "four dimensions of careers: Pace, Workload, Location/Schedule, and Role."[9] Each of the four dimensions can be adjusted like "the sound equalizer on a home entertainment system, where you move the sliders up or down the vertical slots."[10] The options within MCC are not infinite. The company decides, for example, how many different Workload options there are: perhaps three options, twenty, thirty, or full-time hours each week. The company defines boundaries for each dimension appropriate to that business.

MASS CAREER CUSTOMIZATION™

PACE	WORKLOAD	LOCATION/SCHEDULE	ROLE
Accelerated	Full	Not Restricted	Leader
Decelerated	Reduced	Restricted	Individual Contributor

Deloitte.

So if MCC had been in place before I got pregnant, I already would have designed an MCC profile with my manager. Once pregnant, my conversation about adjusting that profile would have been teed up in an existing framework that was part of the culture. I would have asked my boss if I could slow down my Pace of promotion, decrease my Workload to twenty hours a week, restrict my Location to California, and decrease my supervisory responsibilities to take on a Role in which I contributed as an individual instead. Over time, he and I would have continued to adjust the profile to match both my needs and the company's needs.

By creating a framework that applies to everyone, sets limits on the options available, and makes everyone's profile transparent, "MCC transforms the idea of fairness from a static assumption—that each employee should . . . conform to the traditional full-time standard— to a more dynamic notion of fairness relative to each employee's profile."[11] Instead of alternative work options awarded as exceptions to mothers or to high performers, all employees have options within boundaries that are determined by the business.

Benko and Weisberg also emphasize that language is important and give us some ready answers to the question, What would we say if we held these beliefs? They avoid the word *flexibility* to make sure people understand that career customization is very different than existing flexible work arrangements. In addition to customization, they prefer to talk about options or adaptability, such as, "Our company provides job options to all employees." Similarly, I try to avoid the phrases *part-time* and *reduced schedule* because I think they reinforce the idea that anything other than a fifty-fifty-fifty job is somehow less than. When asked, I don't say I'm employed part-time, I just say I'm employed. When talking about my ideal job or the types of jobs mothers want, I refer to them as customized jobs or job alternatives or jobs that fit our lives. Changing our language starts the process of breaking down mental maps—our own and those others may have.

Mass Career Customization is only one example of the ways in which organizations are going beyond the old mental maps and beyond the standard work-family programs in ways that embrace whole new beliefs about employment and family and life. Benko and

Weisberg point to the implementation of similar principles at places like SAS, the largest private software company; Arnold & Porter, a corporate law firm; and Ogilvy & Mather, a global marketing communications company. I have stacks of books and articles on my shelf going back ten to fifteen years describing research and real organizations implementing new work cultures. Many business executives speak to the need for a new approach. Lawrence Perlman, president, chairman, and CEO of Ceridian Corporation, said, "It is time for companies to acknowledge the primacy of family in the value systems of both men and women. Too many women still have to choose between career and family. And too often men sacrifice participation in the lives of their families to meet the demands of their jobs. The cost to both people and the companies they work for is too high."[12]

Mothers share real-life examples, like one who said, "I have a job-share as a Medical Writer for a pharmaceutical company. Each of us works three full days/week. We each receive three-fifths of the full-time salary plus 401K, full medical benefits, and pro-rated vacation and personal time." And the examples I hear about aren't just in big companies, they are in small web development companies and small-town law firms and in the federal government. That's not to say that these, or any other companies, have this challenge all solved, or that everyone who works in companies like these has a customized job. What these organizations show us is that a new view of career-life fit is possible, and they open up our minds by challenging our assumptions about employment.

The Mass Career Customization framework can also help individual couples think about how to customize their ideal jobs and career paths to fit together. Benko and Weisberg encourage people to create their own MCC profiles of past jobs and future possibilities, which when they are connected together represent what they call "career sine waves." They provide an online MCC profile tool (www.masscareercustomization.com), which I wish had been around when David and I were wrestling with how to do this. Identifying our ideal jobs was one of the first steps David and I took in making our jobs fit together.

HOW DAVID AND I MADE OUR JOBS FIT TOGETHER

Once David and I agreed that his job was the biggest barrier to getting the shared employment we both wanted, we wisely concluded he shouldn't quit the very next day. So we embarked on a two-year plan. We needed to identify our ideal jobs and how they would fit together. We both looked carefully and felt that in our respective professions, the chances were slim that we could find standard jobs that would let us have the partnership we wanted in which both of us worked thirty to thirty-five hours a week. I knew I wanted control over when I worked, didn't want to travel too often for a few years, wanted to work about thirty hours a week, and was willing to accept a slow down in advancement and a role without supervisory responsibilities. David wanted control over his schedule and a workweek closer to forty hours, but he also felt he would be more fulfilled running his own business than he was as a lawyer for other businesses. So we both decided to become self-employed. We knew this path had big financial risks and meant giving up seniority at any organization and access to stable benefits. We needed to plan carefully.

> **Lesson Learned:** Know your ideal jobs and what it will take for the two jobs to fit together.

David started seeing a career coach and investigating options for starting a business. At one point, he got a job offer at another law firm that promised better hours. So he announced to his boss that he was leaving. "No, don't go!" came the reply. "What do you need? We didn't know you were unhappy." "Fine," David said. He told them he wanted to work 90 percent, meaning he wanted to move from sixty to seventy hour workweeks to fifty-five to sixty-two hour workweeks. As if to confirm our conclusion about how deeply his workplace assumed a real job is 24/7, he got the 90 percent alternative schedule but was sidelined faster than a quarterback with a dislocated shoulder. He was still working more than fifty hours a week yet the shift he felt in how he was perceived was palpable. Fortunately, even that small change gave both of us enough breathing room to continue exploring other options and demonstrated to me that he was really committed to making changes.

Lesson Learned: Small steps in a shared direction can make everyone feel better.

Every year, around New Year's Eve, David and I go out to dinner to review the past year and make resolutions for the coming year. At this point in our path, a major resolution was for each of us to develop the plan we needed to turn our ideal jobs into reality. So shortly after we made that resolution, we asked Grandma and Grandpa to take care of Kate for the day. At home, I sat at my computer in the back of the house. David fired up his laptop in the living room. All morning, we each worked on business plans for ourselves. We met in the kitchen for lunch to talk about our plans and get feedback. Then we went back to our respective corners of the house and worked all afternoon. At the end of the day we each had a draft of what we were going to do and how we would get from here to there together. We cut back on expenses so we could start putting away some savings for when he left his job. We researched and found health insurance we could purchase on our own. We remodeled our garage into a home office.

As David continued working with the career coach and fleshing out the plan for his business, I did what I could to get ready to start taking consulting projects. We couldn't figure out a way for me to work for pay yet, but I could volunteer. So we continued to invest in some childcare for Kate even though I wasn't earning money yet. She was approaching three years old so we transitioned her to three days a week at a nearby preschool that we loved. Because I was already serving as the president of the board of Mothers & More, the preschool arrangement meant I could continue to do my organizational change work by teleconference and e-mail. I gained valuable experience in a way that fit with my life at the time. I leaned on Grandma and Grandpa for help with Kate in the evenings so I could volunteer locally on a task force to network and get more chances to keep my skills up. Over time, I took an online writing class and accepted a couple of very small projects I could do during nap time or at night. David and I didn't have much more time together yet, but when we did, we talked about how we were working the plan together.

Lesson Learned: Have a regular time to review progress and make plans together.

Lesson Learned: Invest money and time in each other to do the planning, plotting, learning, networking, whatever it might take to make progress toward the vision.

Lesson Learned: If not employed, volunteer strategically in ways that keep up skills and contacts or build new ones.

Lesson Learned: Ask for help from friends and family.

By the next New Year's Eve, when we went out to dinner together, David and I were ready for two big New Year's resolutions. Mine was to "Get back in the game," by starting to take consulting projects. David's resolution was to quit the firm that year and start his own business.

By the end of February, I'd gotten my first major project. Then, on a sunny Friday in May, Kate and I spent the day painting a big banner for David. When he arrived home that night after his last day at the law firm, his new home office was decorated with a hand-painted sign for his new business. Soon after that, I remember coming home from a client meeting in time for dinner. Just as I got out of the car, David pulled into the driveway from picking Kate up from preschool, something he'd rarely done before. I hugged them both and said, "Now this—*this* is how I thought it would be."

Lesson Learned: Celebrate small victories along the way.

AFTER THE HAPPY ENDING

I'm sharing our story to illustrate the lessons but the details are unique to us. Not everyone can or wants to be self-employed. David and I know we may not be able to sustain being self-employed forever, the economic downturn keeps threatening our arrangement. Not everyone wants to split employed hours fifty-fifty. Not everyone has Grandma and Grandpa five minutes away willing to pitch in. However, the underlying lessons we learned can be applied to how couples think about what they want and how to get there together. As one mother explained, "I think all parents must look at themselves as a unit, as a couple, decide what each is willing to change in their lives, and if the situation changes, then the couple needs to renegotiate their situation. Assumptions must go out the window."

This isn't a real fairy tale, so this happy ending wasn't really "The End." Since the time David and I made that big shift when Kate was in preschool, we've had our share of successes and flops and the journey continues. We're constantly adjusting the dimensions of our jobs up or down in concert with each other. Sometimes we get a lucky break, like when David's mother retired shortly after we made our big switch. Her willingness to pitch in makes the whole dance much more doable. Sometimes we miscalculate and get way out of whack. For example, while I was writing this book, I was also doing a lot of consulting, so my average employed hours climbed closer to sixty hours a week. Between us we were working nearly a hundred hours a week, and boy did we feel it. I was exhausted. Stuff I'd been doing at home went undone. David and Kate let me know I wasn't myself, and they wanted me back. Getting so out of whack also confirmed for me that David and I were right. A family workweek of a hundred hours was too much for us. So we adjusted, asking for more help from family and friends and getting creative with our schedules until I could bring my hours back down again.

The experience David and I have had with employment and family has made me stop using the phrase *work-family balance.* It doesn't describe at all what we are trying to do. The word *balance* just reinforces the old mental map that *family and employment are separate* and makes mothers especially feel like it's our fault when we can't achieve or maintain a perfect balance. That phrase makes me think of the deadly playground fixture, the teeter-totter. Work marches up and sits on one end, and the board slams to the ground under the weight. Family lightly skips to the other end. She tries but can't pull down her end so she climbs up to the seat and sits suspended in midair. Hmm, how do we get balance? I know, we hand Family the phone number for a childcare center that stays open until 7:00 P.M., and a laptop so she can do work at home after the kids go to bed, and backup childcare for when the kids are sick. Work lifts a few inches off the ground, and Family comes down a few inches. If we just add enough tricks and tools and supports to Family's load, at some point we'll approach that elusive, perfect, precarious place where Work and Family are separate but in equal amounts—and somehow they'll stay there.[13]

My reality and my ideal are that family and employment are both a part of my life, each ebbing and flowing sometimes within a single day and certainly over the years. So I've tossed out the word *balance* and try to use some of the alternatives I've come across. I like *work-family integration* and *flow* and *harmony* better. Or *work-life effectiveness,* a phrase from the organization Catalyst, or *career-life fit,* a term Benko and Weisberg use with career customization.

David and I decided that integrating family and employment is not my problem but *our* problem to solve together by continually adapting. There is no single fix to making our jobs fit together. Over time, our daughter's needs change, our jobs change, our lives change, so customizing our careers together is a process that requires constant tinkering and collaboration.

THE IMPORTANCE OF ASKING FOR WHAT WE WANT

Customizing our jobs also requires asking for what we want. By the time Kate was in kindergarten, I had significantly remodeled my beliefs about what's fair and what's feasible and that changed what I asked for and how I asked for it in my employment. I was working off and on as a consultant for a client, and they wanted to hire me as a part-time employee. The stability of a permanent position was tempting, as was the opportunity to really be part of their team. They told me part-time employees don't receive health or retirement benefits. The salary they offered was much lower than my consulting fees. This time, I knew not to let good fortune cloud my ability to see what was fair. We negotiated for weeks, and finally agreed that I would remain a consultant. We settled on a monthly retainer that saved them some money in return for some stability for me. My fees would cover a proportional set of my own benefits. I customized the job to my life and at the same time asked for what was fair. I'd learned a thing or two since I was pregnant, and this time I felt both lucky and fairly treated.

Asking can be hard, especially for women. One reason women earn less is that they don't ask and they feel uncomfortable negotiating.[14] Monica went to a bridal shower where most of the young mothers expressed a desire to work part-time but were too terrified to ask. "When I suggested it was important they ask for other women in their companies as well as themselves, they glared at me as if I'd said something crazy and radical." Asking is one of those experimental actions we can take that extends out beyond our own lives. When Seana found a part-time position at a local college, she had two kids under the age of four. She offered to work ten hours in the office and ten hours at home each week. "No one had considered that this person didn't have to work right outside the Dean's office. Because I was confident in my abilities and could show that as a consultant, I was used to working on my own at home, I was able to get through the interview process. It turned out to be a great thing for them, as a few years later they hired another part-time person and he was able to use my cubicle when I was at home. Later, my replacement worked from home too. I certainly opened eyes to show that administrative employees could work from home, just like the faculty and students had been doing for years!"

Often mothers will say they don't ask for prorated health benefits because their husbands have health insurance. So what? Why should your employer save money on the back of your husband's employer? Why should you get less compensation because you happen to be married? Why not ask for your employer to pay you for the extra premium you might be paying for your coverage? Why not ask so that next time maybe someone who doesn't have a husband with health insurance will get prorated health insurance? Each time a mother— or a father—asks clearly for the customized job they want and fair compensation, the ripple effect helps remodel the house for all of us.

Mothers and fathers can help others feel confident about asking for the career-life fit they want. I had a former colleague call me when she returned to work after her first child arrived. Sharing my experience and what I'd learned helped her see that even if she decided to ask for a customized job, she didn't have to settle for less than her fair share of pay and benefits. My friend Felita, when she was still in the hospital with her newborn, had a lactation consultant tell her, "You've had a life and career for twenty years before becoming a mom. Remember that it's okay to ask for what you need and what you want." Later, when her employer asked her to come back to work, she laid out exactly what type of job would work for her, and they gave it to her. Felita said, "With what that woman told me, she empowered me to ask for what I want." We won't always get what we ask for, but we'll never get what we want if we don't ask.

Asking can take many forms. For example, we can ask questions that simply challenge what is feasible. Not all jobs or industries can offer all options under the sun; however, most jobs could offer more alternatives than they do today. So we can ask ourselves and our employers to think about what's possible. Which job requirements are necessary for results, and which are merely "corporate convenient" or simply the way we've always done it?[15] When we challenge what is feasible, we can be ready with the basic evidence that shows business benefits when family and employment are integrated. When we look for a new job or evaluate our current jobs, we can be sure to analyze the work culture not just the policies. We can ask things like: How many mothers with children at home are employed here? How many are in management roles? How many mothers and fathers use the career-life fit policies that are available? How many people in general use the career-life fit options?

Asking for what we want may sometimes mean having to over-compensate to break through the assumptions we know are out there. Most of us would like to believe we'll be successful in getting jobs and getting ahead simply by being good at what we do. However, knowing those subconscious assumptions are out there, we may have to change our approach. For example, we know that people tend to think that:

Mother
+ part-time job
————————————————
dimwit slacker employee who is selfish and neglects her family

So it might not be a good idea to advertise we are looking for a part-time job. Is that deceptive? Only if we are assuming that all jobs must be one-size-fits-all. Why not give the employer the benefit of the doubt and assume instead that both you and the employer are open to anything? As one mother explained, "I am currently looking for a part-time job (three to four days per week) and have found that employers have no interest in speaking with candidates who mention 'part-time.' My approach now is to apply to a full time job and once I receive an offer, I will try to negotiate a more flexible schedule."[16]

In talking with current employers we can try to explicitly address the subconscious assumptions that may be lurking. For example, we might say, "I'm willing to travel" or as I have said explicitly to clients, "I hope you know that just because I'm a consultant and working twenty-five hours a week doesn't mean I'm any less committed to the work." My career coach, Susan W. Miller of California Career Services, recommends saying in interviews that "everything in my home life is totally supportive of my being here and doing the best job possible." Sometimes the best way to address the silent assumptions is to say the opposite out loud.

Asking, challenging, saying things out loud isn't always easy. As Laura says, "I wonder how many employees don't even *ask* for part-time, telecommuting, or new work arrangements for fear of how it will reflect on them. *Or* because they assume 'they'll say no.' How many can push their institutions?" Many mothers and fathers are in situations in which they can't risk challenging their own employer because they'd be the lone ranger, calling even more negative attention to themselves. That was David's problem too. As much as I wanted him to make his entire law firm operate differently, speaking up all by himself would have put his career at risk. Each mother or father has to weigh his or her own situation. However, whatever our situation, we can always connect with other mothers and fathers and colleagues to find out who else is feeling the conflict among work, family, and life. If we feel we can't risk asking for changes with our own employer, we can still work with others on remodeling employment for everyone.

IF WE REMODELED OUR BELIEFS ABOUT EMPLOYMENT, HOW WOULD THE WORLD OPERATE?

What if everyone believed:

- A variety of job structures to fit various stages of personal lives is best for people, families, businesses, and communities.
- Family and employment can be integrated and complementary.[17]
- Mothers and fathers share the responsibility and are equally capable of employment and contributing to the family's financial security.

How would the world operate? The fairy tale ending David and I had come up with wouldn't be far-fetched. Mothers and fathers could make that wish David and I did and believe it could come true.

If the world operated on our new beliefs, then it would be just as important to organize jobs to make it possible for people, families, and communities to have vibrant lives as it is for people, families, and communities to adapt to support vibrant businesses. Customized careers and customized jobs would be just the way things are done. Companies would have budget and payroll systems that support a reasonable variety of job structures defined by the business and the work to be done. Our public policies would do their part by providing a level playing field for all organizations—for example, by requiring a minimum number of paid sick days for all employees. That way, as Tanya says, no mother or father would have "the stress of deciding if her kids are sick enough to stay home and miss work or to take [the kids to school] not feeling well." Leslie wishes that no mother or father would have to "go back to work early due to no paid maternity/paternity leave." Access to health insurance wouldn't necessarily be linked to full-time jobs or employment, making it possible for employers to offer customized jobs and for people to take them without giving up benefits. Laws that govern employee benefits and the Family Medical Leave Act, along with state unemployment and disability insurance programs, would apply to employees with customized jobs, not just jobs that are fifty-fifty-fifty. Employers would all provide proportional pay, benefits, and promotional opportunities to employees based on the person's customized job. Family responsibilities discrimination would be explicitly prohibited. Employers would ask both mothers and fathers what they want rather than assuming mothers don't want to travel or all fathers can work long hours.

In a world built on these new beliefs, society would invest in providing quality childcare that is affordable and flexible. Schools would adapt their yearly and daily schedules to the realities of working families. At the same time, employers would give people the flexibility they need to adapt to school schedules and be active participants in their children's education and in their communities.

Everyone, with children and without, would be able to adapt jobs to life and life to jobs. Everyone would have a right to at least request a customized schedule without worrying about getting dinged just for asking. Given Deloitte's experience with Mass

Career Customization, more employees, especially younger ones, are likely to ask to dial up their employment than those who ask to dial down.[18] The resulting customization would get rid of the resentment employees who don't have family responsibilities sometimes feel toward those who do. Any employee could dial up and get rewarded, or dial down and keep proportional pay and benefits. All options would be available to everyone according to a new definition of what is fair.

To get to this world, business and government would need to actively encourage fathers to customize their careers. When fathers and people without kids are just as likely as mothers to adapt their jobs to family and to life, the culture will shift enough for mothers to customize, too, without being demoted to the mommy track. Companies could persuade fathers in high-level positions to be customized career role models. To motivate more fathers to take time off when a child arrives, families could get an extra month of family leave that only the father can use.[19] When fathers are just as likely as mothers to take time off for a new infant or dial down their job when the kids are in middle school, then mothers will be just as likely as fathers to be in high-level positions. In a world where people encounter mothers and fathers every day who don't fit the old stereotypes, the stereotypes will start to fade away.

Today, a few couples, with a lot of struggle and sacrifice, find their way to a reasonably happy ending, in which employment and family are integrated in a way that works for them, at least for a time. But happy endings aren't supposed to be filled with caveats like "a few" or "with a struggle" or "reasonably" or "for a time." By the time Kate grows up, I want happy endings to be for everyone. I want her fairy tale to be much simpler and shorter, something like this:

There once was a young and idealistic couple who said to each other, "When our children arrive we will both be home for family dinner together every night in our castle. We will both have time to read to and play with and care for our children. We will share employment in a way that works for us and lets us earn enough money to support our family. We will both have time for our own interests and for each other. We'll simply customize our jobs over the years to make a family workweek that works for us!"

And then, the baby arrived . . . and they lived happily ever after.

REMODELING TOOLS

▶ A lessons learned cheat sheet.

◆ Change the conversation with your spouse by stopping the blame game. Help each other see the bigger picture and the mental maps and vicious cycles getting in the way.

◆ Know your ideal—individually and together. Paint a picture of what you want life to be like. Include a goal for a family employment week, the combined weekly employed hours right for your family. Be willing to experiment. Be open to different strategies for getting there.

◆ Know what's fair and what's not fair.

◆ Know the workplace culture not just the policies. Don't assume that certain fields or jobs are always more family-friendly than others because so much depends on the particular employer and the individual manager.

◆ Invest money and time in yourself and each other to reach the vision.

◆ Challenge what's feasible.

◆ Overcompensate for subconscious assumptions you know are out there.

◆ Ask for it all—for yourself and for all mothers and fathers.

▶ Go to the interactive exercise at www.masscareercustomization.com. You can plot several stages of your career using the model and even plot what you hope the future will be like. This is a great tool for reflecting on your path so far and for getting clear about your ideal going forward. Under ONLINE FEATURES, you can download an MCC minibook that provides an overview of the concept of Mass Career Customization. Use it to start a conversation with other mothers. Hand it off to your manager or human resources department. Host a discussion or workshop for employers in your community. Call the chamber of commerce or write them a letter about MCC.

► For another example of how completely rethinking work is a win-win for employers and employees, visit www.caliand jody.com to learn about Results-Only Work Environment (ROWE). Their book, *Why Work Sucks and How to Fix It,* describes the successful implementation of ROWE at Best Buy. As Cali and Jody said in an e-mail conversation, "There are a lot of beliefs that keep us operating in the 1950's 'Model T' structure in office environments. Work happens Monday-Friday 8:00 a.m. to 5:00 p.m. Work happens in cubes. People who put in lots of hours are more dedicated than people who put in few hours. People with kids never put in more than 40 hours. . . . Managers need to direct work. And on and on. All of the beliefs we have about the way work needs to happen create the stability of the workplace today. To change the workplace structure, we have to change people's beliefs."

► Discuss with spouse, friends, or family this question: What aspects of the workplace make it difficult for you to integrate work and life? What do our answers say about workplace culture, "how work is structured, how time is spent, and how employees demonstrate commitment and competence"?[20]

► If we held these beliefs, what would we say? How would we behave differently? How would the world operate?

◆ A variety of job structures to fit various stages of personal lives is best for people, families, businesses, and communities.

◆ Family and employment can be integrated and complementary.

- ◆ Mothers and fathers share the responsibility and are equally capable of employment and contributing to the family's financial security.

▶ Learn negotiating skills. Start with resources and information about women and negotiation from experts Linda Babcock and Sara Laschever, authors of *Women Don't Ask* and *Ask for It*. They provide tons of resources at www.womendontask.com and www.askforit.com, including a tool for preparing for negotiation. Check out Harvard's Program on Negotiation (www.pon.org/catalog/index.php), which has videos, links, free downloads, and books—including the best-seller *Getting to Yes*.

▶ If you are proposing a customized job with a new or existing employer, Cynthia Calvert, deputy director at the WorkLife Law Center, gives this advice. First work on your own mind-set. Remember that you are not asking for a favor or begging. You are asking for what is fair. Remember the value you bring to the employer and the benefits they reap when they retain good employees. Next, make a specific proposal about how to accomplish the work part-time, think about it from the employer's perspective, and anticipate any objections. Finally, ask for more than you think you will get and make sure you are clear with the employer. Do you want me at 70 percent schedule and salary or not at all? Often the boss is actually thinking the choice is between 70 percent and 100 percent. Know what your bottom line is, make it clear to the employer, and know when you are willing to walk away.

▶ Take a quick quiz on Family Responsibilities Discrimination (www.hrhero.com/hriq/index.cgi?FRD). Visit the website for the WorkLife Law Center at UC Hastings Law School, headed by Joan Williams, to read more about family responsibilities discrimination (www.worklifelaw.org). The center has a network of attorneys willing to take cases in this emerging field of law. Visit the U.S. Equal Opportunity Commission to review their "Employer Best Practices for Workers with Caregiving Responsibilities (www.eeoc.gov/policy/docs/care giver-best-practices.html). Send the links to friends and to your human resources department.

► Ask the media to stop portraying mothers' difficult decisions about employment as simply a voluntary choice or opting out. Ask them to stop painting too rosy a picture about how easy it is to find flexible work or opt back in.[21]

► Experiment with new language.

INSTEAD OF	TRY
• Choice or opting	• Decision
• Work-family balance	• Work-family flow or integration or harmony
	• Career-family fit[22]
	• Work-life effectiveness[23]
• Part-time job	• Customized job
• Reduced schedule	• Job that fits

► Challenge assumptions about fathers. For example, once Kate was in school, friends would send me e-mails about school events that were sent to all the mothers. I would reply and add all the fathers. Brian Reid, who owns the blog Rebel Dad (www.rebeldad.com), picked apart a survey question in a highly publicized study. The question asked, "In general, what is the ideal situation for CHILDREN—mothers working full-time, mothers working part-time, or mothers not working at all outside the home?" Brian's pointed observation was, "This is asinine. It assumes there is no room for father involvement. It assumes the working status of dads means absolutely nothing. It assumes that child care is solely a mother issue. This is the worst possible assumption to perpetuate if we seriously want to get to a point where we can think about childrearing as a gender-neutral thing."[24]

▶ Send the link to Harvard's project on implicit bias (https://implicit.harvard.edu/implicit) to your husband and other fathers you know. Tell them to take the ten- to fifteen-minute Gender-Career IAT. Encourage your husband to find other fathers to talk to about work and family issues.

▶ Go to www.evolutionofdad.com to view clips from Dana Glazer's *The Evolution of Dad,* which is "a documentary-in-progress about what it means to be an involved, contemporary American father." Send the link to fathers you know.

▶ Pick up a book.

   ◆ *Unbending Gender: Why Work and Family Conflict and What To Do about It* by Joan Williams.

   ◆ *The Naked Truth: A Modern Woman's Manifesto on Business and What Really Matters* by Margaret Heffernan.

   ◆ *Mass Career Customization: Aligning the Workplace with Today's Nontraditional Workforce* by Cathleen Benko and Anne Weisberg.

   ◆ *Opting Out? Why Women Really Quit Careers and Head Home* by Pamela Stone.

   ◆ *Women Don't Ask* and *Ask for It* by Linda Babcock and Sara Leschever.

9

pits and privates

or why am i obsessed
with saving time?

∽

I N MY LIFE before motherhood, I led time management training sessions for employees of a big company. I indoctrinated everyone in the Franklin-Covey system for managing time. I kept my own binder-size day-planner and later a Palm Pilot at my side to manage my own time. I figured all my well-honed time management techniques would translate neatly to family life. But they were no match for what happened to my time once I had a child. I still track all my appointments and keep a running to-do list. David and I have "calendar meetings" each week to try to stay on top of life. It doesn't matter. Employed or not, I can't make it all fit.

I'm not the only mother with time on my mind and not on my hands. My friend Maggie, mother of two toddlers, lamented, "I was simply so thrilled the other day to have time to clip my toenails. And then I cried because I thought about how crazy it was that I didn't have time to clip my own toenails." Pressed for time, mothers manage only minutes for personal hygiene. I strategize how often I really need to shower before someone notices, as in "I won't see anyone tomorrow, so I can put on a baseball cap and wait to wash my hair until Saturday." We do the same with our kids. One mother told me, "We do a lot of 'rinse offs' in our house—where we count to thirty and focus on the 'pits and privates.'"[1] My friend Rosemary refers to the same system for speed bathing of children as "face, feet and fannies." Toenails, pits, and privates; face, feet, and fannies, something's just not right here.

In a Mothers & More survey of more than fifteen hundred mothers, mothers worried more about not having enough time than about divorce. They worried more about time than they did about the death or disability of their spouses. Mothers' top three worries about their future were—in priority order:

- Not having enough time for their children.
- Not having enough time for their marriages.
- Not having enough time to meet their own needs.[2]

Pollster and political strategist Frank Luntz once said that for employed women with young children, "The issue of time matters to them more than anything else in life."[3] My friend Christine, who has three kids, told me she keeps having the same conversation with her husband, pronouncing to him, "We just have to figure out a way to manage our time better!" When Alice responded to one of my requests for stories, she said, "Oh, I never have enough time. . . . I feel horrible spending time doing this right now. At least I do have a second load of clothes in the wash machine. I cry and berate myself trying to figure out what I do wrong and why I can't get everything done."

Plenty of people are willing to help us with this worry. In fact, there's an entire genre of magazines and books and talk shows advising us how to save time and selling us products to do just that. I have to confess I love the magazines. The glossy pictures of put-together families and spotless homes with coordinated throw pillows lure me in. I try to follow the tips for exercising in ten minutes, dinners in fifteen minutes, and cleaning the house in twenty. Yet, I am still always racing against the clock. I rush both my daughter and my husband along. I try to do two or five things at once. I wonder in passing when I'll have just a few spare minutes for myself. I don't remember my own mother, or father, being this squeezed for time. Am I really a time management expert who's a failure at managing my own time?

As someone who's been known to interrupt executives mid-sentence if they go over their allotted time on the agenda, I had trouble believing that I was a time management failure. So I looked for other villains. Why do mothers feel as if they have no time? Why do mothers and fathers feel more pressed for time than their parents were? What are we doing with our time anyway?

OVERWORK IS PART OF THE PROBLEM, BUT IT'S NOT THAT SIMPLE

I wanted to blame overwork for my time squeeze. To be perfectly accurate, at first I wanted to blame David's boss—for making him stay in the office for so many hours. Along with David's boss, I wanted to blame my past and future employers, who I knew also expected fifty hours a week or more from me. Overwork simply had to be the problem.

- "Americans now work the longest hours in the industrialized world."[4]
- "Workers' access to paid leave and flexible scheduling has declined in the United States."[5]
- "The United States is the only advanced economy in the world that does not guarantee its workers paid vacation."[6]

A ha! I had my villain. Not just my husband's former boss, who really is a nice guy, but an epidemic of overwork sweeping the country, stealing time from our families and our lives. More hours a week on the job, more weeks a year, and less vacation must leave everyone feeling they have no time.

Then I discovered one small problem.

Employed fathers in 1970 worked an average of 45 hours a week. In 2000 they worked a whopping—45 hours.[7]

Well, two small problems.

Employed mothers in 1970 worked an average of thirty-two hours a week. By 2000, that number rose, but only by three hours to thirty-five hours a week.[8]

Wait, where was my epidemic of fifty-, sixty-, and seventy-hour workweeks? Are we working more today or not?

NOT EVERYONE IS OVERWORKED

The overwork epidemic I wanted to blame turns out to be most common among my friends; college-educated people with professional and managerial jobs. Since 1970, a growing percentage of these folks are working a lot more, and over a third put in more than fifty hours a week. At the same time, the number of people working less than thirty hours a week has increased too, in part because so many women have entered the workforce and are more likely to work shorter workweeks.[9] A number of people who work less than thirty hours a week would prefer to work more, in many cases likely because they don't have enough hours to make ends meet or to qualify for benefits.[10] Today, more people are overworked and more are underemployed, but between the two changes the average stayed about the same.[11]

These shifts toward both longer and shorter workweeks are encouraged by the same job structures that make mothers and fathers feel like square pegs in the workplace. Take David and his law firm job. Although the Fair Labor Standards Act established overtime pay for working over forty hours a week, David, as a professional/manager type employee, was "exempt" from those overtime laws. He received a salary and didn't get paid overtime for his long hours.[12] In fact, it was much cheaper for his firm to work him close to eighty hours a week than to hire two forty-hours-a-week employees. A second employee would cost the firm a second set of expensive health insurance and other benefits. Plus, for every dollar David made over $90,000, his employer didn't have to pay Social Security taxes anymore, making his extra hours even cheaper. Maxing out the hours David worked was a financial savings for his firm.

On the other hand, offering short workweeks with no benefits can save money for a company as well. Recall my friend Diane (Chapter 6), whose employer scheduled her to work just under twenty-four hours a week. Her employer saved money by limiting the hours Diane worked as an engineer, which meant they didn't provide her with costly benefits. Plus, part-time employees are often paid a lower hourly wage.[13] Kathleen Gerson and Jerry A. Jacobs point out in their book, *The Time Divide*, that while people, and especially families, "face new needs for balance and flexibility in their working lives, employers have good reasons to offer jobs with either long or short workweeks."[14] Longer than desired workweeks steal time from some people; shorter than desired workweeks steal money from others.

CONTROL OVER WORK TIME MATTERS AS MUCH AS AMOUNT OF TIME

One of the primary reasons I eventually decided to become self-employed was that I wanted to control my own paid work time. I was willing—especially once Kate was in grade school—to put in thirty or more hours a week; I simply wanted to have control over when and where I worked them and when I took vacations. I had watched while that customer service representative who wanted to start at 6:30 A.M. instead of 6:00 was turned down. I had once been the cubicle worker who knew she needed to wait until the boss left before leaving herself. I knew that few companies were really ready and willing to give employees a lot more control over when and where they did their work. The unspoken assumptions always seemed to be that *time belongs primarily to the employer not the employee* and that *face time on the job is more important than results.*

Employer control over work time has been built into our labor laws. While hourly employees must be paid more per hour if they work overtime, what if you don't want to work overtime or can't, say because your child's after-school program ends at 6:00 P.M.? As Lonnie Golden of the Economic Policy Institute explains, "In the U.S., it is entirely legal for an employer to require an employee to work beyond his or her scheduled shift with no advance notice, *and* to take disciplinary action against a worker who refuses."[15]

Even employees who have professional or managerial jobs and are exempt from overtime rules find that their time is not their own. In David's law firm job and in my job before Kate was born, we both effectively faced mandatory overtime too. We just didn't get paid extra for it. The workloads couldn't be done in forty hours a week and everyone put in more than fifty hours a week so being the lone person who didn't was risky for your career. Far too often, David would get handed something late Friday afternoon that was due Monday morning. No matter how much I complained that he should refuse to do it, he really couldn't—not without huge penalties to his reputation and future. Yet there was no cost or consequence to his employer for working him over the weekends and late into the night.

Few employees have the flexibility they need or want, and those who earn less money are less likely to have much control over their employed time.[16] This lack of flexibility and control over employed time is not just unfortunate for employees—it's unfortunate for businesses, too. People who have the ability to customize where they work and when they start and stop find that they can work many more hours in a week and still feel better about their career-life fit than those who don't have flexibility.[17] The less control we have over our employment time to make it fit our lives better, the more we feel we don't have enough time.[18]

OVERWORK IS A FAMILY AFFAIR

With far more mothers in the workforce and far more single parent families today, far more families feel time starved because all the adults in the family are employed—not necessarily because any single adult is working longer weeks.[19] Among married couples with kids, the shift to having two earners has been seismic. My own mother and father, in a traditional "he's employed and she isn't" arrangement, were solidly in the majority in 1970. By 2008, everything had changed, and six in ten couples had both parents employed.[20]

The common presumption is that in a family with two employed parents, both must be working really long hours. That's actually relatively rare, especially when kids are little.[21] What's more common is that he is employed more than forty-five hours a week, and she puts in far fewer hours,[22] a sort of modified traditional family.[23] However, even if she's employed less than he is, their *combined* employed hours are almost sure to be much greater than a single earner family from 1970.

Imagine a typical family in 1970 in which the father works about forty-five hours a week and the mother isn't employed.[24] Their combined hours are, well, forty-five hours. Now imagine a family today where both parents are employed. They need two incomes but can't find two jobs that are both forty hours a week or less. So they modify the traditional arrangement. He'll work forty-five hours a week and she'll work, say, twenty for a total of sixty-five per week.[25] Over a year, her twenty hours a week means our modified traditional couple has about *twenty-five more full weeks of employment a year* to fit into their family life than the traditional 1970 family. Even two-job families today who aren't that far from the traditional single-earner model feel far more squeezed than families in 1970 felt with one job between them.

Of course, families with two earners did exist back in the 1970s, and they had many of the same time challenges as families with two earners do today. However, there are two big differences between two-earner couples then and now. First, these families are far more common today, making the time crunch a much more common problem.[26] Second, families with two earners today are working longer *combined hours* than they have ever worked. Families with both parents employed today are working five hundred more hours a year or *twelve and half full weeks more each year* than those same two-job families did in the late 1970s.[27] While the average workweek for individuals hasn't changed much, the combined hours parents are spending on the job per week and per year have climbed.[28] Overwork is a family problem, not an individual problem.[29]

WHERE DID THE TIME FOR MOTHERS TO BE EMPLOYED COME FROM?

There are only so many hours in the day. If so many more mothers are employed, and if couples' combined employed hours have gone up so much, where did that time come from? Conventional wisdom says that mothers especially must be spending less time with children; therefore, mothers moving into the workforce hasn't been good for kids. People assume employment steals time mothers spend with their children and that assumption contributes to the mental map that *mothers who are employed or pursue personal fulfillment are selfish*. The presumption that being employed steals time from kids is also a source of my own guilt. If I'm employed, I figure, I must be spending much less time with Kate than my mom did with me back in the 1970s. I also figure that when I'm employed I must spend a lot less time with her than when I'm *not* employed.

But I learned two stunning facts. Employed mothers today spend just as much time with their kids as *non*employed mothers did back in the 1970s. Plus, employed mothers today have managed an Elastigirl move that allows them to spend nearly as much active time caring for their children each week as nonemployed mothers do today.[30]

How did that happen? Let me illustrate how families accomplished this by showing you how David and I zipped through a version of that generational shift all by ourselves in a mere six years. In

2000, I wasn't employed and by 2006 I was. The number of available hours in our week stayed the same: seven days times 24 hours times two of us equals 336 hours; no more, no less. Somehow, we found room for me to be employed. Our combined workweek grew by about 20 hours a week, and yet we protected our time with Kate. How we shifted our time may not be ideal, and it certainly wasn't the result of planning on our part, but it is common. We ended up moving time around the same way families in general have over the past thirty-five years.

TIME DIARY FOR DAVID AND KRISTIN: 2000

When I wasn't employed but David was working sixty to seventy hours a week, our days followed a particular rhythm. I'd stay in bed for as long as Kate would let me before she started shouting, "Juice! Juice! Juice!" from her crib. I'd get the orange juice order and make breakfast for both of us. David was usually already gone. Kate and I would go to the park a block away, and I would push her in the swing. As the kids played in the sand, I'd chat with other mothers or caregivers who happened to be there. After the park, Kate and I would do a grocery store run together. In the afternoon, while she napped, I'd test myself to see how much I could get done before she woke up. Empty dishwasher, put laundry in, pay a few bills, check my e-mail, call my mother, get a head start on making dinner, and maybe steal the last fifteen minutes for myself to relax or read. During the witching hours of 3:00 to 6:00 P.M., if I could keep the meltdowns to a minimum, we would play together or, gasp, she would watch a little TV while I made dinner. Whether David made it home or not, we ate dinner and moved into the bath and bedtime routine.

At night when she was asleep, David and I might have enough time to catch up on each other's lives or watch TV. I might get out to a Mothers & More chapter meeting. He might do the dishes or take out the trash. I managed my evenings to be sure to get to bed by 10:30 or 11:00 so I could survive the next day if Kate woke up twice in the night or decided she needed juice at 5:30 A.M. instead of 7:00. Thanks to me, most of the household stuff got done during the week. Our weekends were mostly our own to schedule around the random trip to the discount store for a year's supply of paper towels and Cheerios and around David's weekend trips back to the office.

TIME DIARY FOR KRISTIN AND DAVID: 2006

Fast-forward to 2006. Life moved to a different rhythm. Kate was in full-day kindergarten. I was employed about forty hours a week and so was David. Combined, we had about twenty more employment hours to fit into our week than we did in 2000. I became Elastigirl again, this time stretching here and there to make sure my time with Kate stayed about the same.

We would all wake up to the alarm, having given ourselves the bare minimum minutes we needed to get out the door. David and I would get dressed and remind Kate three times to get out of bed and get dressed. Then I would make our breakfast and try to sit down with Kate as we ate most mornings. We packed Kate's lunch and made sure she had her homework. If all went well, David would get Kate to school just in time to put her at the end of her class line as they went in the school building. David and I went our separate ways for our jobs. Both of us had a few family tasks to get done during the day— dropping off dry-cleaning or calling to get an appointment to get the car fixed. We often skipped lunch and rushed to pack in as much work as we could so we could both leave work as early as we planned.

Around 3:00 or 4:00 in the afternoon, I would walk up to school and pick up Kate. I listened to her talk about school—mostly about recess—and checked her homework. David had planned dinner and gotten groceries over the weekend, so I tried to start a quick dinner while Kate got some down time. David and I made 5:30 to 8:30 P.M. sacred family time. On good days, by 6:00 we were all sitting down together for dinner. Often we ended up picking up dinner or going out instead. If we had time after dinner, we'd play a game of Clue or walk the dog together. Baths for Kate came just once or twice a week, or whenever it would be patently obvious to anyone else that she hadn't washed her hair in days. Kate and I would settle into her bed to read her newest fairy book while David cleaned up the kitchen.

David and I would collapse on the couch for a while as she got to sleep. We both would survey the house, which was a disaster despite David's efforts in the kitchen. The wet laundry in the washer had been there so long it smelled funky and probably had to be rewashed. The mail and newspapers were stacked up on the dining room table. There was a "courtesy call" on our voice mail reminding us that our auto insurance payment was due last week. A pile of clean laundry loomed next to us on the couch, piling up since the last week. I would strategize in my head, "Will I see any clients tomorrow? Do I need to take a shower tonight or can I wait another day without embarrassing myself?" We would take a bit of down time together to talk about our days. Usually, one or both of us returned to a computer to finish up some paid work. David watched more TV and folded the laundry. I was usually in bed by midnight and David by 1 A.M. On the weekend, there would be more household stuff left to do so we would tag team as much as we could: David got the groceries while I hung out with Kate or I paid the bills while David went to her soccer game.

WHERE WE STOLE THE TIME

Between 2000 and 2006, David and I made room for my employed hours in our week the same way families as a whole shifted their time between 1965 and 2000 as more mothers moved into the workforce. We were trying to fit about twenty more combined hours of employment into our lives each week, which is about what families as a whole did over the decades.[31]

Most of the hours I needed for my job I got by dropping a lot of housework. David picked up some of that housework, we paid for some of it, at the local pizza place for example, or by hiring someone to clean the house, and a whole lot of it just stopped getting done. Thus the funky smelling laundry. Another big chunk of hours came out of my own free time and TV time. I got nearly an hour a day for my job by sleeping less and gained a bit by doing a lot more multitasking. I did gain some time by doing less childcare, but not as much as I thought. School took some of the childcare, David picked up some, and most of the childcare hours I dropped were the ones where I was really doing something else, like grocery shopping, and watching Kate at the same time. I made up for time I lost with Kate during the week by spending more time with her on the weekend. The hours I spent directly caring for Kate went down less than an hour a day from 2000.[32] Ta da! Elastigirl conquers again!

Thanks to the American Time Use Survey and some wonderful researchers poring through the data the survey generated, we know that employed mothers today spend about eleven hours a week in what's called "primary childcare," time when you report that your kids are your main activity, like when you are bathing them, or helping with homework, or reading to them. Back in 1975, *non*-employed mothers spent about eleven hours a week on the same activities.[33] As Tamyke recalls from her childhood, "My mom was a stay-at-home mom, but after our homework was done and we had a snack we went outside to play or watched TV or read in our rooms, so she wasn't really with us more than working moms are now with their kids after work." Employed mothers today feel squeezed for time because they've stolen time from just about everything else in order to protect the amount of time they spend with their children.

MOTHERS WHO ARE NOT EMPLOYED ARE SQUEEZED TOO

Okay, but even when I wasn't employed I still felt I never had enough time for everything. Remember our Mother of All To-Do Lists? That ever-expanding set of responsibilities mothers have? Mothers who are not employed today are spending more time on unpaid family work each week than the same mothers did in 1975.[34] The expectations on that Mother of All To-Do Lists expanded to take over the time I had available. When I wasn't employed, I spent more time with Kate.[35] Plus, I constantly felt internal pressure to spend even more: to go to the museum, take a music class together, do crafts with her. As another mother told me, "I have a fantastic mother who raised four kids (I only have two) but I know my mom didn't spend the hours I do doing things like researching preschools, worrying about feeding the kids organic foods, worrying about how neat and organized her closets were, thinking about whether vaccines could cause autism, etc."

Now, mothers who are not employed have dropped some hours of housework over the years, but the increase in time spent with children and on other types of family tasks—like shopping and medical appointments—have more than made up for it. When I wasn't employed, there were myriad ways my magazines told me I could shop better, cook better, be more organized, or clean more often. Because I had the mental map that *caring for family isn't really work, it's just what mothers do*, I didn't think of family work as taking time or energy. So I felt like I should be doing even more for my family because I wasn't employed.

On the plus side, when I wasn't employed, I slept a bit more and had more free time. Though most of it was still not so free since I was also taking care of Kate at the same time, reading the newspaper while she played, for example. I felt time squeezed even when I wasn't employed in part because I was doing more family work than nonemployed mothers used to do and in part because what I was doing never felt like enough. In the end, I didn't have a whole lot more time left over, but I did have laundry that didn't smell moldy and fewer dinners from the pizza place. In other words, I had enough time to cover the basics, barely.

Employed or not, mothers pretty much have the same laments about time and the lack of it. Tamyke, a teacher, says, "I feel like everyone, including me, is getting the short end of the time stick! I think guilt is a major factor because I am always telling myself I could be doing more. More at work, more with my kids, more with my husband, mom, etc." Haley, whose work is taking care of three young children says, "As I sometimes tell people, I don't even have time to sit on the toilet—certainly not by myself. Making breakfast, packing lunches, cleaning, shuttling kids, cooking, homework time, playing with kids. There is little time for me to do what I want or even need to do. . . . I have continually felt that I cannot give my all to anyone—be it each of my children, my spouse, volunteer commitments, friends, and me." Employed or not, mothers feel they don't have enough time for their children or their spouses or themselves, just for different reasons. Employed mothers have stolen time from just about everything else to protect their time with their kids. Non-employed mothers are doing more family work than they used to and always feeling they should be doing even more.

FATHERS ARE DOING FAR MORE FAMILY WORK— BUT ARE STILL BEHIND

So as employed mothers pull a generational Elastigirl move to protect time with their kids and all mothers try to meet an ever expanding expectation of what mothers should do for families, what are fathers doing? Conventional wisdom says fathers haven't picked up their fair share at home and that is why mothers are the ones with no time. True? Well, yes and no.

Today's universal kitchen argument between mothers and fathers goes like this. She says, "I'm doing everything. You're not doing your fair share!" Then he says, "But honey, I'm doing a ton. Way more than my dad ever did. You just don't appreciate it." No one wins, because they are both right. Whether fathers are doing enough depends on who we compare them with. As one Mothers & More member said, "My husband tends to compare his efforts to that of his father's years ago instead of comparing to everything I do."[36] Compared to his father, he's doing twice as much family work. He's a hero. Compared to her, he's only doing half as much. He's a slacker.

If we look at the changes in how mothers and fathers share family work since 1965, two sequential trends pop out. When it comes to housework, we seem to be stuck in 1985. By then mothers had already dropped half the housework they were doing in 1965, fathers had increased their housework to half of what she was doing, and there couples have stayed. The other trend takes off in 1985. When it comes to childcare, fathers were doing only a couple hours a week until 1985, but boy then things changed fast. By 2003, fathers had nearly tripled the time they spent directly caring for children. Fathers stole time for their children from their free time and a bit from paid work time.[37]

At the same time though, mothers increased their time caring for children too. So fathers are still behind—doing about half the direct childcare mothers do.[38] Fathers aren't slackers, they are just rushing to catch up. More employed mothers hasn't translated into neglected kids, in part because employed mothers protect that time but also in part because fathers have so dramatically increased their time with children. Contrary to popular belief, parents today are spending almost double the amount of time engaged with their kids as they did in either 1965 or 1985.[39]

How Times Have Changed

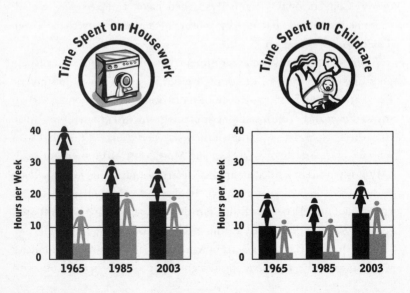

It would be easy to assume that if mothers are doing twice as much family work as fathers, then fathers must have a lot more free time and that must be why mothers are the ones obsessed with saving time. I know that's what I assumed. It was part of my logic for pestering David to do more family work. Well, the reality is that mothers and fathers on average have about the same weekly workload, about 65 hours, if you count both paid work and unpaid work in the total.[40] Fathers have more paid work in that total, and mothers have more family work. As for other activities, fathers already sleep a bit less than mothers and spend less time on "personal care"—that is, doing their hair. Fathers spend more time commuting while mothers spend more time shopping. In the end, fathers have just a few hours more free time than mothers each week.[41]

What fathers do tend to have more of is child-free time, a valuable resource and rare for many mothers. Mothers are more likely to do free-time activities while they watch kids at the same time.[42] When Kate was a baby, I'd take her to play groups where the real purpose was for me to catch up with friends, even though we were interrupted every five minutes by a child. Now that Kate's older, I walk with friends around the field during Kate's soccer practices, which lets me do three things at once: socialize, watch Kate, and exercise. When mothers shop or do housework, they are also more likely to have the kids in tow than fathers are. Everyone knows that going to the grocery store without kids is a completely different experience—a treat even—from the same trip with two young children along. Fathers spend more time employed, which is child-free. A lunch meeting with colleagues is a different experience from lunch with children, not necessarily better or worse but different. While time with our children makes us happy, too much if it can also make a person stir-crazy. Child-free time is time that a person has more control over how to spend and more options for activities that recharge our batteries like uninterrupted conversations with friends or reading a good book or going to a movie that isn't animated. So while mothers and fathers have similar overall workloads, their experiences of the time they have are often quite different.

Many mothers would like fathers to do more family work, but to be fair fathers will have trouble making progress as dramatically as they have recently even if they want to. Fathers continue to be more likely to be employed full-time. If we want fathers to increase family work, where would it come from? The handful of hours of free time fathers have that mothers don't isn't enough to steal to make things fifty-fifty. Fathers could do what mothers do and steal more time from things like sleeping but they already sleep less. One of the only other places to steal from is paid work, but since jobs are one-size-fits-all and he's more likely to be the one with the full-time job, it's hard for him to steal time from employment. Plus, there's another reason neither father nor mother can decrease their employed hours to find more time; they need the money.

WE CAN'T SIMPLY STEAL TIME FROM OUR JOBS BECAUSE WE NEED THE MONEY

When Kate was a baby and David and I were both frustrated with his long work hours, his boss once asked him why we didn't just hire more help for me. He certainly didn't want David cutting back at work to contribute more at home. I suppose this friendly suggestion seemed logical to him because he was paying David a large salary, probably much larger than his own starting salary. But we were puzzled. Despite the large salary, neither of us felt like there was room in our budget for significant hired help. Why did he assume we had a lot of extra cash when we felt like we were just able to take care of the basics of a comfortable middle class life?

As I talked with more mothers, I discovered that no matter what our family income was, no matter if both parents were employed or not, no matter where we lived in the country, we were all anxious about the family finances. Newspaper and magazine articles told us that we were all just spending too much on frivolous stuff we didn't really need. In the advice column, "Ask Marilyn," someone asked the woman with the highest IQ why a man used to be able to support his family on his income but now the family needs the wife's income, too. Marilyn's answer was that "back then people didn't even pay for television, let alone satellite radio . . . Diapers were washed, not discarded at greatly increased cost." Her conclusion was that families need two incomes today because, "Yesterday's luxuries and dreams have become today's routines."[43] If families were better at cutting out the extras and managing our money, so the argument goes, we might even be able to afford to have one parent not employed at all. Conventional wisdom seems to be that families today—so many with two earners—are better off than their parents were but less financially responsible.

Yet, that didn't seem to be my experience or the experience of the mothers I knew. Alicea said, "I have to work . . . for the pay and the insurance. We have made a choice to have two 'lesser' jobs for each of us, but that gives us the time to spend with the kids. . . . Of course finances are very tight—contrary to what a lot of folks think when both parents work—they think you are rolling in the dough!" I felt like somehow David and I were failing if we couldn't get ahead, even with his great job. Then I read *The Two Income Trap: Why Middle-Class Mothers and Fathers Are Going Broke* by the mother-daughter team, Elizabeth Warren and Amelia Warren Tyagi, and learned how wrong the conventional wisdom is and why so many families feel like they can't get ahead—even with two incomes.

On the income side, we're right in assuming that most families have more dollars to spend these days. While fathers' wages have stayed flat, many more mothers are employed since the 1970s and typically add another 75 percent of the father's salary to the family income.[44] Where we're wrong is on the expense side. We aren't blowing that extra money on SUVs and iPods. We're spending it on the increased cost of things like housing, childcare, and healthcare.

When David and I went house hunting before Kate was even born, she dictated our housing criteria: safe neighborhood, good schools, not too far away from David's job in downtown Los Angeles or my job in Pasadena. We were searching for the Holy Grail of middle-class life. And so was every other family we knew. People told us we couldn't live in certain cities or even neighborhoods because of the schools or had to avoid other neighborhoods because they weren't safe enough for children. We were making very good money, but the few houses that fit the bill had multiple desperate families bidding on it. Because adults without children can look for housing without worrying about the schools and only need to know the neighborhood is safe enough for adults, they have more options and less competition. David and I, and families in general, though, end up paying more for housing than those without kids because we drive up the prices by competing with each other to buy houses in safe neighborhoods with good schools.[45] The Warrens confirm that what families pay for housing has gone up much faster than what people without children pay for housing.[46]

Families today also spend more on childcare at several stages of their children's lives. When I grew up in a small town in Minnesota, I remember going to morning preschool a few days a week the year before I started kindergarten. At that point, not everyone went to preschool; it was a "nice to have." By the time we had Kate, families were recommending preschools to us while I was still pregnant. Today, given research in child development and the expectation that kids be ready for kindergarten the first day, most families and our communities consider preschool a "must have" for at least one and often two years before kindergarten. Yet preschool is usually something families pay for themselves. For families with two earners, preschool costs kick in after three or four years of paying for childcare. The childcare costs continue once the kids are in grade school. Kate goes to the public elementary school at the end of our block, but each year we pay for after-school care and scramble to find three months worth of quality summer programs we can afford. Preschool, childcare, after-school care are all fixed costs that most families didn't have thirty years ago.

When Kate was born, we had health insurance through David's employer. In the five years he was there, we saw our share of the premiums triple. When we both became self-employed, we found an individual health insurance plan for about the same monthly premium, but to keep the premium at that level we had to choose a plan that had a much higher deductible so we pay more out of pocket than we did before. Just since 2001, "Health insurance premiums have increased by 78 percent—that's four times as fast as the increase in wages and more than four times as fast as inflation."[47] Health insurance, if they can get it, and medical expenses are taking up a larger share of families' incomes today than ever before.

Then there's transportation. When my middle sister was born in the early 1970s, my mom was not employed, and my dad used the only car to go to work and school. David and I have two jobs in two different locations. So we have two used cars. Families today do spend more on cars, but not because everyone drives fancy cars with DVD players. Families today actually spend less per car than they used to because they hang on to their cars longer. They spend more total because the average family now has two cars and two auto insurance bills to handle transportation to two jobs.[48]

There are a few more surprising notes on the expense side. Back in the 1960s, the federal tax exemption for dependents—that is, children—was so high that many of our parents didn't even pay income taxes. That exemption for dependents was never adjusted for inflation, so families today pay a much larger percentage of our income in taxes than our parents did.[49] What about all that money families waste on luxuries? Well, we may have more clothes, but they are cheaper so we spend less. We spend more on restaurants, but less on groceries and a lot less on meat so overall we spend less on food. Families' total discretionary expenses then and now are about the same. Honestly, we can't spend more on extras, because we don't have it. Given the increased percentage of the family income going to housing, preschool and childcare, health insurance, having two cars, and taxes, families today are spending *more than double* on our fixed costs compared to our parents in the early 1970s.[50]

I've adapted Warren and Warren Tyagi's conclusions into a couple of simple equations. When today's two-income family compares themselves to a single-earner family from their parents' generation, today's family has:

Not quite double the income of their parents
– More than double the fixed costs
_____
Less left to spend on discretionary expenses and savings[51]

Of course, the situation is even worse for a single-earner family today comparing itself to the single-earner family from their parents' generation; today's single-earner family is trying to survive among even more two-earner families but has

Same income as parents' generation
– More than double the fixed costs
_____
Half as much left to spend on discretionary expenses and savings[52]

That extra income from mothers' employment has become necessary for families to simply try to keep up with the increases in their major fixed expenses over time. Advising mothers and fathers that in order to have more money they simply need to spend less on luxuries or in order to have more time they should simply work fewer hours ignores the reality of what's happened to our time and our budgets over the last thirty years. Families have shifted more of their time to more employed hours—by mother or father or both—to earn the money they need to support their families. Annie described her situation this way, "I've finally resigned myself to accept the next good-paying full-time job offered me, after turning down a few that just seemed like the workload would be too much to juggle with my home life, or the pay too low for a person with almost fifteen years' experience in my field. . . . The reason for my recent choice? Our little family, in our very modest home in the outskirts of real estate crazy Boston . . . who drives seven- and nine-year old fuel efficient cars, needs the money. My husband's salary has remained pretty flat while our health insurance, property taxes, food and gas bills, and pretty much everything else have increased." Yet the myth that families are simply overspending on luxuries is so persistent that families today blame themselves and feel like failures when they can't keep up or get ahead financially.

The truth is that families today, whether both parents are working or not, are maxing out their combined time on the job to pay for fixed expenses and along the way trying to save for retirement and college. They can't simply work less to gain more time without going broke.

FAMILIES AGAINST THE WALL AND OUT OF TIME

Contrary to our own self-flagellation, mothers aren't time management drop-outs. How families allocate their time has fundamentally shifted. While the total time mothers and fathers spend together on housework and childcare in a week is exactly the same as it was in 1965—forty-nine hours—the allocation of that time has changed. Ten hours of it moved from housework to childcare. Ten hours of it moved from mother to father.[53] At the same time though, more families have both parents employed and their combined work hours have climbed. In families with one earner, that person may work longer hours to make enough to get by in a world where most families have two earners. Our fixed costs for family basics have more than doubled leaving us scrambling to get ahead by working more combined hours. All the while, that Mother of All To-Do Lists expands the expectations of the time mothers should be spending to do more for our children and families. Families are against the wall. We can't drop any more housework without living in filth and eating McDonald's every day. We can't drop employed hours without worrying about losing the job, or the house, or the health insurance. We can't drop time with our kids because our kids need us and we'll be seen as bad parents and we don't want to! Running out of time and money, increasingly families are forced to make tough decisions between time and money in order to integrate family and employment.[54]

Families just don't have many places to find extra time so we find ourselves stealing time from fundamental parts of our lives. Suzanne Bianchi, a time use researcher, says, "Parents keep time with children high by multitasking, spending more of their leisure time with children than in the past, and curtailing time with a spouse, extended family and friends."[55] That sure sounds like my life and most mothers and fathers I know. We spend our weekends at the soccer field. We spend our Friday nights with our kids and a DVD and a pizza because we're exhausted and because we're making up for lost family time during the week. Mothers, and even fathers, give up healthy habits, like those Jodi gave up, "Time for exercise, time for meal planning and cooking healthier. Oh, and sleep." Couples increasingly say they have little time left over for each other.[56] Kimberley says, "I find that my exercise gets pushed to the side a lot. But my husband begs to differ, he says, 'He' gets pushed off to the side!" Mothers and fathers find they rarely socialize outside of the parents they see at school or weekend sports, and as Barb says, "Many times we have the kids along while we try to socialize, practically ruining the pleasure." Mothers especially spend most of their leisure time with kids underfoot, and that's if they have leisure time at all.[57] Mothers overwhelmingly told me that the first thing to go when they are pressed for time is "me time." Mothers stop doing things that recharge us. We stop giving ourselves the oxygen we need.

Another victim of our lack of time is that we have less time for volunteer work and other ways of being involved in our communities. When David was commuting thirty minutes each way to downtown Los Angeles for ten-hour workdays, he wasn't able to be involved in our community at all. When he became self-employed and moved his office five minutes from our home, he was able to serve on our school PTA, get involved in a local political campaign, and join the board of a community housing group. Our communities used to rely on women who were not employed to do the volunteer work that makes communities healthy, but women are spending fewer hours each week on civic activities than they used to.[58] In a report on the decline of community activity, researchers cited this shift as one factor saying, "Women have poured into the formal labor force, opening new doors for them but also sapping the neighborhood and voluntary organizations that used to flourish under unpaid female leadership."[59] Shifts in allocations of our time are not without costs to our families, to our communities, and to ourselves.

Without an understanding of the ways family time has changed, mothers tend to blame themselves for not being able to fit it all in and to assume everyone else is managing better, saying things like this mother said. "I *constantly* feel like other moms must have been given a secret to time management that I missed out on!! They seem to get so much more done than I do. Their houses are neat and clean, their kids are dressed in unwrinkled clothes, they make dinner and volunteer at school. I feel like I am never caught up. If I get the house clean it's because no one has clean clothes and we ate pizza for three nights!! I don't know what I'm doing wrong but there must be something." She isn't doing anything wrong and there is no secret time management tip. The secret is how dramatically our family time has shifted invisibly under our feet over the years. A fifteen-minute dinner recipe is not going to solve this problem for us. The time management tips we are so drawn to are sort of like saving for retirement by skipping a latte each day. Sure, it's better than nothing, but in the end it might just make you feel like a failure because it won't help much. It's just tinkering on the edges. We have to go to the root of the relationship between family time, family money, family employment, and family work to remodel enough to make a real difference in our lives.

WHAT IF WE THOUGHT DIFFERENTLY ABOUT TIME?

Rethinking time means rethinking the ways our biggest blocks of time are being spent. Not having enough *time* is linked to our challenges with *money* and *employment* and *family work*. Couples feel as if they don't have enough time in large part because of the time demands of employment and family work. Families need employment to earn enough money. Families could find more time if they could do less employment or if they could spend more money to buy more time, in the form of things like pizza delivery. Thinking differently about time is connected to rethinking all of these and the connections between them.

In previous chapters we imagined new beliefs about employment and family work:

- Mothers and fathers share the responsibility and are equally capable of caring for children and home.
- Mothers and fathers share the responsibility and are equally capable of employment and contributing to the family's financial security.

In other words, we experimented with thinking about family work and employment as family resources and family responsibilities shared by couples. Time is the same. What if we thought of time as a shared family resource and responsibility? What if we believed that the freedom to spend time as one wishes is fundamental to life and to self-determination so everyone should have the maximum possible control over their own time? What would we do differently if we believed:

- A person's time belongs first and foremost to that person.
- Time is a shared family resource and responsibility.

Within a family, mothers and fathers would then share a responsibility to allocate time as equitably as possible to balance the needs of each parent and the family as a whole, including the children. Just as couples might sit down to discuss joint investments of money, they might sit down to discuss how they plan to invest their time. What if a couple had goals for their ideal investment of time? How will we invest the finite number of hours available to the adults in the family each week? Because the largest portion of a family's time is spent on the "fixed time expenses" of employment and family work, most couples probably have to look at making changes to one or both of those big blocks to allocate time differently. This is the path David and I went down when we identified targets for a family employment workweek. Our path was to become self-employed, giving us more control over our employed time, both how much and when we did it. We moved toward a more equal division of employed time and family work time between the two of us. To gain some time, we spent some of the family money to take care of some of the family work—like dinners out and someone to clean our house. None of this was easy or solved everything, but at least we were dealing with the right stuff—rather than me beating myself up for not being able to manage our time better on my own.

Even with the changes David and I have made, like most mothers, I still often feel that Kate doesn't get enough time with me.[60] I try to keep in mind that my expectation of how much time I should spend with Kate and in what ways has been artificially inflated by parenting advice and that Mother of All To-Do Lists. I try to trust my own concrete observations about what Kate needs rather than my guilt. David and I try to think in terms of how much parent time Kate gets in any given week and even how much parent and grandparent time she gets, as opposed to how much she gets with me.

Ellen Galinsky, from the Families and Work Institute, was smart enough to ask children directly what they want. What if they could have one wish to change how their mothers' and fathers' employment affects their lives? Most parents predicted the kids would wish for more time.[61] What the children actually wished for was for their parents to be less tired and stressed.[62] Arlene told me that when she's crunched for time, her children "suffer the most since I'm tired, grumpy, stressed out, and behind on absolutely everything that my 'jobs' demand." Our kids notice when we haven't gotten a chance to breathe and need some oxygen. How we are when we are with our children is just as important as what we do with them and how many hours we spend. Yet, when squeezed for time, the first thing mothers—and fathers—give up is oxygen.

MANAGING OXYGEN

The authors of a book called *The Power of Full Engagement* are performance consultants who suggest that managing our energy is often

more important than managing every minute of our day.[63] I've mem-
orized a line from *The Power of Full Engagement* that says that the goal
is to "Burn as brightly as possible as long as possible in the service
of what really matters."[64] For a fire to burn steadily and brightly, it
needs oxygen. If I think of managing my oxygen supply for the long
term, rather than managing my time, that helps me remember that
funky smelling laundry doesn't matter. Getting enough sleep and
exercise to have the energy for myself and my family and for my
long-term health really matters. Kate going one more day without a
shower doesn't matter. Having half an hour at night to reconnect to
my husband to keep our marriage strong really matters.

What counts as oxygen is different for everyone. When David was
employed those long hours and I wasn't, I viewed his time at the office
as oxygen because he got to hang out with adults and do cool stuff.
He viewed my time at home as oxygen because I didn't have to deal
with looming deadlines and stressed-out clients. However, each of us
actually felt we needed a break from our respective work. Oxygen is
in the eye of the beholder. My friends Maggie and Chris created a way
to make sure each person has time to get the oxygen they need. Each
of them wrote down three things they needed to do each week to stay
sane and energized and then they shared the lists with each other. The
lists turned out to be simple gifts of time for oxygen. Maggie wanted
to sleep in one weekend morning. Chris wanted one time each week to
exercise for as long as he wanted. It is not surprising that each of them
wanted a bit of child-free time each week to do things that recharge
them. If time is a family resource, then mothers and fathers would
work together to make sure each parent has time to get the oxygen
each needs to burn as brightly as possible for as long as possible.

WHAT WOULD WE SAY IF TIME
IS A SHARED FAMILY RESOURCE?

Knowing how families have shifted their time over the years and why,
how might we talk differently if we believed *time is a shared family*

resource and responsibility? Mothers would stop scolding ourselves or our spouses that we just need to "manage our time better." Other people wouldn't claim that families don't have time because they are working too hard to earn money to waste on luxuries. We might talk less about "managing time" and more about "managing energy." We wouldn't talk about kids needing "mommy time" and might instead talk about a need for "parent time," or a need for time with family members. When Galinsky asked the children about their lives, she concluded that both the amount of time and what we do with the time we have with our children matter. But she encourages us to move away from the typical "quality time" concept because "quality time" makes us think every moment we spend has to be idyllic to be worthwhile. It doesn't. Galinsky suggests we think and talk about it as spending both "focused time" and "hanging-out time" with our children.[65]

HOW WOULD THE WORLD WORK IF WE RETHOUGHT TIME?

Time is a resource families invest in each other that returns benefits to our communities and the future. The investment of time mothers and fathers make in caring for family translates to fewer employment options, less money, and less time for themselves and other community activities. For families to have more time, we would have to remodel our workplaces, bring down the cost of families' fixed expenses or increase what they can earn, and find ways for society to make sure people have time to care.[66] So let's expand our imagination to ask, How would the world operate if we remodeled our beliefs about time?

- A person's time belongs first and foremost to that person.
- Time is a shared family resource and responsibility.

Much of what we imagined could be different about employment would also help families with time. For example, guaranteeing paid sick days and the ability to use them to take care of sick kids gives parents time. Community investments in quality childcare and education at all ages—childcare, preschool, K–12 education, after-school, summer care, college—would help offset the rapidly increasing amounts of time and money families spend on childcare and education. Labor laws, Social Security taxes, and access to affordable health insurance would be designed to encourage a variety of job structures, rather than providing incentives for employers to divide jobs into workweeks that are too long to have free or family time or workweeks that are too short to have enough money and benefits. If customized jobs were widely available, then families would have more options for allocating their time. Families could decide to take jobs that earn a bit less to gain more time without losing health insurance. Depending on the demands of the job and the business, employees would have far more control over when to start and stop employment and where to do it, giving them the control of their work time they need for a better career-life fit. Overtime would be voluntary. Employers would have to give advance notice of over-time needs, and employees would be able to accept or refuse without being penalized.[67]

Rethinking family work will also help us rethink time. If we believed *caring for others is a vital human and economic activity and a public service*, then society might decide to support the investment of time families are making in that care—for example by adjusting the tax deduction for dependents for inflation. Just as families consider how to invest their own time, our local communities would pay attention to how its citizens are able to invest their time, just as they might analyze how the community invests its money. Do families have the time to care and thrive? Do all our citizens have time to participate in our community? Do our people have time for life? The American Time Use Survey and tools like it help us measure family work, and the same tools would make it possible to monitor our investments of time as a community or as a nation alongside our investments of money.

THE SECRET IS THERE IS NO SECRET

I wish I could say I've found a secret time management tip. I haven't. I still feel rushed. I still feel like I can't fit it all in. However, knowing that mothers and fathers today have less time and fewer options for saving or stealing time than ever, I cut myself more slack. The knowledge that my options for managing my time are limited by forces outside my family and often outside my control, like employers, and economic trends, and cultural expectations, and public policy, gives me a bit of peace. I know I'm not a time management failure, and I don't expect that saving five minutes here or ten minutes there is going to make it all better. I also know that though I may still be the keeper of the family calendar, I can't manage *our* time all by myself. Figuring out how to invest the family time we have is something David and I have to do together.

REMODELING TOOLS

▶ Knowing that time demands on families these days are greater than ever, cut yourself some slack, be confident saying no when you need to and avoid comparing yourself to other parents or families. Surround yourself with friends who tend to be in sync with your own idea of how much time you need to spend with your kids and on your kids, rather than people who ratchet up your anxiety. Avoid the magazines, books, or people who make you feel more stressed rather than less.

▶ What's your favorite example of a time management tip that in reality sets a crazy standard for what we should be doing and how much? One of mine was a magazine article that literally provided long lists of the things in our house that should be cleaned, every day, every week, every month, and every year.

▶ Take Back Your Time is an initiative out of Cornell University focused on changing "the epidemic of overwork, overscheduling and time famine that now threatens our health, our families and relationships, our communities and our environment." To find out more about the initiative and the book of the same name, visit www.timeday.org.

▶ If we held these beliefs about time, what would we say? How would we behave differently? How would the world operate?

◆ A person's time belongs first and foremost to that person.

◆ Time is a shared family resource and responsibility.

▶ Together with your spouse make your respective Oxygen Lists, what you each need each week to maintain your energy, and try to make them happen for each other.

▶ Use the following table to talk to your spouse about how you currently invest your combined family time, 336 hours a week, and how you want to invest it. You may want to break out free time into more detail. [68]

WEEKLY ACTIVITIES	AVERAGE MOTHER (WEEKLY HOURS)	AVERAGE FATHER (WEEKLY HOURS)	YOUR CURRENT WEEK (MOTHER)	FATHER'S CURRENT WEEK	YOUR FAMILY'S GOALS	
					MOTHER	FATHER
Sleep	60	57				
Employment	21	39.5				
Commute	1.5	3				
Meals	7	7.5				
Primary child-care (feed, clothe, play, transport)	14	7				
Housework	18	10				
Shopping/ services	7	5				
Grooming	8.5	7				
Free time (exercise, TV, friends, leisure)	31	32				
Child-free free time	~ 7	~10.5				
	168	168	168	168	168	168

- ◆ What would the ideal allocation of your family time be? How does that ideal affect employment, family work, and money? What changes to employment, family work, or money might get you closer to your ideal in the short-term or in the long-term?
- ◆ Do you agree on how much focused parent time and hanging out parent time your children need each week? Does your division of that parent

time between you work for both of you and your children?

◆ Do you each have the child-free time you feel you need each week?

◆ Is one of you considering a major increase in employed hours? How will you find the time in your family week for those hours?

10

that sinking feeling

or why do i feel financially vulnerable?

AFTER TEN YEARS of financial independence, Kate arrived and overnight I became completely financially dependent on David. On the surface, nothing about our marriage had changed, but below the surface everything had changed. Before Kate, we had been two independent, self-sufficient people choosing to be together. During that time I knew, somewhere in the back of my head, that I could walk away and stand on my own two feet if I had to do it. Once Kate arrived, I felt a nagging anxiety in my stomach. Walking away wasn't an option anymore. I couldn't imagine putting Kate through that and I had no paycheck. I did my best to set aside my worry because I felt guilty and embarrassed the thoughts even crossed my mind.

Then when Kate was a few months old, I read Ann Critten-den's book *The Price of Motherhood*. In addition to jump-starting my obsession with Social Security, the book's chapter about what happens to mothers in a divorce shook me to the core and turned a nagging worry into full-fledged panic. I fumbled around trying to talk to David and suggested, "Maybe, um, I don't know, I was thinking perhaps we could consider a post-nuptial agreement?" He hit the roof. To him, I was implying that he was going to walk out and that I was planning for a divorce. I backed off, fast. But I was still scared, and I didn't really know why, or what to do about it, or how to talk about it. I hadn't dreamed money and who made it could create this kind of turmoil in our marriage. I hadn't dreamed I'd ever be financially dependent on anyone. Not having my own income and, honestly, not having the power that goes with it, made me fearful. Knowing I was fearful made David angry. Fear and anger, not good emotions to insert into a marriage of two sleep-deprived people.

I'm not the only mother who finds that "money and who makes it" messes with a marriage. In hushed tones in a kitchen at a party, a friend admitted that one of the reasons she kept working for pay when her son was born was that she didn't want to hand all the power over to her husband. MaryAnne said that one of her biggest shocks about becoming a mother was, "How much I hate being economically dependent upon my husband. It has really shifted (in my mind—and I guess that's what counts) the power in our relationship. . . . My husband knows that I hate being dependent upon him, and I can't ever make him feel like the money he brings in is 'our' money and not 'his' money." In a Mothers & More member survey, employed or not, mothers ranked as a top worry "Financial dependency on spouse" beaten out only by worries about having enough time.[1] The power shift that comes with a feeling of dependency is often unexpected and collides with our sense of ourselves as independent women. Katie said, "I also feel like I am 'mooching' off of him frequently since he makes the majority of the money. . . . I feel kind of odd depending on him to pay for so many things . . . while at the same time wanting to be a strong independent woman." I thought of myself as a strong independent woman too, so how did I get to this place where I felt so vulnerable? Was this really just all in my own head?

PIN MONEY FOR PIANO LESSONS

I started to notice patterns in the way I and other mothers talked about money. For example, many mothers talk about how their paychecks barely paid for childcare. "I don't want to spend my paychecks just on daycare!" said one.[2] Many mothers talked about their incomes as paying for extras such as piano lessons and vacations. Like Gin, who told me, "I like my job . . . and I am making the extra money we need to keep the kids in swim lessons and Kung Fu." As Frances explains, "My income most definitely pays for the extras. We can pay the basic bills on my husband's paycheck, but we use my paycheck for vacations, gymnastics, toys, etc." She adds, "I have heard other mothers say many times that their paycheck is just extra income. I think this is because in many households the husband is still considered the primary breadwinner, and the income that the wife brings in isn't really a necessity." In fact, the reality today is that for most families, mother's income is a necessity, yet our assumption tends to be an outdated one that:

- Mothers are financially dependent on fathers; mothers' earnings are pin money, just extra.

You might reasonably ask, what is pin money? The term goes back to Henry VIII. One of his wives who was eventually beheaded, Catherine Howard, had a fondness for pins from France. Of course, this meant that most ladies soon shared that fondness for French pins. Pins were quite expensive at the time, so husbands gave a bit of money to their wives for pins. Eventually pins became much cheaper, but the term *pin money* continued to be used to describe money husbands gave to their wives to pay for luxuries and extras.[3]

Come on now. Henry VIII? Why would the idea of pin money still be around today? Well, during the nineteenth and twentieth centuries this assumption contributed to the birth of the family wage concept. Everyone assumed that the ideal was for mother not to work for pay. Economists and union workers argued that "men should be guaranteed a wage sufficient to support their wives and children, a so called 'family wage.'"[4] For union activists a family wage was an argument for increasing pitifully low wages.[5] In a time of high unemployment, a family wage reflected a belief that jobs should go to those most in need, married men with families. For both men and women reformers, giving men a family wage was a way to address family poverty by ensuring that women and children would be cared for as dependents of a man earning enough money to support them.[6] For companies, the family wage was a strategy for creating a stable workforce and heading off union demands.[7] In other words, many well-intentioned and intelligent people promoted the goal of providing a family wage to men, which meant mothers' earnings were just extra—or pin money.

However, having the family wage concept entrenched in the fabric of society over a hundred years caused problems for women. For example, at the turn of the century, Henry Ford did not hire married women unless their husbands were "unable to work," and women were fired if it was discovered that their husbands were working.[8] Not so long ago, public school districts required women teachers to resign upon marriage[9] and had two pay scales, a higher one for men and a lower one for women.[10] Elizabeth Warren, a professor and co-author of *The Two-Income Trap*, worked in a school district then. She said at the time no one questioned the different pay scales because everyone believed "men needed the higher wages to support a family at home."[11] The family wage concept also led to arguments for higher minimum wage levels for men than for women because at some point the man would have a dependent family, even if he didn't at the time.[12] While paying men and women differently for the same work has since been prohibited, the assumptions about pin money and a family wage are still around. In a recent pay equity class action suit brought by women working at Wal-Mart, a woman reported that when she applied for a raise, her manager said, "Men are here to make a career, and women aren't. Retail is for housewives who just need to earn extra money."[13] As distant as Henry VIII and pin money may seem on the surface, these mental maps about money, employment, mothers, and fathers were embedded in major public policies and practices designed long ago and are still with us today.

CAN I MAKE ENOUGH TO PAY FOR CHILDCARE?

After Kate was born, David and I sat down together the way we normally do when we have big financial decisions to make together. He had just started his second year at a law firm and I had just been laid off from my part-time job. The question was whether I should look for a new job or not. Estimating the income we thought I could make in a job with reasonable hours, we subtracted taxes, childcare, and work expenses. There wasn't much left. Working for pay didn't pay much. So we decided I wouldn't, because we could afford for me not to.

Several months later, after my sister Sarah had her first child, she found part-time work as a nurse in an assisted living facility. She told me she was pretty sure she wasn't making much at all after her salary paid for childcare, but they couldn't afford for her *not* to work. While it seemed like Sarah and I were making rational financial decisions, I felt uneasy. I found myself wondering, why do we both assume *our* income alone has to pay for childcare? Why are we both asking ourselves, "Can I make enough to pay for childcare?"

Even mothers have a mental map that *mothers are responsible for and are naturally better at children and family*. If mothers aren't taking care of the kids ourselves at any given moment, we usually assume that we are the ones responsible for finding and paying for someone else to care for them. If mothers also assume *mothers' earnings are pin money, just extra,* then we also feel like it's only okay to be employed if we *have* to be. Our mental maps about money encourage us to think that if a mother's income is only for extras, why would she be employed instead of caring for family? As a result, mothers—and the people around us—think of childcare as our responsibility and as one of those extras our income covers. As one mother explained to me, "I've always had to look at the bottom line to see how much my expenses would be, such as childcare, to see if it is worth my time to work.

It's always been assumed that my paycheck would pay for childcare because in my household if I wasn't working I would be at home with my child. Eliminating the need for childcare."

Now, I don't mean to imply that mothers are deluding themselves into this train of thought. Mothers are engaging in quite sophisticated economic analysis given the way jobs are structured. Couples, faced with needing at least one of the one-size-fits-all jobs for the money and benefits, but finding that two of those jobs often don't leave room for caring for family, often decide to prioritize his job. Once that decision is made, he's likely making more money. His income is primary and hers considered extra even if it is a necessity. Once that happens, it makes economic sense for her to ask herself, "Can I make enough to afford childcare and then some or should I care for family myself?" The answer any mother gives depends on a lot of things, including the cost of quality care, the number of children, her own earning potential, the family finances, the degree to which she feels it is important to care for her children herself, and . . . tax policy. Huh? Tax policy? Yup, tax policy.

MY OBSESSION WITH INCOME TAX POLICY

Just as I didn't expect to become obsessed with Social Security when I had a child, I never expected to become obsessed with income tax policy. Then I read *Taxing Women* by Ed McCaffery. McCaffery is a professor in my backyard, at Caltech and USC Law School. Not long after I read his book, I found myself, a mother of a preschooler, along with my friend Kim, another mother of a preschooler, sitting like college groupies at a café table with him. We quizzed him about tax policy and its effects on women and mothers. I showed him my dog-eared, highlighted copy of his book, and he said his own students' copies of the book never looked as well-read as mine did. See? Obsession.

Like Social Security had done a few years earlier, income tax policy presented me with an opportunity to exercise my brain and understand how assumptions about mothers and fathers and money have been embedded in the walls of our collective house and have become invisible. David and I had assumed that when it came to paying taxes, money was money regardless of who earned it. From up on the balcony, though, I discovered that who earns the money matters a lot. The one who earns less, usually the woman, will be taxed more, which acts as a powerful but unseen disincentive for her to be employed.

As it turns out, that is exactly how the policy was expected to work. Before World War II, the United States used an income tax system of separate filing for married couples in which tax rates applied to each spouse's income separately.* When the war ended and the costs of war went away, Congress saw an opportunity to reduce taxes, and they did so by eliminating separate filing and replacing it with mandatory joint filing for couples. At the time, Congress also had an interest in wanting families to return to normal, in other words, wanting mothers who had entered the workforce during the war to go back home. Joint filing had the added bonus of encouraging them to do just that. [14] As the legislative counsel of the treasury at the time remarked, "Wives need not continue to master the details of . . . business, but may turn . . . to the pursuit of homemaking."[15] The move to joint income tax filing distributed a postwar bonus to married men with nonemployed wives by lowering taxes on families with only one earner. At the same time, joint filing discouraged married women from employment by taxing their incomes more without explicitly saying, "Now we're taxing women more." Joint filing introduced what McCaffery calls the "secondary earner bias,"[16] which I can illustrate for you because the system has the same effect today as it did back then. The secondary earner bias is yet another way outdated assumptions about mothers and fathers affect our decisions today and lead mothers to ask themselves, "Can I make enough to pay for childcare?"

---

* This is not to be confused with today's "married, filing separately" category, which is used in rare circumstances, such as when one spouse wants to avoid the tax problems of the other.

Married couples filing jointly are required to combine their incomes, no matter who earns what. However, the money doesn't go into a common pool that is all taxed at the same rate. As my friend Kim explained in an article she wrote for Mothers & More,

Our federal income tax system uses *progressive marginal rates*. This basically means that as you earn more, you are taxed at higher rates. Imagine each dollar that your family earns in a stack, one on top of the other. Next, see a slice of a large layered cake next to the stack of dollar bills. Each layer of the cake has a corresponding tax rate that increases as you go up each layer. For example, the bottom layer might be 0 percent, the next layer 10 percent, the next 20 percent, and so on. When you calculate your taxes, the first part of your stack of bills ($1 to $10,000) gets taxed at 0 percent, the next part ($10,001 to $20,000) gets taxed at 10 percent, the next part ($20,001 to $40,000) gets taxed at 20 percent and so on. You only incur the higher tax rate if your stack of bills reaches that layer. After the taxes on the various layers are tallied, the percentage of your income that actually goes to tax is called your *effective rate*.[17]

The goal of taxing the top layers more is for individuals who earn more to pay a higher percentage of their income in taxes compared to those who earn less.

For a couple, combining the incomes into one stack and then applying the different rates to each layer has another effect—the secondary earner bias. When David and I faced the question of whether I should find a job after we had Kate and I got laid off, the only jobs immediately available to us were the one-size-fits-all variety. Pushed to prioritize one of our careers, we chose David's because he was earning a lot more. We thought of his job and his income as primary. My income was secondary. We could decide whether it was needed or not or how much. We then asked ourselves, "Would we be better off if I add income on top of his and pay for childcare and other work expenses or if I'm not employed and care for our baby myself?"

We were effectively deciding that his salary comes first in the stack and trying to decide if it was worth it for me to earn money on top of that. So we did some basic math. We didn't think of childcare as coming out of David's income because we wouldn't need childcare unless I was employed. So we counted the cost of childcare against my potential income. Since David and I are a bit geeky, and David had learned about McCaffery's work back in law school, we also knew we were dealing with progressive marginal tax rates. Although many families may not know the details of the tax rates, most are at least familiar with the idea that making more money might push them "into a higher tax bracket." Since David and I thought of his income as primary, we also thought of it as first in the stack—where it would get taxed at lower rates. The very first dollar I earned would be in a layer on top of that where it would get taxed at a higher rate.

David's income
− lower tax rate
David's higher take-home pay

Kristin's income
− higher tax rate
− childcare
Kristin's lower take-home pay

HOW JOINT FILING WORKS

In joint filing, the income from each spouse is combined and then the stacked income is subject to progressive federal tax rates. In 2009 earnings on the first $16,700 were taxed 10 percent; earnings from $16,700 to $67,900 were taxed 15 percent; and earnings up to $137,050 were taxed 25 percent.

So for example, if David earned $67,900, we would pay 10 percent on the first $16,700 and then 15 percent on the rest, for a total of $9,350. His effective tax rate would be about 14 percent.

If we consider me the secondary earner, the first dollar I might earn on top of that would be taxed at the next rate, 25 percent. If I earn $ 20,000, my effective tax rate would be 25 percent. We would pay $9,350 on David's first $67,900. We would pay another $5,000 of my $20,000.

In contrast, if I were not married or could file separately, my $20,000 would be taxed at 10 and then 15 percent, or just $2,270.

Now, that's just federal income tax. If we add an estimated 8 percent Social Security contribution and a 10 percent state tax, David would make 68 cents for every dollar earned. For me, adding those tax contributions plus an average annual cost of childcare of $6000, I would make **only 27 cents on the dollar**—not counting other work expenses like clothes and meals. That's an effective tax rate of 73%.

I wanted to be employed, but because we could live comfortably on David's salary alone and I would net so little from a job, we decided it wasn't worth it for me to be employed—at least in the short-term.

While nothing in the tax code requires couples to identify a primary and secondary earner, one-size-fits-all jobs and joint filing push families in that direction. Once couples go down the well-paved path that makes his job and income primary, and her income linked to childcare, mothers don't need a Ph.D. in economics or tax policy to understand the math well enough to respond with financially practical decisions. As Yvonne told me, "One reason I quit after getting pregnant (with my second) . . .

was the realization that 2x childcare/preschool would be most of my after-tax salary. I think I only would have netted a few hundred bucks a month." What mothers and families don't realize is that our income tax policy was designed decades ago to make the math work against mothers being employed. When federal income tax is combined with Social Security taxes and state taxes, secondary earners can pay more than 50 pecent and even up to 100 percent of their earnings to taxes.[18]

The secondary-earner bias influences mothers' decisions and options at all income levels, not just for those who can afford not to be employed. Mothers in middle-income families who have a harder time giving up even their small contribution as a second earner face an "all or nothing" decision about employment.[19] Sarah, a mother who e-mailed me, was employed thirty hours a week when her second child arrived. She calculated that, "After taxes, health insurance and day-care, I would have been clearing a dollar a day for a six-hour shift." She was trying to decide either to go back to full-time employment "in order to clear more than five dollars a week" or quit when her husband relocated and she had to quit. Working part-time just wasn't worth it. She had to decide all or nothing for it to be worthwhile. At even lower income levels, the wages of a second earner can put a couple over a threshold that means the loss of a tax break called the earned income tax credit. At these income levels—typically a household income of less than $40,000 a year—the secondary earner bias is even greater. If these parents work more, or if they aren't yet married and then get married, they see little gain and may even lose money.[20]

Husbands who are secondary earners face the same bias, but even today the majority of secondary earners—those making less than 40 percent of a couple's income—are women.[21] Mostly, joint filing shapes mothers' employment options and decisions in just the way it was intended over sixty years ago when the policy was written to discourage women from employment. Today, the invisible influence of this outdated policy nudges mothers in well-off families out of the workforce, and sets up middle-income mothers to decide between full-time jobs or nothing because part-time isn't worth it. Plus, in some cases, married mothers at the lowest income levels lose money if they are employed. Once public policies based on old mental maps about mothers and fathers, men and women, have been built into the walls of society, as McCaffery observes, "They seem to stay in place and shape our lives, generally unconsciously, forever."[22]

HERE COMES THAT SINKING FEELING:
Why Do I Feel So Financially Vulnerable?

So there I was, three months into motherhood, having made the decision the federal income tax policy wanted me to make. I decided not to be employed, at least for a while. Somehow it didn't matter that David and I still managed our money together and that as far as we were concerned, I still had as much control over our money as I had ever had. I couldn't shake the feeling that the money he earned was his, not mine. Not only had we fallen into assuming *mothers are financially dependent on fathers; mothers' earnings are pin money, just extra,* I also seemed to be assuming *he who earns it, owns it.*[23] Even so, I had no reason to doubt David's commitment to me and to our family, so why did I feel so vulnerable?

Because I was.

Our growing collection of mental maps sets mothers up for financial vulnerability. Elizabeth Warren and Amelia Warren Tyagi conclude from their research in *The Two-Income Trap* that "[h]aving a child is now the single best predictor that a woman will end up in financial collapse."[24] In *The Price of Motherhood,* Ann Crittenden concludes that "motherhood is the single biggest risk factor for poverty in old age."[25] Young or old, the financial vulnerability of mothers is real and affects our lives and our marriages whether we stay married or not.

THE WAGE GAP BETWEEN MOTHERS AND EVERYONE ELSE

I'd never really given much thought to the wage gap between men and women before I had Kate, mostly because the women I knew

usually made as much or more than their husbands. There's virtually no wage gap between childless young women and men who are
employed full-time.[26] In fact, there are a few industries where women
earn more on average.[27] I reasonably concluded that the wage gap
issue was a thing of the past.

What I hadn't counted on was becoming that square peg in a
round hole at work once I had a child. As we saw, mothers don't work
like everyone else, which means they don't earn like everyone else
either. Even mothers who continue to be employed full-time contort
themselves to continue to fit their jobs. Some switch companies to
find more flexible positions and in the process take a lower salary
and give up the seniority at a company needed for promotions and
pay increases. Some switch from more lucrative jobs to lower-paying
government or non-profit jobs with regular hours and more flexibility. Some mothers stay full-time at the same place but switch to jobs
that don't require overtime or travel or find that taking maternity
leaves puts them behind their colleagues. Some face family responsibilities discrimination at work, probably without even realizing it.
They may have been passed over for a promotion no one ever even
asked them about; maybe they were given a lower starting salary;
perhaps they were given less challenging work after they had children, making it harder to get promoted. Some mothers, like me,
switch to self-employment for the control over their schedules, but
that also typically comes with lower earnings, greater risk, and loss of
future promotions within a company. Even long before they had children, some mothers decided on a particular lower-paying career field
because they hoped it would give them the flexibility they may need
in the future. For all these reasons, even mothers who are employed
full-time earn less than their male counterparts earn, whether or not
the men are fathers.[28]

Now, that's just the wage gap for mothers employed full-time,
but mothers are more likely than others to work alternative schedule—earning less simply because they work fewer hours. Plus, as
we saw earlier, the need for a customized job and schedule means
mothers are likely to work in the lowest-paying jobs in the lowest-

paid industries. Mothers tend to adjust employment up and down over the years more than others do. As Joan Williams explains, "The typical wage gap data is useless, because it compares men working full-time and women working full-time. Women are far more likely than men to work part-time, and those who do suffer a huge 21 percent pay penalty. The classic gender gap statistic, by focusing only on women who work full-time, greatly exaggerates the extent of women's economic equality." In the process, that typical wage gap statistic hides exactly what I had missed. As the wage gap has dramatically closed between men and women who do not have children, the wage gap is actually widening between mothers and women without children.[29] Young women with no children now earn 90 percent of men's wages, while employed mothers earn just 73 percent or less.[30] The wage gap is now specifically a mothers' issue and less and less a women's issue.

On top of all that, mothers also spend more years out of the workforce than anyone else, usually to care for family.[31] While typical wage gap data give only a single snapshot in time, the financial impact of mothers' employment patterns becomes clear only when we look across the years. From that balcony view, the lifetime earnings of mothers are just 38 percent of the lifetime earnings of men.[32]

Whoa. Let's translate that into dollars. Let's pretend Father earns the median income for men of $43,255.[33] Over a forty-five year employment lifetime, he'd earn $1,946,475.[34] If Mother earns 38 percent of that over forty-five years, she'd earn $739,660. That's a gap of more than a million dollars. I have a sinking feeling in my stomach just writing those numbers down, especially because I know that when we talk about retirement it gets even scarier.

SOCIAL SECURITY AND TODAY'S MOTHER

One of the ways to understand why financing retirement is so tough for mothers is to understand Social Security. The way Social Security treats the relationship between women, men, and the control and

ownership of money has spilled over into our other retirement support systems as well. So let's begin with a bit of the history. Social
Security enshrined in policy and practices two mental maps about
money from the late 1930s.

- Mothers are financially dependent on fathers; mothers' earnings are pin money, just extra.
- He who earns it, owns it.

The Social Security Act was adopted in 1935 and then amended
further in 1939 based on recommendations from a Federal Advisory
Council. That council was charged with several tasks, one of which
was to figure out how to distribute a growing surplus of contributions that posed a risk to the economy.[35] As described by historian
Alice Kessler-Harris in *U.S. History as Women's History*, the council's
deliberations reveal the beliefs about men, women, and money that
guided their recommendations. For example, they wanted to discourage women from employment. One participant noted approvingly
that their proposal would "take away the urge [of married women] to
go back [to work]."[36] The council assumed women should depend on
men financially, but also that men couldn't take care of themselves.
One council participant argued for lower benefits for widows since a
single woman can live more cheaply than a single man because "she
is used to doing her own housework whereas the single man has to
go out to a restaurant."[37] Kessler-Harris summarizes this way: "The
document brilliantly conveys a set of messages about how people
should live. Women would be well advised to marry older men and
stay married. . . . Men could expect little benefit from sending their
wives out to work and women who earned wages would have to work
mighty hard to exceed the pensions offered them for being stay-at-
home wives."[38] Social Security encouraged men to work by linking
benefits to employment and providing greater benefits to men who
worked more years and earned more money. Designing the program
to fit men's employment patterns seemed logical because, at the time,
most men were employed and most married wives were not.

HOW SOCIAL SECURITY RETIREMENT BENEFITS WORK

Social Security today works largely the way it was designed in the 1930s. When you work and pay Social Security taxes on your earnings, you earn credits toward Social Security eligibility. In 2008, you received one credit for every $1,050 you earned, up to a maximum of four credits per year. You need forty credits to be eligible for retirement benefits based on your own employment record. For example, working full time for ten years would earn forty credits.

Once you earn forty credits, your monthly retirement benefit is calculated using your thirty-five highest earning years over your lifetime. These earnings numbers are tweaked and massaged by the Social Security Administration accountants to factor for various things, but the bottom line is that the higher your earnings and the more years you work, the higher your monthly retirement benefit. Of course, the reverse is also true—the lower your lifetime earnings and the fewer years you work, the lower your monthly retirement benefit. As we've seen, even when they are employed, mothers earn less for a variety of reasons. They also work fewer years. Although the gap is projected to narrow, women are expected to continue to work fewer years over their lifetimes. Men who retired in 2000 worked a median forty-four years. They would have no trouble posting earnings in the thirty-five years used by the Social Security Administration to calculate monthly retirement benefits. In fact, nine of their lowest-earning years will be dropped out, leaving only the highest earning years. On the other hand, mothers who retired in 2000 worked a median thirty-two years and will have three zero years averaged into their calculations.[39] Plus, they'll have to count all their lowest earning years like that first job after high school or college or the year they were out for three months on unpaid maternity leave. So while nearly as many women as men today earn the forty credits, because of the lower lifetime earnings and fewer years in the workforce, the benefits women earn are lower than men's.

HOW YEARS OUT OF WORKFORCE
IMPACT SOCIAL SECURITY

Even if two people have the same annual income, say $43,255, if one is out of the workforce for several years then that person will have a lower average lifetime earnings plugged into the Social Security calculations.

Average annual earnings $= \dfrac{35 \text{ years} \times \$43,255}{35} = \$43,255$

Average annual earnings $= \dfrac{32 \text{ years} \times \$43,255}{35} = \$39,547$

HISTORY OF THE SPOUSAL BENEFIT

When the advisory council amended the Social Security Act in 1939, they decided to give the growing surplus to men with dependent wives. They created a "supplementary allowance on behalf of an aged wife" equal to 50 percent of the man's benefit amount.[40] The motivation for wives' benefits was that "you are doing something real for the man who would enjoy the security of the additional income."[41] Wives' benefits weren't put in place because she had earned benefits by caring for family while her husband was employed or because as a citizen she simply deserved protection from poverty in old age. No, the assumption was that mothers would be financially dependent on their husbands during old age so he needed an additional benefit to support her. The proposal ultimately submitted to Congress literally used the terms "husband," "he" and "him" when referring to the person eligible for "Primary Insurance Benefits," and the terms "wife," "she" and "her" when referring to "Wife's Insurance Benefits." However, that didn't mean those benefits were really "hers" at all.[42] The check for the wife's retirement benefits was written and sent to her husband and not to her.[43]

The supplementary allowance for wives is one of the ways the council discouraged women from being employed. Married mothers who were employed—and their husbands—would get no additional benefit from the Social Security contributions employed women made out of their paychecks. Most would end up claiming the 50 percent spousal benefit anyway because that amount would be greater than their own benefit. In other words, if their husbands' incomes were identical, a mother who was employed and making Social Security contributions for thirty-five years and a mother who was never employed would receive identical benefit amounts if both claimed the spousal benefit. For women, more employment wouldn't translate to more benefits. The advisory council noted that this was a way to "control the cost of the system" because more and more women would be employed and contribute taxes, but rarely would they receive any greater benefit for being employed and contributing dollars to the system.[44] As historian Kessler- Harris explains, "The Advisory Council fully expected that married women would work occasionally and that their contributions . . . would both be absorbed by the system and help to sustain its financial health without necessarily yielding any direct benefit to the female contributor."[45] Given their assumption that women would spend most of their lives financially dependent on men, the council felt comfortable balancing Social Security's books on extra revenue from employed women.

Men weren't eligible for the supplementary allowance if their wives had earned benefits.[46] Widowers weren't eligible for widows' benefits. Not until a series of Supreme Court decisions in the late 1970s did Social Security become gender neutral—at least on the surface. This supplementary allowance is now referred to as a "spousal benefit," but despite the gender neutral label, in practice the spousal benefit has pretty much the same effects on men, women, and money as it did when it was designed as the "wife's benefit."

HOW THE SPOUSAL BENEFIT WORKS

At retirement age, you can choose to claim 100 percent of the benefits based on your own work record or 50 percent of the benefits your spouse has earned, whichever is greater. Even today, nearly six in ten women claim the spousal benefit, whether they were ever employed or not. Virtually no men claim the spousal benefit.[47] A third of the women at retirement age in 2006 had been employed enough to be eligible for retirement benefits, but received the same benefit (50 percent of their spouse's) as if they hadn't been employed at all.[48] Think Social Security is in financial trouble now? Imagine how much trouble it would be in if all those women hadn't moved into the workforce over the years and contributed taxes but then received the same benefits as if they hadn't. Will the number of women taking the spousal benefit go down over time as women earn more? Sure, but surprisingly slowly. Estimates are that even by 2060, four in ten women will still be receiving the spousal benefit because their own lifetime earnings will still be less than their spouse's.[49]

Even though spousal benefit checks no longer go to the husband, we haven't escaped the assumption that *he who earns it, owns it*. Social Security was designed assuming that the husband and wife would stay married and the two would use the 150 percent benefit to support them both during retirement. However, the higher-earner still controls more of the money. If the wife takes the spousal benefit and stays married, in old age her husband receives his check for 100 percent and she receives hers for 50 percent of that. Technically, he's in control of two thirds of that portion of the retirement funds.

If they divorce, the wife still gets just the 50 percent check and he gets his 100 percent check. So instead of each getting half of the total after a divorce, the lower earner is left with only a third of the total. To make matters worse, if they divorce the day before their tenth anniversary, she can't claim the spousal benefit at all.* Since the average length of a marriage today is eight years, this ten-year requirement can leave mothers high and dry.[50] A mother who divorces after nine years of cutting back or staying out of the workforce to care for the children and family of an employed spouse, will not be able to claim the 50 percent spousal benefit even though her unpaid work

---

* I pointed out to David that our tenth anniversary was extra-special for this reason, but he didn't think that was a very romantic way of looking at it.

made it possible for him to earn the money. The mental map embed-ded in the policy is that she hasn't earned that benefit, he has—so it stays with him. To add insult to injury, the Federal Social Security Act prohibits transfer of benefits, so the benefits cannot be divided upon divorce. (Though some state courts are moving toward allow-ing differences in Social Security benefits to be offset by other assets in a divorce.)[51]

Yet another way that Social Security reinforces that *mothers are financially dependent on fathers* and *he who earns it, owns it* is that the 50 percent spousal benefit disappears if she remarries, no matter the finances of the new spouse. The presumption is that the new husband will provide for her. The spousal benefits she could claim in the first marriage are not really considered hers. They were designed to give the husband a supplementary allowance to sup-port a dependent wife.

Of course, today the wife and husband in any of these scenarios could be in reverse roles, though couples where the wife earns a lot more money over her lifetime is still much less common.[52] Whoever earns more has more control of Social Security money during mar-riage and takes more away in a divorce. The one who pays the price is the lower earner, often the one who provides most of the care to the family. I've used the words *he* and *she* here on purpose because today the lower earner is still overwhelmingly women. As a result, in 2007, "the average annual Social Security income received by women 65 years and older was $10,685, compared to $14,055 for men."[53] The financial impact of the out-of-date and out-of-sync Social Security policies falls mostly on women, no matter how gender-neutral the language.

WHAT ABOUT RETIREMENT SAVINGS?

I wish I could tell you the picture is much rosier because there are so many additional ways people save for retirement these days. Social Security was never meant to be anyone's sole source of retirement income. It was supposed to be part of a three-legged stool: Social Security, pensions, and personal retirement savings. Unfortunately, mothers' employment patterns over their lifetimes affect both pensions and personal retirement savings, too. Plus, the mental maps built into Social Security spilled over into the way pensions and personal retirement savings have been structured.

Pensions are what are called "defined benefit" plans. In other words, once earned, your benefit stays the same no matter how long you live. Pensions are often awarded after a certain number of years of service. Mothers, however, are less likely to have the years at one employer that they need to qualify. More mothers work part-time and only one in four part-time workers are included in their employer's pension plan.[54] As I mentioned in Chapter 6, the federal law that governs employee benefits has thresholds that in effect prevent part-time workers from receiving pension benefits. Mothers are less likely to have pensions than other workers, and when they do the pensions are worth less.[55]

Pensions are increasingly rare for everyone these days because employers have been getting rid of them in favor of offering "defined contribution" plans that help people build personal retirement savings. Defined contribution plans are the acronyms most of us have heard of and hopefully have. They include 401(k), Individual retirement account (IRA), Roth IRA, and SEP accounts.* Defined contribution means you contribute a defined amount. Sometimes that amount is defined by you; sometimes your employer defines an amount they contribute. Your annual benefit amount depends on how much you save. If you run out before you die, well, you run out. The more you earn, the more you can save, and then the more you have to live on when you retire. However, even when women are eligible to participate in a 401(k) plan or IRA, fewer participate than men.[56] The effectiveness of retirement savings also depends on saving money early so that it can earn interest for years and years

---

* The 401(k) plans are employer-sponsored retirement savings accounts. SEP and Roth are specific types of individual retirement plans.

before you need it. So if you have lower earnings or no earnings earlier in your employed life—say because you are caring for two young
children—you lose the contributions you would have made. You
also lose the annual interest the contributions would have earned for
more than thirty years. As a result, the balance in women's retirement accounts is typically far lower then men's—in one large survey
women's accounts held an average of $56,320 while men averaged
over $100,000.[57]

Not long after I left the workforce, it dawned on me that my
retirement savings had come to a halt, while David's were growing even more rapidly. As one mother said, "My husband receives
retirement benefits directly out of his paycheck. We try to make
up the difference by putting additional savings in a Roth under
my name only, but it doesn't come close to the retirement benefits
in his name." David and I had always had an unspoken agreement that our retirement savings belonged to both of us. The
reality was that in the years right after Kate was born he had
much greater control than I did over what had become the bulk
of our money. That type of imbalance made Kaki uncomfortable,
too. "While I know it is 'our' retirement money, the reality is that
it is his name on the account and his paycheck that contributes to
it, and he is the one who allocates the investments. But we have
different investment strategies, and I would like some portion of
'our' retirement money to be 'mine' to allocate according to my
investment strategy."

When it comes to retirement accounts, the law generally follows a *he who earns it, owns it* rule with few exceptions. Federal
law does require my consent before David could name anyone but
me the beneficiary of his retirement savings if he dies, and vice
versa. He can't roll an employer plan like a 401(k) into an IRA
without my consent. After that, the laws get pretty inconsistent
across plans and across states. For example, David could take out a
loan against his plan without my permission. When he leaves his
employer, he can choose whether to get one lump sum or annual
payments without my consent. For an IRA, only community prop-

erty states* would make David get my permission before naming someone else the beneficiary. And even if we wanted to, David and I couldn't transfer retirement money between us to make it equal.[58] While David and I may think of our retirement savings as "ours," the laws that govern those savings assume simply that *he who earns it, owns it.*

THE TRIPLE PENALTY

So, now I have good news and bad news. Which do you want first? The good news? I thought so. The good news is that women live longer than men do.[59] The bad news? Because they live longer, women are more likely to run out of other retirement assets and depend solely on those lower Social Security benefits. Right now, without Social Security, more than half of all elderly women would live in poverty.[60] Chances are good that for many more decades women will still be relying on Social Security much more than men.

Let's use some numbers to illustrate. First, I must beg forgiveness from my own college economics professor and any other financial planning gurus out there. I'm simplifying to make a point and I'll confess to all those simplifications in the endnotes.[61] That said, let's pretend a father makes the median income, $43,255, for forty-five years until he's about sixty-five, and the mother makes 38 percent of those lifetime earnings—our wage gap. Then let's estimate the retirement savings with interest each would have after forty-five years of employment based on those earnings—our retirement savings gap. Then let's add the Social Security benefits each would start to receive at age sixty-seven for twenty years until they are eighty-seven—our Social Security gap. In the end, the total lifetime financial gap between the father and the mother is nearly $2 million, simply assuming the median income. Now, this is a simplified illustration; the point is that mothers pay a triple penalty for modifying their employment to care for their children and family.

---

* In 2008, there were nine community property states.

They earn less over their lifetime, and as a result they have less in private retirement savings and they get less from Social Security.

SAMPLE ILLUSTRATION OF THE TRIPLE WHAMMY

	45 YEARS OF EARNINGS	RETIREMENT SAVINGS AFTER 45 YEARS	20 YEARS OF SOCIAL SECURITY BENEFITS	TOTAL
His	$1,946,475	$1,263,903	$281,100	$3,355,225
Hers	$739,660	$480,283	$213,700	$1,381,868
			Life Time Gap	$1,973,357

Note: The totals for His and Hers are not simple addition since that would double count the portion of earnings put into retirement savings. For the totals I have included the saved amount only once.

THE THREE D'S:
Death, Disability, and Divorce

Let's see, we've dealt with taxes and old age. While we're at it, we might as well deal with death, disability, and divorce. The specter of the death or disability of a spouse is a nightmare by itself, but one made even more frightening on the financial front for someone who depends on a spouse's earnings to support the family. This is true whether both spouses are employed or not. Often, the family depends on both incomes to pay all the bills. Losing either one would put the family on the financial edge.

Motivated by the need to protect our children, many families who can afford to do it make contingency plans for death and disability. After Kate was born, some of our first financial steps were to increase David's life insurance, add life insurance for me, and sign David up for his employer's long-term disability insurance. We had health insurance through David's employer so if one of us got seriously ill or injured, the medical bills wouldn't sink us. We also met with an estate attorney and created a will and a family trust. If something happened to David, Kate and I were covered. If something happened to both David and I, Kate would still get the care and support she needed.

HISTORY OF SOCIAL SECURITY DISABILITY INSURANCE

In the mid to late 1950s the Social Security Act was amended again to include disability benefits both for workers and their dependents. Like the retirement benefits, disability benefits were based on earnings history.

While nine in ten families with children have some life insurance, over half say they don't have enough life insurance. Experts agree and estimate that most families need twice as much life insurance as the average family currently has in order to meet the industry recommended coverage. Nearly half of families say they could only survive a few months if the primary earner dies.[62] Disability insurance is even less common. Six in ten employed people do not have short-term disability coverage and seven in ten don't have long-term coverage. Yet, at the age most of us have children, we are far more likely to become disabled than to die before retirement.[63] It is not surprising that disability and medical bills are some of the most common reasons families find themselves in a financial tailspin. In their book *The Two-Income Trap*, co-authors Elizabeth Warren and Amelia Tyagi Warren estimate that if all families had access to disability insurance, it could "help as many as 300,000 families avoid bankruptcy courts *every year*—and hundreds of thousands more who are on the brink of collapse."[64]

HOW SOCIAL SECURITY DISABILITY INSURANCE WORKS

Most workers need 20 credits—5 years of full employment—earned in the 10 years immediately before they become disabled to be eligible for Social Security's disability benefits. Mothers are less likely to have the necessary credits in the required timeframe so they are less likely to be eligible for Social Security disability benefits. Even if they are covered, their lower earnings mean their disability benefit is lower.

David and I were lucky to live in one of only five states that provide short-term disability insurance to workers.[65] However, we knew the benefits weren't enough so we purchased more for him. What was frustrating is that when I wasn't employed, I wasn't eligible for either the state disability insurance or private disability insurance. You have to have earnings to be eligible. Yet we knew that if I became disabled, we'd need to pay to replace the care I was providing. One of my imperfect solutions to this risk was to make sure I earned enough to remain eligible for disability benefits through Social Security. This was an imperfect solution because Social Security disability benefits take five months to kick in and are only available for disabilities that will last a year or more. Plus, the majority of claims are initially turned down and the benefits are very low. Still, I figured it was better than nothing. Later on, when I was self-employed, getting my own private disability insurance was expensive and difficult; I had to prove at least two years' worth of consistent earnings.

In other words, David and I had just about everything going for us. His employer provided some life and disability insurance and we could afford to purchase more. We had access to the financial advice we needed to sort through it all. We could afford to purchase life and disability insurance for me. We had access to health insurance first through his employer, and then later we were able to get and afford an individual health insurance policy. We were willing to talk about and plan for the unpleasant risks of death and disability. Still, the process of managing all this risk was complex, time-consuming, and expensive. In their rushed lives, families—and especially mothers—often just don't get around to learning about and planning for these risks and often can't afford to anyway.

The Third D: Divorce

It is interesting that most mothers I talk to find it easier emotionally to plan for a spouse's death or disability than to think about the risk of divorce. In a Mothers & More member survey, mothers said disability and death of a spouse were high on their worry list. Divorce was near the bottom even though divorce is more likely.[66] Death and disability are external events that are out of our control. Worrying about the risk of divorce means having to contemplate that one half of our partnership might do something that would lead to such a disaster. Worrying about the pain of a potential divorce is directly at odds with our desire to unconditionally believe in our partners and in our marriages. Our mind helps us avoid this conflict by convincing us that it won't happen to *us* so we don't have to think about it. As if to prove the point, this particular section of the book was very difficult for me to write. Writing about the risk of divorce meant returning to that time just after Kate was born when I was scared and angry and felt more powerless than I ever had before. My mind did not want me to go there.

Before we had Kate, I had it in my head that by the year 2000 divorce law must have evolved enough to match how couples like David and I thought about our money as *our* money. Community property must be the law of the land. Besides, I was well-educated and could get good jobs if the worst ever happened. David and I had many unspoken agreements between us about money; agreements like "No matter who earns it, we share our income," and "We'll share our retirement money," and later on, "I'll earn less for awhile to care for the family so you can earn more which means we're both better off now and later." Given all that, divorce was not something I worried about.

Then, in that first year of Kate's life, when I had no paycheck, I read both *The Price of Motherhood* and *Unbending Gender* and began to understand that things had not evolved as I had expected. Reading the sections on divorce in both books was like reading Stephen King horror novels, each page sending another stabbing pain through my chest.

- "Just because a wife is entitled to a *share* of the marital assets, doesn't mean she is entitled to *half*."[67]
- "A breadwinner's income is legally his alone, and he can do whatever he wants to with it: share it, spend it on himself, or stash it away in a secret bank account."[68]
- "[N]early 40% of divorced mothers end up in poverty."[69]

- "[M]en's standard of living increases while women's and children's declines sharply upon divorce."[70]
- "[N]o law . . . requires an equal standard of living for all members of postdivorce households."[71]
- "80% of women assume they will be able to get alimony if they need it, but only 8% are awarded alimony today."[72]
- "The overwhelming impression one gets from review-ing judicial decisions on spousal support is their striking arbitrariness."[73]

It seemed that those unspoken agreements David and I, and many married parents make about money meant nothing in a divorce. I learned that community property was the law in just nine states. Crittenden also told stories about mothers who sounded a lot like me that revealed that even my good education and professional career wouldn't help much in a divorce. While my time out of the workforce to care for family was derailing my earning potential and increasing David's, my previous jobs would mean I didn't "need" financial support from my spouse after a divorce. If I didn't need a portion of his income, I wouldn't get it because it wasn't mine or even ours, it was his.[74] As my friend Joy, who went through a divorce, explained, "Even if you've been careful and all assets are in both names, you have no access to your partner's paycheck unless the person gives it to you. Even before a divorce is final, if he leaves, he has the paycheck."

Divorce laws historically stem from a time when the money was his property and the wife was literally his property as well.[75] The outdated mental maps that *he who earns it, owns it* and *mothers are financially dependent on fathers* and even that *caring for family isn't work, it's just what mothers do* are all fixtures in divorce law. Divorce turned out to be yet another place where outdated mental maps have been invisibly embedded in the way things work. Whether or not I ever experienced a divorce, the laws were so out of sync with how David and I thought about our marriage and our money that when I wasn't earning any money the risk hung over my head anyway.

My worried mind couldn't help playing out the full unpleasant scenario. I might spend five, ten, even twenty years modifying my employment to care for family—sacrificing income, retirement savings, and earning potential. I would do this on the unspoken agreement that David could then earn more, and who made the money wouldn't matter because we would treat it as our money. We'll use it to support Kate and our family now and support both of us in the future when she is grown.

Then, what if the worst happened and we ended up in a divorce? That agreement we had would go out the window. Instead, the judge would assume that the income and property are David's because he earned them. The law says the judge is supposed to take into account contributions of spouses, including unpaid family work. However, there's no direction given about the weight to give that family work, and what if the judge's subconscious assumption that *caring isn't really work, it's just what mothers do* guides him? Loathe to attach a financial value to a mother's love and care, my family work that allowed David to earn his income is given little weight.[76]

So the judge would then go to divide the assets and property acquired during our marriage. His guidelines are to be equitable, not to be confused with fifty-fifty.[77] Only in community property states would the court assume property like retirement and savings accounts should be divided in half unless someone proves otherwise.[78] In fact, the more assets David and I have, the more likely it would be that I would get only a small fraction.[79]

Now most families don't have much money to divide up when they divorce.[80] The big question is how to divide the future income going forward after the divorce. Future income isn't covered under community property, even though in the large majority of families the ability to earn income is the primary if not the only asset.[81] So the judge assumes the future income belongs to David, the one who earns it or at least earns most of it. The judge might award me spousal support based on what I "need" to get by, even if David is left with far more. Spousal support is something the earner gives, not something the spouse in question has earned the right to share. If I had custody of Kate, the judge awards child support based on what is "enough," whatever he thinks that means.

In my worried scenario, divorce would stink for both David and me. Our one household would be divided into two households; two households cost more to maintain so both of us are going to have less money than we did before. If I have primary custody of Kate, my household supports two people, and I'm still going to have trouble keeping good jobs because I'm still doing most of the family work. Yet, the judge would have left David with more assets and more income for his household of one, than for mine with two. Williams explains that "the cause of women's impoverishment upon divorce is not the level of child support payments, but a double application of the ideal worker norm: women first are marginalized at work because of their inability to perform as ideal workers, and then upon divorce are cut off from the ideal worker wage they helped create."[82]

If I were lucky, I would have a receptive judge and a good lawyer who argued that I could never have the standard of living that David will have given the way we had agreed to divide employment and family. So my spousal support would be greater and last longer. Unless I increase my employment and earnings, because then I wouldn't need the support anymore and the judge may reduce the support.

Shocked and scared by the realistic scenario I'd spun, I decided I needed to talk to David. I didn't want to bring up divorce, and if the laws hadn't been so completely at odds with how we thought about our marriage and our money I wouldn't have brought it up at all. I fumbled around and asked David for a postnuptial agreement. My argument to him was that we have a contingency plan if either of us dies by having life insurance. We have contingency plans if either of us is disabled by having disability insurance. We hope we never have to use those plans either. Would it be so crazy to have a contingency plan for divorce, which statistically is much more likely?

Turned out, David felt quite strongly that it was crazy. We couldn't have a calm conversation about it. The emotions for both of us were just too raw. From his perspective, I was questioning his commitment to me and his commitment to the agreements we had as a couple.

I really wasn't, but I knew those unspoken commitments weren't worth much in a court of law. So I found myself stuck between two lousy options. I could do something else to protect myself and risk that David might see it as evidence that I didn't trust him. Or I could do nothing and risk feeling like a sucker later on if anything happened. Emotionally, doing nothing is easier.

When I asked my friend Joy about this dilemma after her divorce, she agreed that when you are married, it is hard to have the state of mind to consider the risks and do something about them. When you are married, she said, "You need to believe in the partnership. It's really hard when you're comfortable to maintain enough awareness of the risk to do something to protect yourself if something happens." Yet mothers who've been through divorce advise others to *always* have their own money. I didn't want to feel I had to protect myself, but I didn't want to feel like a sucker either. Over the years, I've taken several steps to have my own money, each accompanied by a measure of guilt. I have always kept a credit card in my own name. Maintaining my own financial footing is one of many reasons I am employed. Being self-employed made it logical to establish bank accounts in my own name. Taking actions like these are tough on our psyche though. One mother was putting away cash in a hiding place at home. A friend of mine suggested that she at least put it in a safe deposit box. "No," her friend responded, because she felt that would mean admitting to herself that she was actually doing it.

No mother wants to go down the mental path of what a divorce would mean. Yet many mothers feel they have to hold on to that little bit of fear and doubt because divorce laws are so different than our unspoken agreements in our marriages. Even for those who will never experience a divorce and don't worry about it, the laws serve as an illustration of the way financial inequality in a marriage has been embedded in the way things work. Even in a solid marriage, divorce law combined with the lifetime earnings gap between mothers and fathers can create both a real and perceived imbalance of money and that can then introduce a new and unsettling imbalance of power.

MONEY, MARRIAGE, AND POWER

Most people who know me well would find it hard to believe I ever had trouble asking David for anything. The honest and embarrassing truth is I was shocked to find how much more reluctant I was to ask for time, or money, or for him to do more of the family work when I wasn't making any money myself. David never did anything to flex that power. He wasn't telling me not to spend money or what I could and couldn't do. Quite the contrary, he was the one encouraging me to take time for myself and to explore my job options. He was quick to say how important the family work was that I was shouldering. In fact if you ask him, he didn't feel a shift in power much at all. It was in my own mind that the power imbalance was real, and for good reason because our only paycheck had his name on it. That paycheck went into our joint account like it always had, but legally he could stop sharing that money with me anytime. In my mind, *he who earns it, owns it* also activated another unwritten rule, *he who has the gold, makes the rules.*

I didn't expect any of this because before we had Kate there were times I made more money and times he made more money and I didn't feel any power shifts then. At that point, the *he who earns it, owns it* assumption didn't phase us. In theory both of us could have walked away from the marriage as independent, self-sufficient people and that put us pretty much on equal footing. It was having Kate that introduced a new kind of interdependence that triggered different power dynamics within our marriage. Once we had Kate it would be tragic if either of us walked away because this lovely little girl was depending on both of us to care for her. However, because David had the paycheck, he could walk away much more easily—practically speaking. I didn't think he *would* walk away. It didn't matter, we weren't on equal footing anymore, and I felt it at a subconscious level and that changed my own behavior.

Sometimes it's hard for mothers to articulate what has changed because on the surface they often control a lot of what goes on in the family. When I wasn't employed, I made plenty of our household decisions on my own and most big ones together with David. However, coordinating the family calendar or handling the day-to-day decisions about how we spent our money didn't feel like power. Managing the household bills wasn't the same as actually having equal ownership of those financial resources. Doing all that family work and making those decisions didn't translate into the power to ask for or simply take the time I needed for myself, or to ask for a different division of the family work at home. In fact, what I really wanted was *less* daily decision making on my plate and for David to take some on his. The image of the clueless father who defers to his organized wife on all things family related can make it hard to recognize or describe the deeper power issues underneath.

Elizabeth Gregory, professor and author of *Ready: Why Women Are Embracing the New Later Motherhood,* said in an online discussion that in her interviews with mothers, she found that because mothers are typically much more financially vulnerable in a divorce that "there is a big threat hanging over women with kids that can have a subtle but large effect in day to day relations." One of the effects can be a reluctance to speak up or ask for what we need or want. As Sherri described, "I say very little about how he spends money, however he lets me know when I spend too much. I probably would have said more in the past, but don't feel I have as much of a right to do so anymore." In other words, the problem is not just that he says she spends too much, it's also that she feels she doesn't have the right or the power to speak up and say otherwise. When Kaki told her husband she was uncomfortable that the retirement accounts were in his name and wanted to be able to have investment control of some of "their" money, her husband was open to putting money into accounts in her name. She then asked herself, "Why is it so hard to ask for something so fair? The rest of our accounts are divided fairly in terms of equal control over investments. It's just the retirement account (which is our largest asset) that feels off-limits to me. . . .but that's because of ME. . . . which is my point: Why do we voluntarily hold back on this stuff? . . . Like housework, this really boils down to discussions between spouses. But how do we give ourselves a collective spine on stuff like this?" It's hard to ask and we hold ourselves back because if we make less and we assume *he who earns it, owns it*, then we feel like we are more vulnerable—because we are, in fact, more vulnerable. So asking feels riskier, no matter how great our husbands are.

Another subtle effect of a power imbalance is who has more control over their own time and how the family time is allocated. When I wasn't employed, David would call to say he'd be late, and I'd tell him he had to come home because I had a volunteer meeting or other plans. His response was often that his job was paying the bills, so I'd just have to adjust. He wasn't trying to be mean or make a power play and I felt I couldn't argue with the logic, but the effect was that because he made more money and his job had priority he had more control over his time than I did over mine. As Sarah adds, "Because my husband earns much more than I do, it is assumed that his job takes precedence, so I am usually the one to pick up the slack with childcare and home management." Tanya agrees, saying, "He definitely gets more breaks than I do and now that I work less outside the home, he has more power since he makes more money." In other words, money buys time, and time is the most important resource any one of us has. As much as I loved him, when he was the only one of us with an income, David possessed the financial power to restrict what I could do with my time and our money. He didn't ever have to overtly use that power for me to feel that my ability to decide how to spend my time, what path to take in life, and how to fulfill my own potential was compromised. Of course, having children changes what both mothers and fathers want for ourselves and what is possible. The problem was that I felt I was sacrificing far more of the control over my own life than David had to give up over his.

Now if I were someone who had always wanted my life to focus on caring for my family, I might not have felt this change as a loss of control. Or if we had been a couple in which both of us kept earning somewhat similar amounts of money before and after children, this whole power dynamic might never have surfaced. If we had been a couple in which the mother earns more, the dynamic might have surfaced in the reverse. Further, not every couple who has unequal earnings feels that power issues insert themselves into the marriage. My story is simply one illustration, and the variations on it are infinite, so it would also be easy to dismiss me or any of the mothers I've talked to and tell us to just snap out of it. If we loved our husbands, we wouldn't be thinking about money and power at all. Yet all that would accomplish is to drive the issue back under the kitchen table. No matter how strong the marriage and even when couples stay happily married, our outdated policies and workplaces and our own mental maps mean that the lower-earner is in a weaker bargaining position at home and more financially vulnerable if the marriage doesn't last. How that plays out in any given couple will be different, but pretending it doesn't exist at all simply leaves mothers who experience it feeling alone and in the dark about what to do differently. As MaryAnne told me, "I won't hide behind the mask that there is no power structure in a truly loving relationship." It was incredibly hard for me to take off this mask and admit to myself that as a strong, independent woman who loved her husband, my financial dependence was a risk I couldn't ignore.

The lever that changed this dynamic in my marriage happened to be my return to employment. Other mothers have told me that power issues factor into their employment decisions. One mother said that her fear of financial dependence was causing so many issues in her relationship with her husband that she started a job search. Yet another mother, Maggie, admitted, "Actually, one of the reasons I work is because I am not comfortable relying on him for money. This is completely self-imposed, as he has never made me feel like I need to work. I don't feel equal when I'm not working, and I feel guilty when I am the one who spends most of the money (grocery store, Target, kids clothes, etc.) and he is the only one making it." My own return to employment was based on a variety of reasons, only one of which was the financial risk I felt, but returning to employment proved further to me the link between money and power. As dramatically as the power had shifted when I stopped earning money, it shifted again when we were equal earners and again when I was the primary earner. When I felt on more equal footing financially, I felt more comfortable asking for time, for family work, for anything—even if it meant an argument—and ultimately our marriage got stronger.

My marriage was really unhappy when I wasn't employed, mostly because I was really unhappy and anxious and felt powerless to do much about it. I felt powerless both because David made the money and also because society made it so hard for us to have what we wanted—jobs for each of us that left time for family too. We are much happier and our marriage is much stronger when we're both employed. I wish our workplaces and public policies made it easier to achieve that. On the other hand, some couples who can afford it are much happier when one isn't employed or isn't employed much, and I wish our laws and policies didn't make it so financially risky for mothers—or fathers—to take that path.

Although the financial risks of dependence are very real today, I'm tired of people using that risk to insist that the easy answer is that all mothers ought to be employed and ought to be employed full-time in the highest paying job they can get. Using the risk of financial dependence to scold mothers about their employment decisions is insulting, ineffective, and irresponsible. Insulting because it implies mothers aren't aware of the risk, and in my experience, most are very aware. Ineffective because given how workplaces are structured, finding and keeping well-paid jobs for both spouses that leave time to care for family are tough, and in the end mothers and couples will make employment decisions based on what's best for their family and especially their children. Irresponsible because blaming mothers for their own financial risk or compromised employment opportunities ignores the layers of mental maps and vicious cycles all around us that push the most independent of women down the path of financial dependence and risk. Caring for family is valuable and important work to families and to everyone. It's not the fault of mothers and fathers today that doing that work is financially risky. What mothers—and fathers—can do is understand the context well enough to make more informed decisions about employment and managing money. We need to entirely remodel our own assumptions about my money, his money, and our money. And then get to work on remodeling everyone else's too.

WHAT IF?:
Rethinking My Money, His Money, and Our Money

Enough of the doom and gloom, time to get to the imagination and action part. So what if, in addition to this new belief about employment:

- Mothers and fathers share the responsibility for and are equally capable of employment and contributing to the family's financial security

we also adopted this new belief about money?

- Family income and wealth are the result of joint work—both family work and employment—so they are owned jointly by both spouses.

I still remember the day I really made the shift to that remodeled belief. I was at a Mothers & More conference in Chicago about the time Kate turned one. It was the first time I met Joan Williams, author of *Unbending Gender*, in person. She gave a keynote address to a room full of mothers. She used an example that could have been my story at the time. "He works full time; today, he's often working lots of overtime. If he's a parent, who makes it possible for him to do that? Who makes sure he has clean shirts? Who makes sure his kids aren't poor little rich kids whose parents never come to a school event? Who makes the play dates, takes the kids to soccer, makes the dinner, perhaps gives parties that help his career? Who takes his mother to the doctor's if she gets ill? The answer is obvious: his wife. Her work is the only reason he can continue to perform as an ideal worker, and at the same time have a family life that lives up to our sense that children need and deserve time with their parents. The only reason he can continue to perform as an ideal worker is because he is supported by a flow of family work by his wife. What we call 'his' wage is really a family wage.* It reflects not only his paid work but her unpaid work."[83]

---

* Williams is using the term *family wage* here differently from how it has been used historically. Here she uses it to describe joint family income as something produced by both paid work and unpaid family work.

Whether we were employed or not, we sat in stunned silence as Williams drove it home by telling us that men married to housewives make up to 30 percent more money than unmarried men or men married to employed wives. For many of us in the room, that was when it dawned on us that in a marriage, the family's financial well-being was just as dependent on the unpaid family work as it was on the work that produced a paycheck. I could see how the interdependence played out in various other scenarios. When one spouse is working a reduced schedule or has a less-demanding job and covers most of the family work, the other spouse can work a full-time job, and they can save money on how much the family needs to pay for childcare and other support. When both parents are employed, they might share the family work that makes it possible for both of them to be employed—maybe by a grueling schedule of working different shifts or by getting other family members to pitch in. No matter how we decide or end up sharing the employment and the family work, the family income is the result of joint effort. Williams was offering us a new way of thinking about our marriages and our money. "An asset produced by two people should be jointly owned by them."[84]

In Chapter 5, we talked about how to value family work by looking at what it would cost to replace that work. Williams offered us that day yet another way of thinking about the value of family work, especially within the context of a marriage. In an e-mail conversation, she explained that one problem with using the cost of hiring someone else to do the family work to calculate the value of the work "is that the wages we pay for child care, housekeeping, etc. are so depressed that we end up underselling ourselves." Williams instead encourages us to move toward a "discussion of who creates the ideal-worker wage. If a wife at home has helped create a $100,000 wage, why do we care how much it costs to replace her services? She should own half the wage— or more: in the event of divorce, she should own enough so that the incomes of the two post-divorce households are equalized."

How would shifting to this belief in jointly owned income change our lives? Take this example. Over lunch, a friend who teaches a few exercise classes a week told me she wanted to pursue a license that would help her professionally. She sighed and explained that given her husband's work schedule and toddler at home she didn't have the time, and she didn't make enough money to justify paying for another day of childcare. She was assuming, encouraged by the world around her, that any childcare had to come out of her income and that her husband's income was his and his alone. So she didn't have any right to spend it on childcare to support an investment in her career.

What if instead she and her husband both believed that *family income and wealth are the result of joint work—both family work and employment—so they are owned jointly by both spouses?* What if they believed that childcare was a family expense not hers alone? What if they believed her family work made it possible for him to earn his paycheck so the total income was a shared resource? Then she would feel that she could use their money for additional childcare to pursue her ambitions. Together, she and her husband would evaluate the cost of the license as an investment in her future and their future. The framework for making her decision would be completely different.

WHAT WOULD WE SAY AND DO IF FAMILY MONEY IS JOINTLY OWNED?

If we believed *family income and wealth are the result of joint work—both family work and employment—so they are owned jointly by both spouses,* mothers would probably avoid saying our income pays for extras or for childcare. That shift to talking and thinking about "our money" can be tougher than it seems because the outdated mental maps are so embedded that it is often logical for us to ask, "Can *I* make enough to pay for childcare?" However, we can experiment with language like, "Does it make financial sense for *us* to pay for childcare or for one of us to care for the kids? In the short-term? In the long-term?" As Amy explains, "In my family, paying for childcare is a family responsibility. So I have never felt the burden of needing enough income to afford it." Thinking and talking this way is often easier when both spouses are employed. Rachel said, "I do have friends who are in careers where it is full time and they don't view their income as paying for the extras. It's part of their whole package—hubby works and wife works and together they bring in the money to pay for the bills." No matter who's earning what, instead of talking about the lower earner's income as paying for extras, we can talk about both spouses' income contributing to the family pot.

The outdated assumptions are so embedded in the world we live in, that it's hard to imagine what an individual couple can do to live their lives more in tune with the belief that *family income and wealth are owned jointly by both spouses*. Half the battle for me and David was knowing what we believed. Then we could experiment with doing things differently. When I wasn't employed and we decided to pay for a day or two of childcare anyway so I could stay active in my profession even on a volunteer basis, we both looked at it as an investment of *our* money in *our* future. We now think of childcare as a joint expense. When the two of us talk about how to customize our jobs to fit together and our goal for our total family workweek, we also discuss the total income we want to achieve for our family. Each of us may dial up or down in terms of how much money we make individually, but together we focus on the total income we need per month and per year. We make a point of working on finances, budget, and investments together. When we make financial decisions and plans, we are careful to weigh the long-term impact on our individual and collective earning potential and individual and collective retirement savings. We've come to think of it as a game. Our team needs to figure out how to work a lousy system to our best advantage.

For example, when I was employed doing just a few projects a year, we had a meeting with our tax accountant who advised that we apply as many tax deductions as possible to my income. I asked why. She said it would minimize our taxes. I pointed out she was trying to make us look like a single-earner family. Then I asked if making me look like I didn't earn anything would mean no Social Security credits and no way for me to contribute to my own retirement account. Yes, she answered, except for a small contribution to a Roth perhaps. I talked with David and pointed out that if we hadn't already been married for ten years, that advice would be risky for my Social Security benefits. I also said I wanted to show enough earnings that year to be able to make a reasonable contribution to my own retirement account and so that's what we did.

Later still, at a time when I was the primary earner, we talked to our tax accountant again. This time, she suggested that David's business not pay him a salary that year. When we got off the phone, I pointed out to David, "See, she's trying to make us look like a single-earner family again because that's better for taxes. Only this time, I'm the single earner and you're the one giving up Social Security and retirement savings." At the time, David's retirement account was still much larger than mine, so we decided that looking like a single-earner family and having me make the big contribution to my retirement account made sense for us. Our tax accountant's advice was not bad. The financial advice couples get is based on how to navigate the existing out-of-date policies. Couples may be led to make decisions based on avoiding taxes to maximize short-term cash flow, without considering the often invisible effect on each person's long-term retirement or the consequences to each if there is ever a divorce.

HOW WOULD THE WORLD OPERATE IF FAMILY MONEY IS JOINTLY OWNED?

If everyone believed,

- Mothers and fathers share the responsibility and are equally capable of employment and contributing to the family's financial security

and

- Family income and wealth are the result of joint—both family work and employment—so they are owned jointly by both spouses

how would the world operate?

In this world, we would want our public policies to let mothers and fathers share employment the way that was best for them and their families. So we might have couples file taxes separately, an option both McCaffery and economist Gary Becker have suggested.[85] In fact, most advanced countries today mandate separate filing like the United States did before 1948.[86] Or we might allow families to choose either joint or separate filing, depending on their current employment and family situation, which would free them to make decisions without the tax code pushing them in one direction or the other. We might allow a secondary earner tax deduction that would offset the extra costs and taxes associated with having a second earner, a suggestion President George W. Bush made in his 2000 campaign.[87] We might offer greater tax deductions for childcare expenses when there is a secondary earner and structure the earned income tax credit so that the poorest families don't lose a tax break for staying married and for having two earners.[88]

As for Social Security, even back in the 1930s when it was being designed, Gerard Swope, a member of the Social Security Council, suggested an "earnings sharing" policy. Swope would have supported wives "by providing that the total wages earned by any married person, one half would be credited to his (or her) account, and that the other half would be credited to the spouse's account."[89] The council rejected this in favor of the 50 percent spousal benefit paid to the husband to care for his wife as his dependent.[90] An earnings sharing policy would give each spouse joint ownership of half the retirement benefits and ensure that even in the event of divorce each received half the total benefits earned during the marriage.

Imagine how the history of our other retirement vehicles might have been different if earnings sharing had been the policy in Social Security instead of the spousal benefit. Maybe when tax-free private retirement accounts like 401(k)'s came along, earnings sharing would have applied to them too. I save for retirement and half goes in an account in my name and half into one in my husband's name. The same happens to his retirement savings. He and I don't have to argue about how to invest. I hope we would still work on our investment strategy together, but we would each have investment control over half the money.

Why limit earnings sharing to retirement? Laura shared, "My husband and I look at everything as 'one family pot' but I know that legally that is not the case. At a Mothers & More meeting several years ago, one woman had a suggestion . . . that I never forgot: Married couples' paychecks should come with two names on them to show that the money legally belongs to both, and retirement accounts should be in both names. I was quite shocked at the time—especially about the paychecks. But now it makes complete sense to me." Splitting paychecks makes sense if we believe family money is truly owned by both spouses.

If Social Security reflected the belief that *caring for others is a vital human and economic activity and a public service,* then we would have ways for people who spend time caring for others to earn protection from poverty in old age. We could provide a number of years of family service credits to the Social Security account of the lower earner of a married couple, or to a single parent, for the years he or she cares for a child under six or a disabled or elderly family member.[91] We might allow a lower-earning spouse or single parent a number of "drop out" years spent caring for children or other family members so that those zero years wouldn't be counted in calculating Social Security benefits.[92]

If we believed that *family income and wealth are the result of joint—both family work and employment—so they are owned jointly by both spouses,* what would happen in a divorce? Divorce would probably look a lot like the joint-property proposal that Williams makes in *Unbending Gender.* First, all the marital assets acquired during marriage would be divided fifty-fifty no matter how large or small those assets are. After the divorce, if the children are still young, the joint income going forward would be split so that the two households had an equal standard of living until all the children were eighteen. Depending on custody arrangements, one parent is likely providing more of the family work, leaving them with more costs and less able to fit into higher paying jobs, so that parent would receive a larger share of the income. Splitting the income to equalize the two households recognizes that even after a divorce there is still joint work going on—both family work and employment—to support the whole family. Finally, if the children are all grown or almost grown when the divorce happens, the income splitting would continue for half the length of the marriage. For example, a twenty-two-year marriage that ended would split the future income for another eleven years, even if the children all left home during that time. This requirement protects a mother or father who cuts back on employment for years and then faces a divorce when the children are near or over eighteeen from being left high and dry.[93]

Using this remodeled family law, divorce settlements would be less arbitrary, and mothers and fathers would both know that they would share equally in the financial challenges of divorce. That knowledge would put mothers and fathers on equal footing in terms of the financial risk of walking away from the marriage. As a result, being the lower-earning spouse would be less risky and less likely to translate to less power in the marriage.

TURNING FRUSTRATION INTO ASPIRATION

David and I never did create a post-nuptial agreement. After some wrenching conversations, I stopped pushing for one. Once we arranged our lives so we could both be employed, my anxiety went down. Mostly though, I decided that inserting lawyers and written contracts into a stable marriage to someone I loved so much might cause more damage to our relationship than I was willing to risk.

What makes me angry is that I ever had to consider taking that risk. If I could have counted on divorce laws making the same assumptions David and I did that our money was really ours not just his, then I never would have felt so vulnerable that I needed to force difficult conversations about a post-nuptial agreement to protect against a divorce that was unlikely to happen. If our paychecks had been split, if half our retirement was automatically in my name, and if half of our income had been credited to my Social Security account, then I wouldn't have harbored this tiny worry that if the worst ever happened, I'd feel like the sucker who hadn't really protected herself. If the world had made it possible for us to remain on equal footing financially, regardless of our employment, I wouldn't have felt a loss of power and control that messed with our relationship. I never wanted to look at my own marriage and worry about protecting against divorce. So instead, David and I found a more aspirational way to express our commitment to sharing the responsibility for our family and to celebrate the ways our marriage had struggled, changed, and grown after we had Kate. We renewed our vows.

REMODELING TOOLS

▶ Talk with your spouse about the belief that *family income and wealth are the result of joint work—both family work and employment—so they are owned jointly by both spouses.* Is this your belief or not? If you adopted it as a belief, what could you do together to make that belief a reality in your family? How would you talk about money? What would you do differently? How would the world operate?

▶ Whenever faced with an employment or financial decision, ask yourself these questions and do enough digging to feel like you really know the answers before you decide.

   ◆ How will this decision affect the short- and long-term finances of my family?
   ◆ How will this decision affect *my* short- and long-term financial security?

▶ Consider all the aspects of long-term financial health— your own and your family's—when making employment decisions. This includes: future earning potential, Social Security, retirement savings and pensions, death, disability, divorce, and health insurance.

▶ Involve both spouses in all the financial decisions for your family. Even if one person is taking the lead on a financial task, involve the other regularly.

▶ Knowledge is power. Today motherhood is financially riskier than fatherhood. Mothers are better off being honest with themselves about the reality and magnitude of that risk. If you don't already have it, get the knowledge you need to be an equal partner in budgeting, monitoring income and expenses, and investment planning. Resolve to take one simple step this month to increase your financial literacy. Pick up a book by guru Suze Orman. Read a few articles from the Women's Institute for Financial Education (WIFE) at www.wife.org. For information on retirement, check the Women's Institute for a Secure Retirement (WISER) at www.wiserwomen.org and download their report, *Your Future Paycheck: What Women Need to Know About Pay, Social Security, Pensions, Savings and Investments,* at www.wiserwomen.org/pdf_files/yfp_women .pdf. To learn about making good decisions about insurance of all types, including life insurance and disability insurance, visit www.lifehappens.org, the website for the nonprofit Life and Health Insurance Foundation for Education (LIFE).*

► With your increased knowledge, resolve to take one step this month to increase your own financial security. Apply for your own credit card. Open your own bank account. Make a savings goal for your own retirement. Invest some of your money. These aren't just steps that protect you in a divorce. Women are more likely to spend a number of years on their own financially for a variety of reasons.

► Do a Social Security checkup.

◆ For more information on Social Security visit www .mothersandmore.org or www.ssa.gov/women. For two of my articles on Social Security and mothers visit www.mothersandmore.org/Advocacy/social_security .shtml. The knowledge can make a difference. For example, I figured out that I could be out of the workforce or cut back for up to five years and still have thirty-five years of high earnings on record. I've used up three and a half years of that so far. How many potential earning years do you have between the time you were first employed and age sixty-seven? How many years could you leave the workforce or cut back on your paid work and still have thirty-five years of high earnings that count toward Social Security?

LIFE is funded by insurance industry professionals.

- ◆ Check your Social Security statement. You should receive an annual statement around your birthday or you can request one at www.ssa.gov or by calling 1-800-772-1213. If you are married, review your Social Security statements together.
- ◆ Do you have the forty credits you need for retirement benefits on your own work record?
- ◆ What would your own retirement benefits be? Your spouse's? When you plan for retirement, include realistic estimates of your Social Security benefits based on reasonable assumptions about your work patterns.
- ◆ Are you currently eligible for disability benefits? What would it take to remain or become eligible? Don't count on Social Security to cover all your disability insurance needs. Do you have other state or private options for disability insurance?

▶ To see the numbers on what the secondary earner bias means to your family, visit the Motley Fool Calculator Should My Spouse Work Too? at www.fool.com/calcs/calculators .htm?source=LN. Enter the tax rates on the primary earner, the secondary earner's income, and the expenses associated with her or him working. Keep in mind that this calculator applies childcare expenses solely to the secondary earner. While this is rational economic thinking, it may not reflect how you and your spouse want to make the analysis.

▶ Do you live in a community property state? What are the laws during marriage and in a divorce in your state?

▶ Pick up a copy of *The Two-Income Trap: Why Middle-Class Parents Are Going Broke* by Elizabeth Warren and Amelia Warren Tyagi. Use their Financial Fire Drill with your spouse to help you walk through and plan for some What if? scenarios, such as, What if one of us loses his job? or What if one of us is injured? You can also search the Internet for the Financial Fire Drill to find short versions of the drill.

▶ Pick up a book.
- ◆ *The Price of Motherhood* by Ann Crittenden.
- ◆ *Taxing Women* by Ed McCaffery.

11

the next wedding

or what happened to our marriage?

"The transition [from partners to parents] is clearly stressful and the consequences of not doing well during the transition can be catastrophic for most marriages. We know what the potential buffers and toxic factors are. Still, most families move inexorably through the gauntlet toward catastrophe, as if all this knowledge were a secret."

JOHN GOTTMAN, FOREWORD TO *WHEN PARTNERS BECOME PARENTS.*

SOMETIME DURING KATE'S first year, on one of those rare nights I slept long enough to dream, I found myself standing under the lights on the side of a grassy football field in my Minnesota hometown. Both David and I were suited up to play. I could smell the fresh-cut grass and the white lime lines marking the field. The bleachers behind us were full and we stood on the sidelines in the midst of our team. The game started, and I watched David trot out to join the others on the field. I smiled and waited my turn. But as the minutes continued to tick off the scoreboard, and I watched David race up and down the field, I realized I wouldn't get a chance to play. My heart sank. I stood on the sidelines, not understanding why. The scoreboard buzzer blared at the end of the game. I jolted awake to my alarm's buzzer, disheartened and confused.

That dream—that nightmare—gave me the metaphor I needed to begin understanding what had happened to our marriage when Kate was born. David and I had been married for nearly seven years when I got pregnant. I remember the months of my pregnancy nostalgically as an idyllic time in our marriage. Every night David would pull out his guitar and sing the rock ballad "Waiting on an Angel" to me and my pregnant belly. He hadn't sung to me since our courtship many years before. My every wish—usually for Thai food—was his command. We took a last pre-baby vacation together and went antiques shopping, went out for dinner, and spent some quality time in our hotel room. Our friends threw baby showers for us celebrating what was clearly perceived as an event that would enrich our marriage now that we would be a true "family."

Then somehow we went from basking in the glow to shouting in the kitchen. You may remember these scenes. Several months after Kate was born I heard myself shouting at David, "If you can't figure out a way to fix this mess and spend more time with us and less time at work, I'm leaving for my parents' house in Minnesota and I'm not coming back until you do!" Not long after that explosion, I awkwardly asked David about a post-nuptial agreement and he blew up, accusing me of planning for divorce.

David and I were not really on the same team anymore. My football dream crystallized it for me. I adored my baby and my husband, but somehow my life felt sidelined and out of my control, while his life marched forward and our marriage struggled. I wanted us to be on the same team again. Instead, becoming parents was driving David and I further and further apart and we couldn't seem to stop the widening gap. What had happened to our connection, to our partnership, to our intimacy . . . to our marriage?

Now, the only thing worse than having other people think you are a "bad mother" is having other people think your marriage is in trouble. Very few of us want to confess to anyone else that becoming parents messes up our marriages even though research says the experience is common. Jay Belsky and John Kelly, the authors of *The Transition to Parenthood*, conducted research that suggests "one in every two marriages now goes into decline" when the first child arrives.[1] In the research Carolyn Pape Cowan and her husband, Philip

A. Cowan, share in their book, *When Partners Become Parents*, 92 percent of couples described more conflict after the baby arrived than before, and both mothers and fathers on average experienced a significant decline in marital satisfaction.[2]

While the experience may be common, we still don't like to admit it. Yvonne told me that when she went to Mommy and Me classes, "Sometimes I would mention something about how my marriage seemed to be falling apart, and would be met by silence and either blank stares or downward glances. It was as though I'd mentioned the unmentionable." I was embarrassed to talk about it, too, especially to people who knew David and me well.

However, bit by bit, the more I opened up about my own marriage, the more I found out that many mothers were struggling with the same issues. Katie shared, "We always used to be a team before we had a child together. . . . After she was born I felt like I was on my own with this infant and it was such an overwhelming and life-altering experience for me. I felt emotionally deserted by my husband and really resented the fact that he wasn't doing much with our baby or to support me emotionally during that stressful time. . . . I never knew that having a child, which is such a blessing, could put such a strain on a marriage." So many of us had been taken completely by surprise. Kathy described it like this, "My husband was unable to help much because of that very same business that made it possible for me to stay home. He was coping there without me, I was coping at home without him, and we felt like a truck had hit us." For many mothers, like me, having children was the first time our marriages were shaky enough that divorce crept into our heads as a real anxiety. Many mothers, on the other hand, told me they felt even more strongly that divorce was *not* an option now that they had children. Yet, they were just as taken aback by how much the quality of their marriage had taken a dive.[3]

Mothers described a huge gap between what they wanted in their marriage—or what they'd actually had in their marriage before kids—and what they'd somehow ended up with instead. The division of labor wasn't what they'd expected. As Barbara said, "Before [children] we were very egalitarian. Then we were Ozzie and Harriet." Time with their spouse had vanished into thin air. Beth said, "I was unaware how challenging it would be to find the time to spend with my spouse. By the time my husband gets home and our son gets in bed, we only have about two hours before our bedtime. I need those two hours to complete chores and attend to responsibilities." Mothers felt a bigger dip in their sex life than they expected. As Krista said, "The biggest change and challenge in our marriage is the amount of time and intimacy we have together. I don't always want to have sex and we do not get a chance until later in the evening when the baby is in bed for the night. That time of the evening is also the only time I get to do what I want." Magazines love to tell us how to put the sex back into a marriage after kids: lingerie, date nights, a lock on the door. No one seems to talk about how having children can push couples so far apart on so many levels that even the fanciest lingerie can't make up for the disconnect.

How do so many of us find ourselves in marriages so different from what we expected, so different from what we had before we had children? What we want from our marriages is totally different today, yet our workplaces, our public policies, and the assumptions of most of the people around us are rooted in the 1930s and 1940s and 1950s. So when we have children, all the outdated mental maps and vicious cycles about mothers, fathers, money, and work come crashing down on our marriages, sending us down a one-way street to a 1950s cul de sac.

WHAT WE WANT

In the late 1960s, the purpose of marriage was to have children. Mother would care for children and family; father would have the job. Selecting a husband was mainly about selecting a provider a woman could depend on. In fact, a 1965 survey showed that "three out of four college women said they would marry a man they didn't love if he fit their criteria in every other way."[4]

Times have changed. When David and I got married thirty years later in 1994, having children was not our purpose. We figured we probably would, but that was years down the road. We wanted to get married because in each other we'd found a partner in life. Today eight in ten women say they would "rather have a partner who can communicate his feelings than one who makes a good living."[5] Increasingly people say the purpose of marriage is to find personal satisfaction and commitment and that having children is less essential.[6] As Rachel told me, "We love our kids but we didn't get married because of our kids. We got married because we chose each other to live with. The kids are the added bonuses." When David and I dated, I never would have considered marrying someone I did not love. Why would I? I didn't need the money; I could earn that myself. I was independent, financially and personally. Our relative independence frees women up to look for soul mates rather than providers.

David and I also assumed we'd both have jobs. Without ever talking about it, we figured that if we did have children, our partnership model would easily translate to sharing family and career responsibilities. More and more people report that sharing household chores is important to marital harmony.[7] Young women today (under twenty-nine) are just as likely as young men to want jobs with more responsibility, and men ages twenty to thirty-nine are nearly as likely as women to say a job schedule that allows for family time is more important than money or status.[8]

Yes, times have changed and our expectations and hopes for our marriages have changed, too. As pollsters Celinda Lake and Kelly-anne Conway have found, women aren't giving up on marriage, they want to improve it; "For the first time in history, women are saying that a strong marriage requires a happy wife."[9] Women have mostly rejected the 1950s idea of marriage as a woman who depends on a man. They've also rejected the idea of marriage as two completely independent people. Women want *inter*dependence in their marriages, a true partnership of equals.[10]

The challenge is that our marriages are at the epicenter of all the outdated mental maps and vicious cycles about mothers, fathers, money, work, and marriage that kick in when we have children. While each couple's relationship and circumstances are unique, when all those invisible forces converge on our marriages, couples get unexpectedly disconnected from each other and puzzled as to why the marriage they want is so hard to have.

All the mental maps we've covered so far create six different disconnects between couples.

- Family work disconnect
- Employment disconnect
- Money disconnect
- Power disconnect
- Time disconnect
- Identity disconnect

These disconnects all feed into each other, adding up to one big Marriage Divide.[11]

FAMILY WORK DISCONNECT:
Why Am I the One Getting Up in the Middle of the Night?

First comes the crunchy waffle effect. David and I both operated with the mental map that *mothers are naturals and fathers are clueless*. So I just did everything that had to do with Kate and family. For example, I made the waffle every morning for Kate. I got more practice making waffles, and inevitably I learned the hard way that crunchy waffles were unacceptable, because they got thrown on the floor or at my face. Along the way I learned about and connected with Kate. This made me feel good, and made me feel like I was living up to that mental map of a "good mother." So what did I do? I kept making more waffles.[12]

David, on the other hand, rarely made the waffle. So he didn't get much practice. So when he found himself one day making a waffle, it was crunchy. Kate threw it at him, and I yelled at him for screwing it up. This made him angry and frustrated. So what did he do? He avoided making waffles. I made more waffles, he made fewer waffles. I got more practice with family work, he got less.

Yet another mental map, *caring for family isn't really work, it's just what mothers do* meant neither David nor I really saw the family work as work that took time and energy. As a result our perception of who was working harder was skewed. He thought he was working harder and I thought I should be able to do more at home because I wasn't employed. Both these mental maps led to a vicious cycle in which I did more family work and David did less, thereby feeding a growing family work disconnect.

EMPLOYMENT DISCONNECT:
Why Don't Either of Our Jobs Fit Anymore?

Now, let's add the mental map and vicious cycles that say *jobs are one-size-fits-all, full-time, full-year* and *family and employment are separate.* When Kate was born, David's job required ten- to twelve-hour days, weekends, and travel. I'd left one company to get a customized job and then been laid off. I couldn't get or keep a job that was less than fifty hours a week. We couldn't find standard employment that would let us have the partnership we wanted, in which both of us worked thirty to forty hours a week. We both felt like square pegs trying to fit into a round hole.

The jobs with benefits that we could find were fifty hours, fifty weeks, fifty years, modeled on old assumptions that *fathers are responsible for and are naturally better at employment and earning money* and *mothers are responsible for and are naturally better at family.* David and I needed one of those jobs for the money and the benefits. Because David earned more, David stayed at his job and spent most of his time there. Practice on the job made him better at his job. He got a bonus. He got promoted. This made him feel successful so he continued to work hard at his job. At the same time, I was out of the workforce so I was not getting much practice at employment. My employability, my connections, and my earning potential went down as his went up. My employed hours went down, and his went up; our employment disconnect.

The family work and employment disconnects feed each other. I got a lot more practice taking care of family. David got a lot more practice earning money. The more we practiced, the better we were at our "specialty" and the harder it was to share them with each other. More and more our daily lives were spent in very different ways.

MONEY DISCONNECT:
Why Do I Feel Financially Vulnerable?

Let's pile on the assumptions that say *mothers are financially dependent on fathers; mothers' earnings are pin money, just extra,* and *he who earns it, owns it.* Given that we needed at least one of those fifty-fifty-fifty jobs, David and I made our employment decisions based in part on the economic realities. David could earn more so his would be the primary job. Because the pin money mental map had been embedded in our income tax policy back in the 1940s to discourage me from employment, the math told us it wouldn't pay much for me to be employed after taxes, childcare, and work expenses. Because we could afford it, I left employment. He earned more, and for a time I earned nothing. At the same time, the *he who earns it, owns it* assumption meant that increasingly the bulk of our retirement savings were in David's name and my Social Security benefits suffered. My earning potential decreased while his increased. He had more money and I had less, fueling our money disconnect.

POWER DISCONNECT:
Why Has the Balance of Power Shifted?

An imbalance of money can lead to an imbalance of power. The combination of having Kate and also introducing a big difference in our earnings changed the dynamics of our marriage. Before Kate, we'd each had equal financial ability to walk away from the marriage, putting us on equal footing. Not anymore. I didn't think either of us wanted to go anywhere, but the paycheck had his name on it, and divorce law would assume *he who earns it, owns it.* At that point, he could walk away far more financially stable than I could. I felt dependent and vulnerable, and that gave him more power, whether he ever used it or not. Feeling vulnerable somewhere down deep, I didn't push for him to do more family work. I didn't want to rock the boat. The unexpected power shift messed with our relationship. He had more money and power, I had less; our power disconnect.

TIME DISCONNECT:
Why Am I Obsessed with Saving Time?

Take all the outdated assumptions about family work, employment, money, and power, and we get our time disconnect. When David was putting in long hours at the office, and I was putting in long hours at home with baby Kate, we had different perceptions of time and how it was being spent. David had far more child-free time than I did but didn't have much free time for himself or time with Kate and felt stressed. I, on the other hand, had far less child-free time, not much free time for myself, too much time with Kate and felt stressed. I felt like David had more control over his time because he was employed. If he couldn't come home, I was stuck picking up the family work. If he needed a break from the work that was paying the bills, that somehow seemed to both of us more legitimate than me needing a break from family stuff. I had a mental map that said Kate was my responsibility, so I felt like the time I took for me was stolen from time that really belonged to Kate. So I was more reluctant to take that time than David was. Out of the little spare time available to either of us, he had more free time and more child-free time, I had less. We spent our time differently. Our time disconnect.

IDENTITY DISCONNECT:
Who am I Now? And Who Are You?

All of these mental maps and vicious cycles introduced a discon-nect between my identity and David's that hadn't been there before Kate was born.[13] One that I didn't really understand until after the fact when I read *When Partners Become Parents* by Pape Cowan and Cowan. Remember my identity pie in Chapter 3 and the trouble I had making room for the Mother piece? Well, David also had to add father to his identity pie. Our assumptions about mothers and fathers dictated how we approached that identity pie dilemma. The mental maps sent us off in opposite directions and at different speeds, with me taking on the mother identity in a much larger and faster way than David took on his father identity.

We started getting out of sync with each other even before Kate was born. My mental maps about the expectations of a good mother kicked in and I was reading parenting books and researching baby gear. People cooed over me and my pregnant belly. Being a mother quickly took over a big chunk of my identity and started crowding out other pieces. Not David. Except for the baby showers and doc-tor's appointments, being a father hadn't really forced itself into his identity yet.

Then Kate was born, and the family work and employment discon-nects accelerated the growing distance between our identities. I spent more time being a mother. He spent more time being a worker. As I made room in my head for the growing size of my mother identity, the Worker and Partner and More pieces shrunk to slivers. David was slower to take on the father identity. He didn't have much time with us to be a father. He made some room for a smaller piece of father identity, but his Worker piece didn't shrink at all. His Partner and More pieces shrunk only a little bit.[14]

I saw the world and talked to David as this person:

A **Mother** who happened to also be a **Partner**, a **Worker**, and once in a long while **Myself**.

David saw the world and talked to me as this person:

> A **Worker** and **Partner** who happened to be a **Father** and sometimes **Himself**.

This was our identity disconnect.

Mothers and fathers incorporate their parent identity in different amounts and on different timeframes, with mothers cramming in a bigger Parent piece faster. These differences in how we integrate the parent role are at the root of a lot of conflict, dissatisfaction, and failure to communicate. When our identities go in opposite directions, we feel like the other person just doesn't understand our perspective. As Tanya explains, "Sometimes I feel a million miles away from him and he doesn't understand what I've gone through after having both kids." Examples of common symptoms of this identity disconnect include the following:

- He's jealous of the attention she gives to the kids. As one friend told me, "He regularly says 'I don't count. I don't matter,' and that he feels like the low man on the totem pole." As Mother, she sees prioritizing time with the children as the right thing for her to do. As Partner, he sees her spending way too much time and attention on the children and not enough on him.
- She's reluctant to get a baby-sitter. As Mother, she feels bad about leaving the children. As Partner, he doesn't understand; he wants to spend time with his wife.

The Cowans also found that the identity disconnect isn't good for either mothers or fathers. At six months after birth, women with a larger investment in the Mother identity have *lower* self-esteem. However, for men, those with a larger investment in the Father piece have *higher* self-esteem. Ultimately, the bigger the difference between husbands and wives in the size of their Parent piece when the baby is six months old, the less satisfied they both are with the quality of the marriage, and the more satisfaction continues to decline through the baby's eighteen-month mark.[15] The larger the identity disconnect, the greater the marriage divide.

The Cowans conclude, "The challenge then is how to allow Parent a central place in one's identity without abandoning or neglecting Partner. The couples who manage to do this feel better about themselves and their lives."[16] My interpretation of that conclusion is that it really means we need to find ways for fathers to be more involved with family, especially early on, and find ways for mothers to hang onto their More piece. Of course, this is no easy task because couples are living in a society that tells us that *mothers are responsible for and are naturally better at children and family* and *fathers are responsible for and are naturally better at employment and earning money.*

THE MARRIAGE DIVIDE

For those first few years after Kate's birth, David and I just kept getting further and further apart on every front. I was overloaded with family work. He was overloaded with paid work. I had more connection to Kate and my role as a mother. He had more connection to his job and his role as the breadwinner and husband. I had less money. He had more money. I had less power. He had more power. I had less time left over, especially time on my own. He had more time left over, but still not very much. As my friend's husband said to her one morning, "When did we start leading separate lives?"

Although any one of these disconnects may create a chasm for one couple, that same area might be a non-issue for another couple. Some of these disconnects may even be reversed. For example, he earns less money and she earns more. While the particular combination of disconnects is unique to each couple, a lot of couples wake up one day to find that their marriages aren't what they expected and they don't know how to fix it.[17]

BRIDGING THE MARRIAGE DIVIDE:
The Fathers Have Margaritas

While I was writing this book, off and on I would reserve a back table at our neighborhood cantina, Amigo's, and invite a bunch of mother friends to talk with me about topics I was writing about at the time. I often couldn't get a word in edgewise. No matter where I started the conversation, inevitably, the mothers returned to venting about who does what at home, peppering their stories with good husband caveats. "*I love my husband, but* . . . he interrupted my phone call yesterday to ask how to make instant ramen noodles for the girls!" Over years of conversations with mothers, I'd come to expect this common theme.

However, I didn't know what to expect the night I bought margaritas and quesadillas for my friends' *husbands*. I wanted to talk with fathers about a few topics so I invited David's crew of poker buddies to talk with me. This group had known each other for several years and most of their wives were members of Mothers & More. I figured that because they already knew each other and knew me, I might have a chance of overcoming the adage that "Real men don't talk about their feelings with each other." David came with me. I was a little nervous. How would I get them to open up? Would I end up doing most of the talking? Then, a funny thing happened. The margaritas came, and they started talking about "who does what." And I couldn't get a word in edgewise.

"I'm at work all day. I'm trying to be the dad. I'm trying to make my wife happy—and yes I want to get laid. So I fold the laundry, but I don't do it right. I feed the kids, but I was supposed to do peas before pears not pears before peas. I can't win."

"I just want to know when quitting time is. If I turn on the TV before some mystery quitting time she has in her head, she freaks out. Just tell me when quitting time is and whenever that is, I'm going to watch an hour of ESPN before I go to bed."

"I'm doing the best I can. Doing more than my father ever did. But it's never enough."

"I used to get home at the end of the day and she would immediately start handing me the kids and stuff to do. I just wanted to retreat into a cave to recover from my day."

Oh, we talked about other things too, but over and over the conversation returned to current or past frustrations with the tension and misunderstandings over who does what and who was working harder. I felt the defensiveness mingling with the scent of tequila. I remembered feeling that defensiveness from David when we argued. Underneath the words, some of the fathers seemed to be assuming, "If I try to do my share of the family work, I get yelled at for not meeting some invisible unspoken standard. If I don't try, I get yelled at. I can't win and I'm tired of getting the blame."

These were not men who were interested in skating by. They weren't joking about avoiding dirty diapers or being clueless about kids. They wanted to be involved. Yet, here they sat in the same booth their wives sat in the night before and they were talking about different versions of the very same frustrations. The fathers were louder, they drank more and ate more, they poked more fun at each other, but other than that, both the mothers and the fathers wanted largely the same thing—an end to the arguing about who does what and to be on the same team again—but neither could figure out how to get there.

WHAT'S AT STAKE

Who does the laundry and who makes pediatrician appointments may seem petty on the surface, but there's so much more at stake. As one mother told me, "Whenever my marriage has hit rocky patches, it has been due to a real or perceived imbalance in family and household responsibilities." The squabbles and resentments about who's doing what at home are the symptom on the surface reminding us of that gap between what we want and expected in our marriages and where we ended up.

Whenever people feel the pain of a big gap between current reality and the way we want things to be, there are two options. Change the reality or change the vision. Reality is tougher to change, so the easiest and fastest way to relieve the pain is to ratchet down our expectations. For example, we tell ourselves mothers are just naturally better at family so it will never change. For a time, we feel better. The painful gap between what we have and what we want is a little less because we've decided to want less. But what have we lost in the process?

I knew what I would lose. I'd lose my marriage. Maybe not literally, but something vital at its core. David and I got married as equals, as best friends, as partners. When we were married, we vowed to "be true to the pursuit of the dreams and goals we both share." The dream we shared now was of a family life with everyone home for dinner, with time for our relationship with each other. We wanted a family life that would allow us to share the family responsibilities so that we both had time to pursue our own dreams and both had a relationship with Kate. How could we hope to have our marriage stand the test of time if we gave up on that vow to be true to the dreams we both share? I would always carry some level of resentment, and he would always feel some defensiveness. If we gave up on the idea that we could share responsibility for our family, effectively we would be giving up on a core value in our marriage.

What would David lose? I knew, in my heart of hearts, that during those first three and a half years, when David was never around, when music class Saturday mornings was often the only alone time he got with Kate that his connection to her, his understanding of her, paled in comparison to mine. He loved her. He didn't know her. She didn't know him. When she was upset, she came to me. When she was excited, she came to me. At times this made me frustrated and put upon. But just as often, it made me sad. I didn't want David to miss out on the richness of the relationship I had with Kate. A richness that came from putting a cold washcloth on her feverish forehead, from reading and giggling about stories in her bed at night, and, yes, from the times she drove me crazy and I yelled and then said I was sorry and she hugged me anyway. I didn't want David to find many years later that he didn't know his own child, had missed her childhood and couldn't have a meaningful conversation with her. I wanted more for him. So badly it brought me to tears. And I was pretty sure he wanted it too.

The arguments David and I had about "who does what at home" weren't really about keeping score on who supervises homework and who gets the groceries. Our wedding vows and our relationships with each other and with Kate were at stake. We simply couldn't give up.

RESISTING THE QUICK FIXES

We couldn't give up, but we also had to resist the quick fixes. There's lots of advice out there about how to share family work so everyone is happy. Some of it may relieve a bit of pain temporarily, but you can't fix a complex problem with simple solutions. One version of the quick fix advice goes like this:

> Mothers should just insist their husbands do more around the house. Mothers have only themselves to blame if they don't demand husbands do their fair share.

or

> Mothers should stop doing all the things they do. Leave the laundry undone. Go on strike and force him to pick up the slack.

Hmmm, I'm already in a tense standoff with the person who shares my bed, and I'm supposed to yell louder and make more demands? Or I'm supposed to pull a passive-aggressive move that leaves everyone—including me—with no clean underwear? I admit, I've been desperate enough to try both. They didn't work. Yelling just triggered David's defensiveness and led us into that lose-lose kitchen argument about who's working harder. The passive-aggressive move punishes me, too. I don't have clean underwear, and he doesn't see the laundry that needs to be done no matter how long I let it pile up.*

---

* To be fair, David would definitely see a pile of dirty dishes before I would.

Another piece of quick fix advice, one that sometimes comes from fathers, sounds like this:

> Mothers should just delegate more to other people. Mothers have only themselves to blame if they don't have enough time or don't have the paid job they need or want. Get more child-care. Hire someone to clean the house.

Delegate more? Wow, I'm overwhelmed by all the assumptions underneath this advice. Where to start? First, this assumes mother can afford to hire help, but as we've seen families have less disposable income than ever. Telling mothers to "just delegate" assumes she can find quality childcare. The just-hand-it-off advice assumes that she should be able to instantly rid herself of her assumptions that a good mother should do it all herself and get over any desire she may have to care for her own children.

I'm not saying parents shouldn't share the family work with other people. David and I sure do. When couples have the family or the money to do so, sharing the work can relieve some tension and open up some time and space to tackle other challenges the couple may be facing. However, telling *her* to delegate still assumes it's *her* responsibility to coordinate all the family work and make sure it gets done well by someone else. I've watched families delegate out nearly everything they can, yet the mother is still responsible for coordinating all that work. Delegating the tasks while mother keeps the responsibility leaves the old mental maps about who does what firmly in place, and the underlying tension between mother and father won't go away.

Another quick fix often found in magazines or when mothers trade tips about how to get fathers to do their share is this one:

> Mothers should strategize or trick or organize fathers into doing more at home. Leave detailed directions when you go out of town. Put one child's clothes on blue hangers and the other child's on white hangers so he dresses everyone in the right clothes.

Okay, the problem here is that we're still operating on the assumption that fathers are clueless. He can't or won't do anything unless mothers write it down or spend our energy setting up everything so that he can't fail. Then we wonder why it doesn't stick or why the success with one task doesn't transfer to other family work or why we still feel resentful and then feel guilty for being resentful because he's doing more. Giving mothers responsibility for the strategies or tricks or safety nets doesn't get to the root of the problem. If mother is in charge of making sure the *tasks* are shared and done right, then we haven't truly succeeded in sharing the *responsibility*.

Now, there is one quick fix I hear doled out to fathers, from mothers and other people:

Fathers should just stop slacking and do more around the house.

Yes! That sounds good. Oh, wait. That assumes he simply lacks the will or motivation to do more. At first, I admit, that was my assumption about David. He didn't really care. He didn't want to do the stuff or else he'd just do it. Once I could see all the mental maps and vicious cycles though, I thought to myself, "Wow, I wouldn't do it if I were him either." The proposition to do more around the house isn't very enticing for fathers in general: "Someone else is doing this work right now but we'd like you to share it with them. The work is often tedious. Given your hours on the job, you don't have much time to do it. You won't get paid. Your friends will think you're a wimp. Your boss will pass you over for promotion. And best of all, your wife will criticize how you do it. How about it?" This advice to fathers to just do it ignores all the invisible barriers steering him away from doing more family work and blames him instead.

These quick fixes aren't fixes at all. They are band-aids, simple solutions to a complex problem. At the beginning of the book, I explained how David and I were each tangled up on opposite sides of a spiderweb of assumptions. David and I couldn't solve Who does what by focusing only on Who does what. We couldn't get our marriage back using lingerie and dates. When everything's connected, there is no one single thing that stops the vicious cycle. We had to do a bunch of little experiments all over the place, until we reached a tipping point at which our downward spiral reversed into an upward one. This entire book up to this point describes how we were trying to untangle all those knots all at the same time. I wish I could say that getting untangled was simple, that we simply listed all the new and improved beliefs out and posted them on the kitchen bulletin board and—*Shazam!*—we both started behaving differently. The reality was far more tortured, more like trial and lots of error. Unfortunately, I didn't read any of the fabulous research on the transition from partners to parents until we'd already clawed and scratched, cried and yelled our way through the toughest parts. Quick fixes lend themselves to bullet points, but the only way to explain how David and I got from here to there is to return to our story.

LIST OF NEW BELIEFS

- Mothers and fathers share the responsibility and are equally capable of caring for children and home.
- All mothers are unique. All fathers are unique.
- A mother is more than any single role she plays at any given point in her lifetime. She is entitled to fully explore and develop her identity as she chooses: as a woman, a citizen, a parent, or an employee.
- The transitions women make into and through motherhood are challenging and can be difficult.
- Caring for others is a vital human and economic activity and a public service.
- Mothers and fathers share the responsibility and are equally capable of employment and contributing to the family's financial security.
- A variety of job structures to fit various stages of personal lives is best for people and organizations and communities.

- Family and employment can be integrated and complementary.
- A person's time belongs first and foremost to that person.
- Time is a shared family resource and responsibility.
- Family income and wealth are the result of joint work—both family work and employment—so they are owned jointly by both spouses.

BACK TO THE STORY

After Kate arrived, we were stuck in a marriage David and I didn't recognize. Me threatening to leave for Minnesota. Him accusing me of planning for divorce. Me plagued with dreams that we were no longer on the same team. Him thinking I had gone completely insane. We each held ridiculously contradictory expectations of ourselves and of each other and didn't even recognize their absurdity. David was doing seventy-hour workweeks same as my father had, but I expected him to do half the family work. I was the independent, modern woman with my own career and interests that David had always wanted to marry, but he still hadn't expected that his work life would change when we had children.

We talked constantly. Correction, we argued constantly. I'd call the office and ask when he was coming home and we'd argue. He'd try to put Kate to bed, and I'd swoop in to rescue and we'd argue. We were in the thick of confronting the brutal reality that when Kate was born, our old marriage ended. We each grieved that loss, often blaming it on the other. Our marriage had been the biggest, most cherished piece of both our lives. Losing it was totally unexpected and completely devastating. We lost that version of our marriage before we could even imagine what a new version could look like or feel like. David's favorite Ending Zone tactic was denial. "Just wait. It will get better once I feel more confident about my job." Or "It will get better when she's a bit older." My favorite tactic was anger, especially at him. "What do you *mean* you can't get home for dinner?" Or "You must be crazy if you think we're having sex when I haven't had a bit of help from you all week."

So we sat together in our misery in the Ending Zone and told each other how awful it all was. It was not fun, but it did serve its purpose. Eventually through the shouting, the grumping, the nights on opposite ends of the couch watching TV, we came to some critical realizations.

This is *not* how it was.

This is *not* how we thought it would be.

This is *not* how we want it to be.

We were emerging from this miserable Ending Zone. Little did we know we'd spend seven messy years flailing around in the Neutral Zone together before we got to a New Beginning.

EXPERIMENTING IN THE NEUTRAL ZONE

David and I began to experiment with ways to relieve critical pressure points. When Kate was seven months old, my most immediate pain was how unhappy I was being on family duty 24/7 with no time for myself and no help from David. Signing Kate up for two days of childcare was a quick win for us. Time for myself made me feel better, happier, or less "insane," as David would say, and that made him happier, too. Taking an action, any action, together, was significant. Acting together told me David cared about and understood—or at least accepted—how difficult this transition was for me. We also signed David and Kate up for a Saturday morning music class. Music is David's thing, not mine. He had no time during the week with Kate, but every Saturday he had something uniquely his to do with her, with the added bonus of giving me more time to myself too.

I had spent the first three to six months of Kate's life trying to take care of everything myself, thinking I shouldn't need help from anyone else. And secretly thinking I didn't want anyone else to judge how well I was doing it. Finally David convinced me to reach out to his parents for more help. Grandma and Grandpa were working during the day, but I started leaning on them for help in the evenings so I could start a Mothers & More chapter or go to a community meeting. David and I also leaned on them to get a night out together regularly. Just two hours over dinner was often enough to reconnect us again for several weeks, though sometimes we ruined the date by falling into an argument.

We even managed to take baby steps toward sharing the family work. In that first year, I would often find myself in the middle of the elaborate, hands-on bedtime routine when I would hear the TV go on in the other room. My blood would boil. How dare David relax when I'm still working? After letting my resentment build for months and months, one night after this had happened yet again, I marched into the TV room and stood over David. I was so frustrated I was practically spitting. In my head I was shouting, "I can't believe you are watching TV while I'm in the middle of all that! You insensitive lout. You don't care about me or Kate." Instead, through gritted teeth, I managed to say, "I need us to agree that the time when we're putting Kate to bed is family work time. Whoever isn't putting her to bed should be doing other stuff, laundry, dishes, whatever." I dug in, preparing for a fight. He looked surprised, and said, "Sure. We can do that." Huh? Where was the fight?

David wasn't trying to slack off; he didn't know that I was assuming quitting time didn't come until Kate was asleep. We came to an agreement that employed or not, both of us were working all day. When we were together at home in the evening, we started another shift of work when we were both on family duty. So we had to negotiate with each other about quitting time and breaks. This was one of my first clues that David wasn't really trying to avoid being involved, that he truly was having a different experience from mine. However, I wasn't ready to read those clues clearly yet. I was still too focused on what was happening to me and what else I had lost.

CLEANING UP MY OWN MESS

Our few quick wins eased the emotions and gave me some time to spend on figuring out what was happening to me. Every other week at my Mothers & More meetings, listening to the stories of other mothers reminded me I wasn't alone. I helped put together meetings on the topics I was wrestling with like identity, money, and employment. The conversations gave me a safe place to vent and to talk through my experience so I could begin to understand it. I read *The Price of Motherhood*, followed quickly by *Unbending Gender* and a host of other books. I joined the Mothers & More POWER online discussion group where I, along with mothers across the country, poured our stories into e-mail and connected them to the things we read, and where we hosted authors like Ann Crittenden and Joan Williams as guest speakers.

Slowly, often painfully, I began to piece together an understanding of why motherhood had thrown me for a loop. Answers to my questions began to take shape. Why am I the one getting up in the middle of the night? Why didn't anyone tell me how hard this is? Who am I now? What did I do all day? Why doesn't my job fit anymore? Why do I feel financially vulnerable? Why am I obsessed with saving time? I started to see my experience within an historical and social context. That balcony view gave me a lot more compassion for myself and other mothers.

The more I understood, the more I also felt I had to *do* something. So I was quickly and willingly swept into the work of Mothers & More. I helped design materials for local chapters to lead meetings on those questions we all had. Mere days after Kate's first birthday, I got on an airplane to Chicago for the national conference and my first trip on my own since Kate had been born. Ann Crittenden and Joan Williams gave keynote addresses and I got to meet my virtual friends in person for the first time. Judith Stadtman Tucker and I led workshops where mothers sat alongside Crittenden and Williams and talked about what mothers of all types need to live a whole life. Once back home in Pasadena, I began writing letters to the editor of our local papers responding to articles about women and mothers. I signed up for an online writing class and started writing an article about Social Security and mothers. By that spring, I became the national president of Mothers & More. Quite literally my job, all my volunteer time, was dedicated to understanding what was going on with mothers and families and being able to talk about it—to our own members and to the media. The more time I spent being a champion for mothers in general, the more strongly I myself believed things could and should be different. Acting and speaking for others boomeranged back into my life to make me more confident in what I believed and what I wanted our own family life to be like.

SEEING *OUR* MESS AND
MOVING TOWARD A NEW BEGINNING

Something else happened. The more I found myself saying things to reporters like, "The world around us is structured in such a way that it is hard to fulfill your caregiving responsibilities and do anything else like paid work," the more I realized that David was trying to make his way in that same warped world.[18] I started feeling more empathy for David and his experience. Speaking out about the changes I wanted for me helped me see David and our marriage in a new light. Another mother, Freda, described the same experience. "I slowly began to regain my power and sense of self, both out of sheer desperation, and due to the 'education' I was receiving through Mothers & More. I started to see motherhood, parenthood, and couplehood in the full context of society, and the struggles started to make sense, on some level, or at least became easier to analyze. No wonder my husband and I couldn't process all the changes and stressors—we were fighting the current of a culture which undermines the health and strength of families. This realization allowed me to channel some of my resentment away from my husband, and into advocacy work, and into respectfully renegotiating some things with my husband.... Seeing our relationship through a wider lens has helped a great deal."

Being up on the balcony to view my own drama within the big picture inevitably gave me the distance I needed to see David was in the drama with me. "It's not his fault," I thought to myself. I didn't blame him as much. More and more, I saw us as in the same boat, and that's a better place from which to have tough conversations. As my frame of mind shifted, the ways I talked with David also shifted. I was less likely to say accusatory things like "You need to . . ." or "You aren't . . ." and more often said things like "I need . . ." and "Can we . . . ?"

Everyday family events turned into opportunities to take the balcony view together. One day David and I took toddler Kate to buy her some new shoes. We measured her foot and discovered that she had been wearing shoes three sizes too small! I was mortified. I felt awful. What kind of mother doesn't notice that her kid's shoes are three sizes too small! David was like, "Whatever. No big deal." We joked about how I felt guilty, but he didn't. Sharing the balcony view, we could see that I was trying to live up to the mental map that a good mother is supposed to be perfectly in tune with her child's needs. He wasn't holding either me or himself to that standard.

Quick wins, sharing the balcony view, my growing empathy, his growing understanding that I was truly unhappy not simply insane, all made the way for deeper conversations. We were relentless about talking with each other. We didn't have time to talk, but we did anyway. Sometimes for fifteen minutes and sometimes for two hours. In hindsight it was all really one conversation with a million different threads. We'd talk about our ideal family life during a date night. I'd read a new book and then share the balcony view with him about the ways workplaces made mothers and fathers feel like square pegs. I'd stew until he got home late at night and then launch a late-night argument about his long hours and how our life was not how I thought it would be. Over the Sunday paper we'd puzzle over what steps we could take.

At different times, we each risked a lot—sticking our necks out to push an issue or make ourselves heard. I would want to keep talking until we resolved it. He would need to cool down first. We learned that an argument or conversation didn't have to result in an answer that moment, as long as we returned to the thread eventually. We learned a five-minute blowup in the kitchen might lead two days later to a deeper conversation late at night. We learned that sometimes whatever was making us feel stuck wouldn't surface unless the discussion got intense and heated. We learned that our relationship was strong enough to handle the risk. In fact, the path of least resistance would continue to take us away from what we really wanted. We had to keep taking risks.

In a lot of these conversations, I continued to rail about David's job, but I started to allow myself to recognize that he was as out of sync with the workplace as I had been. The men he worked for had wives who were not employed and that seemed to work for them, so they seemed to figure that arrangement worked for everyone. The men—and a few women—that were his peers were not married. They spent long hours at the office along with long lunches and late nights out on the weekends. As the father of an infant, married to me who wanted him far more involved at home and wanted to get back to work myself, he was a major square peg.

Slowly, over many conversations, we revisited what we wanted for our family and for each other. We took the balcony view of his job and what we wanted our lives to be like. Together we concluded that he would need to leave his job and we would have to completely remodel our employment to get the life we wanted together. At that moment, our relationship took an important step back on track. We were no longer focused on avoiding a catastrophe in our marriage, instead we were working together toward a shared vision. We were moving from that messy Neutral Zone toward a New Beginning.

That summer, in the midst of all our plotting and planning about our jobs, David and I took preschool Kate along on a vacation with David's family to Lake Tahoe. We took advantage of the built-in baby-sitting to go out for dinner. We talked about our dreams for the future, for Kate, for our family. As the sun set over the lake in front of us and the wine loosened us up, I asked David, "Do you ever wish you had married someone else? Someone who was more willing to do all the family work so you could focus on your career?" No, he said vehemently. "The first time I brought you home when we were dating, my mother said you were everything I'd always wanted—smart, ambitious, and opinionated—and she was right. Even if making it all fit together is harder, I want you. Together, we'll make it work." My heart lightened, relieved of a worry I'd carried without even allowing myself to realize it.

On our way home that night, we found a dark, out-of-the-way spot, parked the rental car and steamed up the windows.

A NEW BEGINNING OR A BACKSLIDE?

All our experiments in the Neutral Zone were paying off. Not long after Tahoe, David left his job and I started mine. I knew David and I had entered a New Beginning that evening I came home from a client meeting as David pulled into the driveway with Kate. I hugged them both and said, "Now this, this is how I thought it would be."

Well, except when it wasn't.

While we'd taken a giant leap on the employment issue and made progress on our relationship and even baby steps on the family work, I continued to feel as if we were taking three steps forward toward the marriage we wanted followed by two steps back. So David and I reached out for help getting a better balcony view. I visited a therapist myself for several months. I wanted a better understanding of my own experience, but the unexpected thing was how it became couples counseling by extension. I would have an appointment and then that night after Kate fell asleep, David and I would get a glass of wine and sit together in our living room and talk. As I talked about what I was discovering about myself, my childhood, my own parents, he would do the same. We began to understand each other better and how our own baggage—good and bad—from childhood was yet another layer of stuff underneath how our own marriage had responded to parenthood.

I shared with David that I had grown up telling myself I would never be in my mother's shoes, that I would never just care for family or depend on someone else for money. Yet overnight, when Kate was born, I found myself in a life a lot like my mother's and I freaked out. Then I felt guilty for freaking out because I felt like I was being disrespectful to my own mother, whom I love, when it was really my own flawed assumptions about homemakers and the work of caring for family that messed me up. David gained a greater understanding of why the transition had been so hard for me. David shared that he felt like his family hadn't had much money growing up so he was very focused on being financially secure. I gained a greater understanding of his desire to be successful in his career.

I suggested to David that we see a couples counselor together. After all, if the research says this transition to parenthood is so hard for a lot of couples, why not get some help navigating it effectively? In those sessions, I first heard about the day David took baby Kate to the park across the street from my parents' home and teared up. In that office, I first heard David get emotional as he talked about how fondly he remembered those first few days together after Kate was born. And then how he had to leave us to go back to the office and felt jealous I got to stay in that cocoon and angry that I resented and complained about feeling trapped in it every day.

Our couples counselor recommended doing regular check-ins with each other on our marriage. For several months David and I had coffee together every Monday morning. We'd ask each other, "So how are you feeling about us? Has anything happened recently that we should talk about but didn't take the time to talk when it happened? Anything coming up that we can anticipate a conflict about? Anything that went well for us this past week?" These conversations rarely lasted more than fifteen to thirty minutes but that was all we needed to monitor our relationship without making it a big deal or leaving things to stew until they blew up.

FINALLY SHARING THE FAMILY WORK

My own employment almost magically led to David taking on more housework. Mostly his response was practical—someone had to do the stuff. I wasn't around as much, and fortunately for me David's a neatnik and could stand dirty dishes for only a day or two. When I asked him to do something, he did. Usually I didn't even have to ask. Sharing the responsibility for earning money made it more critical logistically that we also share responsibility for everything else. Now that I was employed, I eased up on my own expectation that I should be able to do all the family work myself. Plus, earning money shifted the power balance so I felt I could ask him to do more. Our conversations about dividing up the housework became more deliberate and less contentious.

One summer, we made a decision for me to take an opportunity to take on a lot more paid work, including a bit of travel every month. David and I sat down at the picnic table on our deck and talked about what the change would mean for our family. I said, "If I'm going to be employed more hours, we need to shift some of the family work to you." "Okay," he said. "What makes sense?" We looked at what I was doing and what he was doing. He was still working full days during the week so what could we shift that he could do on the weekend or at night? "What I really want," I told him, "is to shift something to you that is a *responsibility* not just a task. Something that you own. Something I don't have to *think* about. Though you can ask for my help if you need it. Like maybe meal planning and the grocery list every week. It's killing me." He said, "Sure." Done deal. David took responsibility for making a weekly meal plan, a grocery list and doing the grocery shopping.

As with anything new there were a few hiccups early on. One day, I got home pretty late and looked at the bulletin board for the day's meal. Chicken and broccoli. I looked in the fridge. No chicken. I looked in the freezer. Rock solid chicken. I called David. "Hey, there's no thawed chicken for the meal on the plan." "Oh, yeah," he said, "I guess I should have put it in the fridge to thaw." I said, "That's one of the pain in the neck things about meal planning, remembering to thaw stuff in advance. Why don't you pick something up on your way home." Practice makes perfect, though, and soon David was doing the meal planning better than I ever did. He created a computer template for planning the meals and making a grocery list and used it every weekend to write the plan then do the shopping. He scoffed at my laziness because I shopped only at the chain grocery store to save time. Instead he got a bunch of our produce cheaper at a neighborhood store and specialty items at an Italian market. He started watching the Food Network and Kate and I ate like royalty the first summer David took over the responsibility for our meals.

As well as we were doing when it came to sharing responsibility for housework, we still struggled to get David truly sharing responsibility for Kate. I was still the one noticing that she needed new clothes and still the one monitoring what she ate every day. Whenever all three of us had to get ready to go somewhere, I was still the one getting both myself and Kate ready to go—and then wanting to strangle David when he acted impatient because we weren't ready on time. We also clearly had different standards for taking care of Kate, differences that in part came from cultural assumptions about what mothers are expected to do and partly from differing parenting philosophies. I was frustrated because I was trying to live up to standards for caring for Kate that, as a mother, were far higher and different from David's, and felt like he used that to let himself off the hook and leave me on my own. David would shrug his shoulders saying things like, "Fine, if you think Kate must have a parent on that field trip, then *you* knock yourself out." So I would give up time for myself, or sleep, or a shower to do it and then resent that David was simply letting me knock myself out. On the flip side, my own standards also meant I prevented David from doing certain tasks, like packing Kate for a trip. And different standards also often led us to our most heated arguments.

One Friday afternoon, while I was gone and unreachable (well, I'd turned off my cell phone), elementary school Kate had an accident at school that chipped off half of one of her top front teeth. When I arrived back home that evening, David was picking up Kate from school and discovering that the envelope with the tooth had been lost in the school transitions that afternoon. I was furious. I grilled David, "What do you mean you didn't rush to school as soon as they called you and then get her to a dentist? Now we can't get in to the dentist until Monday and the tooth is lost." As a mother, I couldn't fathom his handling of the situation. If I'd gotten the call, I would have rushed to school, called the dentist on the way, and made sure I had that tooth in my own possession as quickly as possible. David, on the other hand, got the call, heard the teachers say Kate was fine and that they had the tooth, considered his busy afternoon, and concluded he didn't need to go to school early.

It was twenty-four hours before I could calm down enough to talk with David. (I called my sister first to vent.) When I did talk with David, I said we needed to talk about what happened because clearly we had different assumptions about what to do and this was an opportunity to get on the same page for next time. A tense and heated conversation ensued, and I think the only reason we got through it without throwing things at each other was by talking about standards we each had and standards we could agree to going forward. In this case, those agreements included me keeping my cell phone on and agreeing that any injury at school that produced a phone call meant one of us had to go in person to check it out, and that any injury on a Friday meant that getting in to the dentist or doctor that day was top priority. My lesson learned was that talking about standards for caring for Kate was critical. Neither of us could assume that the other had the same standards or philosophy. Both of us had to acknowledge that cultural assumptions played at least some role in the standards we each had. And most importantly, neither of us should be able to use any difference in our standards to either get out of family work or keep the other person away from doing certain tasks.

For a long time, my strategy for getting David to do more of the childcare was to nag and complain that the division of labor wasn't fair, but nagging rarely seemed to work. Then late one night, when I again found myself the one getting up in the middle of the night to comfort a scared preschooler, somehow in the middle of my frustrated thoughts, something dawned on me. Yes, getting up in the middle of the night sucks. But at the same time, some of my most treasured memories are of moments in the middle of the night with Kate that David had never had. The time baby Kate smiled at me for the first time as the moonlight streamed through the window. The time I laid in bed with toddler Kate and she told me about her dream that someone was chasing her and I curled up around her and we both fell asleep.

My frustration turned to sadness—for David—because his opportunities to connect to his daughter in these ways were so much fewer and farther between. I knew it made him sad, too. He was visibly upset when preschool Kate walked right past him to get to me when she was upset. And then there was that time at the swingset in the park, he and baby Kate alone together playing for one of the only times since she'd been born, and him tearing up. He'd told me that he resented my first few years taking care of Kate and didn't understand my difficulty with it because it was an experience with her that he would never, ever have.

I realized that sharing all the various responsibilities for taking care of Kate needed to be more about David wanting and needing a relationship with Kate, and less about my need for equity. The idea that David should have a rich relationship with our daughter was something we both fully agreed upon. Both of us knew that a relationship like that meant David being involved in all the mundane childcare tasks. He told me, "I have to have daily responsibilities for Kate to know and understand her." To do that, he needed to be more available, and that was a big part of his motivation to change his own employment so drastically. Sharing responsibility for Kate got better the more we both focused on his relationship with her as the motivation and the goal. David sharing responsibility for Kate became its own self-fulfilling prophecy. He spent time taking care of Kate, she turned to him more often, and he felt the rewards of a richer relationship with her and in turn did more with her.

David and Kate's relationship with each other grew and in valuable ways is different from the one Kate and I have. Any weekend morning that Mommy isn't around, David and Kate head to the donut shop, something I frown upon. When I get home, Kate always revels in telling me about this rebellious Daddy-and-Kate ritual. When Kate came home from school one day and complained that a friend had been mean to her, I empathized and hugged her. When David got home later, he joked, "Well, did you slug him?" and she laughed. I am still more likely to do some things, like buy clothes for Kate, and David still gets the cars fixed and takes out the trash. David does dentist appointments and I do the pediatrician, but we don't keep score. We still backslide from time to time, but the important thing is that we both feel the responsibility for family and the workload is being shared fairly, and if not we have ways to talk about it. We've gotten untangled. We're back on the same team again, reconnected— which works better than lingerie if you know what I mean. Our old marriage is gone, but we've rebuilt something different and amazing in its place.

THE NEXT WEDDING

As our marriage began the move from the messy Neutral Zone to a New Beginning, I was suddenly struck with the idea that David and I should renew our wedding vows. In Anna Fels' book *Necessary Dreams*, I'd read how anthropologist Margaret Mead had suggested many years ago that a marriage before kids was very different than a "parental marriage," which included new and different levels of commitments.[19] In another book, I'd read about a writer in the 1970s who had found that both she and her husband were dissatisfied with how their marriage had changed after kids and had written a new marriage contract promising to share responsibility and opportunities.[20] Nearly every day, I passed a corner shop in town whose display cases were filled with gorgeous wedding gowns and found myself thinking, "We celebrate a new marriage publicly at a wedding, and people often celebrate a fiftieth wedding anniversary, but why don't we do anything in between?" So I mentioned the idea of renewing our vows to David—and to Kate.

Kate loved the idea and started referring to the hypothetical event as our "next wedding." David was open to the idea from the beginning; he thought it sounded like fun and made sense given what we'd gone through. The two of us love to throw parties and here was a chance to throw one on a grand scale. Still, at first I felt like the whole thing was mostly my idea and he was going along.

Over the next couple of years, the idea popped up in our conversations. When David and I had our New Year's dinners each year we'd talk about what renewing our vows would mean to us. We talked about how it seemed in today's world, there weren't many models for the kind of marriage and shared family commitments we really wanted for our relationship. So much had changed even since our own parents got married that we felt like pioneers. We asked ourselves why we wanted to renew our vows and came up with answers like wanting to acknowledge that marriage with kids is different and wanting to celebrate our own journey to create a new relationship with each other as parents. Over time and conversation, what had been my idea became our idea.

One New Year's Eve we decided that 2008 would be the year of the next wedding. We picked a day in March when my family would be in California visiting anyway and once we started telling everyone, we were committed—no turning back now. Yet, we were so busy in the months leading up to the next wedding that the whole thing nearly sneaked up on us. Perhaps that was a good thing, because if we had thought too hard about what we were doing—inviting 140 people to an event that required a lengthy explanation—we might never have done it. Because we were inviting so many kids, we chose a summer camp lodge in the hills for a location. David and I had fun picking out wine and music for the DJ together. In some ways, preparing for the event was like the first time around; I tried on at least six pairs of earrings; I whitened my teeth and bought special undergarments. This time, though, instead of Victoria's Secret it was Spanx to keep my tummy flat. Kate and I went to the west side of Los Angeles to look for my dress in fancy department stores and had tea together after we picked out a stunning coral evening gown. We ordered Kate a white flower girl dress with pink trim and a crown of white flowers, plus a matching outfit for her American Girl doll. We sent out invitations to all our friends.

With only a couple of months to go, the one task we hadn't gotten to was designing a ceremony of some sort. So David and I spent a few late evenings trying to figure it out. We revisited our reasons: reaffirming our original vows, acknowledging that having kids can challenge a marriage, and celebrating having tackled that challenge and making it to the other side. David questioned me, "Why do we have to do it publicly though? It seems self-centered." I replied, "I think we celebrate publicly for the same reasons first weddings are shared with friends and family. Making a public declaration of our commitment means we are asking our community to both hold us to our promises and support us in keeping them. Plus, we have a whole new community of friends now who didn't know us back then and I want to celebrate with the people who are part of our lives at this stage." That made sense to David and we got to the point where we could explain why we wanted to renew our vows, but we couldn't seem to hit upon what the ceremony should look like. Then David made the breakthrough. He said, "You know, the promises we made to each other when we got married were bidirectional, between you and me, but now the promises are tridirectional, they include Kate too."

With that insight, a ceremony took shape. We wanted to reaffirm our original promises to each other, we wanted to make new promises to each other now that Kate was our shared responsibility, and we wanted to make promises to Kate. One more date night dinner, and we had hammered out the ceremony and the vows we wanted to make. David insisted that he would be the one to welcome everyone to the event to start the ceremony, which told me this was really just as much his event as it was mine. David and Kate and I rehearsed together a few times in the hallway at home. Even with the event a few weeks away, all the time we spent talking and planning was already having an impact. I would think about David or look at him across the room and get that queasy feeling in my chest that I remembered from when our love was brand-new.

When the day arrived, Kate and I spent the morning getting our hair done with Kate chattering with excitement to everyone in the salon. At home, we all rushed to get dressed in our finery. As we drove up the hill late in the afternoon, I squeezed David's hand. "I've got butterflies," I said. "I do too," he replied.

The evening was wonderfully and unseasonably warm for a March day in Los Angeles. David and I stood at the gate in the shade-dappled late afternoon sun and welcomed our friends and family. We could hardly get Kate to sit still long enough to get her picture taken. She was too busy hugging her cousin Jack and running around with all her favorite friends. When she did stand still, we later discovered she'd stuck out her tongue in the middle of the picture.

White tablecloths and flowers had done wonders for an old lodge, and as the adults took their seats, forty kids gathered on the floor just in front of a small stage. Kate took her spot in the back corner, carrying a white basket that held her doll and a pile of pink rose petals. David, looking handsome in his tux, took the stage to welcome everyone and then I joined him and we explained to everyone what we were doing and why. I looked out at all those tables filled with friends and family and explained that we would begin the ceremony with Kate. We had chosen to play "Waiting on an Angel," the song David had sung to me when I was pregnant. As the music played, Kate walked slowly through the tables, scattering pink petals and smiling with her entire face. She stepped lightly to the side of the stage with David's brother Bob and my sister Jane, who then asked that everyone who had attended our first wedding in Minnesota please stand.

As a handful of our family and long-time friends stood, David and I held hands and turned to each other, smiling and, yes, unexpectedly nervous. David spoke first, repeating our original wedding vows. "Kristin, I promise to strive to be someone who is worthy of your love and respect. I promise to be true to you and to the pursuit of the dreams and goals we both share. I promise to love and cherish you, comfort and encourage you, and never cease to give thanks that we have found each other." Shaking, I did the same. "David, I promise to strive to be someone who is worthy of your love and respect.

I promise to be true to you and to the pursuit of the dreams and goals we both share. I promise to love and cherish you, comfort and encourage you, and never cease to give thanks that we have found each other." Saying those words again to David, I was taken with how good it felt, how even "new" it felt inside.

Everyone sat down and Kate then joined us at the microphone, smiling out at the audience as she stood between us and took our hands. "Kate," I said to her, "Daddy and I have a new promise we are making to each other because you are part of our family now." I turned to David and said, "David, because we share responsibility for Kate for the rest of our lives, I promise to share the time, the money, and the care for her and for our family." Squeezing Kate's hand, David looked at me and repeated, "Kristin, because we share responsibility for Kate for the rest of our lives, I promise to share the time, the money, and the care for her and for our family."

David turned to Kate and said, "Kate, now we have some promises to make to you." We both smiled at Kate and said in unison, "We promise we will always be a family. We promise to help you pursue your dreams and goals. We promise to love and cherish you, comfort and encourage you, and never cease to give thanks that you've come into our lives."

Now it was time for Kate's line. She reached her arms up and declared, "Time for hugs and kisses!" David picked her up into a big group hug. He kissed me and then we both planted kisses on Kate, leaving a big lipstick mark on my side of her cheek. The room applauded and the party began. As parents led toddlers along the buffet table, David and I mingled. People said they hadn't known what to expect but loved it. Our friend Chris said we'd passed his wife's "cry test"; she'd started crying when Kate walked through the room. Another friend said we'd made him tear up and his wife had poked fun at him for being mushy. Our friends and family were as moved by it as we had been.

We started up the music. David and I had a short first dance and then we invited Kate and everyone else to join us to dance to "We Are Family" and the party really got started. The floor was full of

kids of all sizes and grown-ups who probably hadn't danced in a long
while. Moms and dads, two-year olds and ten-year olds all did the
Hokey Pokey and the Chicken Dance. David and his guy friends, a
group someone that night called the "cool dads," danced with their
kids. We played music from *High School Musical 2* and *Hannah Montana* and the 1970s and everyone danced to everything. Off and on I
would catch a glimpse of Kate running through the room, her pink
sash undone and streaming behind her, having the time of her life.

The entire evening was unforgettable.

When it was all over, David and I sat at home recovering and
reliving it. Going in, we had wondered how we would feel making
the promises since a renewal doesn't have the gravitas of a wedding.
Instead, we found that as we had exchanged vows we had each felt
the same excited, happy, emotional feelings as we had the first time
around. David said that forcing ourselves to go through with renewing our vows was hard because it was risky, it took time, and money,
but we had to do it. "It's special," he said. "It's worth it because it
is such a unique moment in time." Neither of us regretted a single
penny or a single moment of time we'd invested in making it all
happen. The next wedding was something Kate, David, and I would
always carry in our memory. David and I had added one last new and
improved belief to our list.

- Having children changes a marriage; the transition couples
  go through and the new commitments they make deserve
  their own celebration.

The next wedding was our own unique way of celebrating the
remodeling we had completed . . . together.

REMODELING TOOLS

▶ Together, try making a list of all the work it takes to maintain your family and home and who is doing what right now. If you need a starter list, visit www.mothersandmore .org/Forum/ChoreWars.shtml. Talk about how you each feel about the way the work gets done now—no commitments, no accusations, no solutions—and what your ideal would be if you could wave a magic wand. Then talk about experimental changes you might make and how.

▶ Carolyn Pape Cowan and Phillip A. Cowan found that couples groups have great potential for easing the transition to parenthood, but very few of these programs exist. They offer a list of recommendations for couples to use on their own and elaborate on them in their book *When Partners Become Parents*. Some of those recommendations include:[21]

- ◆ "Share expectations" of family life in advance.
- ◆ "Give yourselves regular 'checkups.' "
- ◆ "Make time to talk with each other."
- ◆ "Adopt an experimental attitude."
- ◆ "Don't ignore sex and intimacy."
- ◆ "Talk with a friend or co-worker."

▶ In their book *The Transition to Parenthood*, Jay Belsky and John Kelly identify six characteristics that help parents weather the transition and illustrate them with couples' stories. I discovered after the fact that David and I had stumbled across many of them on our own.[22]

- ◆ "Surrender individual goals and needs and work together as a team."
- ◆ "Resolve differences about division of labor and work in a mutually satisfactory manner."
- ◆ "Handle stresses in a way that does not overstress a partner or a marriage."

- ◆ "Fight constructively and maintain a pool of common interests despite diverging priorities."
- ◆ "Realize that however good a marriage becomes postbaby, it will not be good in the same way it was prebaby."
- ◆ "Maintain the ability to communicate in a way that continues to nurture the marriage."

▶ Remember the identity pie chart idea from Pape Cowan and Cowan that I suggested back in Chapter 3? Try having both spouses create one and compare. Consider the different aspects of your life, and then draw a pie chart showing how big each part feels, regardless of how much time you spend on it.[23] How big is the difference between the two charts? What is one small thing you could do to close the gap?

▶ Is something changing in your family? A new baby, a new job, a child going to school for the first time? Before any major change, sit down to look at the list of family work and what impact the change will have. Having this conversation regularly transforms it into just a normal conversation to have.

▶ Marc and Amy Vachon have a website and seminars dedicated to what they call equally shared parenting. "In a world set up to expect mothers to be in charge at home, it does take purpose and intent to keep things equal. Hence, the extra work an Equally Shared Parenting (ESP) couple has to do as a team to keep their equality alive. But this work is *not* 'you against me'—it is the team of two parents against societal norms." Visit www.equallysharedparenting .com to learn more.

▶ Jessica Degroot, a work-life expert, founded The ThirdPath Institute to help find "new options for men and women to approach family and new and innovative ways to redesign work and create more time for life." The ThirdPath calls its new work-family model "Shared Care." Visit www.thirdpath .org to learn more about ThirdPath resources for couples.

▶ Pull out your original wedding vows. What don't they cover about being married with children? What if you believed that *having children changes a marriage; the transition couples go through and the new commitments they make deserve their own celebration*? What would you do or say? Talk together about the assumptions you both have about the commitment of time, energy, and money you are making to be a family. Imagine together what vows you might make to each other now. Imagine how you might like to celebrate a new commitment in a way that is unique to you.

▶ Pick up a book.

◆ *When Partners Become Parents: The Big Life Change for Couples* by Carolyn Pape Cowan and Philip A. Cowan.

◆ *The Transition to Parenthood: How a First Child Changes a Marriage and Why Some Couples Grow Closer and Others Apart* by Jay Belsky and John Kelly.

◆ *The Lazy Husband: How to Get Men to Do More Parenting and Housework* by Joshua Coleman. A good book with an unfortunate title that uses all this good research to provide mothers with strategies and includes a chapter for husbands to read.

AFTERWORD

remodeling motherhood for ourselves,
our families, and our future

IN THE SUMMER of 1997, a few years before Kate was born, David and I went with some friends to the game that launched the Women's National Basketball Association. The Los Angeles Sparks were playing the New York Liberty at the Great Western Forum, the arena where the legendary Lakers played. We got our popcorn and nachos. We found our seats. We laughed and talked while the players warmed up. Then we all stood for the national anthem. As the first notes played, I started crying. My tears took me by surprise. I watched the players with their eyes on the flag and their hands on their hearts. I took in the packed stadium and the TV cameras. I realized that if I ever had a daughter, she would never know a world where girls couldn't play basketball. Our country's view of girls and women had been irreversibly changed. Playing my own small part in that change had changed me. My own view of the world and my role in it had been irreversibly changed. The tears ran down my cheeks and wouldn't stop.

As a young girl, at first I challenged the way things were simply because I wanted to play ball. If the girls didn't get the good gym, then I'll play with the boys. If the varsity boys team gets a band and concession stand at the games, then I wanted our team to get them too. Along the way though, what began as a personal issue transformed into something more. As I piped up at people and poked at the system to get what I wanted, both the people and the system reacted to what I was saying and doing. Sometimes the responses I got signaled, "Girls shouldn't play." I didn't like that answer, so I got better and better at articulating to myself and to other people what I wanted and what I believed was fair. At other times I got praise from my parents and a few teachers for taking action when I felt something was unfair. Over time, I came to think of myself as someone who stands up for what I believe in. My own poking and prodding and the responses I got gave me an understanding of who I was and how the world worked. I was contributing to a larger paradigm shift and experiencing one myself. All simply because I wanted to play basketball. Without those interactions, I would not be who I am today.

When you set out to remodel the world, it changes you too. When you want to remodel your own life, it helps to do your part to change the world.

WHEN A TREE CRASHES THROUGH THE ROOF

Have you ever known someone who was forced to remodel their house? Maybe a storm dropped a tree on the roof or mold grew in the walls and they had to overhaul the whole place. A lot of the seismic social shifts in world history have been remodels forced by other economic, demographic, political, technological, or environmental shifts—the proverbial tree crashing through the roof. For example, the invention of the printing press transformed the social order by making reading available to all classes, not just the rich and the clergy. The Industrial Revolution transformed the relationship between labor and management.

In just the same way, seismic events like widespread drought, the Great Depression, and World War II converged in the late 1930s and 1940s to force a remodel of our economic, political, and social structures. Ultimately, public policy is an expression of people's values and beliefs. Social and economic structures spring from the assumptions people have at the time about the way the world works and the way they'd like it to work. So when this forced remodel happened, people used a blueprint with a set of mental maps about mothers, fathers, money, marriage, and work that were commonly shared at the time. In a span of ten years, the foundation was laid and the walls were put up.

- The creation of Social Security codified the assumptions about men, women, and money.
- The Fair Labor Standards Act established the forty-hour work week and overtime laws.
- Companies attached benefits to full-time jobs.
- The switch to joint filing of taxes for married couples discouraged women from employment.
- The publication of Dr. Spock's *Baby and Childcare* captured and spread expectations about how mothers should care for children.

As distant and arcane as some of these may seem, they and the assumptions behind them impact our lives everyday. Why? *Because mental maps are the connection between the personal and the political.* The same assumptions that trip us up every day are the ones built into the political, social, and cultural walls of the house back in the 1930s and 1940s.

For example, from the mental map that *caring for family isn't really work, it's just what mothers do* we get both the personal:

- "What did you do all day?"
- "When are you coming back from your baby vacation?"

and the political:

- No Social Security credit for years spent caring for family.
- Welfare policies that require single parents to take a low-pay or no-pay job to get some help rather than care for their own children.

From the mental maps that *mothers who are not employed are dull* and *mothers who are employed are selfish,* we get both the personal:

- Identity Whiplash.
- "You can't have it all."

and the political:

- Family responsibilities discrimination.

From the mental map that *jobs are one-size-fits-all* we get both the personal:

- Mothers and fathers feel like square pegs at work.
- Mothers feel "lucky" if they can find a customized job with low pay and no benefits.

and the political:

- Health insurance attached to full-time jobs.
- A wage gap between mothers and everyone else.

From the mental maps that *he who earns it owns it* and *mothers' earnings are just extra, pin money,* we get both the personal:

- "Can I make enough to pay for childcare?"
- Power shifts in our marriages.

and the political:

- Income tax policy that taxes secondary earners more.
- Family law that penalizes the spouse who gives up earnings to be able to care for family.

The outdated mental maps are the common denominator across both our personal experience and the political systems and their consequences. Families have changed over the years. The commonly stated beliefs about mothers, fathers, marriage, money, and work have changed. Yet we've only made incremental changes to our house. We haven't really been forced to remodel since the last storm. So families feel out of sync, uncomfortable, like they can't win no matter what they do.

But guess what?

The tree is crashing through the roof again.

As the 2008 financial crisis began to take hold, newspapers and magazines and politicians increasingly compared the crisis, the challenges it presented, and the solutions required to the Great Depression. Yet the financial crisis is just one of a collection of converging seismic shifts likely to force a remodel on the scale of the late 1930s and 1940s.

The largest generation of our time, the Baby Boomers, is entering retirement and living longer. They are requiring more care by families already stretched to care for their children, and they are drawing more money from Social Security. When combined with an increasing high school drop-out rate, the Boomers' retirement has led to projections of a severe shortage of college-educated workers. At the same time, colleges now graduate more women than men every year, and during the recession more men than women have lost their jobs and more women have needed to reenter the workforce or increase their employment hours. Employers and the economy as a whole will need women even more and families will increasingly depend on their incomes.[1] The financial crisis has proved beyond a doubt that our economy is now a global one in which companies and workers must compete around the world, and our country's economic fortunes are tied to countries across the sea. Add terrorism, global warming, and digital and biomedical technology advances and we have the perfect storm—one that will send a tree crashing through the roof that will force us to remodel as a nation.

While all these trends will present challenges for mothers and families, as they converge they will also present opportunities.

- Will employers' need for educated workers—largely women and family-focused Gen Y workers—force companies to provide a larger variety of job structures to attract and retain workers?
- Will retiring Boomers find they need and want to stay employed but not at full-time jobs—adding pressure on employers to restructure jobs to hang on to experienced and educated workers?
- Will more mothers be the primary earner and more fathers the primary care provider—giving fathers more and more motivation to push for changes that were once the sole concern of mothers?
- Will the need to restructure Social Security to make it financially sustainable present an opportunity to remodel it to be more in sync with modern families?
- Will the urgency of reforming healthcare present an opportunity to restructure the relationship between jobs and health insurance such that companies can offer a variety of job structures and people can use them without losing health insurance?

We don't know if these opportunities or others will come or when. Yet we can and should be hopeful that now more than ever change is possible. Change is inevitable. The question is whether the change follows the old blueprint about mothers, fathers, money, marriage, and work or follows our new one.[2]

OLD BLUEPRINT	NEW BLUEPRINT
• Mothers are responsible for and are naturally better at children and family.	• Mothers and fathers share the responsibility and are equally capable of caring for children and home.
• Fathers are responsible for and are naturally better at employment and earning money.	• Mothers and fathers share the responsibility and are equally capable of employment and contributing to the family's financial security.
• Mothers are completely fulfilled by caring for family.	• All mothers are unique. All fathers are unique.
• Mothers who are employed or pursue personal fulfillment are selfish.	• A mother is more than any single role she plays at any given point in her lifetime. She is entitled to fully explore and develop her identity as she chooses: as a woman, a citizen, a parent, or an employee.
• Employment is women's path to fulfillment and equality.	
• Mothers who are not employed are dull.	
• Caring for family isn't really work, it's just what mothers do.	• The transitions women make into and through motherhood are challenging and can be difficult.
• Jobs are one-size-fits-all, fifty hours a week, fifty weeks a year, for fifty years of our lives.	• Caring for others is a vital human and economic activity and a public service.
• Family and employment are separate.	• A variety of job structures to fit various stages of personal lives is best for people, families, businesses, and communities.
• Mothers are financially dependent on fathers; mothers' earnings are pin money, just extra.	• Family and employment can be integrated and complementary.
• He who earns it owns it.	• A person's time belongs first and foremost to that person.
• Time belongs primarily to the employer not the employee.	• Time is a shared family resource and responsibility.
• Children and marriage go together.	• Family income and wealth are the result of joint work—both family work and employment—so they are owned jointly by both spouses.
	• Having children changes a marriage; the transition couples go through and the new commitments they make deserve their own celebration.

WILL WE BE READY WHEN OPPORTUNITY KNOCKS?

We never know when an opportunity to remodel using the new blue-print will knock at our door. Back when I was spending time writing and learning about Social Security, it wasn't exactly a hot topic. I did it as a way to understand what was happening to me and why. Four years later, President George W. Bush's proposal for privatizing Social Security made it front page news for over a year. I was ready. Although most analyses focused on the straight economics of the proposal, dealing with questions like What would it cost? and Would retirees end up with more or less money? I analyzed the proposal from a different perspective. Would the proposals perpetuate the old mental maps about mothers, fathers, and money or align more closely with the new ones? I wrote articles and letters to the editor pointing out where the proposal got it right and where it remained out of date. Bush's proposal died, but what if it hadn't? What if we had remodeled Social Security without getting rid of all the outdated assumptions embedded in it the first time around? We might have been stuck with them for another seventy years. When the opportunities knock, if we're not ready to share our new blueprint, if we haven't made our voices heard, even people with the best of inten-tions may design policies that perpetuate the old mental maps. And then those old mental maps will continue to shape our personal experience.

We need to make sure that when the opportunity comes to change things, as many people as possible share our updated beliefs. We need to ask ourselves: When the opportunity to remodel something presents itself, will your congressperson understand that *mothers and fathers share the responsibility and are equally capable of caring for children and doing family work?*

When the opportunity presents itself, will your state representa-tive understand that *family income and wealth is the result of joint work so both partners own and control it equally?*

When the opportunity presents itself, will your city council person know that *caring for others is a vital human and economic activity and a public service?*

When the opportunity presents itself, will your employer know that *a variety of job structures to fit various stages of personal lives is best for people, families, businesses, and communities*?

They will know these things if you are in one of those positions yourself. They will know these things if these people are your family, your friends, or your community members who you've talked and worked with. They will know if you've told them and keep telling them every chance you get.

WHERE DO I START?

That night I was speaking in Minnesota about mothers and employment, I told the group about family responsibilities discrimination and how it stems from mental maps about mothers and fathers and jobs. At the end of my talk someone asked, "But what can we do about family responsibilities discrimination?"

I answered, "First, don't wait for someone else, or some advocacy organization to prioritize FRD and tell you what to do. We don't have to wait for a national court case or even a state statute. Did you know that Atlanta, Georgia, and Milwaukee, Wisconsin, and Tacoma, Washington, have all adopted local laws prohibiting discrimination on the basis of 'familial status'?"[3] To drive the point home I said, "Imagine if next week all sixty-five of you showed up at your city council meeting, with your children, with your husbands, and told them you want them to prohibit family responsibilities discrimination in your city? Imagine the power. They would have to listen." The room paused as they looked around at each other and imagined a crowd of families in front of the city council and the potential dawned on them. I think their assumption was that my answer would be to tell them about a big organization working on the issue and what e-mails they could send or money they could donate, but instead I told them the power lay with them—together.

I imagine at this point you too might expect or hope for me to tell you exactly what to do and what policies or practices you should support. But I've found that telling someone else what's important and what to do is the opposite of what works and what's right. No one else knows what you care about or which issues will help you personally. No one else knows how much or how little room in your life you have right now. No one else knows how to fit activism into your life—except you.

I hope that my story has illustrated what I care about and how activism fits into my everyday life and helps me transform my everyday life. I hope the remodeling tools at the end of the chapters give you some ideas with which to experiment. I can tell you what I think about *how* to do something. One, start small. The first action I ever took around these issues was sending an e-mail, not to my congressperson but to my friends and family. I sent it when Kate was four months old during her naptime.

From: Kristin Maschka
Sent: Wednesday, February 28, 2001 12:46 PM
To: Everyone I Know
Subject: Must-Read Book!

Hello all!

I've just finished reading a new book that should be required reading for all mothers! I can't recommend it highly enough!

It's called. . . . *The Price of Motherhood: Why the Most Important Job in the World Is Still the Least Valued* by Ann Crittenden.

It just came out this month, and it is amazing. Buy it, read it, lend it to a friend, discuss it. Hope you enjoy it as much as I did!

Start with what you care about. Pick a chapter of this book that made you particularly excited or confused or angry and experiment. Get together with a few friends. Share your stories. Find the hidden mental maps. The minds you open because you talk over coffee make a big contribution. Read a book to learn more about a topic that interests you. Lend the book to a friend. I keep several copies of my favorite books on hand so I can hand them out when I have the opportunity. See if your library has them and donate copies. Take a cue from Amy Richards, author of *Opting In: Having a Child Without Losing Yourself*. In an e-mail discussion she advised, "Look for things that upset you or anger you and try to build projects from there. The last thing I want to do is to add more to someone's list—my goal is that people incorporate activism into their lives rather than add more to their lives." Or take a cue from Tara, a mother in upstate New York, who created a campaign for her Mothers & More chapter called "Power of a Purse," which collected donated purses to give to homeless mothers while at the same time sending a powerful symbolic message about the economic risks of motherhood.

Don't get paralyzed by how much there is to do, just take your piece of the remodeling job. Start local. If the conversation and stories bubble up a need to do something more, have confidence that as my friend Judy is fond of saying, "Making change is not rocket science. Most of the hands-on work of grassroots activism involves things you already know how to do. If you've organized a bake sale, you can organize for change." And she adds, "Everything else you need to know can be learned." So when you need to, find the people in your community who know how to get on the city council agenda or who run the chamber of commerce or who know how to get a meeting with your congressperson and learn from them. Find out who else works on issues you care about locally, in your state, or nationally. Connect with a few of the organizations that are made up primarily of mothers and focused on issues facing mothers and families. They are listed in the Resources section of this book.

Finally, let me add just one more idea. Let's all make Mother's Day resolutions each year about the small steps each of us will take that year in our own life or together with other mothers to get rid of the outdated mental maps. Share your resolutions and find more remodeling tools at www.remodelingmotherhood.com. Hopefully any remodeling work you tackle will make a difference in someone else's life. But because mental maps are the connection between the personal and the political, you can be certain it will make a difference in your own. We'll all be one step closer to remodeling motherhood for ourselves, our families, and our future.

ACKNOWLEDGMENTS

THE TWO PEOPLE who come first, last, and always for me are David and Kate. They've let me share our story in intimate detail and put up with me while I wrote about it for so long, so they get to come first here too. Before this book was even an idea, David Hitchcock took on the project of a lifetime with me—bucking just about everything around us and our own preconceived notions of "success" to remodel our family life into what we wanted. Then, David was the one who, when I said what I really wanted to do was write a book, simply said, "Then you have to do it. We'll make it work." David was a rock of support. He rehashed our first years of parenthood with me. He took over when I went away for weekend writing retreats. He got his father friends together to talk with me and listening to him explain this stuff to his friends over margaritas made me fall in love with him all over again. I'm so glad I married him . . . twice.

This book wouldn't exist without Kate. Exuberant, grinning, boisterous Kate, who never met anyone she couldn't befriend. Kate read chapters for me to make sure everything passed the eight-year-old humor test. She still laughs uncontrollably every time she reads the vomit on the wall story. One day as I approached the end of writing this book, I was in the kitchen while Kate was watching Saturday morning TV. She shouted at the top of her lungs, "Mama! Come here! Come here! You have to see this!" Expecting to see an ad for a toy she wanted, or a new song from Hannah Montana, I joined her. She pushed the rewind button and said, "You have to see this commercial for juice."

A commercial for Juicy Juice came on the screen. Images of a mother and child in the sun at the park and chasing each other around a house with shiny wood floors came onto the screen. As the two smiled on the screen, the voiceover said:

> Motherhood means victories are rewarded; dolls are rescued; dinosaurs are saved. Motherhood means climate control, special orders, and teamwork.
>
> Motherhood means always giving 100 percent because it's the little things you do for them now that make all the difference later.
>
> Juicy Juice. The very best juice for the very best kids.

Kate turned to me with a huge grin on her face. "Do you see that Mommy? They think that mommies are the only ones who take care of kids, but that's not true." Kate gets it, and that all by itself is reward enough for the whole thing.

I want to thank my mother, Kathleen, for all her support and for giving me my love of books and words, and my father, Jerry, for playing ball with me and making sure I knew I could do anything I wanted to in life. My sisters, Sarah and Jane, for always being there and making sure I don't take myself too seriously. My mom's sister, Ann, for being a comforting and constant source of support for this book. And my best friend for twenty-five years, Tammy Shain, who's pretty much family now, for always knowing in her gut when I was having a bad writing day and from miles away calling at just the right moment to rescue me. David's parents, John and Ida Hitchcock, are truly the added bonus I got for marrying David. I am so grateful to have them in my life and am especially thankful for Ida's unconditional willingness to share in taking care of Kate. Kate and David and I are all richer for having both of them play an integral part of our everyday lives.

A huge thank-you to my agent, Laura Nolan, at The Creative Culture, and to my editor, Denise Silvestro, at Berkley, for their unwavering support and capable guidance. Both are mothers who understood right away what I was trying to do with this book. I guess they wanted to make sure they *really* understood the need for this book because both had their second child in the middle of the whole process! Also at Berkley, I want to thank designer Rita Frangie for capturing the essence of my book in her beautiful cover design.

I am so grateful to all my friends at Mothers & More, especially Debra Levy, Joanne Brundage, and Judith Stadtman Tucker, with whom I've had a nine-year conversation about these issues that I hope never ends. As I was writing, Debra shipped me books I needed from her library, called to check on me, and e-mailed me articles and her late-night musings. Judy pointed me to key resources, and her papers and our conversations about social change have helped me tremendously in thinking about how to write about all these issues through the lens of my own experience. Joanne, well, where would I be if she hadn't founded Mothers & More? Mothers & More has been so generous with providing me access to data and member stories and helping me put out the call for more stories as I needed them. The stories here that come from "e-mail conversations" largely come from the POWER Loop and some from other member e-mail loops. So a big thank-you goes to Mothers & More members all over the country and over the years who have contributed to this book simply by being part of Mothers & More. Plus my own Mothers & More chapter in Pasadena has been and continues to be a source of enlightenment, laughter, and lifelong friends. Thanks go as well to the hundreds of additional mothers and fathers who contributed to my surveys and who gave me permission to use their stories here.

My writing group, Kim Tso and Bev Belling, let me monopolize our conversations for more than two years. They were gentle with me when I needed it, yet offered up feedback that made the book so much better at each step. How ridiculously lucky for me to have a writing group while writing this particular book that included Bev, a life coach with an artist's soul, and Kim, whose knowledge about women's issues, economics, and public policy goes even deeper than my own.

Filling the role of number one cheerleader was my friend Rosemary Baxter Baker, who comforted me when I was sobbing and convinced I would never find my voice, who listened when I was on a roll and wanted to share it, and who kept telling me how much she and everyone she talked to needed this book. Thanks Rosie. And thank you to your husband, Clif, along with our friends Anne and Eric, and Lee and Lisa, for moral support, picking up Kate at school, and making sure we all had wine and food on Friday nights.

Then there's the team of mother friends I hired to help me get all this done, starting with my long-time career coach, Susan W. Miller, who helped me get from thinking about writing a book to doing it. Christine O'Brien, who edited every chapter. Cathy Nathan, who tracked down all the random tidbits of research I needed and then put together all the endnotes. Nancy Stiles and Maggie Brandow who helped her. Nancy Dufford, who helped me with marketing and promotion. Neighbor Sue Zamparelli, who created the diagrams. And Rebecca Little, who did just about anything I needed, including tracking all the permissions and, most important, coordinating the "next wedding." I am also incredibly fortunate to have friends willing to volunteer their time as well, so thank you to Margaret Thomas, Susan Williams, and Tara Brettholtz for pitching in on the promotion team.

I hosted several margarita nights so thank you to anyone else who ever had a margarita with me, shared their stories, and let me talk through ideas. That includes you Felita, Beth, Amy, Emily, Julie R., Edie, Kelly, and Jackie. A special thank-you to all the dads who joined me that one night. You know who you are. And a special thank-you to our friends Julie and Tod Cole, who both went above and beyond to lend me their feedback and support.

I was fortunate to have a series of amazing English teachers in public school in Mankato, Minnesota, and I am indebted to them all, especially Mrs. Kudela, Mr. O'Brien, Mr. Dorn, and Ms. Etzell for nurturing both my writing and my love of writing. Reconnecting with my high school composition teacher, Gretchen Etzell, was one of the unexpected benefits of writing this book. Thanks Gretchen, for believing in me and coaching my voice back then and helping me find that voice again twenty years later.

I also want to express my unending gratitude to all the authors and researchers I've read and referred to here. Especially those who've talked with me over the years—Ann Crittenden, Joan Williams, Ed McCaffery, and Margaret Heffernan. I hope I've struck a properly humble and grateful tone that matches how I feel about all the great work all of you have done and how much it helps me and so many families. Plus a thank-you to Sandra Tsing Loh for supporting a fellow "Mother on Fire" along the way.

Finally, I have a few places to thank. The Starbucks at Washington and Allen in Pasadena, my second office, where the staff always asked how the book was coming along. The Hampton Inn in Arcadia, my home away from home when I needed a writing retreat. And Amigo's Restaurant on Colorado, which always saved the big booth in the back for me when I needed to get mothers or fathers together to talk things out.

The margaritas are on me, everyone! Thanks so much.

NOTES

INTRODUCTION

1   The "balcony view" is a common concept in organizational change, especially in education. My own use of the term came from reading Garmston and Wellman many years ago. Garmston and Wellman, *The Adaptive School*, 56.

2   Senge et al., *The Fifth Discipline Fieldbook*, 235. See also Senge, *The Fifth Discipline*, 174–204.

3   Senge et al., *The Fifth Discipline Fieldbook*, 235.

4   "The trend in organized sports reveals girls and women are participating in sports in record numbers at all levels—from youth to high school, up through college and professional sports." In 1972, one in twenty-seven girls were actively participating in sports; by 2007 that ratio had increased to one in three. "Girls 6 to 17 years of age now account for approximately 44% (11.4 million) of sports team members." Tucker Center for Research on Girls & Women in Sport, *The 2007 Tucker Center Research Report*, 2.

5   "Generating new mental models, if they are to take hold, can take place only by linking imagination to action. Ask yourselves, 'If we did hold better models of our customers, how would we behave?' Then try the new behavior and over time see if the new view of the world feels closer to reality." Senge et al., *The Fifth Discipline Fieldbook*, 242. See also Pipher, *Writing to Change the World*, 103; Blair and Lenton, "Imagining Stereotypes Away."

6   To satisfy my history of science professors from the University of Chicago, I just want to note that I know Copernicus was really the one who developed the mathematical model for heliocentrism. Galileo just took the heat for it from the church. And I know the sun is not really at the center of the universe, but in the interests of metaphor and language, I ended the introduction with the same heliocentric view.

CHAPTER 1

1   Jacobsen, "Chore Wars," 5.

2   Mucinex advertisement, seen in *Parents* magazine, Oct. 2007, p. 267. (emphasis added)

3   Dimetapp advertisement, seen in *Parents* magazine, Nov. 2007, p. 31. (emphasis added)

4   "MEN AND WOMEN: SAME DIFFERENCE: In contrast to the media focus on gender differences, a new consensus challenging this view is emerging from

the research literature. Many well-designed studies find no significant gender
differences with respect to such cognitive and social behaviors as nurturance,
sexuality, aggression, self-esteem, and math and verbal abilities. The big story
is that there is far greater within-gender variability on such behaviors than
there is between-gender difference. For example, when young boys act up and
get physical we are accustomed to hearing their behavior explained away by
their high levels of testosterone. In fact, boys' and girls' testosterone levels are
virtually identical during the preschool years when rough-and-tumble play is
at its peak." Barnett, "Unconventional Wisdom."
5   Senge et al., *The Fifth Discipline Fieldbook*, 242.
6   Coltrane, "Families and Gender Equity."
7   Jacobsen, "Chore Wars," 5.

CHAPTER 2
1   Sanders and Bullen, *Staying Home.*
2   Mothers & More. "Connections Survey." 2007.
3   Mohler, "Are Stay at Home Moms 'Letting Down the Team?' "
4   T. Berry Brazelton quoted by Hulbert, *Raising America,* 324.
5   Smith, *A Potent Spell,* 85
6   Ibid., 89.
7   "A mother may blunder on, as most of them do, till she has killed a number
    of children, before she is capable of rearing one." William Buchan, MD, 1817,
    quoted in ibid., 117.
8   Freedman, *No Turning Back,* 48–49.
9   Hays, *The Cultural Contradictions of Motherhood,* 2; Smith, *A Potent Spell,* 106–
    119.
10 Hays, *The Cultural Contradictions of Motherhood,* 29.
11 Abbott, *The Mother at Home;* Smith, *A Potent Spell.*
12 William Buchan, a nineteenth-century doctor, advised mothers that in "all
    cases of dwarfishness and deformity, ninety-nine out of a hundred are owing to
    the folly, misconduct or neglect of mothers." Quoted in Smith, *A Potent Spell,*
    117.
13 Abbot wrote, "The mother of [George] Washington is entitled to a nation's
    gratitude." Abbot contrasted Martha Washington with Lord Byron's mother,
    "the mother who fostered in his youthful heart those passions which made
    the son a curse to his fellow-men." Both quotations from *The Mother at Home,*
    11–12.
14 Smith, *A Potent Spell,* 109.
15 "According to a 1981 study, 97% of American mothers read at least one
    child rearing manual. Nearly ¾ consult two or more manuals for advice on
    how to rear their young. (Geboy, 1981)" Hays, *The Cultural Contradictions of
    Motherhood,* 51.
16 "*Dr. Spock's Baby and Child Care* (1985) has sold 40 million copies in its six
    editions, outselling all other books in the history of publishing with the single
    exception of the Bible. (Hackett 1967; "At S & S" 1992)." Ibid.
17 Ibid., 39–45.
18 Smith, *A Potent Spell,* 126–164.

19   Spock, *Dr. Spock's Baby and Child Care*, 1.
20   Hays, *The Cultural Contradictions of Motherhood*, 48.
21   Hulbert's *Raising America* covers the last century of the rise of scientific expert
     advisers to mothers. Hulbert, *Raising America*, 314.
22   Hays, *The Cultural Contradictions of Motherhood*, 43.
23   Hulbert, *Raising America*.
24   Ibid., 365.
25   Hays, *The Cultural Contradictions of Motherhood*, 42–43.
26   *The Mommy Myth* provides a more detailed analysis of the idealization of
     mothers and the supermom phenomenon. Douglas and Michaels, *The Mommy
     Myth*, 79–80, 110–139.
27   The National Center for Public Policy and Higher Education, *Measuring Up
     2008*, 8.
28   Levy, "The Mask of Motherhood," 1.
29   Adapted from Mothers & More belief. "All mothers, all children and all families
     are unique. We respect the wisdom of each mother to decide how to care for her
     children, her family and herself." Mothers & More's Mission Statement & Core
     Beliefs (http://mothersandmore.org/AboutUs/mission.shtml).
30   "According to some cognitive theorists, changes in short-term everyday mental
     models, accumulating over time, will gradually be reflected in changes in
     long-term deep-seated beliefs." Senge et al., T*he Fifth Discipline Fieldbook*, 237.
31   See www.brainchildmag.com/about.

CHAPTER 3

1   Maschka, "Put on Your Own Oxygen Mask First," 1.
2   Pape Cowan and Cowan, *When Partners Become Parents,*80.
3   Mothers & More. "Connections Survey." 2007.
4   W. Bridges, *Managing Transitions*, 3–10.
5   Fels, *Necessary Dreams*, 3.
6   Apparently I was not alone in concluding motherhood might be a trap.
     Ruth Rosen's essay describes how common this feeling was for young adult
     women to express in the late sixties and seventies. Rosen, Ruth. "The Female
     Generation Gap: Daughters of the Fifties and the Origins of Contemporary
     American Feminism." In *U.S. History as Women's History,* edited by Kerber et
     al., 319–321.
7   Fels, *Necessary Dreams*, 14.
8   Ibid., 9–10, 72–98.
9   Ibid., 237.
10   De Marneffe, *Maternal Desire*, 3.
11   Levy, "Talking With: Maternal Desire," 12.
12   Fels, *Necessary Dreams*, 237.
13   First statement is adapted from a longer statement, "All mothers, all children
     and all families are unique. We respect the wisdom of each mother to decide
     how to care for her children, her family and herself." Mothers & More Mission
     Statement and Core Beliefs. See www.mothersandmore.org/AboutUs/mission
     .shtml.
14   These guiding questions are adapted from *ManagingTransitions*. Bridges,
     Managing Transitions, 25; Bridges, *Transitions*, 5.

15 Maschka, "Put on Your Own Oxygen Mask First," 7.
16 Ibid.
17 Pape Cowan and Cowan, *When Partners Become Parents,* 80.
18 Morgan Roberts et al., "How to Play to Your Strengths."

CHAPTER 4

1   Fels, *Necessary Dreams,* 74–78.
2   "A person is a person because of other people." Senge et al., *The Fifth Discipline Fieldbook*, 26.
3   Rosenthal and Jacobson, *Pygmalion in the Classroom;* Fels, *Necessary Dreams,* 81–82.
4   Mothers & More. "Connections Survey." 2007.
5   Project Implicit, "General Information"; Though I already new about implicit biases, reading *Blink* for reasons unrelated to writing the book helped me see the connections between implicit bias and our everyday experiences as mothers. Gladwell, *Blink.*
6   Implicit associations "can produce behavior that diverges from a person's avowed or endorsed beliefs or principles." Greenwald and Krieger, "Implicit Bias," 945.
7   Lane et al., "Understanding and Using the Implicit Association Test: IV What We Know (So Far) about the Method."
8   Bertrand and Mullainathan, "Are Emily and Greg More Employable Than Lakisha and Jamal?"
9   Nosek et al., "Harvesting Implicit Group Attitudes and Beliefs from a Demonstration Web Site," 108–109.
10 Fiske et al., "A Model of (Often Mixed) Stereotype Content: Competence and Warmth Respectively Follow From Perceived Status and Competition."
11 Etaugh and Study, "Perceptions of Mothers"; Jacobs and Gerson, *The Time Divide;* Bridges and Etaugh, "College Students' Perceptions of Mothers."
12 Epstein, Cynthia Fuchs et al. quoted in Stone, *Opting Out?,* 92–93.; Eagly and Steffen, "Gender Stereotypes, Occupational Roles, and Beliefs About Part-Time Employees," 258.
13 William Buchan, quoted in Smith, *A Potent Spell,* 109.
14 Smith, *A Potent Spell,* 110.
15 Schrobsdorff, "Some Day My 9-to-5 Job Will Come."
16 Cardoza, *Sequencing.*
17 Ibid.
18 "Deferred life" is a term I picked up from reading *The Monk and the Riddle.* Komisar, *The Monk and the Riddle,* chap. 4.
19 Heffernan, *The Naked Truth,* 130.
20 Mothers & More Programs. www.mothersandmore.org/Advocacy/programs .shtml.
21 For excellent analyses of the mommy wars phenomenon, see Douglas and Michaels, *The Mommy Myth;* Peskowitz, *The Truth behind the Mommy Wars,* 20–56; and DiQuinzio, "The Politics of the Mothers' Movement in the United States."
22 Project Implicit, "FAQs"; Blair, "The Malleability of Automatic Stereotypes and Prejudice"; Dasgupta and Asgari, "Seeing Is Believing."

23 Blair and Lenton, "Imagining Stereotypes Away."

24 "Living in a diverse neighborhood does not in itself seem to reduce bias, but having close friendships with people from other ethnic groups does appear to lower bias, the IAT researchers have found." Dasgupta and Greenwald, "On the Malleability of Automatic Attitudes." See also Vedantam, "See No Bias."

25 "In group bias designates favoritism towards groups to which one belongs." Greenwald and Krieger, "Implicit Bias." See also Brauer et al., "The Communication of Social Stereotypes" and Lane et al., "Understanding and Using the Implicit Association Test."

26 Project Implicit, "FAQs."

27 Nosek et al., "Harvesting Implicit Group Attitudes and Beliefs from a Demonstration Web Site,"108–109.

28 Third Wave Foundation, "I Spy Sexism."

29 Ibid.

CHAPTER 5

1 Crittenden, *The Price of Motherhood,* chap. 3.

2 Many examples can be found. One such example is Ellen Key, "all motherhood would be looked upon as holy." Quoted by Smith, *A Potent Spell,* 131.

3 "In the language of love, women are called angels; but this is a weak and silly compliment; they approach nearer to our ideas of the Deity." William Buchan, quoted by Smith, *A Potent Spell,* 109; Wallace, "What Rules the World."

4 Mohler, "Are Stay at Home Moms 'Letting Down the Team?' "

5 Lukas, "Mothers Don't Go on Strike."

6 Crittenden, *The Price of Motherhood,* 77, 194.

7 Kessler-Harris, Alice. "Designing Women and Old Fools: The Construction of the Social Security Amendments of 1939." In *U.S. History as Women's History,* edited by Kerber et al., 104–105.

8 Crittenden, *The Price of Motherhood,* 135.

9 U.S. Department of Health and Human Services, "Office of Family Assistance (OFA)"; The result of being forced to take unwaged employment to get a welfare check, says Pat Gowens of Welfare Warriors, is that "moms will take any job for any pay to avoid NO pay." Gowens, "Congress Betrays US People and the Constitution"; Peskowitz, *The Truth behind the Mommy Wars,* 176–186.

10 Folbre, *Valuing Children,* 101–102. Folbre discusses this concept in more detail, including its limitations.

11 De Marneffe, *Maternal Desire,* chap. 4.

12 Mothers & More. "Day After Time Use Survey." May 9, 2005.

13 Lukas, "Mothers Don't Go on Strike."

14 LIFE Foundation, "Who Needs Life Insurance?"; Elliott, "All Women."

15 Hanrahan, "Six Figure Moms."

16 In this instance, Folbre adapts a key question that drives her book. "If parents were unwilling or unable to provide care to their children, what would society need to pay to provide substitute care of acceptable quality?" to apply to an individual family. Folbre, *Valuing Children,* 121.

17 Ibid., 128–132.

18 Ibid., 39.

19 Folbre, *The Invisible Heart,* 32.

20   Folbre, *Valuing Children*, 180.
21   Ibid., 121 (emphasis added).
22   In 2006, there were 73.7 million children under age 18 in the United States.
     U.S. Census Bureau, *Annual Estimates of the Population by Selected Age Groups and
     Sex for the United States*, table 2.
23   Talberth et al., *The Genuine Progress Indicator 2006;* Family Caregiver Alliance,
     "Selected Caregiver Statistics."
24   Folbre, *Valuing Children*, 135.
25   "On December 26, 2007, President Bush signed into law the 2008
     Consolidated Appropriations Act. The bill provides $544.3 million in funding
     to the Bureau of Labor Statistics for the 2008 fiscal year that began on October
     1, 2007. This funding level is $30.2 million (or 5.3 percent) less than the
     President requested." U.S. Department of Labor, "Impact of the 2008 Federal
     Budget on the Availability and Quality of Data."
26   The total budget for calculating the GDP comes from the budget for
     development of the National Economic Accounts, the Regional Economic
     Accounts, and the Industry Economic Accounts. U.S. Department of
     Commerce. *Economic and Statistical Analysis Budget.*
27   U.S. Department of Commerce, "Glossary 'G.' "
28   McLaughlin, "Making Mothers Count."
29   Bianchi et al., "Maternal Employment and Family Caregiving."
30   Ibid., table 1.
31   Folbre also describes a Human Development Index as an option. Folbre,
     Valuing Children, 74.

CHAPTER 6
1   Mothers & More. "Part-Time Work Survey." 2005–2008.
2   Lovell, *No Time to Be Sick.*
3   Of workers who needed but did not take leave, 77.6 percent said they could
     not afford to lose income. Waldfogel, "Family and Medical Leave," 20.
4   Williams, *Unbending Gender*, 4.
5   Ibid., 111.
6   Mink and O'Connor, *Poverty in the United States;* May, "The Historical Problem
     of the Family Wage."
7   The National War Labor Board froze wages and implemented price controls
     in order to make sure labor disputes or economic disruptions didn't interfere
     with the production of weapons and war supplies. Montgomery, "Why
     Does America's Health Care System Rely on Job-Based Coverage?: A
     Brief History"; Employee Benefits Research Institute, "History of Health
     Insurance Benefits."
8   Montgomery, "Why Does America's Health Care System Rely on Job-Based
     Coverage?: A Brief History"; Employee Benefits Research Institute, "History
     of Health Insurance Benefits."
9   Williams, *Unbending Gender*, 111.
10   In comparing the 2002 NSCW with the 1977 Quality of Employment Survey
     for employees who work 20 or more hours per week, we find:
     • Men work 49 paid and unpaid hours on average at all jobs or the only job
       they have, up from 47 hours in 1977.

- The increase in hours worked by women is even larger—women work an average of 43.5 paid and unpaid hours now at all jobs, compared with 39 hours in 1977.

Many of us still think of 40 hours as the standard work week and in fact, it is for many. In 2002, 72 percent of men and 55 percent of women reported that their regularly scheduled work week in their main jobs was 40 hours, with the average being 39.3 hours per week for men and 35 hours for women.

But the reality is that *unscheduled* hours have been climbing:

- Total paid and unpaid time per week at employees' main jobs was 46 hours in 2002 for men (5 hours more than their regular scheduled hours on average) and 39.8 hours for women (3.8 hours more than their regular schedule).
- Employed parents (defined as having at least one child under 18 living at home half time or more) report working a total of 44 hours a week on average at their main jobs.
- Employed fathers work 48.3 paid and unpaid hours per week at their main jobs. Fathers in dual-earner couples work 49 hours at their main jobs— perhaps surprisingly, even longer hours than fathers in single earner-couples, who work 47.3 hours (Galinsky et al., "*When Work Works*" 1-2.).

11 Williams, *Unbending Gender,* 2–3.

12 Williams, personal communication, July 12, 2005.

13 "Among working mothers with minor children (ages 17 and under), just one-in-five (21%) say full-time work is the ideal situation for them, down from the 32% who said this back in 1997, according to a new Pew Research Center survey. Fully six-in-ten (up from 48% in 1997) of today's working mothers say part-time work would be their ideal, and another one-in-five (19%) say she would prefer not working at all outside the home." In the same study, 33 percent of mothers who are not employed said part-time work would be their ideal. Pew Research Center, *From 1997 to 2007.*

14 Data refer to hours worked in all jobs and to all mothers and fathers, married or not. U.S. Department of Labor, "Table 5." Some data indicate that among married mothers even fewer are working full-time. "Forty-three percent of married mothers and 88 percent of married fathers were employed full-time. Full-time workers are those who usually work 35 hours or more per week." U.S. Department of Labor, "Married Parents' Use of Time Summary." Williams cites research that shows that nearly two-thirds of mothers "are not ideal workers even in the minimal sense of working full time full year. One-quarter still are homemakers, and many more work part time in an economy that rigorously marginalizes part-time workers." She adds that "jobs requiring extensive overtime exclude virtually all mothers (93 percent)." In other words, 93 percent of mothers work forty-nine hours a week or less. Williams, *Unbending Gender,* 2.

15 The results of a Harvard Business School Study showed "While 89% of the men were working full-time five years or more after graduation (their prime career-building years), only 56% of the women were—and of the women with more than one child, only 38% were working full time. The remaining 62% of women with more than one child were working part-time or not at all." Hart, "Models of Success." Of women with children under 3, 56% were employed in 2006. 59.1% of women with children under 6 were employed, and 73.7% of women with children between 6 and 17 were employed. U.S. Department

of Labor, *Women in the Labor Force,* 13; "Mothers' employment is also far more responsive to the number and ages of children than fathers' employment is." Bianchi et al., *Changing Rhythms of American Family Life,* 46.

16   Hewlett, *Off-ramps and On-ramps,* 41; Benko and Weisberg, *Mass Career Customization,* 41.

17   Williams, *Unbending Gender,* 2.

18   Only 6 percent of the top earners in Fortune 500 companies are women, and only 3 percent of Fortune 500 CEOs are women. Catalyst, "U.S. Women in Business."

19   The pyramid shows that 46.3 percent of the workforce is women and 50.6 percent of management, professional and related occupations are filled by women. Ibid.

20   Mothers & More. "Part-Time Work Survey." 2005–2008.

21   Ibid.

22   Ibid.

23   Ibid.

24   Galinsky et al. *When Work Works,* 22.

25   Bailyn, *Breaking the Mold,* 50; Benko and Weisberg, *Mass Career Customization,* 63.

26   Bell, "Ohio Health Staff Getting Some Help."

27   Catalyst, *Women and Men in U.S. Corporate Leadership;* Benko and Weisberg, *Mass Career Customization,* 64.

28   Bailyn, *Breaking the Mold,* 51.

29   Mothers & More. "Part-Time Work Survey." 2005–2008.

30   Mothers & More. "Connections Survey." 2007.

31   Wyn et al., *Issue Brief,* 2.

32   Williams, *Unbending Gender,* 112.

33   Wenger, *Share of Workers in 'Nonstandard' Jobs Declines,* 18.

34   Williams, *Unbending Gender,* 112.

35   Ibid., 111.

36   King cites data from the national compensation survey showing that economy-wide, part-timers earn an average $8.89 per hour versus $15.77 per hour for full-timers. King, "Part Time Workers' Earnings." Warner cites research by Janet Gornick, a professor of sociology and political science at City University of New York, and Elena Bardasi, a labor economist: "Women on a reduced schedule earn almost 18 percent less than their full-time female peers with equivalent jobs and education levels." Warner, "The Full-Time Blues."

37   Wenger, *The Continuing Problems with Part-Time Jobs.*

38   Williams and Westfall, "Deconstructing the Maternal Wall."

39   National Women's Law Center, *Paycheck Fairness Act.*

40   The Equal Pay Act in the UK covers part-time and temporary workers' pay and benefits. Equality and Human Rights Commission, *Pay Benefits and Workplace Conditions.*

41   Mothers & More. "Connections Survey." 2007.

42   When asked if the increase in working mothers of young children working was a good thing for our society, a bad thing for our society, or makes no difference, 22 percent said it was a good thing, 41 percent said it was a bad thing, and 32 percent said it makes no difference. When asked, in general, what is the ideal situation for children, 42 percent said mother not working, 41 percent said mother working part time, and 9 percent said mother working

full time. Pew Research Center, *From 1997 to 2007*, 7–8. "One recent survey found, for example, that close to half of all Americans (48 percent) believe that preschoolers suffer if their mothers work. (National Opinion Research Center 2002). Another, conducted by the Families and Work Institute, found that even among employed parents, more than two out of five (42 percent) are concerned that many working mothers care more about succeeding at work than meeting their children's needs (Galinsky 1999, p. 11)." Quoted in Jacobs and Gerson, *The Time Divide*, 54.

43 Correll et al., "Getting a Job."

44 "Not only are [working mothers] viewed as less competent and less worthy of training than their childless female counterparts, they are also viewed as less competent than they were before they had children. Merely adding a child caused people to view the woman as lower on traits such as capable and skillful, and decreased people's interest in training, hiring, and promoting her." Cuddy et al., "When Professionals Become Mothers, Warmth Doesn't Cut the Ice."

45 Williams and Calvert, *WorkLife Law's Guide to Family Responsibilities Discrimination.*

46 Ibid., sec. 1-15.

47 Ibid., sec. 1-36.

48 Ibid., sec. 1-15.

49 Ibid., sec. 9-2.

50 Ibid., sec. 1-18.3.

51 Ibid., sec. 1-15.

52 From 1996 to 2006, there was a 400 percent increase in cases. Still, "Litigating the Maternal Wall."

53 Center for WorkLife Law, "Frequently Asked Questions about FRD."

54 Williams and Calvert, *WorkLife Law's Guide to Family Responsibilities Discrimination*, sec. 1-29.

55 *Nevada v. Hibbs.* Quoted in ibid., sec. 1-34

56 In the 2004, Mothers & More member survey, members cited the following reasons for making a change to their employment. Best situation for their children (76 percent), best situation for their family (71 percent), and/or best for themselves personally (50 percent). Mothers & More. "Membership Survey." 2004.

CHAPTER 7

1 Data refer to hours worked in all jobs and to all mothers and fathers, married or not. U.S. Department of Labor. "Table 5." Among fathers, "12% say they would prefer to work part-time and 16% say they would prefer not working outside the home. Pew Research Center, *From 1997 to 2007*. "13 percent of men who are full-timers would prefer to be working part-time." About 49 percent of men would prefer to have part-year work schedules. Galinsky et al., *When Work Works*, 12–13.

2 Levine and Pittinsky, *Working Fathers*, 103; Galinsky et al., *When Work Works.*

3 Women would prefer to be employed about nine hours less than they are. Men would like to be employed about ten hours less than they are. In part because they are actually working more hours. Jacobs and Gerson, *The Time Divide*, 64–65.

4   In 2001, "husbands were still the sole (25%) or major provider (39%) in a majority (64.5%) of couples." Raley et al., "How Dual Are Dual-Income Couples?"

5   Lewin, "Men Whose Wives Work Earn Less, Studies Show."

6   "Earnings contributions to the family become less equal between mothers and fathers once children arrive… Gornick and Meyers (2003) show that mothers' wages lag behind fathers in virtually all developed economies: U.S. mothers average about 28% of a family's labor market earnings…" Bianchi et al., *Changing Rhythms of American Family Life*, 46.

7   Cornell Couples Career Study quoted in Zuboff, "Career Taxidermy."

8   Kmec, "Multiple Aspects of Work-Family Conflict."

9   Between 5 and 15 percent of men eligible for paternity leave actually take advantage of it. Levine and Pittinsky, *Working Fathers,* 136–137.

10   Sakiko and Waldfogel, "Effects of Parental Leave and Work Hours on Fathers' Involvement with Their Babies."

11   Lewin, "Father Awarded $375,000 in a Parental Leave Case."

12   *Chavkin v. Santaella.* Quoted in Williams and Calvert, *WorkLife Law's Guide to Family Responsibilities Discrimination,* sec. 7-9.

13   *Tisinger v. City of Bakersfield,* 2002 WL 275525 (Cal. Ct. App., 2002).

14   Families and Work Institute, *Generation and Gender in the Workplace,* 4 and 14–15.

15   About 71 percent of men twenty-one to thirty-nine would give up some of their pay for more time with family. Radcliffe Public Policy Center, *Life's Work,* 3.

16   Elias, "The Family-First Generation."

17   "Gen-X fathers spend significantly more time with their children than Boomer fathers with children of the same age, an average of 3.4 hours per workday versus an average of 2.2 hours for Boomer fathers—a difference of more than 1 hour." Families and Work Institute, *Generation and Gender in the Workplace,* 4. "In 2002, married men spend significantly more time on workdays (1.9 hours) doing household chores than married men did 25 years ago (1.2 hours)." "Although married women are spending significantly less time doing household chores—down from 3.3 hours in 1977 to 2.7 hours in 2002—on days when they are working, the reduction in women's time doing chores—approximately 42 minutes less—is made up by their spouses, who are spending approximately 42 minutes more on chores." Ibid., 11.

18   Alfano, "PTA Set to Elect First Male President."

19   Families and Work Institute, *Generation and Gender in the Workplace,* 4.

20   Families and Work Institute, quoted in Gibbs, "Viewpoint."

21   Reid, "Daddy Wars Definition."

22   Kimmel, Interview with Dana Glazer. *The Evolution of Dad.*

23   The estimated numbers of stay-at-home dads per year are 2003 = 105,000, 2004 = 98,000, 2005 = 143,000, 2006 = 159,000, 2007 = 159,000, 2008 = 140,000. U.S. Census Bureau, *Facts for Features.*

CHAPTER 8

1   Bailyn proposes a similar belief. Bailyn, *Breaking the Mold,* 109.

2   Families and Work Institute, *National Study of the Changing Workforce.*

3   Mothers & More. "Part-Time Work Survey." 2005–2008.

4   "Estimates of the total cost of losing a single position to turnover range from 30 percent of the yearly salary of the position for hourly employees (Cornell University) to 150 percent, as estimated by the Saratoga Institute, and independently by Hewitt Associates." Taleo Research, *Strategic Talent Management*.

5   Mothers & More. "Part-Time Work Survey." 2005–2008.

6   Putnam, *Bowling Alone*, 406.

7   Benko, "CMC Women in Real Life."

8   Benko and Weisberg, *Mass Career Customization*, 81.

9   Ibid., 90.

10 Ibid., 83.

11 Ibid., 87.

12 Perlman, "What If She Has A Baby?"

13 Heffernan talks about a similar concept, that "work-life balance suggests that the key to these issues is to find some perfect equilibrium and then preserve it." Heffernan, *The Naked Truth*, 121.

14 Babcock and Laschever, *Women Don't Ask*, 119.

15 The term "corporate convenient" comes from *Breaking the Mold*. Bailyn, *Breaking the Mold*, 89.

16 Mothers & More. "Part-Time Work Survey." 2005–2008.

17 See also Ibid., 109.

18 Benko and Weisberg, *Mass Career Customization*, 137.

19 "There is a social consensus in Sweden that women should have jobs and fathers should be involved in care." Bailyn, *Breaking the Mold*, 57. In Sweden, "One month [of the 12-month leave] is available only to the father and lost if not used by him." Kimmel, "Gender Equality."

20 Rapoport and Bailyn, *Relinking Life and Work*, 27.

21 Williams et al., *"Opt Out" or Pushed Out*.

22 Adapted from *career-life fit*, a term used by Benko and Weisberg, *Mass Career Customization*, 161.

23 Catalyst, *New Work-Life Approach Benefits both Employers and Employees*.

24 Reid, "How Pew Got It Wrong."

CHAPTER 9

1   Maschka, Kristin. "Warm-up." www.kristinmaschka.com, January 2008.

2   Mothers & More. "Membership Survey." 2004.

3   Luntz, *"Now"* with Bill Moyers."

4   Golden, *Working Time*, 5; Moen, quoted in Bailyn et al., *Integrating Work and Family*.

5   Levin-Epstein, *Getting Punched*, 2.

6   Ray and Schmitt, *No-Vacation Nation*, 1.

7   Jacobs and Gerson, *The Time Divide*, 44.

8   Mean weekly hours comparing wives with some children under 18 in 1970 to those in 2000. Ibid.

9   Bernstein and Kornbluh, *Running Faster to Stay in Place*, 3, n. 3.

10 About one fifth of both men and women said they would prefer to work more hours than they do currently. Jacobs and Gerson, *The Time Divide: Work, Family, and Gender Inequality*, 64, table 3.1.

11 Ibid., 34, table 1.2.
12 "The structure and distribution of benefits, such as health care and other services, also give employers incentives to divide the labor force. By hiring part-time workers with no benefits and simultaneously pressuring some full-time employees—especially salaried workers—to work longer hours, work organizations can lower their total compensation costs." Ibid., 37.
13 King cites data from the national compensation survey showing that economywide, part-timers earn an average $8.89 per hour versus $15.77 per hour for full-timers. King, "Part Time Workers' Earnings," Warner cites research by Janet Gornick, professor of sociology and political science at City University of New York, and Elena Bardasi, labor economist: "Women on a reduced schedule earn almost 18 percent less than their full-time female peers with equivalent jobs and education levels." Warner, "The Full-Time Blues."
14 Jacobs and Gerson, *The Time Divide*, 63.
15 Golden and de Graaf, *Take Back Your Time*, 29.
16 Levin-Epstein, *Getting Punched*, 10.
17 Hill, "Finding an Extra Day a Week."
18 "Employees who believe they cannot change their work schedule so that they can work the hours or days they prefer feel more overworked: 45% of those who say they cannot change their work schedules to be able to work their preferred hours experience high levels of feeling overworked versus 33% of those who can change their work schedules." Galinsky et al., *Feeling Overworked*, 7.
19 Jacobs and Gerson, *The Time Divide*, 46, 52.
20 U.S. Department of Labor, "Employment Characteristics of Families in 2008," 2.
21 The percentage of couples with kids in which both parents work forty-five hours or more is less than 23 percent for all ages of kids. Moen, Phyllis and Stephen Sweet. "Time Clocks: Work-Hour Strategies." In *It's About Time*, edited by Moen, Phyllis, 25.
22 Ibid., fig. 2.2, 25.
23 Moen and Sweet call it *neotraditional*. Ibid, 20.
24 A total of 44.8 hours for fathers with children under eighteen in 1970. Jacobs and Gerson, *The Time Divide*, 44, table 2.1.
25 The average is forty-five for fathers/men in 2000 when both parents work. Ibid. I chose the twenty hours to make the point that even when mother isn't working too much, the time impact is big. Average for mothers/women in 2000 is actually higher, around thirty-five hours. However, looking at time use data instead, twenty hours a week is about the average time of paid work mothers have reported since 1985. Bianchi et al. "Maternal Employment and Family Caregiving."
26 Jacobs and Gerson, *The Time Divide*, 42.
27 Bernstein and Kornbluh, *Running Faster to Stay in Place*, 1. For evidence of the increase see also Gerson and Jacobs, "The Overworked."
28 Bernstein and Kornbluh, *Running Faster to Stay in Place*, 4, fig. 2 and 3.
29 Bernstein and Kornbluh, *Running Faster to Stay in Place*, 3; "Focusing on families rather than individuals provides a fuller, potentially more fruitful lens for making sense of the changing balance of paid work, family work, and leisure time." Jacobs and Gerson, *The Time Divide,* 41.
30 Bianchi et al. "Maternal Employment and Family Caregiving," 16–17.

31 Ibid., table 1.
32 Ibid., 15, fig, 2, table 3.
33 Ibid., 16, table 3.
34 Bianchi et al., *Changing Rhythms of American Family Life*, 57.
35 Betweeen four and six hours a week. Bianchi et al., "Maternal Employment and Family Caregiving," table 3.
36 Jacobsen, "Chore Wars," 5.
37 The comparisons and the data used for the illustrations come from "Maternal Employment and Family Caregiving." Childcare here refers to "primary childcare," time when childcare is your primary activity. It doesn't include hours of "secondary childcare" when you are doing something else and also watching your kids. These numbers are averages and include mothers who are employed and those who are not employed. That's why the total primary childcare number is high. Employed mothers have stayed the same and non-employed mothers went up even higher, making for a moderate average increase. The numbers, from 1965, 1985, and 2003, are as follows: fathers' housework went from 2.5 to 2.6 to 7.0 hours per week, mothers' housework went from 31.9 to 20.4 to 18.1, fathers' childcare went from 2.6 to 2.6 to 7.0, and mothers' childcare went from 10.2 to 8.4 to 14.1. Bianchi et al., "Maternal Employment and Family Caregiving," 13, fig. 1, table 1.
38 Ibid., 13, fig. 1, table 1.
39 Ibid., fig. 1. Combined primary childcare in 1965 was 12.7 hours per week. In 2003 it was 21.1 hours per week.
40 Bianchi et al., *Changing Rhythms of American Family Life*, 115.
41 There are differences here between the 2000 data and the 2003 data. Looking at both, fathers have between one and three hours more free time each week. Bianchi et al., "Maternal Employment and Family Caregiving," table 1.
42 "Married mothers provided secondary childcare for about 67 percent of the total time they engaged in leisure and sports activities (2.0 hours out of 3.0 hours)." Allard and Janes, "Time Use of Working Parents."
43 Vos Savant, "Ask Marilyn."
44 All figures adjusted for inflation, and compared to average family of four in early 1970s. Text refers only to increase in family income because of her income. Warren and Warren Tyagi, *The Two-Income Trap*, 50.
45 Burggraf, *The Feminine Economy and Economic Man*, 60.
46 Warren and Warren Tyagi, *The Two-Income Trap*, 22.
47 Kaiser Family Foundation, *Employee Health Benefits 2007 Annual Survey*, 18.
48 Warren and Warren Tyagi, *The Two-Income Trap*, 47.
49 Folbre, *The Invisible Heart*, 111.
50 Warren and Warren Tyagi, *The Two-Income Trap*, 50–51.
51 Ibid., 51–52.
52 Ibid., 52.
53 Bianchi et al., "Maternal Employment and Family Caregiving," fig. 1.
54 Workers are forced to "choose between time and income—a difficult decision that clashes with the exigencies of the new family economy." Jacobs and Gerson, *The Time Divide*, 63.
55 Bianchi's profile at www.popcenter.umd.edu/people/bianchi_suzanne/index .shtml.
56 Galinsky et al., *When Work Works*, 3.

57 Allard and Janes, "Time Use of Working Parents," 43.
58 Bianchi et al., *Changing Rhythms of American Family Life*, 106–107.
59 Saguaro Seminar on Civic Engagement in America, *Better Together*, 6.
60 Parents who work typically feel their children are deprived of their time.
    "67 percent of employed parents say they don't have enough time with their
    children, about the same proportion as 10 years ago." Galinsky et al., *When
    Work Works*, 3.
61 Fifty-six percent of parents predicted that their children would wish for more
    time with them. Galinsky, *Ask the Children*, 93.
62 Taken together, children's wishes for mothers and fathers to be less tired and to
    be less stressed accounted for 34 percent of their wishes for their mothers and
    27.5 percent of their wishes for fathers. These were higher percentages than for
    either "make more money" or "spend more time with me" alone. Ibid., 93–94.
63 Loehr and Schwartz, *The Power of Full Engagement*, 4.
64 Ibid., 199.
65 Galinsky, *Ask the Children*, 309–310.
66 Take Back Your Time uses "Time to Care" to describe their policy agenda.
    Take Back Your Time. "Time to Care Public Policy Agenda."
67 Golden and de Graaf, *Take Back Your Time*, 36.
68 Table uses 2003 data and rounds to achieve 168 total hours for each. In
    particular there are discrepancies between the 2000 and 2003 data on free time
    so I did my best to illustrate that mothers have between one and three hours
    less free time a week. These data are the average of all mothers and fathers,
    regardless of employment status. Bianchi et al., "Maternal Employment and
    Family Caregiving," table 1. The data on child-free time refers instead to
    married mothers and fathers who are both employed full-time, more than
    thirty-five hours a week. The difference could be even greater for couples
    sharing employment in other ways. Allard and Janes, "Time Use of Working
    Parents," 14.

CHAPTER 10
1   Mothers & More. "Membership Survey." 2004.
2   Mothers & More. "Connections Survey." 2007.
3   "Pin money." *Merriam-Webster Online Dictionary;* Edwards, *Words, Facts, and
    Phrases*, 428.
4   Folbre, *The Invisible Heart*, 93.
5   May, "The Historical Problem of the Family Wage," 400.
6   "Family wage assumptions led virtually all welfare reformers to assume that
    women's and children's poverty would usually be corrected by supporting
    husbands' and fathers' incomes. That is, the social-insurance programs for men
    would take care of men's dependents." Gordon, Linda. "Putting Children First:
    Women Maternalism, and Welfare in the early Twentieth Century." In *U.S.
    History as Women's History*, edited by Kerber et al., 81.
7   May, "The Historical Problem of the Family Wage," 415.
8   Ibid., 413.
9   Folbre, *The Invisible Heart*, 93.
10 Dubeck and Borman, *Women and Work*, 174–175.
11 Warren and Warren Tyagi, *The Two-Income Trap*, 101.

12 The reasons cited as arguments for a family wage also "resulted in arguments for different minimum wage levels for women and men. Male minimum wages were based on the possibility of a dependent family at some point in the male wage earner's life cycle." May, "The Historical Problem of the Family Wage," 405.

13 National Women's Law Center, *The Paycheck Fairness Act*.

14 McCaffery, *Taxing Women*, 51–52, 54, 56.

15 Ibid., 56.

16 Ibid., 19.

17 Kim Tso helped me tremendously with this entire chapter and with the income tax piece especially. Tso, "Work, Motherhood and Taxes."

18 McCaffery, *Taxing Women*, 17.

19 The tax policy provides incentives "to work full time, to make a certain 'all or nothing' decision in regard to the labor force." "At the middle-income levels, the laws encourage women to work full time or stay at home." McCaffery, *Taxing Women: How the Marriage Penalty Affects Your Taxes*, 142-144, 159.

20 Carasso and Steuerle, "The Hefty Penalty on Marriage Facing Many Households with Children"; McCaffery, *Taxing Women: How the Marriage Penalty Affects Your Taxes*, 138-141.

21 Raley et al., "How Dual Are Dual-Income Couples? Documenting Change From 1970 to 2001," 11–28.

22 McCaffery, *Taxing Women*, 103.

23 Ann Crittenden's book introduced me to this concept: "Under current family law, 'He who earns it owns it.'" Two pages alone are worth reading the book for her easily understood explanation of this economic assumption. Crittenden, *The Price of Motherhood*, 110–111. Williams, *Unbending Gender*, 120–123.

24 Warren and Warren Tyagi, *The Two-Income Trap*, 6.

25 Crittenden, *The Price of Motherhood*, 6.

26 In 1991, young women with no children earned 90.1 percent of the mean wage of all men. Waldfogel, "Understanding the Family Gap in Pay for Women with Children," 145.

27 Overall, there were only a handful of occupations in which women's median earnings were equal or nearly equal to those of men (in addition to dining room and cafeteria attendants, these occupations include dietitians and nutritionists, meeting and convention planners, postal service clerks, postal service mail sorters and processors, and five occupations falling into two occupational groups with very low percentages of female workers: construction and extraction occupations and installation, maintenance, and repair occupations). Weinberg, *Evidence from Census 2000 about Earnings by Detailed Occupation*.

28 A 2007 AAUW report found that "Even among women who are employed full-time, having children exacts a pay penalty." In 2003, among men and women who had earned bachelor's degrees in 1992–93, women with children employed full-time earned 63 percent of men with children and also less than men without children. Dey and Hill, *AAUW—Behind the Pay Gap Research Report*, 2.

29 The pay gap between mothers and non-mothers actually expanded from 10 percent in 1980 to 17.5 percent in 1991. Waldfogel, "Understanding the Family Gap in Pay for Women with Children," 145.

30 Given that the figures are from 1991, young women with no children
    may even have narrowed the gap with men even further. 73% refers to all
    young mothers (mean age 30). Waldfogel shows that married mothers as a
    subset fare a few percentage points better while single mothers fared much
    worse. Waldfogel, "Understanding the Family Gap in Pay for Women With
    Children," 145.

31 Social Security Administration, quoted in OWL, *Older Women and Poverty*, 2.

32 The analysis in *Still a Man's Labor Market* uses data from 1983 to 1998
    and includes all prime-age workers (twenty-six to fifty-nine years old) who
    have at least one year of positive earnings during that period and who have
    provided information on labor market activity for each of the fifteen years.
    Rose and Hartmann, *Still a Man's Labor Market*, as summarized by English
    and Hegewisch, *Research-In-Brief Still a Man's Labor Market*, iii. Other
    studies show similar lifetime gaps in pay. "Women may lose $434,000
    in income, on average, over a 40 year period due to the career wage gap."
    Aarons, *Lifetime Losses*.

33 Bishaw and Semega, *Income, Earnings, and Poverty Data from the 2007 American
    Community Survey*.

34 The total for men takes the median income in 2007 for men of $43,255
    multiplied by forty-five years ($1,946,475). The total for women is derived
    from the idea that women earn 38 percent of the lifetime earnings; applied
    to the men's total that means $739,660. I realize I am simplifying to make a
    point. The 38 percent figure was found over the specific fifteen-year period in
    the IWPR study, and I am applying it to a forty-five year period. I'm also not
    controlling for inflation, but inflation would affect both men's and women's
    earnings equally. The 38 percent figure also may not account for more recent
    work patterns of men and women since 1998.

35 Kessler-Harris, Alice. "Designing Women and Old Fools: The Construction of
    the Social Security Amendments of 1939." In *U.S. History as Women's History*,
    edited by Kerber et al., 92.

36 Ibid., 101.

37 Ibid., 137.

38 Ibid., 104.

39 Through 2031, "Using both marital and earnings histories to estimate
    unreduced Social Security benefits,we find that men are projected to continue
    receiving higher benefits than women, although the gap is expected to narrow
    as the baby boomers near retirement age." Butrica and Ians, "Projecting
    Retirement Income of Future Retirees with Panel Data: Results from the
    Modeling Income in the Near Term (MINT) Project," 3; Men work a median
    44 years and women work a median 32 years. Aleksandra Todorova, "The
    Girl's Guide to Retirement"; Zero years reduces average. "Each zero year
    reduces a woman's lifetime benefit calculation. In 1998, women retiring at
    age 62 averaged 6 of these zero years in their lifetime calculation for benefits."
    Hounsell, *Your Future Paycheck*, 18.

40 Kessler-Harris, Alice. "Designing Women and Old Fools: The Construction of
    the Social Security Amendments of 1939." In *U.S. History as Women's History*,
    edited by Kerber et al., 92.

41 Ibid, 98.

42 Social Security Act Amendments of 1939.

43 Kessler-Harris, Alice. "Designing Women and Old Fools: The Construction of the Social Security Amendments of 1939." In *U.S. History as Women's History,* edited by Kerber et al., 92.

44 Ibid., 100.

45 Ibid.

46 Ibid., 87.

47 In 1998, "63 percent of female Social Security beneficiaries age 65 and over receive benefits based on their husband's earnings record. (Only 1.2 percent of male Social Security beneficiaries receive benefits based on their wife's earnings record)." National Economic Council, *Women and Retirement Security.* See also Butrica et al., "Using Data for Couples to Project the Distributional Effects of Changes in Social Security Policy."

48 "The proportion of women aged 62 or older who are receiving benefits as dependents (that is, on the basis of their husband's earnings record only) has been declining—from 57% in 1960 to 30% in 2006. At the same time, the proportion of women with dual entitlement (that is, paid on the basis of both their own earnings record and that of their husband) has been increasing— from 5% in 1960 to 28% in 2006." I find the use of the term *dual entitlement* here misleading. Dual entitlement simply means being entitled to benefits both on her own record and on the spouse's record, but benefits on the spouse's record is greater. So women with dual entitlement are simply receiving the spousal benefit. To use the word dual entitlement implies that somehow the benefit is based on their own earnings record, but it isn't. Thus the number of women receiving the spousal benefit is the combination of the two numbers, or 58 percent. Social Security Administration, *Fast Facts and Figures about Social Security 2007.*

49 "Therefore, the percentage of women receiving benefits based solely on their own earnings history is expected to rise from 37 percent today to 60 percent in 2060. However, this means that 40 percent of women will continue to receive benefits based on their husband's earnings." National Economic Council, *Women and Retirement Security*, 4. See also Levine et al., "A Benefit of One's Own."

50 Kreider and Fields, "Number, Timing and Duration of Marriages and Divorces," 70.

51 Lewis and Shankle, "Social Security Benefits."

52 In 2001, 12 percent of wives made substantially more than their husbands. Raley et al., "How Dual Are Dual-Income Couples?," 11–28.

53 Social Security Administration, "Press Office."

54 Wenger, *Share of Workers in "Nonstandard" Jobs Declines.*

55 Social Security Administration, "Press Office"; Wu, *Sources of Income for Women Age 65 and Over*, 2.

56 Springstead and Wilson, "Participation in Voluntary Individual Savings Accounts," 37.

57 Hoffman, "Can Women Bridge the Retirement Savings Gap?"

58 "Under our current system it is not possible to have retirement savings in joint name. It is also not possible for one spouse to transfer part or all of his retirement plan to the other except in divorce or death." Cox, "Peaceful Revolution."

59 "With longer life expectancies than men, elderly women tend to live more years in retirement and have a greater chance of exhausting other sources of

income. They benefit from Social Security's cost-of-living protections because
benefits are annually adjusted for inflation. Women reaching age 65 in 2006
are expected to live, on average, an additional 19.7 years compared with 17.2
years for men." Social Security Administration, "Press Office."

60 Data from 2006. Wu, *Sources of Income for Women Age 65 and Over*, 1–2.
61 Figures all calculated based on $43,255 median income for men in 2007 cited
previously. I have not factored for inflation. I have assumed a constant income
of $43,255 a year for him, which of course doesn't reflect the typical arc of
earnings where you earn less when you are young and earn more when you
are older. Her lifetime earnings are 38 percent of his. I took 38 percent of
his lifetime earnings and divided it equally over 45 years, which works out to
$16,436.90 per year. Again this doesn't reflect a natural arc of earnings. For
the mother, this may even overstate the retirement savings since she may be
out of the workforce or have very low earnings in a number of the earlier years.
Money not saved early hurts more since it doesn't earn interest and this may
slightly understate the gap. Note that the 38 percent number from IWPR was
calculated over 15 years and specifically the years 1983 to 1998, so it's possible
that since then that number has changed as women's earnings increase. In these
figures, I have applied the 38 percent to a longer span of years—45 years. I
have assumed actual national average savings rate of 7 percent and the standard
rule of thumb of annual interest of 8 percent on retirement savings. Of course,
the economic challenges of 2009 may adjust that rule of thumb downward.
My calculations apply the interest rate to the full savings amount that year for
the full year, which may inflate the total interest earned for each and slightly
inflate the gap. For the Social Security estimates, I used the 2007 annual
benefit amounts for women, $10,685, and $14,055 for men and multiplied by
20 years; National average savings rate referenced by Schwab, Charles Schwab,
"Schwab Retirement Advice Indicators Reveal Savings Rates Continue to Rise
Among Advice and Managed Account Users in 401(k) Plans."
62 "The typical married couple would need to double its current coverage to meet
the expert recommendation of having enough life insurance to replace income
for seven to ten years." For this and all statistics in this paragraph, see LIMRA
International, *American Families at Risk.*
63 37 percent of all employees have short-term disability coverage and 29 percent
have long-term disability coverage. LIFE, *What You Need To Know About
Disability Insurance*, 4. "According to the American Council of Life Insurers
(ACLI), a person age 35 is six times more likely to become disabled than to die
before he or she reaches age 65." Halverson, "MoneyWise."
64 Warren and Warren-Tyagi, *The Two-Income Trap*, 94.
65 States that offer short-term disability insurance are California, New York, New
Jersey, Hawaii, and Rhode Island. LIFE, *What You Need to Know about Disability
Insurance*, 4.
66 Mothers & More. "Membership Survey." 2004.
67 Crittenden, *The Price of Motherhood*, 133.
68 Ibid., 111.
69 Williams, *Unbending Gender*, 115.
70 Ibid.
71 Crittenden, *The Price of Motherhood*, 151.
72 Williams, *Unbending Gender*, 122.

73 Crittenden, *The Price of Motherhood*, 157.

74 Ibid., 140–147.

75 Williams, *Unbending Gender*, 115–120.

76 In the Uniform Marriage and Divorce Act (UMDA), "Contributions as a homemaker are named as one factor to be considered, but no weights or presumptions are provided to direct courts how to balance the many factors enumerated. In this context, most courts have given little weight to family work, or have ignored it completely. . . . Consequently husbands are awarded the bulk of the property." Ibid., 121.

77 Crittenden, *The Price of Motherhood*, 157.

78 "In only three states—California, New Mexico, and Louisiana—does marital property have to be divided fifty-fifty. . . . In six other states—Idaho, Nevada, Arkansas, West Virginia, North Carolina, and New Hampshire—judges start with a presumption that property should be split fifty-fifty." Ibid.

79 Williams, *Unbending Gender*, 121; Crittenden, *The Price of Motherhood*, 133.

80 Williams, *Unbending Gender*, 129.

81 "In other words, the chief asset of most marriages—the ideal-worker's wage—continues to be treated as the property of the husband." Ibid., 115.

82 Ibid., 139.

83 Williams, "Celebrating Mothers' Choices."

84 Williams, *Unbending Gender*, 125.

85 Becker, "How to Eliminate the Marriage Tax Penalty"; McCaffery, *Taxing Women*, 277–278.

86 McCaffery, *Taxing Women*, 280; Carasso and Steuerle, "The Hefty Penalty on Marriage Facing Many Households with Children," 171.

87 Becker, "How to Eliminate the Marriage Tax Penalty."

88 Carasso and Steuerle propose basing EITC on individual wages so marriage doesn't impact the level of support. Carasso and Steuerle, "The Hefty Penalty on Marriage Facing Many Households with Children," 170. McCaffery suggests among several options, "a more generous child-care deduction or credit, allocated to the lesser-earning spouse." McCaffery, *Taxing Women*, 278.

89 Kessler-Harris, Alice. "Designing Women and Old Fools: The Construction of the Social Security Amendments of 1939." In *U.S. History as Women's History,* edited by Kerber et al., 97.

90 Ibid., 97–98.

91 Hartmann and Hill, "Strengthening Social Security for Women," 15.

92 Women spend an average of twelve years out of the workforce. Social Security Administration, quoted in OWL, *Older Women and Poverty,* 2. "A third approach would be to allow the lower-earning spouse a certain number of family care 'drop out' years, i.e., years that would not be counted in calculating Social Security benefits." Hartmann and Hill, "Strengthening Social Security for Women," 15.

93 Williams, *Unbending Gender*, 129–131.

CHAPTER 11

1 Belsky and Kelly, *The Transition to Parenthood*, 6, 14–15.

2 Pape Cowan and Cowan, *When Partners Become Parents*, 107–110.

3   Some research shows marriages with children are more stable. Waite et al.,
    "The Consequences of Parenthood for the Marital Stability of Young Adults."
    Pape Cowan and Cowan point out there is a distinction between marital
    stability and marital quality. Pape Cowan and Cowan, *When Partners Become
    Parents,* 119. Belsky and Kelly's research showed 50 to 51 percent of parents
    had challenges, for 30 percent there was little or no change, and 19 percent
    became closer. Belsky and Kelly, *The Transition to Parenthood,* 14–15.

4   Lake and Conway, *What Women Really Want,* 30.

5   Ibid.

6   "Just four-in-ten respondents (41%) now say that children are very
    important to a successful marriage, compared with 65% who said this back
    in 1990." "By a ratio of nearly three-to-one, more Americans say that the
    main purpose of marriage is 'forming a lifetime union between two adults for
    their mutual happiness and fulfillment' (65%) than say its main purpose is
    'forming a lifetime union between two adults for the purpose of bearing and
    raising children' (23%)." Taylor et al., *Generation Gap in Values, Behaviors,*
    27, 29.

7   Ibid., 27. When asked what makes a successful marriage, "sharing household
    chores" was the only item that "has risen sharply, from 47% in 1990 to 62%
    this year."

8   About 66 percent of women and 67 percent of men under twenty-nine express
    a desire to have jobs with greater responsibility. Galinsky et al., *Times Are
    Changing,* 1; Men are as likely as women to want a job schedule that allows for
    family time. Radcliffe Public Policy Center, *Life's Work.*

9   Lake and Conway, *What Women Really Want,* 29.

10 Ibid.

11 Both Belsky and Kelly and Pape Cowan and Cowan talk about the polarizing
    effects of having children on couples. Both sets of researchers point to a variety
    of social, cultural, and biological factors, some of which I've illustrated here.
    Belsky and Kelly, *The Transition to Parenthood,* 5; Pape Cowan and Cowan,
    When Partners Become Parents, 92.

12 Folbre talks about this cycle of commitment. "When we spend time with
    people who need our care, we often become attached to them. An initial
    decision to care for someone can lead to a cascading level of commitment. It
    can change our preferences and our priorities." Folbre, *The Invisible Heart,* 38.

13 Both Pape Cowan and Cowan, and Lake and Conway point to data indicating a
    disconnect between the mother's identity and the father's identity. Pape Cowan
    and Cowan, *When Partners Become Parents*; Lake and Conway, *What Women
    Really Want.*

14 Pape Cowan and Cowan, *When Partners Become Parents,* 80–81.

15 Ibid., 81.

16 Ibid., 84.

17 Belsky and Kelly, *The Transition to Parenthood,* 6, 14–15.

18 Uy, "More Parents Making Choice to Stay at Home."

19 Fels, *Necessary Dreams,* 244–245.

20 Douglas and Michaels, *The Mommy Myth,* 42–43.

21 Pape Cowan and Cowan, *When Partners Become Parents,* 206–209.

22 Belsky and Kelly, *The Transition to Parenthood,* 16.

23 Pape Cowan and Cowan, *When Partners Become Parents,* 80.

AFTERWORD

1   "Fortunately, a single but very important number suggests this will happen:
    That is the percentage of college and university degrees going to women
    today, and it means that only 43 percent of degrees are going to men. Given
    the high value our economy places on education, that number means we
    will see more and more families where the woman earns more than the man.
    Simple economics tells us that more dads are going to want part-time in the
    future. Savvy employers and policy-makers will start making the 'dad-friendly'
    workplace a reality." Drago, "More Part-time for Moms?" See also Norris, "In
    This Recession, More Men Are Losing."

2   Although I had formulated my ideas about a new set of beliefs and
    assumptions before reading it, Nancy Fraser's article "After the Family
    Wage" helped validate and clarify for me what I found wanting in the most
    prominent efforts to make change for mothers, fathers, and families. As
    she points out, there are two primary approaches to achieve gender equity
    currently, "one aiming to make women more like men are now, and the other
    leaving men and women pretty much unchanged, while aiming to make
    women's difference costless." Neither does the job. Her third possibility—"to
    induce men to become more like most women are now—that is, people who
    do primary care work" and that the "key to achieving gender equity, . . . then,
    is to make women's current life patterns the norm"—helped me feel confident
    that David's story was just as important to tell as mine to illustrate that third
    possibility. Fraser, "After the Family Wage," 611.

3   Williams and Calvert, *WorkLife Law's Guide to Family Responsibilities
    Discrimination*, sec. 7-11.

RESOURCES

REMODELING TOOLS

- To share your remodeling projects, make remodeling resolutions, and access more remodeling tools, visit www.remodelingmotherhood.com.

MOTHERS' ORGANIZATIONS

- Mothers & More. www.mothersandmore.org
- National Association of Mothers' Centers and their Mothers Ought To Have Equal Rights initiative. www.motherscenters.org and www.mothersoughttohaveequalrights.org
- MomsRising. www.momsrising.org
- National Organization of Women Committee on Mothers and Caregivers Economic Rights. www.now.org/issues/mothers
- The Mothers Movement Online. www.mothersmovement.org

BOOKS LISTED AS REMODELING TOOLS

- *The Mask of Motherhood: How Becoming a Mother Changes Our Lives and Why We Never Talk About It* by Susan Maushart.
- *A Potent Spell: Mother Love and the Power of Fear* by Janna Malamud Smith.
- *Brain, Child: The Magazine for Thinking Mothers.*
- *Transitions: Making Sense of Life's Changes* by William Bridges.
- *Necessary Dreams: Ambition in Women's Changing Lives* by Anna Fels.

- *Maternal Desire: On Children, Love and the Inner Life* by Daphne de Marneffe.
- *Mojo Mom: Nurturing Your Self While Raising a Family* by Amy Tiemann.
- *The Truth behind the Mommy Wars: Who Decides What Makes a Good Mother?* by Miriam Peskowitz.
- *The Mommy Myth: The Idealization of Motherhood and How It Has Undermined Women.* Susan Douglas and Meredith Michaels.
- *The Invisible Heart: Economics and Family Values* by Nancy Folbre.
- *Unbending Gender: Why Work and Family Conflict and What to Do about It* by Joan Williams.
- *The Naked Truth: A Modern Woman's Manifesto on Business and What Really Matters* by Margaret Heffernan.
- *Mass Career Customization: Aligning the Workplace with Today's Nontraditional Workforce* by Cathleen Benko and Anne Weisberg.
- *Opting Out?: Why Women Really Quit Careers and Head Home* by Pamela Stone.
- *Women Don't Ask* and *Ask for It* by Linda Babcock and Sara Leschever.
- *The Price of Motherhood: Why the Most Important Job in the World Is Still the Least Valued* by Ann Crittenden.
- *Taxing Women: How the Marriage Penalty Affects Your Taxes* by Ed McCaffery.
- *The Two-Income Trap: Why Middle-Class Parents Are Going Broke* by Elizabeth Warren and Amelia Warren Tyagi.
- *When Partners Become Parents: The Big Life Change for Couples* by Carolyn Pape Cowan and Philip A. Cowan.
- *The Transition to Parenthood: How a First Child Changes a Marriage and Why Some Couples Grow Closer and Others Apart* by Jay Belsky and John Kelly.
- *The Lazy Husband: How to Get Men to Do More Parenting and Housework* by Joshua Coleman.
- *Opting In: Having a Child Without Losing Yourself* by Amy Richards.

REFERENCES

Aarons, Jessica. *Lifetime Losses: The Career Wage Gap*. Washington, D.C.: Center for American Progress Action Fund, Dec. 8, 2008. Available at www.ameri canprogressaction.org/issues/2008/pdf/equal_pay.pdf. Accessed June 2009.

Abbott, John. *The Mother at Home, or The Christian Mother*. Worcester, Mass.: American Tract Society, 1933.

Alfano, Sean. "PTA Set to Elect First Male President." June 27, 2007. Available at www.cbsnews.com/stories/2007/06/27/national/main2987126.shtml. Accessed June 2009.

Allard, Mary Dorinda, and Marianne Janes. "Time Use of Working Parents: A Visual Essay." *Monthly Labor Review* 131 (June 2008): 3–14. www.bls.gov/opub/mlr/2008/06/art1full.pdf. Accessed June 2009.

Babcock, Linda, and Sara Laschever. *Women Don't Ask: Negotiation and the Gender Divide*. Princeton, N.J.: Princeton University Press, 2003.

Bailyn, Lotte. *Breaking the Mold: Redesigning Work for Productive and Satisfying Lives*. 2nd ed. Ithaca, N.Y.: Cornell University Press, 2006.

Bailyn, Lotte, Robert Drago, and Thomas A. Kochan. *Integrating Work and Family Life: A Holistic Approach*. MIT Sloan School of Management: Sloan Work-Family Policy Network. Sept. 14, 2001. Available at http://web.mit.edu/workplace center/docs/WorkFamily.pdf. Accessed June 2009.

Barnett, Rosalind Chait. "Unconventional Wisdom—A Survey of Research and Clinical Findings." Paper presented at the Tenth Anniversary Conference of the Council on Contemporary Families, Chicago, 2007.

Becker, Gary S. "How to Eliminate the Marriage Tax Penalty—Fairly and Simply." *Business Week*, Sept. 18, 2000, 34.

Bell, Jeff. "Ohio Health Staff Getting Some Help—Concierge Available for Errands." *Columbus Business First*, Dec. 17, 2004. Available at http://www.biz journals.com/columbus/stories/2004/12/20/story2.html. Accessed June 2009.

Belsky, Jay, and John Kelly. *The Transition to Parenthood: How a First Child Changes a Marriage; Why Some Couples Grow Closer and Others Apart*. New York: Dell Publishing, 1994.

Benko, Cathleen, "CMC Women in Real Life: The Work/Family Challenge." Paper presented at the Claremont McKenna College, Berger Institute for Work, Family and Children, Athena Award Presentation. Claremont, Calif., Mar. 24, 2007.

Benko, Cathleen, and Anne Weisberg. *Mass Career Customization: Aligning the Workplace with Today's Nontraditional Workforce.* Boston: Harvard Business School Press, 2007.

Bernstein, Jared, and Karen Kornbluh. *Running Faster to Stay in Place: The Growth of Family Work Hours and Incomes.* Washington, D.C : New America Foundation, June 2005.

Bertrand, Marianne, and Sendhil Mullainathan. "Are Emily and Greg More Employable Than Lakisha and Jamal? A Field Experiment on Labor Market Discrimination." Department of Economics Working Paper Series. Boston, Massachusetts Institute of Technology, May 27, 2003. Available at http://papers.ssrn.com/sol3/papers.cfm?abstract_id=422902. Accessed June 2009.

Bianchi, Suzanne M., John P. Robinson, and Melissa A. Milkie. *Changing Rhythms of American Family Life.* New York: Russell Sage Foundation, 2006.

Bianchi, Suzanne M., Vanessa Wight, and Sara Raley. "Maternal Employment and Family Caregiving: Rethinking Time with Children in the ATUS." Paper presented at the ATUS Early Results Conference, December 2005, Bethesda, MD. Available at http://www.atususers.umd.edu/papers/atusconference/authors/Bianchi.pdf. Accessed June 2009.

Bishaw, Alemayehu, and Jessica Semega. *Income, Earnings, and Poverty Data from the 2007 American Community Survey.* Washington, D.C.: U.S. Census Bureau, Aug. 2008. Available at www.census.gov/prod/2008pubs/acs-09.pdf. Accessed June 2009.

Blair, Irene V. "The Malleability of Automatic Stereotypes and Prejudice." *Personalilty and Social Psychology Review* 6, no. 3 (2002): 242–261.

Blair, Irene V., Jennifer E. Ma, and Alison P. Lenton. "Imagining Stereotypes Away: The Moderation of Implicit Stereotypes Through Mental Imagery." *Journal of Personality and Social Psychology* 81, no. 5 (Nov. 2001): 828–841.

Brauer, Markus, Charles M. Judd, and Vincent Jacquelin. "The Communication of Social Stereotypes: The Effects of Group Discussion and Information Distribution on Stereotypic Appraisals." *Journal of Personality and Social Psychology* 81, no. 3 (2001): 463–475.

Brazelton, T. Berry, M.D. *Touchpoints: Your Child's Emotional and Behavioral Development.* New York: Perseus Books, 1992.

Bridges, Judith S., and Claire Etaugh. "College Students' Perceptions of Mothers: Effects of Maternal Employment—Childrearing Pattern and Motive for Employment." *Sex Roles: A Journal of Research* 32, no. 11–12 (June 1995): 735–751.

Bridges, William. *Managing Transitions: Making the Most of Change.* 2nd ed. Cambridge, Mass.: Da Capo Press, 2003.

Bridges, William. *Transitions: Making Sense of Life's Changes.* Rev. 25th anniversary ed. Cambridge, Mass.: Da Capo Press, 2004.

Buchan, William, M.D. *Advice to mothers: on the Subject of their own health, and on the means of promoting the Health, Strength, and Beauty of their Offspring.* New York: Richard Scott, 1815.

Burggraf, Shirley P. *The Feminine Economy and Economic Man: Reviving the Role of Family in the Postindustrial Age.* Reading, Mass.: Basic Books, 1998.

Butrica, Barbra A., and Howard M. Ians. "Projecting Retirement Income of Future Retirees with Panel Data: Results from the Modeling Income in the Near Term (MINT) Project." *Social Security Bulletin* 62, no. 4 (1999): 3-8.

Butrica, Barbara A., Howard M. Iams, and Steven H. Sandell. "Using Data for Couples to Project the Distributional Effects of Changes in Social Security Policy." *Social Security Bulletin* 62, no. 3 (1999): 20–27. Available at www .socialsecurity.gov/policy/docs/ssb/v62n3/v62n3p20.pdf. Accessed June 2009.

Carasso, Adam, and C. Eugene Steuerle. "The Hefty Penalty on Marriage Facing Many Households with Children." *The Future of Children* 15, no. 2 (fall 2005): 157–175. Available at www.urban.org/UploadedPDF/1000844_marriage _penalty.pdf. Accessed June 2009.

Cardoza, Arlene Rossen. *Sequencing*. Minneapolis: Brownstone Books, 1996.

Catalyst. *New Work-Life Approach Benefits Both Employers and Employees, Advancing Workplaces into the 21st Century*, Aug. 13, 2008. Available at www.catalyst.org/ press-release/135/new-work-life-approach-benefits-both-employers-and -employees-advancing-workplaces-into-the-21st-century. Accessed June 2009.

Catalyst. *Women and Men in U.S. Corporate Leadership: Same Workplace, Different Realities?* 2004. Available at: www.catalyst.org/file/74/women%20and%20 men%20in%20u.s.%20corporate%20leadership%20same%20workplace,%20 different%20realities.pdf. Accessed June 2009.

Catalyst. "U.S. Women in Business—Pyramids." Feb. 2, 2009. Available at www .catalyst.org/publication/132/us-women-in-business. Accessed June 2009.

Center for WorkLife Law. "Frequently Asked Questions about FRD." *WorkLife Law*. Available at http://worklifelaw.org/FRDFAQ.html. Accessed June 2009.

Charles Schwab. "Schwab Retirement Advice Indicators Reveal Savings Rates Continue to Rise among Advice and Managed Account Users in 401(k) Plans," Apr. 28, 2005. Available at www.prnewswire.com/cgi-bin/stories .pl?ACCT=104&STORY=/www/story/04-28-2005/0003491202&EDATE. Accessed June 2009.

Coltrane, Scott. "Families and Gender Equity." *National Forum* 77 (Mar. 22, 1997): 31–34.

Correll, Shelley J., Stephen Benard, and In Paik. "Getting a Job: Is There a Motherhood Penalty?" *American Journal of Sociology* 112, no. 5 (Mar. 2007): 1297–1339.

Cox, Elizabeth. "Peaceful Revolution: Joint Parenting, Joint Retirement Accounts?" *The Huffington Post*, July 7, 2008. Available at www.huffingtonpost.com/eliza beth-cox/peaceful-revolution-joint_b_111255.html. Accessed June 2009.

Crittenden, Ann. *The Price of Motherhood: Why the Most Important Job in the World Is Still the Least Valued*. New York: Holt, 2002.

Cuddy, Amy J. C., S. T. Fiske, and P. Glick. "When Professionals Become Mothers, Warmth Doesn't Cut the Ice." *Journal of Social Issues* 60 (2004): 701–718.

Dasgupta, Nilanjana, and Anthony G. Greenwald. "On the Malleability of Auto- matic Attitudes: Combating Automatic Prejudice with Images of Admired and Disliked Individuals." *Journal of Personality and Social Psychology* 81, no. 5 (Nov. 2001): 800–814.

Dasgupta, Nilanjana, and Skaki Asgari. "Seeing Is Believing: Exposure to Counterstereotypic Women Leaders and Its effect on the Malleability of Automatic Gender Stereotyping." *Journal of Experimental Social Psychology* 40 (2004): 642–658.

De Marneffe, Daphne. *Maternal Desire: On Children, Love, and the Inner Life.* New York: Little, Brown, 2004.

Dey, Judy Goldberg, and Catherine Hill. AAUW—*Behind the Pay Gap Research Report.* Washington, D.C.: AAUW Educational Foundation, April 2007. Available at www.aauw.org/research/behindPayGap.cfm. Accessed June 2009.

DiQuinzio, Patricia. "The Politics of the Mothers' Movement in the United States: Possibilities and Pitfalls." *Journal of the Association for Research on Mothering* 8, no. 1–2 (winter–summer 2006): 55–71.

Douglas, Susan J., and Meredith Michaels. *The Mommy Myth: The Idealization of Motherhood and How It Has Undermined All Women.* New York: Free Press, 2004.

Drago, Robert. "More Part-time for Moms?" Sept. 14, 2007. Available at www.huffingtonpost.com/robert-drago/a-peaceful-revolution-mo_b_64335.html. Accessed June 2009.

Dubeck, Paula, and Kathryn M. Borman. *Women and Work: A Handbook.* New York: Taylor & Francis, 1996.

Eagly, Alice H., and Valerie J. Steffen. "Gender Stereotypes, Occupational Roles, and Beliefs About Part-Time Employees." *Psychology of Women Quarterly* 10, no. 3 (1986): 252–262.

Edwards, Eliezer. *Words, Facts, and Phrases: A Dictionary of Curious, Quaint, and Out-of-the-Way Matters.* Picadilly, London: Chatto & Windus, 1882.

Eisenberg, Arlene, Heidi E. Murkoff, and Sandee E. Hathaway. *What to Expect When You're Expecting.* 2nd ed. New York: Workman Publishing Company, 1996.

Elias, Marilyn. "The Family-First Generation." *USA Today,* Dec. 12, 2004. Available at www.usatoday.com/life/lifestyle/2004-12-12-generation-usat_x.htm.

Elliott, Susan. "All Women—Especially Mothers—Need to Have Life Insurance." *Denver Business Journal,* June 6, 2008. Available at www.bizjournals.com/denver/stories/2008/06/09/focus3.html?ana=from_rss. Accessed June 2009.

Employee Benefits Research Institute. "History of Health Insurance Benefits." Mar. 2002. Available at www.ebri.org/publications/facts/index.cfm?fa=0302fact. Accessed June 2009.

English, Ashley, and Ariane Hegewisch. *Research-In-Brief: Still a Man's Labor Market: The Long-Term Earnings Gap.* Washington, D.C.: Institute for Women's Policy Research, Feb. 2008. Available at www.iwpr.org/Publications/pdf.htm. Accessed June 2009.

Epstein, Cynthia Fuchs, Carroll Serron, Bonnie Oglensky, and Robert Saute. *The Part-Time Paradox: Time Norms, Professional Lives, Family and Gender.* New York: Routledge, 1999.

Equality and Human Rights Commission. *Information for Employers: Pay Benefits and Workplace Conditions.* Available at http://www.equalityhumanrights.com/your-rights/information-for-employers/pay-benefits-and-workplace-conditions. Accessed June 2009.

Etaugh, Claire, and Gina Gilomen. "Perceptions of Mothers: Effects of Employment Status, Marital Status, and Age of Child." *Sex Roles: A Journal of Research* 20, no. 1 (Jan.1989): 59–70.

Families and Work Institute. *Generation and Gender in the Workplace*, 2004. Available at http://familiesandwork.org/site/research/reports/genandgender.pdf. Accessed June 2009.

Families and Work Institute. *National Study of the Changing Workforce—Executive Summary*. 1997. Available at http://familiesandwork.org/site/research/summary/curvesumm.pdf. Accessed June 2009.

Family Caregiver Alliance. "Selected Caregiver Statistics." Available at www.caregiver.org/caregiver/jsp/content_node.jsp?nodeid=439. Accessed June 2009.

Fels, Anna. *Necessary Dreams: Ambition in Women's Changing Lives*. New York: Pantheon, 2004.

Fiske, Susan T., Amy J. C. Cuddy, Peter Glick, and Jun Xu. "A Model of (Often Mixed) Stereotype Content: Competence and Warmth Respectively Follow from Perceived Status and Competition." *Journal of Personality and Social Psychology* 82, no. 6 (June 2002): 878–902.

Folbre, Nancy. *The Invisible Heart: Economics and Family Values*. New York: New Press, 2001.

Folbre, Nancy. *Valuing Children: Rethinking the Economics of the Family*. Cambridge, Mass.: Harvard University Press, 2008.

Fraser, Nancy. "After the Family Wage: Gender Equity and the Welfare State." *Political Theory* 22, no. 4 (Nov. 1994): 591–618.

Freedman, Estelle B. *No Turning Back: The History of Feminism and the Future of Women*. New York: Ballantine, 2003.

Galinsky, Ellen. *Ask the Children: The Breakthrough Study That Reveals How to Succeed at Work and Parenting*. New York: Harper Paperbacks, 2000.

Galinsky, Ellen, Kerstin Aumann, and James T. Bond. *Times Are Changing: Gender and Generation at Work and at Home*. New York, New York: Families and Work Institute, 2009. Available at www.familiesandwork.org/site/research/reports/Times_Are_Changing.pdf. Accessed June 2009.

Galinsky, Ellen, James T. Bond, and E. Jeffrey Hill. *When Work Works—A Status Report on Workplace Flexibility—Who Has it? Who Wants It? What Difference Does It Make?* Families and Work Institute, 2004. Available at http://familiesandwork.org/3w/research/downloads/status.pdf. Accessed June 2009.

Galinsky, Ellen, James T. Bond, and E. Jeffrey Hill. "Why Workplace Flexibility? Why Now?" Available at www.familiesandwork.org/3w/research/status.html.

Galinsky, Ellen, Stacy S. Kim, and James T. Bond. *Feeling Overworked: When Work Becomes Too Much*. New York: Families and Work Institute, 2001.

Garmston, Rob and Bruce Wellman. *The Adaptive School: A Sourcebook for Developing Collaborative Groups*. Norwood, Mass.: Christopher-Gordon, 1999.

Gerson, Kathleen, and Jerry Jacobs. "The Overworked—and Underworked—Americans." http://sociology.fas.nyu.edu/docs/IO/220/Overworked_and_Underworked_Americans.pdf. Accessed June 2009.

Gibbs, Nancy. "Viewpoint: Bring On the Daddy Wars." *Time,* Feb. 27, 2006. Available at www.time.com/time/nation/article/0,8599,1168125,00.html?iid =sphere-inline-sidebar. Accessed June 2009.

Gladwell, Malcolm. *Blink: The Power of Thinking Without Thinking.* 1st ed. New York: Little, Brown and Company, 2005.

Golden, Lonnie. *Working Time: International Trends, Theory and Policy Perspectives.* London: Routledge, 2000.

Golden, Lonnie and John de Graaf. *Take Back Your Time: Fighting Overwork and Time Poverty in America.* San Francisco: Berrett-Koehler, 2003.

Gordon, Linda. "Putting Children First: Women Maternalism, and Welfare in the Early Twentieth Century." In *U.S. History As Women's History: New Feminist Essays,* edited by Kerber, Linda K., Alice Kessler-Harris, and Kathryn Kish Sklar, 63 –86. Chapel Hill: University of North Carolina Press, 1995.

Gowens, Pat. "Congress Betrays US People and the Constitution." Press release by Welfare Warriors. Milwaukee, WI. (Feb. 2006).

Greenwald, Anthony G., and Linda Hamilton Krieger. "Implicit Bias: Scientific Foundations." *California Law Review* 94 (July 2006): 945.

Halverson, Richard. "MoneyWise—Disability Insurance: The Biggest Gap in the Financial Plans of Many Families." *Meridian Magazine,* 2004. Available at www .meridianmagazine.com/moneywise/040427disability.html. Accessed June 2009.

Hanrahan, Meredith. "Six-Figure Moms." Available at www.salary.com/personal/ layoutscripts/psnl_articles.asp?tab=psn&cat=cat011&ser=ser032&part=par901. Accessed June 2009.

Hart, Myra M. "Models of Success." Harvard Business School, Cambridge, Mass., 2006.

Hartmann, Heidi and Catherine Hill. "Strengthening Social Security for Women." Paper presented at the Working Conference on Women and Social Security, Washington, D.C., 2000.

Hays, Sharon. *The Cultural Contradictions of Motherhood.* New Haven, Conn.: Yale University Press, 1996.

Heffernan, Margaret. *The Naked Truth: A Working Woman's Manifesto on Business and What Really Matters.* San Francisco: Jossey-Bass, 2004.

Hewlett, Sylvia Ann. *Off-Ramps and On-Ramps: Keeping Talented Women on the Road to Success.* Boston: Harvard Business School Press, 2007.

Hill, E. Jeffrey. "Finding an Extra Day a Week: The Positive Influence of Perceived Job Flexibility on Work and Family Life Balance." *Family Relations* 50, no. 1 (2001): 49–58.

Hoffman, Ellen. "Can Women Bridge the Retirement Savings Gap?." *Business Week,* Aug. 11, 2008. Available at http://www.businessweek.com/investor/ content/aug2008/pi2008088_307392.htm. Accessed June 2009.

Hounsell, Cindy, Pat Humphlett, and Jeffrey Lewis. *Your Future Paycheck: What Women Need to Know About Pay, Social Security, Pensions, Savings and Investments.* Washington, D.C.: Women's Institute for a Secure Retirement (WISER). May, 2002. Available at www.wiserwomen.org/pdf_files/yfp_women.pdf. Accessed June 2009.

Hulbert, Ann. *Raising America: Experts, Parents, and a Century of Advice about Children.* New York: Knopf, 2003.

Jacobs, Jerry A., and Kathleen Gerson. *The Time Divide: Work, Family, and Gender Inequality*. Cambridge, Mass.: Harvard University Press, 2005.

Jacobsen, Kristin. "Chore Wars." Elmhurst, IL: *Mothers & More Forum* 18, no. 3 (June 2005): 5–7.

Kaiser Family Foundation and Health Research and Educational Trust. *Employee Health Benefits 2007 Annual Survey*. 2007. Available at www.kff.org/insur ance/7672. Accessed June 2009.

Kerber, Linda K., Alice Kessler-Harris, and Kathryn Kish Sklar, eds. *U.S. History As Women's History: New Feminist Essays*. Chapel Hill: University of North Carolina Press, 1995.

Kessler-Harris, Alice. "Designing Women and Old Fools: The Construction of the Social Security Amendments of 1939." In *U.S. History As Women's History: New Feminist Essays,* edited by Kerber, Linda K., Alice Kessler-Harris, and Kathryn Kish Sklar, 63–86. Chapel Hill: University of North Carolina Press, 1995.

Kimmel, Michael. Interview with Dana Glazer. *The Evolution of Dad* [Video]. Dir. Dana Glazer. Dec. 8, 2007. Available at www.evolutionofdad.com/clips.html. Accessed June 2009.

Kimmel, Michael. "Gender Equality: Not for Women Only." Paper presented at the International Women's Day Seminar, European Parliament. Brussels, Mar. 8, 2001. Available at www.europrofem.org/audio/ep_kimmel/kimmel.htm. Accessed June 2009.

Kimmel, Michael. *Manhood in America: A Cultural History*. New York: Free Press, 1996.

King, Jerome. "Part Time Workers' Earnings: Some Comparisons." *Compensation and Working Conditions* (summer 2000): 27–36.

Kmec, Julie A. "Multiple Aspects of Work-Family Conflict." *Sociologial Focus* 32, (1999): 265–285.

Komisar, Randy. *The Monk and the Riddle: The Education of a Silicon Valley Entrepreneur*. Boston: Harvard Business School Press, 2000.

Kreider , Rose M. "Number, Timing and Duration of Marriages and Divorces: 2001." *Current Population Reports* (Feb 2005): 70–97.

Lake, Celinda, and Kellyanne Conway. *What Women Really Want: How American Women Are Quietly Erasing Political, Racial, Class, and Religious Lines to Change the Way We Live*. New York: Free Press, 2005.

Lane, Kristin A., Mahzarin R. Banaji, Brian A. Nosek, and Anthony G. Greenwald. "Understanding and Using the Implicit Association Test: IV What We Know (So Far) about the Method." In *Implicit Measures of Attitudes*. Ed. Bernd Wittenbrink and Norbert Schwarz. New York: Guilford Press, 2007, 59–102.

Levin-Epstein, Jodie. *Getting Punched: The Job and Family Clock*. Washington D.C.: Center for Law and Social Policy, July 2006.

Levine, James A., and Todd L. Pittinsky. *Working Fathers: New Strategies for Balancing Work and Family*. Reading, Mass.: Addison-Wesley, 1997.

Levine, Philip B., Olivia S. Mitchell, and John W. R. Phillips. "A Benefit of One's Own: Older Women's Entitlement to Social Security Retirement." *Social Security Bulletin* 63, no. 3 (2000), 47–53. Available at www.socialsecurity.gov/policy/docs/ssb/v63n3/v63n3p47.pdf. Accessed June 2009.

Levy, Debra. "Talking With: Maternal Desire, Author Daphne de Marneffe." *Mothers & More Forum* 17, no. 5 (Oct. 2004): 12–14.

Levy, Debra. "The Mask of Motherhood." *Mothers & More Forum* 14, no. 2 (Mar.–Apr. 2001): 1, 16–18. Available at www.mothersandmore.org/Advocacy/MaushartForum.shtml. Accessed June 2009.

Lewin, Tamar. "Father Awarded $375,000 in a Parental Leave Case." *New York Times*, Feb. 3, 1999, sec. A.

Lewin, Tamar. "Men Whose Wives Work Earn Less, Studies Show." *New York Times*, Oct. 12, 2004. Available at http://query.nytimes.com/gst/fullpage.html?res=9505E2DC163CF931A25753C1A962958260. Accessed June 2009.

Lewis, Eugene B., and Jessica A. Shankle. "Social Security Benefits: Clarified by the Supreme Court." *Columbus Bar Briefs* (suppl. to *The Daily Reporter*) (spring 2005), 33.

Life and Health Insurance Foundation. *What You Need to Know about Disability Insurance*. Arlington, VA.: Life and Health Insurance Foundation for Education, 2008. Available at www.lifehappens.org/pdf/printable-consumer-guide/disability-pcg.pdf. Accessed June 2009.

Life and Health Insurance Foundation. "Who Needs Life Insurance?" Available at www.lifehappens.org/life-insurance/who-needs-it#stay-home-parent. Accessed June 2009.

LIMRA International. *American Families at Risk—Facts About Life Insurance*. Sept. 2007. Available at www.limra.com/PDFs/NewsCenter/Materials/07USFAQ.pdf. Accessed June 2009.

Loehr, Jim, and Tony Schwartz. *The Power of Full Engagement: Managing Energy, Not Time, Is the Key to High Performance and Personal Renewal*. New York: Free Press, 2003.

Lovell, Vicky. *No Time to Be Sick: Why Everyone Suffers When Workers Don't Have Paid Sick Leave*. Washington, D.C.: Institute for Women's Policy Research, 2004. Available at www.iwpr.org/pdf/B242.pdf. Accessed June 2009.

Lukas, Carrie. "Mothers Don't Go on Strike." *National Review Online*, May 12, 2006. Available at http://article.nationalreview.com/?q=M2Q3YmMwYzRjN2MzMWMwMTViOTJhNmE4M2UwOWZiNDI=#more. Accessed June 2009.

Luntz, Frank. *"Now* with Bill Moyers." July 2, 2004. Available at www.pbs.org/now/transcript/transcript327_full.html. Accessed June 2009.

Malamud Smith, Janna. *A Potent Spell: Mother Love and the Power of Fear*. New York: Houghton Mifflin, 2003.

Maschka, Kristin. "Put on Your Own Oxygen Mask First." *Mothers & More Forum* 19, no. 3 (summer 2006): 1, 6–8.

May, Martha. "The Historical Problem of the Family Wage: The Ford Motor Company and the Five Dollar Day." *Feminist Studies* 8, no. 2 (summer 1982): 400–405.

McCaffery, Edward J. *Taxing Women: How the Marriage Penalty Affects Your Taxes*. Chicago: University of Chicago Press, 1997.

McLaughlin, Margaret. "Making Mothers Count: New Economic Statistics May Help Unpaid Caregiving Become Visible." Mothers & More Forum 17, no.1 (Jan/Feb. 2004): 3–4.

Mendel, Richard. *Family Values at Work: It's about Time!* Multistate Working Families Consortium, Sept. 2007. Available at www.9to5.org/resources/publications/family-values-at-work. Accessed June 2009.

Mink, Gwendolyn, and Alice O'Connor. *Poverty in the United States: An Encyclopedia of History, Politics, and Policy.* Santa Barbara, CA: ABC-CLIO, 2004.

Moen, Phyllis, ed. *It's about Time: Couples and Careers.* Ithaca, N.Y.: Cornell University Press, 2003.

Moen, Phyllis, and Stephen Sweet. "Time Clocks: Work-Hour Strategies." In *It's About Time: Couples and Careers.* Edited by Moen, Phyllis. Ithaca, N.Y.: Cornell University Press, 2003.

Mohler, Albert. "Are Stay at Home Moms 'Letting Down the Team?' " Available at www.albertmohler.com/commentary_read.php?cdate=2006-02-24. Accessed June 2009.

Montgomery, Kelly. "Why Does America's Health Care System Rely on Job-Based Coverage?: A Brief History." *About.com,* September 30, 2006. Available at http://healthinsurance.about.com/od/jobbasedcoverage/a/jobbasedhistory.htm. Accessed June 2009.

Morgan Roberts, Laura, Gretchen Spreitzer, Jane Dutton, Robert Quinn, Emily Heaphy, and Brianna Barker. "How to Play to Your Strengths." *Harvard Business Review* (January 1, 2005): 1-6.

"Mothers & More Mission Statement and Core Beliefs." Available at www.mothersandmore.org/AboutUs/mission.shtml. Accessed June 2009.

National Center for Public Policy and Higher Education. *Measuring Up 2008—The National Report Card on Higher Education.* San Jose, CA.: Dec. 3, 2008. Available at http://measuringup2008.highereducation.org/print/NCPPHEMU NationalRpt.pdf. Accessed June 2009.

National Economic Council Interagency Working Group on Social Security. *Women and Retirement Security.* Oct. 27, 1998. Available at www.ssa.gov/history/pdf/sswomen.pdf. Accessed June 2009.

National Legal Research Group. *Social Security Benefits and Equitable Distribution.* 2005. Available at www.divorcesource.com/research/edj/socialsecurity/95nov121.shtml. Accessed June 2009.

National Women's Law Center. *The Paycheck Fairness Act: Helping to Close the Wage Gap for Women.* Apr. 2005. Available at www.pay-equity.org/PDFs/Paycheck FairnessAct_April2005.pdf. Accessed June 2009.

Norris, Floyd. "In This Recession, More Men Are Losing." *New York Times,* Mar. 13, 2009. Available at www.nytimes.com/2009/03/14/business/economy/14charts.html. Accessed June 2009.

Nosek, Brian A., Mahzarin R. Banaji, and Anthony G. Greenwald. "Harvesting Implicit Group Attitudes and Beliefs from a Demonstration Web Site." *Group Dynamics: Theory, Research, and Practice* 6, no. 1 (2002): 101–115.

OWL. "Older Women and Poverty." [Fact Sheet] OWL: The Voice of Midlife and Older Women. Arlington, VA. Available at www.owl-national.org/Issues _Fact_Sheets_files/OlderWomenandPoverty.doc. Accessed June 2009.

Pape Cowan, Carolyn, and Philip A. Cowan. *When Partners Become Parents: The Big Life Change for Couples.* Mahwah, N.J.: Lawrence Erlbaum, 1999.

Perlman, Lawrence. "What If She Has a Baby?" Center for Ethical Business Cultures. Minneapolis, MN, May 1993. Adapted from the keynote speech at "Work-Family Issues and the Work Ethic," a conference sponsored by The Conference Board and the Families and Work Institute. Available at www.cebcglobal.org/index.php?/ceos-corner/comments/what-if-she-has-a-baby/. Accessed June 2009.

Peskowitz, Miriam. *The Truth Behind the Mommy Wars: Who Decides What Makes a Good Mother?* Emeryville, Calif.: Seal Press, 2005.

Pew Research Center. *From 1997 to 2007: Fewer Mothers Prefer Full-Time Work.* July 2007. Available at pewresearch.org/assets/social/pdf/WomenWorking.pdf. Accessed June 2009.

Pipher, Mary. *Writing to Change the World.* New York: Riverhead, 2007.

Project Implicit. "FAQs." Available at https://implicit.harvard.edu/implicit/demo/background/faqs.html#faq13. Accessed June 2009.

Project Implicit. "General Information." www.projectimplicit.net/generalinfo.php. Accessed June 2009.

Putnam, Robert D. *Bowling Alone: The Collapse and Revival of American Community.* New York: Simon & Schuster, 2001.

Radcliffe Public Policy Center with Harris Interactive. *Life's Work: Generational Attitudes toward Work and Life Integration.* Cambridge, Mass., 2000.

Raley, Sara B., Marybeth J. Mattingly, and Suzanne M. Bianchi. "How Dual Are Dual-Income Couples? Documenting Change from 1970 to 2001." *Journal of Marriage and Family* 68 (Feb. 2006): 11–28.

Rapoport, Rhona and Lotte Bailyn. *Relinking Life and Work.* New York: Ford Foundation, 1996. Available at www.fordfound.org/archives/item/0299. Accessed June 2009.

Ray, Rebecca and John Schmitt. *No-Vacation Nation.* Washington, D.C.: Center for Economic and Policy Research, May 2007. Available at www.cepr.net/index.php/publications/reports/no-vacation-nation. Accessed June 2009.

Reid, Brian. "Daddy Wars Definition." Mar. 21, 2006. Available at www.rebeldad.com/2006_03_01_archive.html. Accessed June 2009.

Reid, Brian. "How Pew Got It Wrong." July 18, 2007. Available at www.rebeldad.com/2007_07_01_archive.html. Accessed June 2009.

Rose, Stephen J., and Heidi Hartmann. *Still A Man's Labor Market: The Long-Term Earnings Gap.* Washington, D.C.: Institute for Women's Policy Research, 2004. Available at www.iwpr.org/Publications/pdf.htm. Accessed June 2009.

Rosen, Ruth. "The Female Generation Gap: Daughters of the Fifties and the Origins of Contemporary American Feminism." In *U.S. History As Women's History: New Feminist Essays,* edited by Kerber, Linda K., Alice Kessler-Harris, and Kathryn Kish Sklar, 313 –334. Chapel Hill: University of North Carolina Press, 1995.

Rosenthal, Robert, and Lenore Jacobson. *Pygmalion in the Classroom: Teacher Expectation and Pupils' Intellectual Development.* Norwalk, CT: Crown, 2003.

Saguaro Seminar on Civic Engagement in America. *Better Together.* Cambridge, Mass.: John F. Kennedy School of Government, Harvard University, Dec. 2000. Available at www.bettertogether.org/pdfs.

Sakiko, Tanaka, and Jane Waldfogel. "Effects of Parental Leave and Work Hours on Fathers' Involvement with Their Babies: Evidence from the Millennium Cohort Study." *Community, Work and Family* 10, no. 4 (Nov. 2007): 409–426.

Sanders, Darcie, and Martha M. Bullen. *Staying Home: From Full-Time Professional to Full-Time Parent.* Boulder, CO: Spencer & Waters, 2001.

Schrobsdorff, Susanna. "Some Day My 9-to-5 Job Will Come." *Newsweek Web Exclusive,* Mar. 10, 2008. Available at www.newsweek.com/id/120362. Accessed June 2009.

Sears, William, M.D., and Martha, R.N. Sears. *The Baby Book: Everything You Need to Know About Your Baby From Birth to Age Two.* 1st ed. New York: Little, Brown & Company, 1992.

Senge, Peter M. *The Fifth Discipline: The Art and Practice of the Learning Organization.* New York: Currency Doubleday, 1990.

Senge, Peter, and Art Kleiner, Charlotte Roberts, Richard Ross, and Bryan Smith. *The Fifth Discipline Fieldbook.* New York: Doubleday, 1994.

Shierholz, Heidi. "Jobs Picture, May 8, 2009." Economic Policy Institute. Available at www.epi.org/publications/entry/jobspicture20090508/. Accessed June 2009.

Smith, Janna Malamud. *A Potent Spell: Mother Love and the Power of Fear.* New York: Houghton-Mifflin, 2003.

Social Security Administration. Office of Policy. Office of Research, Evaluation, and Statistics. *Fast Facts and Figures about Social Security 2007.* Washington, D.C. Sept. 2007. Available at www.socialsecurity.gov/policy/docs/chartbooks/fast_facts/2007/fast_facts07.pdf. Accessed June 2009.

Social Security Administration. "Press Office: Social Security Is Important to Women." *Social Security Online,* Oct. 2008. Available at www.ssa.gov/pressoffice/factsheets/women.htm. Accessed June 2009.

Springstead, Glenn R., and Theresa M. Wilson. "Participation in Voluntary Individual Savings Accounts: An Analysis of IRAs, 401(k)s and the TSP." *Social Security Bulletin* 63, no. 1 (2000): 34–39. Available at www.ssa.gov/policy/docs/ssb/v63n1/v63n1p34.pdf. Accessed June 2009.

Spock, Benjamin, M.D., and Steven J. Parker, M.D. *Dr. Spock's Baby and Child Care.* 7th ed. New York: Pocket Books, 1998.

Still, Mary C., "Litigating the Maternal Wall: U.S. Lawsuits Charging Discrimination against Workers with Family Responsibilities." San Francisco: Center for WorkLife Law at UC Hastings Law School. July 6, 2006. Available at www.worklifelaw.org/pubs/FRDreport.pdf. Accessed June 2009.

Stone, Pamela. *Opting Out?: Why Women Really Quit Careers and Head Home.* Berkeley: University of California Press, 2007.

Take Back Your Time. "Time to Care Public Policy Agenda." Available at www.timeday.org/time_to_care.asp. Accessed June 2009.

Talberth, John, Clifford Cobb, and Noah Slattery. *The Genuine Progress Indicator 2006—A Tool for Sustainable Development.* Redefining Progress, Feb. 2007. Available at www.rprogress.org/publications/2007/GPI%202006.pdf#search=%22genuine%20progress%20indicator%202006%22. Accessed June 2009.

Taleo Research. *Strategic Talent Management: Calculating the High Cost of Employee Turnover.* 2003. Available at www.taleo.com/research/articles/strate gic/calculating-the-high-cost-employee-turnover-15.html. Accessed June 2009.

Taylor, Paul, Cary Funk, and April Clark. *Generation Gap in Values, Behaviors: As Marriage and Parenthood Drift Apart, Public Is Concerned about Social Impact.* Pew Research Center. July 1, 2007. Available at www.pewresearch.org/assets/social/ pdf/Marriage.pdf. Accessed June 2009.

Third Wave Foundation. "I Spy Sexism." Available at www.thirdwavefoundation .org/advocacy/i-spy. Accessed June 2009.

Thomas, Marlo. *Free to Be . . . You and Me.* CD. New York: Arista Records, distributed by Sony BMG Music Entertainment, 1972.

Tiemann, Amy. *Mojo Mom: Nurturing Your Self While Raising a Family.* New York: Gotham Books, 2009.

Todorova, Aleksandra. "The Girl's Guide to Retirement." *comcast.net Finance*, February 27, 2008. Available at http://finance.comcast.net/personalfinance/view. html?x=retirement/planning/planningforwomen. Accessed June 2009.

Tso, Kim. "Work, Motherhood and Taxes." *Mothers & More Forum*, Apr. 2004: 3–5.

Tucker Center for Research on Girls & Women in Sport. *The 2007 Tucker Center Research Report, Developing Physically Active Girls: An Evidence-Based Multidisciplinary Approach.* Minneapolis, Minn.:University of Minnesota 2007. Available at http://cehd.umn.edu/TuckerCenter/projects/TCRR/2007-Tucker-Center-Research-Report.pdf. Accessed June 2009.

U.S. Census Bureau, *Annual Estimates of the Population by Selected Age Groups and Sex for the United States: April 1, 2000 to July 1, 2006.* Washington, D.C.: U.S. Census Bureau (Population Division, May 17, 2007), Table 2. Available at www.census.gov/popest/national/asrh/NC-EST2006/NC-EST2006-02.xls. Accessed June 2009.

U.S. Census Bureau, *Facts for Features—Father's Day.* June 2004. Available at www .census.gov/Press-Release/www/releases/archives/facts_for_features_special_edi tions/013535.html. Accessed June 2009.

U.S. Department of Commerce. Bureau of Economic Analysis. "Glossary 'G.'" Available at www.bea.gov/glossary/glossary.cfm?key_word=GDP&letter=G#GDP. Accessed June 2009.

U.S. Department of Commerce. Economics and Statistics Administration. *Economic and Statistical Analysis Budget. Budget Estimates Fiscal Year 2009.* Feb. 2008. Available at www.osec.doc.gov/bmi/Budget/09CBJ/ESA-BEA%20 FY2009Congressional%20Justification.pdf.

U.S. Department of Health and Human Services. Administration for Children and Families. "Office of Family Assistance (OFA)." Available at www.acf.hhs.gov/ opa/fact_sheets/tanf_factsheet.html. Accessed June 2009.

U.S. Department of Labor. Bureau of Labor Statistics. "Employment Characteristics of Families in 2008," May 27, 2009. Available at www.bls.gov/bls/budgetim pact.htm. Accessed June 2009.

U.S. Department of Labor. Bureau of Labor Statistics. "Impact of the 2008 Federal Budget on the Availability and Quality of Data," Mar. 28, 2008. Available at www.bls.gov/bls/budgetimpact.htm. Accessed June 2009.

U.S. Department of Labor. Bureau of Labor Statistics. "Married Parents' Use of Time Summary." May 8, 2008. Available at www.bls.gov/news.release/atus2 .nr0.htm. Accessed June 2009.

U.S. Department of Labor. Bureau of Labor Statistics. "Table 5. Employment Status of the Population by Sex, Marital Status, and Presence and Age of Own Children under 18, 2006–07 Annual Averages." May 20, 2008. Available at www .bls.gov/news.release/famee.t05.htm. Accessed June 2009.

U.S. Department of Labor. Employment Standards Administration. Wage and Hour Division. *The Family and Medical Leave Act: A Report on the Request for Information*. June 2007. Available at www.dol.gov/esa/whd/fmla2007report .htm. Accessed June 2009.

U.S. Department of Labor. Bureau of Labor Statistics. *Women in the Labor Force: A Databook*. Sept, 2007. Available at www.bls.gov/cps/wlf-databook-2007 .pdf. Accessed June 2009.

Uy, Erin. "More parents making choice to stay at home." *The Gazette*, Sept. 17, 2003. Available at www.gazette.net/gazette_archive/2003/200338/potomac/ news/178382-1.html. Accessed June 2009.

Vedantam, Shankar. "See No Bias." *Washington Post*, Jan. 23, 2005, W12.

Vos Savant, Marilyn. "Ask Marilyn." *Parade Magazine*, Oct. 23, 2005, 8.

Waite, Linda, Gus Haggstrom, and David E. Kanouse. "The Consequences of Parenthood for the Marital Stability of Young Adults." *American Sociological Review* 50, no. 6 (Dec. 1985): 850–857.

Waldfogel, Jane. "Family and Medical Leave: Evidence from the 2000 Surveys." *Monthly Labor Review* 124 (Sept. 2001): 17–23. Available at www.bls.gov/ opub/mlr/2001/09/art2full.pdf. Accessed June 2009.

Waldfogel, Jane. "Understanding the Family Gap in Pay for Women with Children." *Journal of Economic Perspectives* 12, no. 1 (winter 1998): 137–156.

Wallace, William Ross. "What Rules the World." In *Beautiful Gems of Thought and Sentiment*. Boston, MA: The Colins-Patten Co., 1890.

Warner, Judith. "The Full-Time Blues." *New York Times*, July 24, 2007. Available at http://select.nytimes.com/2007/07/24/opinion/24warner.html?_r=1. Accessed June 2009.

Warren, Elizabeth and Amelia Warren Tyagi. *The Two-Income Trap: Why Middle-Class Mothers and Fathers Are Going Broke (With Surprising Solutions That Will Change Our Children's Futures)*. Reading, Mass.: Basic Books, 2003.

Weinberg, Daniel H. *Evidence from Census 2000 about Earnings by Detailed Occupation* [Census 2000 Special Reports]. Washington, D.C.: U.S. Census Bureau, May 2004. Available at www.census.gov/prod/2004pubs/censr-15.pdf . Accessed June 2009.

Wenger, Jeffrey. *Share of Workers in "Nonstandard" Jobs Declines* [Briefing Paper]. Washington, D.C.: Economic Policy Institute, 2003. Available at http:// epi.3cdn.net/dd020a269eeca98ff5_2xm6bxkay.pdf. Accessed June 2009.

Wenger, Jeffrey. *The Continuing Problems with Part-Time Jobs* [Issue Brief]. Washington, D.C.: Economic Policy Institute, 2001. Available at www.epi.org/page/-/ old/Issuebriefs/ib155/ib155.pdf. Accessed June 2009.

Williams, Joan. "Celebrating Mothers' Choices: Making New Ones." Keynote address. Mothers & More National Conference, Chicago, Oct. 19, 2001. Available at www.mothersandmore.org/Advocacy/Williams-Keynote_Chicago2000. PDF. Accessed June 2009.

Williams, Joan. *Unbending Gender: Why Family and Work Conflict and What to Do About It*. New York: Oxford University Press, 2001.

Williams, Joan C. and Cynthia Thomas Calvert. *WorkLife Law's Guide to Family Responsibilities Discrimination*. San Francisco: Center for WorkLife Law, 2006.

Williams, Joan, Jessica Manvell, and Stephanie Bornstein. *"Opt Out" or Pushed Out: How the Press Covers Work/Family Conflict*. University of California Hastings College of Law, Center for WorkLife Law, 2006. Available at www .worklifelaw.org/pubs/OptOutPushedOut.pdf. Accessed June 2009.

Williams, Joan C. and Elizabeth S. Westfall. "Deconstructing the Maternal Wall: Strategies for Vindicating the Civil Rights of 'Carers' in the Workplace." *Duke Journal of Gender Law & Policy* 13 (2006): 31.

Wu, Ke Bin. *Sources of Income for Women Age 65 and Over* [Data Digest]. Washington, D.C.: AARP Public Policy Institute, Nov. 2007. Available at http:// assets.aarp.org/rgcenter/econ/dd161_income.pdf. Accessed June 2009.

Wyn, Roberta, Victoria Ojeda, Usha Ranji, and Alina Salganicoff. *Issue Brief: Women, Work, and Family Health: A Balancing Act*. Menlo Park, Calif.: Henry J. Kaiser Family Foundation, 2003. Available at www.kff.org/women shealth/loader.cfm?url=/commonspot/security/getfile.cfm&PageID=14293. Accessed June 2009.

Zuboff, Shoshana. "Career Taxidermy." *Fast Company*, June 2004. Available at www.fastcompany.com/magazine/83/szuboff.html. Accessed June 2009.

INDEX

73920